solutions@syngress.com

With more than 1,500,000 copies of our MCSE, MCSD, CompTIA, and Cisco study guides in print, we continue to look for ways we can better serve the information needs of our readers. One way we do that is by listening.

Readers like yourself have been telling us they want an Internet-based service that would extend and enhance the value of our books. Based on reader feedback and our own strategic plan, we have created a Web site that we hope will exceed your expectations.

Solutions@syngress.com is an interactive treasure trove of useful information focusing on our book topics and related technologies. The site offers the following features:

- One-year warranty against content obsolescence due to vendor product upgrades. You can access online updates for any affected chapters.

- "Ask the Author" customer query forms that enable you to post questions to our authors and editors.

- Exclusive monthly mailings in which our experts provide answers to reader queries and clear explanations of complex material.

- Regularly updated links to sites specially selected by our editors for readers desiring additional reliable information on key topics.

Best of all, the book you're now holding is your key to this amazing site. Just go to **www.syngress.com/solutions**, and keep this book handy when you register to verify your purchase.

Thank you for giving us the opportunity to serve your needs. And be sure to let us know if there's anything else we can do to help you get the maximum value from your investment. We're listening.

www.syngress.com/solutions

SYNGRESS®

D0620132

1 YEAR UPGRADE
BUYER PROTECTION PLAN

BUILDING A
Cisco
Wireless LAN

Eric Ouellet

Robert Padjen

Arthur Pfund

Ron Fuller Technical Editor

Tim Blankenship Technical Editor

KEY	SERIAL NUMBER
001	5T54T94DGH
002	RT4MPE4AKT
003	63NER5VM4N
004	9UND34B3SG
005	7U88MNVU6H
006	4NFGRN4TEM
007	B46HTWBVRT
008	R5B962P5MR
009	8AS3N54BMR
010	2ZFGYH2CT6

PUBLISHED BY
Syngress Publishing, Inc.
800 Hingham Street
Rockland, MA 02370

Building A Cisco Wireless LAN

Printed in the United States of America

1 2 3 4 5 6 7 8 9 0

ISBN: 1-928994-58-X

Technical Editor: Ron Fuller, Tim Blankenship
Technical Reviewer: Ron Fuller
Acquisitions Editor: Catherine B. Nolan
Developmental Editor: Kate Glennon
Cover Designer: Michael Kavish
Page Layout and Art by: Shannon Tozier
Copy Editor: Darren Meiss
Indexer: Robert Saigh

Distributed by Publishers Group West in the United States and Jaguar Book Group in Canada.

Acknowledgments

We would like to acknowledge the following people for their kindness and support in making this book possible.

Ralph Troupe, Rhonda St. John, Emlyn Rhodes, and the team at Callisma for their invaluable insight into the challenges of designing, deploying and supporting world-class enterprise networks.

Karen Cross, Lance Tilford, Meaghan Cunningham, Kim Wylie, Harry Kirchner, Kevin Votel, Kent Anderson, Frida Yara, Bill Getz, Jon Mayes, John Mesjak, Peg O'Donnell, Sandra Patterson, Betty Redmond, Roy Remer, Ron Shapiro, Patricia Kelly, Andrea Tetrick, Jennifer Pascal, Doug Reil, and David Dahl of Publishers Group West for sharing their incredible marketing experience and expertise.

Jacquie Shanahan, AnnHelen Lindeholm, David Burton, Febea Marinetti, and Rosie Moss of Elsevier Science for making certain that our vision remains worldwide in scope.

Annabel Dent and Paul Barry of Elsevier Science/Harcourt Australia for all their help.

David Buckland, Wendi Wong, Marie Chieng, Lucy Chong, Leslie Lim, Audrey Gan, and Joseph Chan of Transquest Publishers for the enthusiasm with which they receive our books.

Kwon Sung June at Acorn Publishing for his support.

Ethan Atkin at Cranbury International for his help in expanding the Syngress program.

Jackie Gross, Gayle Voycey, Alexia Penny, Anik Robitaille, Craig Siddall, Darlene Morrow, Iolanda Miller, Jane Mackay, and Marie Skelly at Jackie Gross & Associates for all their help and enthusiasm representing our product in Canada.

Lois Fraser, Connie McMenemy, Shannon Russell and the rest of the great folks at Jaguar Book Group for their help with distribution of Syngress books in Canada.

Thank you to our hard-working colleagues at New England Fulfillment & Distribution who manage to get all our books sent pretty much everywhere in the world. Thank you to Debbie "DJ" Ricardo, Sally Greene, Janet Honaker, and Peter Finch.

Contributors

Eric Ouellet (CISSP) is a Senior Partner with Secure Systems Design Group, a network design and security consultancy based in Ottawa, ON, Canada. He specializes in the implementation of networks and security infrastructures from both a design and a hands-on perspective. During his career he has been responsible for designing, installing, and troubleshooting WANs using Cisco, Nortel, and Alcatel equipment configured to support voice, data, and video conferencing services over terrestrial, satellite relay, wireless, and trusted communication links.

Eric has also been responsible for designing some of the leading Public Key Infrastructure deployments currently in use and for devising operational policy and procedures to meet the Electronic Signature Act (E-Sign) and the Health Insurance Portability and Accountability Act (HIPAA). He has provided his services to financial, commercial, government, and military customers including the U.S. Federal Government, Canadian Federal Government, and NATO. He regularly speaks at leading security conferences and teaches networking and CISSP classes. Eric is a co-author of *Hack Proofing Your Wireless Network* (Syngress Publishing, ISBN: 1-928994-59-8) and is a contributor to the forthcoming *Sniffer Network Optimization and Troubleshooting Handbook* (Syngress Publishing, ISBN: 1-931836-57-4).

Eric would like to acknowledge the understanding and support of his family and friends during the writing of this book, along with Walter Allan and "The Boys" for being who they are.

Robert Padjen (CCNP-Security, CCNP-Switching, CCDP) is Director of Technology Solutions for a large financial institution. He has written eight texts on network administration, troubleshooting, and design and is recognized as an expert witness in computer networking and intellectual property litigation. Robert's experience over the past ten years includes design and implementation of wireless, ATM, Frame Relay, and security solutions for a wide variety of clients. Robert served as subject matter expert on 802.11b services for Callisma, a network consulting firm, and has previously contributed to *Cisco AVVID & IP Telephony Design and Implementation* (Syngress Publishing, ISBN: 1-928994-83-0). An avid flyer and motorcyclist, Rob, and his wife, Kristie, live in Northern California and have three children. Robert is on the Board of Directors for the Chernobyl Children's Project, a non-profit organization that provides respites for children affected by the disaster, and he is also on the Cisco Technical Advisory Board.

Arthur Pfund (CCIE#7249, CCNP, CCNA) is a Principal Engineer with a Fortune 500 company. Currently, he is responsible for the strategic and tactical evolution of a large multi-data center network environment. Specializing in Cisco routers and switches, he has hands-on experience working with a wide range of networking equipment. In addition to network design and engineering, Arthur's background includes extensive experience with implementation, operational support, and troubleshooting LAN and WAN systems in a large network environment.

Sean Thurston (CCDP, CCNP, MCSE, MCP+I) is a Senior Solution Architect with Siemens Business Services. He provides network and data center design solutions for large-scale deployment. His specialties include implementation of multivendor routing and switching equipment and XoIP (Everything over IP installations). Sean's background includes positions as a Technical Analyst for Sprint-Paranet and the Director of a brick-and-mortar advertising dot com. Sean is also a contributing author to the following books from Syngress Publishing, *Building a Cisco Network for Windows 2000* (ISBN: 1-928994-00-8), *Cisco AVVID and IP Telephony Design and Implementation* (ISBN: 1-928994-83-0), and the forthcoming *Managing Cisco Network Security, Second Edition* (ISBN: 1-931836-56-6). Sean lives in Renton, WA with his fiancée, Kerry. He is currently pursuing his CCIE.

Technical Editors and Reviewers

Ron Fuller (CCIE #5851, CSS-Level 1, CCNP, CCDP, MCNE) is a Senior Network Engineer with a large financial institution in Columbus, OH. He currently provides design and engineering support for the network infrastructure. His specialties include Cisco routers and LAN switches, strategic network planning, network architecture and design, and network troubleshooting and optimization. Ron's background includes senior systems engineering responsibilities for Cisco and Novell resellers in Central Ohio. Ron has also acted as contributing author to the book *Administering Cisco QoS in IP Networks* (Syngress Publishing, ISBN: 1-928994-21-0). He currently resides in Sunbury, OH with his family, Julie and Max.

Tim Blankenship (CCNP, CCDA, CNE-5, CNE-4, CNE-3, MCP, CSEC–Wireless Field Engineer) is a private consultant responsible for leading the design and implementation efforts involving Local and Wide Area Networks to clients in the mid-west region of the United States. His specialties include Cisco wireless networking, routers and LAN switches, Novell design and implementation, strategic network planning, network architecture and design, and network troubleshooting and optimization. Tim currently resides in Grove City, OH with his family, Connie, Morgan, Ben, and Emily.

Contents

**Common Practice for
Subnetting TCP/IP
Address Space**

This practice serves many
purposes:

- It does not use regis-
  tered IP space for wireless devices; which
  typically do not include
  servers.

- It enables the organization to subnet the
  address space without
  any restrictions.

- It allows for easy identification of WLAN
  traffic on the network
  because it is not
  sharing address space
  with the wired net-
  work.

Phase Modulation

The following modulation techniques are used in Cisco Aironet radios:

- Binary Phase Shift Keying (BPSK)

- Quadrature Phase Shift Keying (QPSK)

- Complimentary Code Keying (CCK)

Answers to Your Frequently Asked Questions

Q: How far can a wireless client communicate to an Access Point (AP)?

A: Client adapters can support 11 Mbps at a range of 400 feet (120m) in open environments and 100 feet (30m) in typical closed/indoor environments. Client adapter can support 1 Mbps at a range of up to 1,500 feet (460m) in open environments and 300 feet (90m) in closed/indoor environments.

Chapter 4 Wireless Network Design   131

**Designing &
Planning...**

**Calculating the Fresnel
Zone**

A bit of mathematics is
required to calculate the
size of the Fresnel zone
radius at its widest point
(midpoint radius). The
following formula will
allow you to calculate the
radius in feet of the
widest point in your
Fresnel zone:

**Fresnel Zone Radius
Formula**

$$R = 72.1 \sqrt{\frac{d_1 d_2}{F_{GHz}\,(d_1 + d_2)}}$$

Setting the WEP Key

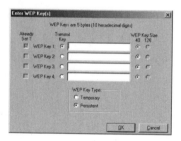

Comparing Traditional Bridges with Wireless Bridges

Cisco Aironet 340 and 350 wireless bridges can be used in one of three modes:

- Wireless bridge between two wired network segments (point-to-point)

- Wireless bridge between three or more wired network segments (point-to-multipoint)

- Wireless bridge used as a repeater (repeater)

Chapter 6 Installation and Configuration of Cisco Aironet Bridges   253

Chapter 7 Installation and Configuration of Cisco Wireless Network Cards   329

Client Adapter Auto Installer

A DOS-based configuration file encryption utility is provided for the safeguard of the INI or TXT configuration file. The utility encrypts the file by using a scrambling algorithm that can be decrypted by the Auto Installer. The utility is called EncryptIni.exe:

1. Select **Start | Run**.

2. In the Open prompt, type **Command** and press **Enter**.

3. Using the DOS commands, navigate to the directory where the EncryptIni.exe and the configuration files are located.

4. Type **EncryptIni.exe <configuration file name>**.

**Designing &
Planning...**

**Preventing Dictionary
Attacks Using EAP**

EAP was designed to support extended authentication. When you implement EAP, you can avoid dictionary attacks by using nonpassword-based schemes such as biometrics, certificates, OTP, smart cards, and token cards.

You should be sure that if you are using password-based schemes that they use some form of mutual authentication so that they are more protected against dictionary attacks.

Yagi Articulating Mount

Foreword

Over the last 10 years, the impact of wireless communications on the way we live and do business has been surpassed only by the impact of the Internet. Cellular phones, pagers, and wireless personal digital assistants (PDAs) have become so commonplace in our lives that it is easy to forget that 10 years ago, they were a rarity. But wireless communications technology is still in its infancy, and the next stage of its development will be in supplementing or replacing the network infrastructure that was traditionally "wired" as well as enabling network infrastructures that previously could only be imagined. From local coffee shops to commercial inventory control systems, within restaurants and throughout public airports, wireless commerce is beginning to challenge the exchange system that our modern world currently embraces, by accessing central pools of information and communicating directly between users and between the devices themselves.

No longer are our choices restricted by the shortfalls of processing and battery power, operating system efficiencies, or heat dissipation within the small footprint of the mobile device. Rather, we are limited only by the practical application of these technologies. How will we access information? How will we integrate multiple hardware and software technologies into intelligent and useable form factors? Not all business models necessarily imply the use of a single terminal to supply the user with voice, video, and data services. Ergonomic factors may dictate that voice services are maintained privately while data exchange and video information is easily viewable from a specified distance, perhaps on complementary devices.

As network engineers, the challenges before us include the seamless distribution of information between seemingly incompatible software and hardware standards. In addition, we will be challenged by narrower bandwidths to develop highly efficient means of transport in order to fully leverage wireless technologies.

Wireless LAN (Wi-Fi) technology is a reliable and convenient method of providing immediate, highly flexible, and pedestrian-speed mobile data network access.

IEEE 802.11-based products offered by Cisco Systems have quickly become one of the foundational technologies fostering the untethering of data communications in the same way cordless telephony enhances local mobility for residential voice communications.

Wi-Fi, however, is significantly more complex than cordless telephony; loss, coverage, and bandwidth requirements are much more stringent, not to mention that direct sequence spread-spectrum (DSSS) is inherently more complicated than frequency division multiple access (FDMA) and time division multiple access (TDMA). More important, the proliferation of wireless LANs in corporate environments has resulted in interesting security challenges.

Many organizations do not invoke IEEE security features. In addition, the current IEEE 802.11 standard authentication techniques of using Service Set Identifiers (SSID) and Media Access Control (MAC) addressing do not provide strong authentication. And although Wired Equivalent Protocol (WEP) combines access control, data privacy, and data integrity using an underlying algorithm, it can also be broken via passive monitoring with freely available monitoring software such as AirSnort. Fortunately, Cisco offers enhanced capabilities to mitigate some weaknesses. Of course, proper design and implementation are critically important; the design should exclude direct wireless access point connectivity to the internal network, strong security mechanisms must be implemented at different levels, and strict security policies must be enforced. With 802.11b access speed ranging from 1 Mbps up to 11 Mbps, and distances reaching from 500 feet indoors to as much as 5 kilometers outdoors, a wireless LAN could offer an unwanted user powerful network access.

Connectivity, availability, and capacity issues are resolved with proper frequency planning and testing. Security concerns are properly addressed with unobtrusive testing, implementation of proper policies, and firewalls. Network addressing must also be implemented consistently.

Callisma regularly assists customers with these considerations. This book will educate readers on some of the theory and practical information required to successfully and safely deploy Wi-Fi.

—*Ralph Troupe*
President and CEO, Callisma

Chapter 1

Introduction to Wireless Local Area Networks

Solutions in this chapter:

- Reviewing Networking Basics
- Understanding How Wireless Fits into the OSI System Model
- Reviewing TCP/IP Basics

☑ Summary

☑ Solutions Fast Track

☑ Frequently Asked Questions

Introduction

Wireless local area networks (WLANs) can be employed to provide network connectivity almost anywhere. Consider the cost savings from not having to run network cable to every possible location that could have a computer or network device connected to it. Consider the convenience of a wireless-enabled conference room. Imagine the increase in accuracy of a medical professional's data entered directly into a tablet computer during his rounds through the WLAN instead of transcribed from a clipboard at a central workstation. Conference rooms, warehouses, indoor and outdoor public access areas, and hospitals are all suitable locations for WLANs. Unfettered access to the network, regardless of physical location, or traditional cable distance limitations is one of the primary drivers for WLANs.

Where can you fit WLANs into your existing infrastructure? Just about anywhere you like. WLANs allow network designers to no longer be constrained by the 100m distance limitation for Category 5 copper cabling. Because WLANs use radio frequency (RF) signals to communicate, users can stay connected to the network almost anywhere.

Many companies are merging WLANs into their traditional wired networks to provide connectivity to the network to large numbers of users. Conference rooms are a great place to start considering wireless in your network. The cost of wiring a conference room and maintaining the hardware required to keep those wired jacks "hot" can be prohibitive. Conference rooms are used for "chalk talk" design sessions, application development sessions, and training. By using WLANs, the need for multiple data jacks in a conference room can be eliminated. A single antenna connected to a WLAN access point (AP) can support many users.

Warehouse applications are also prime candidates for WLAN. Real-time inventory control can be implemented using wireless. Imagine having your inventory control software connected to mobile devices on the warehouse floor tracking inventory as it fluctuates during the course of a day. WLANs can be a very important business driver, enabling a company to gain a competitive advantage.

Hospital bedside access is also a popular application for WLANs. The ability for a hospital staff member to check in a patient at bedside rather than waiting in line at an admissions desk is much more efficient. Bedside access can also enable a doctor to write a prescription or check medical records on a patient instantaneously.

College campuses and some companies are also extending the network infrastructure to public access areas both indoors and outside. This no longer restrains the user to just her desk, or even in the building, to be productive. For the growing mobile workforce, wireless provides the connectivity.

Reviewing Networking Basics

Before we delve into the topic of WLANs, we need to cover networking in general. A *network* is defined as a series of points or nodes interconnected by communication paths. The points or nodes may be devices dedicated to a single function, such as a PC dedicated to client applications, or a router dedicated to interconnecting networks. This chapter covers some fundamental theories, technologies, and applications for networks. LAN Technologies such as Ethernet, Fast Ethernet, Gigabit Ethernet, Token Ring, and Fiber Distributed Data Interface (FDDI) are prevalent in the networking industry today.

There are three primary types of networks, the local area network (LAN), metropolitan area network (MAN), and the wide area network (WAN). The distinguishing feature of these networks is the spatial distance covered. LANs, as the name implies, are typically contained in a single structure or small geographic region. Groups of LANs interconnected may also be referred to as a *campus* in larger environments. MANs connect points or nodes in a geographic region larger than a LAN, but smaller than a WAN. Some of the same LAN technologies may be employed in a MAN, such as Gigabit Ethernet. WANs are geographically diverse networks and typically use technologies different from LANs or MANs. WANs typically are comprised of high-speed circuits leased from a telecommunications provider to facilitate connectivity. WANs rarely use the same technologies as LANs or MANs. Technologies such as Frame Relay, Integrated Services Digital Network (ISDN), X.25, Asynchronous Transfer Mode (ATM), Digital Subscriber Line (DSL) and others may be used. This is because of the larger distances WANs service.

Defining Topologies

Within the definition of a network, points or nodes are connected by communication paths. These paths may vary significantly depending on the paths implemented. We cover four primary topologies: *bus*, *star*, *ring*, and *mesh*. Each topology has strengths and weaknesses, as well as different associated costs. A good network design will take each topology into consideration to determine the best solution.

> **NOTE**
>
> The word *topology* can refer to either the physical or logical layout of the network. For example, an Ethernet network with a hub would have a star topology, but the logical topology would be a bus.

Bus Topology

A bus topology is a linear LAN architecture in which transmissions from network devices or stations propagate the entire length of the medium and are received by all nodes on the medium. A common example of a bus topology is Ethernet/IEEE 802.3 networks, as illustrated in Figure 1.1.

Figure 1.1 Bus Topology

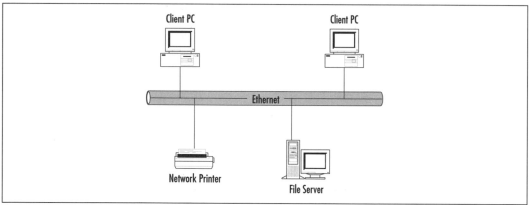

Star Topology

A star topology is a LAN architecture in which the devices or stations on a network are connected to a central communications device, such as a hub or switch. Logical bus and ring topologies are often physically implemented in star topologies. Figure 1.2 shows a typical star topology.

Ring Topology

A ring topology is a LAN architecture in which the devices or stations on a network are connected to each other by unidirectional transmission links to form a single closed loop. Common examples of ring topologies are Token Ring/IEEE 802.5 and FDDI networks, as illustrated in Figure 1.3.

Figure 1.2 Star Topology

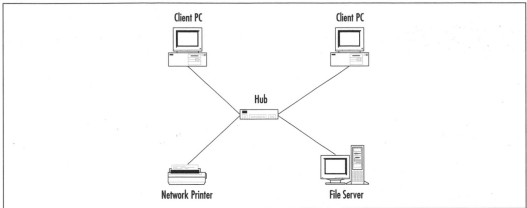

Figure 1.3 Ring Topology

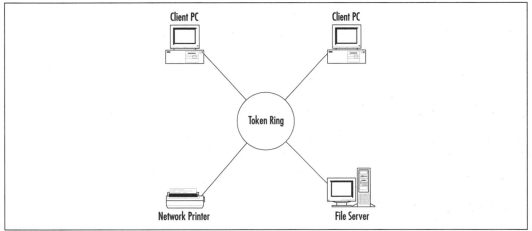

Mesh Topology

A mesh topology is a LAN architecture is which every device or station on a network is connected to every other device or station. Mesh topologies are expensive to deploy and cumbersome to manage because the number of connections in the network can grow exponentially. The formula used to calculate the number of connections in a fully meshed network is as follows:

(N x (N–1))/2

where N is the number of devices on the network. Divide the result by 2 to avoid double counting the device A-to-device-B connection and the device

B-to-device-A connection. To illustrate the large numbers that a fully meshed environment can reach, review the following examples:

- A small network with 50 users wants to implement a fully meshed topology. The number of connections required to do this would be $(50 \times (50–1))/2$, which equals 1,225. That is a lot of connections for a small LAN!

- A medium network with 500 users wants to implement a fully meshed topology. The number of connections required to do this would be $(500 \times (500–1))/2$ which equals 124,750 connections!

Now for the reality check on fully meshed networks. Fully meshed networks are typically implemented in a small handful of situations. The most common deployment model for fully meshed networks would be in the WAN arena. Frame Relay and ATM are technologies that are well suited for fully meshed networks with high availability requirements. Figure 1.4 depicts a typical mesh network.

Figure 1.4 Mesh Topology

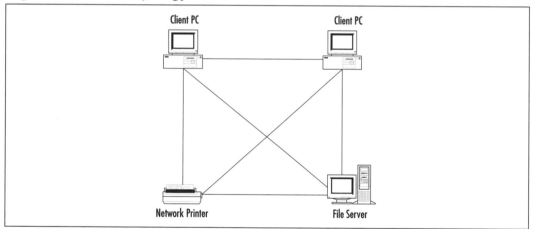

CSMA/CD versus Deterministic Access

In LANs, there are two predominant methods of controlling access to the physical medium: Carrier Sense Multiple Access with Collision Detection (CMSA/CD) and deterministic access. CSMA/CD is the access method for Ethernet. CSMA/CD is best described as the same set of rules you would follow in a meeting. In a meeting, everyone in the room has the right to speak, but everyone follows the generally accepted rule of "Only one person can talk at one time." If you want to speak, you need to listen to see if anyone is else is speaking before you begin. If someone else is speaking, you must wait until they are finished before you can begin. If nobody is speaking, you can speak, but will continue to listen in case someone else decides to speak at the same time. If they do, both speakers must stop talking, wait a random amount of time, and start the process again. If a speaker fails to observe the protocol of only one speaker at a time, the meeting will quickly lose all effective communication. (Sounds too familiar, doesn't it?)

In Ethernet, the multiple access (MA) is the terminology for many stations connected to the same cable and having the opportunity to transmit. No device or station on the cable has any priority over any other device or station. All devices or stations on the cable do take turns communicating per the access algorithm to ensure that one device on the LAN does not monopolize the media.

The CS (carrier sense) refers to the process of listening before speaking in an Ethernet network. The carrier sense operation is performed by every device on the network by looking for energy on the media, the electrical carrier. If a carrier exists, the cable is in use, and the device must wait to transmit. Many Ethernet devices maintain a deferral or back-off counter defining the maximum number of attempts the device will make to transmit on the cable. If the deferral counter is exceeded, typically 15 attempts, the frame is discarded.

The CD (collision detect) in Ethernet refers to the capability of the devices on the wire to know when a collision occurs. Collisions in Ethernet happen when two devices transmit data at the same time on the cable. Collisions may be caused by the cable distance being exceeded, a defective device, or a poorly written driver that does not adhere to Ethernet specifications. When a collision is detected, the participants generate a collision enforcement signal. The enforcement signal lasts as long as the smallest Ethernet frame size, 64 bytes. This sizing ensures that all stations know about the collision and do not attempt to transmit during a collision event. After the collision enforcement signal has finished, the medium is again open to communications via the carrier sense protocol.

Deterministic access is the protocol used to control access to the physical medium in a token ring or FDDI network. Deterministic access means that a control system is in place to ensure that each device on the network has an equal opportunity to transmit.

Cabling

The physical infrastructure of a LAN is one of the most important components of a network. If the physical medium that data is traversing is faulty or installed incorrectly, network performance and operation will be impacted. It is analogous to the foundation of a building. Everything in the building is set upon the foundation, typically strong reinforced concrete or other equally durable and reliable building materials. If the foundation is not installed properly, everything built on this foundation is suspect. A LAN is the same, a faulty foundation can be disastrous to a network. You can install all of the high-end gear, switches, routers, servers, but if they don't have the physical infrastructure to communicate effectively, your network will fail.

There are two primary forms of physical medium a network will utilize: copper and fiber. Between these two forms, there are sometimes many different standards of cable. For example, copper may be shielded, unshielded, twisted, untwisted, solid core, or braided core. We explore copper and fiber cable in more detail to provide a solid understanding of the importance of cabling in your network. You may be asking yourself "Why are we covering cabling in a book on wireless?" That is a very good question. Wireless, as its name implies, does not use physical cabling to provide communications to the wireless network. However, it does use copper cabling to connect to your *existing* LAN. If your existing LAN has out-of-spec or faulty cabling, your WLAN may not meet your expectations. (Or more importantly, your boss's expectations!)

The most common form of LAN cabling installed today is copper. Copper has been the "preferred" installation since networks starting taking hold in the corporate world in 1980 when Xerox developed Ethernet. Copper is relatively cheap, easy to install, and can meet most distances that LANs were designed to cover. The original Ethernet specification used what is called thick coaxial cable. This cable lived up to its name for sure! Thick coax is much bigger than the traditional copper cable you might be familiar with. After thick coax came thin coax. Thin coax was a cheaper and easier to handle and install cable alternative. Both of these cable types are implemented in a bus topology. As we covered earlier, a bus topology is linear LAN architecture. Each device or station on a bus is connected to the same medium. One of the major downsides to thick and thin coax was that it created a single point of failure. If the bus were to experience a failure or cut, the network became nonfunctioning.

With the advances made in copper technology, twisted pair cable became a popular LAN medium. There are two main types of twisted pair cable: shielded and unshielded. Shielded, as its name implies, contains smaller copper cables, twisted among themselves with a shielded jacket around them. Shielded twisted pair allows copper cable to be installed in facilities where there is significant interference to the electrical signals passed along the cable. The shielding—as well as the twisting of the cables—plays a role in protecting the cable from this interference. Twisted pair cables are less prone to interference than flat, or nontwisted cables.

Among the twisted pair cabling family are a number of different levels of cables. These are commonly referred to as *categories*, or *CAT* for short. The primary differences between the categories is the number of twists per foot in the cable. More twists per foot equals less susceptibility to outside interference. Some of the newer, higher categories of cabling also have internal dividers intertwined with the copper cabling to further reduce interference. These higher standards allow faster communications such as Fast Ethernet at 100 Mbps and Gigabit Ethernet at 1000 Mbs over copper cabling.

Designing & Planning...

The Blame Game

When planning your WLAN implementation, you need to consider the wired network and its physical plant. Connecting a WLAN to a wired network with a questionable physical plant is a plan for trouble. Troubleshooting connectivity to a new technology is difficult enough because the new technology is the first to be blamed. On man occasions, problems have been blamed on the wireless network when in fact the wired network and the wiring itself was to blame. Approximately 60 percent of all network problems can be tracked to the physical layer. Don't let your wired network create havoc in your wireless network.

Understanding How Wireless Fits into the OSI System Model

Wireless technology, as a networking component, is guided by the same standards processes and organizations defined for all other networking components in the industry. Although working in the networking industry can be difficult at best, there are many components to a network that can either make or break the system. In order to help standardize and define the areas a manufacturer must build their equipment to service, the International Organization for Standardization (ISO) created the Open Systems Interconnection (OSI) reference model. This model is a seven-layer approach to data networking. Each layer encompasses a specific set of tasks or standards that must be met in order for the network to function. We'll review each layer in greater detail because this is a *very* important concept to understand. A comprehensive understanding of the OSI system model is of paramount importance for the internetworking designer, installer, or support team.

The seven layers to the OSI system model are as follows:

- Physical layer
- Data-link layer
- Network layer
- Transport layer
- Session layer
- Presentation layer
- Application layer

We start at the bottom with the Physical layer. The Physical layer of the OSI system model is responsible for defining the electrical and mechanical aspects of networking. Topics such as cabling and the methods for placing the 0's and 1's of binary data on the medium are covered in great detail here. Standards such as Category 5, RS-232, and coaxial cable fall within the realm of the Physical layer.

The next layer is the Data-link layer. The Data-link layer defines the protocols that control the Physical layer. Issues such as how the medium is accessed and shared, how devices or stations on the medium are addressed, and how data is framed before transmission on the medium are defined here. Common examples of Data-link layer protocols are Ethernet, Token Ring, FDDI, and PPP.

Within the Data-link layer are two sublayers: the Media Access Control (MAC) and Logical Link Control (LLC). These two sublayers each play an important role in the operation of a network. We start with the MAC first. The MAC sublayer is responsible for uniquely identifying devices on the network. As part of the standards of the OSI system model, when a network interface in a router, switch, PC, server, or other device that connects to a LAN is created, a globally unique 48-bit address is burned into the ROM of the interface. This address must be unique or the network will not operate properly. Each manufacturer of network interfaces has been assigned a range of addresses from the Institute of Electrical and Electronics Engineers (IEEE). The MAC sublayer is considered the lower of the two sublayers and is also responsible for determining the access method to the medium, such as token passing (Token Ring or FDDI) or contention (CSMA/CD). Figure 1.5 shows an example of MAC addresses "on the wire" after being passed from the MAC layer to the Physical layer and being converted to 0's and 1's.

Figure 1.5 MAC Layer to Physical Layer

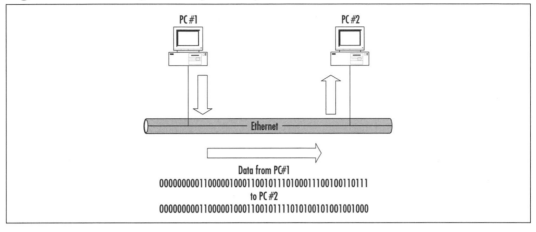

The next sublayer is the LLC layer. The LLC sublayer is responsible for handling error control, flow control, framing, and MAC sublayer addressing. The most common LLC protocol is IEEE 802.2, which defines connectionless and connection-oriented variants. IEEE 802.2 defines Service Access Points (SAPs) through a field in the Ethernet, Token Ring, or FDDI frame. Two SAPs are associated with LLC: the Destination Service Access Point (DSAP) and the Source Service Access Point (SSAP). These SAPs in conjunction with the MAC address can uniquely identify the recipient of a frame. Typically LLC is used for protocols such as SNA that do not have a corresponding network layer.

The next layer defined by the OSI reference model is the Network layer. The Network layer is responsible for addressing a network above the Data-link layer. The Network layer is where protocols such as Transmission Control Protocol/Internet Protocol (TCP/IP), Internetwork Packet Exchange (IPX) and AppleTalk tie into the grand scheme of things. Routing functions are also performed at the Network layer. TCP/IP routing protocols such as Routing Information Protocol (RIP), Open Shortest Path First (OSPF), and the Border Gateway Protocol (BGP) operate at the Network layer. We focus more on TCP/IP in the upcoming "Review of TCP/IP Basics" section.

The three previous layers we covered, Physical, Data-link, and Network, are considered the *lower level* protocols in the OSI reference model. These are the protocols that will more than likely consume the majority of your time as a network engineer. However, that does not mean that the next four layers are not important to the operation of a network. They are equally important, because without the next four layers, your network doesn't even need to be in existence.

The fourth layer of the OSI system model is the Transport layer. The Transport layer defines the protocols that control the Network layer, similar to the way the Data-link layer controls the Physical layer. The Transport layer specifies a higher level of flow control, error detection, and correction. Protocols such as TCP, User Datagram Protocol (UDP), Sequenced Packet Exchange (SPX), and Name Binding Protocol (NBP) operate at this layer. These protocols may be connection-oriented, such as TCP and SPX, or connectionless, such as UDP.

The fifth layer of the OSI system model is the Session layer. The Session layer is responsible for establishing, managing, and terminating communication sessions between Presentation layer entities and the Transport layer, where needed. Lightweight Directory Access Protocol (LDAP) and Remote Procedure Call (RPC) are examples of Session layer protocols.

The sixth layer of the OSI system model is the Presentation layer. The Presentation layer is responsible for ensuring that data sent from the Application layer of one device is comprehensible by the Application layer of another device. IBM's Network Basic Input Output System (NetBIOS) and Novell's NetWare Core Protocol (NCP) are examples of Presentation layer protocols. The ISO also developed a Presentation layer protocol named Abstract Syntax Notation One (ASN.1), which describes data types independent of various computer structures and representation techniques. ASN.1 was at one time thought to be the Presentation layer protocol of choice, when the ISO's protocol stack was going to sweep the networking industry. Now we know that some components of ISO, such as Intermediate System to Intermediate System (IS-IS) as a routing protocol, and the X.500 directory services protocol have been widely deployed, while the majority of the protocol stack has been neglected.

The seventh, and final, layer of the OSI system model is the Application layer. The Application layer is responsible for providing network services to applications such as e-mail, word processing, and file transfer, which are not implicitly defined in the OSI system model. The Application layer allows developers of software packages to not have to write networking routines into their program. Instead, developers can utilize programming functions to the Application layer and rely upon Layer 7 to provide the networking services they require. Some common examples of Application layer protocols include Simple Mail Transfer Protocol (SMTP), Hypertext Transfer Protocol (HTTP), and Telnet.

Tracking Data through the OSI System Model

Understanding how data moves across an internetwork is a very important component of being a network engineer. You need a comprehensive grasp of the technologies and the standards they support, and you also need to know how those technologies and standards relate to the actual network. The OSI system model bridges that gap for you. Knowing the details of the network as well as the way end-user applications interact with the network is a powerful trouble-shooting tool.

One of the easiest analogies used to understand the OSI system model is that of sending a letter through the mail. A number of items must be completed for your letter to be delivered to the appropriate recipient. We walk a letter through the postal system and illustrate the parallel connections to the OSI system model.

The first thing that you need to do to send a letter is to write it. You sit down at your desk and write a letter to your friend that lives on the other side of the country. After you finish writing the letter, you get an envelope and address it to your friend. You then walk to your mailbox and place the letter inside. These actions correlate to the OSI system model layers nicely. Writing the letter corresponds roughly to the Application layer. If you used a word processor to write the letter, then print it out to place in the envelope, the act of printing the letter would be similar to what happens at the Application layer. The fact that you printed the letter means that you relinquished control of the letter to the network, the postal system in this case. Your actual words on the paper correspond to the Presentation layer in that you needed to ensure that the recipient, your friend, can read the letter. You presented your thoughts in a format your friend can read and comprehend. Addressing the letter can correspond to the Session, Transport, and Network layers. In networking terms, the steps of sealing the letter in the envelope and addressing it relate to the actions of UDP in a TCP/IP network. The data, your letter, was encapsulated in the envelope and passed down through the OSI model to the Network layer where it was addressed. Without the address, your letter cannot be delivered and the same principle applies to networking. Data cannot be delivered without an address. Placing the envelope in the mailbox is comparable to what happens at the Data-link and Physical layers of the OSI system model. The envelope was placed or encapsulated in the correct format for delivery on the network where it will be transmitted to the recipient. The mailbox maps to the Data-link layer and the postal carrier that picks up the envelope would be the Physical layer, responsible for ensuring that the envelope is delivered.

Now that the envelope is in the network, the postal system, it may pass through many different offices. If you view these offices as nodes on a network, they would correspond to routers. The envelope reaches your local post office, or default gateway in a TCP/IP network, and is scanned by a computer to determine if the envelope requires routing for proper delivery. In this example, your friend lives across the country, so the envelope does need to be routed. The computers in the post office review the destination address and determine the best path for the envelope to take to reach its final destination. The next office, or hop, on the path the envelope takes may be a regional office or some other central location with routes to the next hop. Your envelope is transported by mail truck, plane, or other form of transportation. The actual path and transmission medium are unimportant to you as you relinquished control of your letter when you placed it in your mailbox. You are trusting that the postal service will ensure that your letter arrives.

Your envelope finally reaches the local post office for your friend. The envelope is delivered to your friend and is opened. Your friend opens the envelope, pulls out the letter, and reads it. These last steps correlate to the OSI system model working in reverse. The data, your letter, is de-encapsulated when the envelope is opened. The contents are then delivered to the recipient when your friend reads the letter, a mapping to the Presentation layer, and comprehends through the Application layer.

OSI and Wireless: Layer 2 and Down

Now that you have an understanding of the OSI system model, we can relate the different technologies used in WLANs to the OSI system model. As the name *wireless LAN* implies, it is networking without wires. The wires you are accustomed to using are replaced by radio signals. A number of various techniques are available for sending data over radio signals—these are covered in greater detail in Chapter 2.

The standards covered by the Cisco WLAN products detailed in this book are based on the IEEE's 802.11 series. The 802.11 standards are responsible for defining the Physical and MAC layers of operation in a WLAN. The primary standard we focus on in the 802.11b standard, which is an extension to the original 802.11 standard. 802.11b's primary objective defines the use of the 2.4 GHz band in radio frequency (RF) for high-speed data communications. 802.11b supports the original 802.11 data rate of 2 Mbps as well as higher speeds up to 11 Mbps.

The frames generated by a WLAN device differ from the frames generated by an Ethernet device in many ways. WLANs are not physically connected by cables like an Ethernet LAN, so new fields in the frames must be created to describe aspects of the WLAN. We first examine a typical 802.2 Ethernet frame and compare it to a 802.11b frame.

An 802.2 Ethernet frame is comprised of six fields each with a specific function. Figure 1.6 illustrates an Ethernet frame.

Figure 1.6 Ethernet Frame Format

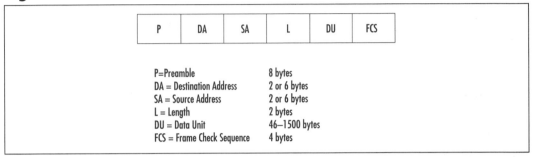

- **Preamble** The first field in an Ethernet frame is the preamble. The preamble is an 8-byte long alternating pattern of 0's and 1's telling receiving devices that a new frame is arriving.

- **Destination Address and Source Address** The next fields are the destination address (DA) and source address (SA). The fields are 2 or 6 bytes long and contain the MAC address of the source device on the network and the destination address. The destination address may be a single MAC address in the case of a unicast, a broadcast to all nodes on the network, or a multicast to a group of nodes on the network.

- **Length** The next field is the length and is 2 bytes long describing the number of bytes of data following this field.

- **Data Unit** The next field is the data unit containing the user data of the frame and is 46–1500 bytes long. This is where the data being encapsulated into the frame is located; for example the graphic in a Web page requested by your system. This field will vary in length based on the data encapsulated.

- **Frame Check Sequence** The last field in an Ethernet frame is the Frame Check Sequence (FCS) field and is 4 bytes long. The FCS is a cyclic redundancy check (CRC) on the frame allowing the receiver of the frame to perform basic error controls on the frame. If a frame fails the CRC check, it is discarded and the upper layer protocol is typically responsible for retransmission.

A 802.11b frame (illustrated in Figure 1.7) is comprised of nine fields.

Figure 1.7 802.11b Frame Format

FC	D/ID	A1	A2	A3	SC	A4	FB	FCS

FC = Frame Control   2 bytes
D/ID = Duration/ID   2 bytes
A1 = Address 1   6 bytes
A2 = Address 2   6 bytes
A3 = Address 3   6 bytes
SC = Sequence Control   2 bytes
A4 = Address 4   6 bytes
FB = Frame Body   0–2312 bytes
FCS = Frame Check Sequence   4 bytes

- The first field in an 802.11b frame is the *frame control* (FC) field and is 2 bytes long. The FC field contains ten subfields including protocol version, type, subtype, to Distribution System (DS), from DS, more fragments, retry, power management, more data, Wired Equivalent Protocol (WEP), and order. These fields are some of the prime differentiators in an 802.11b frame and are described in greater detail here:

  - **Protocol Version** The protocol version field is the first field within the frame control field and is 2 bits long. The default value for this field is 0 with all other values being reserved at this time.

  - **Type** The type field is 2 bits long and works in conjunction with the 4-bit subtype field to identify the function of the frame. The possible combinations and their descriptions are illustrated in Table 1.1.

  - **To Distribution System** The To DS field is 1 bit long and is set to 1 in all frames sent by an associated station with an AP to signify that the frame is destined for the network behind the AP, such as a server connected to the same Ethernet network as the AP. All other frames have the To DS bit set to 0.

  - **From Distribution System** The From DS field is 1 bit long and is set to 1 on all frames exiting the DS. All other frames have the From DS bit set to 0.

  - **More Fragments** The More Fragments (MF) field is 1 bit long and is set to 1 in all frames that contain another fragment of the current MAC Service Data Unit (MSDU) or MAC Management Protocol Data Unit (MMPDU). All other frames have the MF bit set to 0.

- **Retry** The retry field is 1 bit long and is set to 1 in all frames, data or management, that are retransmissions of earlier frames. Frames that are not retransmissions of a previous frame are set to 0.

- **Power Management** The Power Management (PM) field is 1 bit long and is used to indicate the power management mode of a station. The value is used to indicate the state in which the station will be in after the successful completion of the frame exchange sequence. A value of 1 is used to indicate that the station will be in power-save mode, whereas 0 indicates that the station is in active mode.

NOTE

The PM field in frames transmitted by a wireless Access Point will always be set to 0, indicating active mode. It would not be desirable for an AP on your network to go into power-save mode.

- **More Data** The More Data field (MD) is 1 bit long and used to tell an associated station in power-save mode that one or more frames are buffered for the station on the AP. The MD field is set to 0 for all other directed frames.

- **WEP** The WEP field is 1 bit long and is set to 1 if the frame body contains data that has been processed by the WEP algorithm. Frames that have not been processed by WEP have a WEP field value of 0.

- **Order** The Order field is 1 bit long and is set to 1 in any data frame that contains data using the *StrictlyOrdered* service class. All other frames have a value of 0 in the Order field.

NOTE

The *StrictlyOrdered* service class is a mechanism built into the 802.11 standard that provides additional protection against out of order frames. This is accomplished by holding any multicast or broadcast traffic that matches addresses for frames that are already queued. Without this mechanism, it would be possible for broadcast or multicast traffic to reach a recipient out of order and create communications problems.

Table 1.1 802.11 Type and Subtype Combinations in the Frame Control (FC) Field

Type Value	Type Description	Subtype Value	Subtype Description
b3 b2		b7 b6 b5 b4	
00	Management	0000	Association Request
00	Management	0001	Association Response
00	Management	0010	Reassociation Request
00	Management	0011	Reassociation Response
00	Management	0100	Probe Request
00	Management	0101	Probe Response
00	Management	0110-0111	Reserved
00	Management	1000	Beacon
00	Management	1001	Announcement traffic indication message (ATIM)
00	Management	1010	Disassociation
00	Management	1011	Authentication
00	Management	1100	Deauthentication
00	Management	1101-1111	Reserved
01	Control	0000-1001	Reserved
01	Control	1010	Power Save (PS) Poll
01	Control	1011	Request To Send (RTS)
01	Control	1100	Clear To Send (CTS)
01	Control	1101	Acknowledgement (ACK)
01	Control	1110	Contention-Free (CF) End
01	Control	1111	CF-End + CF-ACK
10	Data	0000	Data
10	Data	0001	Data + CF-ACK
10	Data	0010	Data + CF-Poll
10	Data	0011	Data + CF-ACK + CF-Poll
10	Data	0100	Null function (no data)
10	Data	0101	CF-ACK (no data)
10	Data	0110	CF-Poll (no data)
10	Data	0111	CF-ACK + CF-Poll (no data)

Continued

Table 1.1 Continued

Type Value	Type Description	Subtype Value	Subtype Description
10	Data	1000-1111	Reserved
11	Reserved	0000-1111	Reserved

- The next field in an 802.11b frame is the *Duration/ID* field and is 16 bits long. It is used to carry the association ID of a station with an Access Point.

- The next fields in the 802.11b frames are *address fields*. If you review an Ethernet frame, you see that there are only two fields for addresses: destination and source. In 802.11b frames, there may be up to four, the basic service set identifier (BSSID), destination address (DA), source address (SA), receiver address (RA), and transmitter address (TA).

    - The BSSID is the MAC address of the Access Point.

    - The DA is the MAC address of the final recipient.

    - The SA is the MAC address of the sending station on the WLAN.

    - The RA is the MAC address of the intended immediate recipient stations on the WLAN.

    - The TA is the MAC address of the sending station on the WLAN.

- The next field in an 802.11b frame is the *frame body* and is 0–2312 bytes long. The frame body is the payload, or data contained within the frame. This is where the data being encapsulated into the frame is located, for example the graphic in a Web page requested by your system. This field will vary in length based on the data encapsulated.

- The final field in the 802.11b frame format, just as in the Ethernet format, is the FCS.

As you can see, there are a number of differences between Ethernet and 802.11b frames. These differences are required to enable high-speed communications on a physical medium of radio waves rather than standard copper or fiber media.

www.syngress.com

OSI and Wireless: Layer 3 and Up

The OSI system model applies to the configuration, management, and trouble-shooting of Cisco WLANs far beyond Layers 1 and 2. Certainly Layers 1 and 2 are key to WLANs, but the other layers play key roles as well. For example, all configuration of wireless APs and bridges are done through Telnet and HTTP, two Application-layer protocols. The Web interface on APs and bridges use HTTP in their graphical interfaces. This is a key topic to understand because if there is a problem accessing the Web interface, you need to be able to use your knowledge of the OSI system model to troubleshoot the problem. Could the problem be caused by an access list on a router between your system and the AP, is it a problem with general network connectivity, can you ping the AP's TCP/IP address? These all come into play in determining the cause of the failure.

Bridges and APs also use other protocols in the OSI system model. Examples include the following:

- Dynamic Host Configuration Protocol (DHCP) at Layer 7 to automatically obtain a TCP/IP address on the network from a DHCP server.

- Extensible Authentication Protocol (EAP) at Layer 7 working with RADIUS.

- Remote Authentication Dial In User Service (RADIUS) at Layer 7 in conjunction with EAP to authenticate WLAN users.

- WEP at Layer 2 to encrypt/decrypt data on the WLAN.

Review of TCP/IP Basics

TCP/IP is one of the most widely deployed protocols on networks today. TCP/IP can be looked upon as the great network communication unifier. Prior to the wide adoption of TCP/IP as the protocol of choice, many disparate and proprietary protocols existed. IPX, Local Area Transport (LAT), and AppleTalk each provided connectivity to their respective operating systems. There was no common protocol to facilitate communications between the different operating systems. Awkward protocol gateway systems were implemented to "covert" communications between the networks. TCP/IP had actually been around since the 1980s, but few vendors felt it was important or dominant enough to implement in their products. Now, looking back, it is almost hard to imagine networking without TCP/IP to provide intersystem connectivity.

TCP/IP was originally implemented as a standard protocol for the pre-fledging Internet called ARPANET for the United States government Advanced Research Projects Agency, which funded the network. As the ARPANET grew, the need to have a standardized protocol became apparent. IP as a protocol was defined in Request for Comments (RFC) 760 in 1980; TCP was defined in RFC 793 in 1981. TCP/IP comprises a suite of protocols. This means that many different protocols fall under the umbrella of TCP/IP.

A few of the more common TCP/IP protocols include HTTP, File Transfer Protocol (FTP), SMTP, Internet Control Message Protocol (ICMP), and Post Office Protocol (POP). Each of these protocols uses IP as their base foundation for moving data on a network. Looking at TCP/IP from the perspective of the OSI system model can be very beneficial to understand how the protocols inter-relate. For example, SMTP, a messaging protocol is defined as an Application layer protocol, and as such, resides at Layer 7 of the OSI system model. SMTP relies on TCP at the Transport layer to establish a reliable connection to a remote system. TCP in turn relies on IP to provide addressing information and routing capabilities to ensure that the data is sent to the proper destination. We cover TCP in more depth later in the chapter.

Understanding TCP/IP Addressing

As with any Network layer protocol, addressing is a key component; TCP/IP is no different. Devices on the network require a unique address to identify themselves as well as other nodes on the network to establish communications. The addressing in TCP/IP is comprised of a 32-bit value, represented by four groups of decimal addresses separated by periods for ease of classification. The decimal numbers represent binary numbers, 0's and 1's, in a format that is much easier for humans to comprehend and remember. For example, the TCP/IP address of 192.168.149.234 is a representation for 11000000.10101000.10010101.11101010. Which number would you rather remember? Furthermore, any IP address can be divided into two portions: the network number and the host number. The network number may be a valid Internet assigned network or may be part of a private TCP/IP addressing scheme. Because there are a limited number of TCP/IP addresses available in the world, the Internet community created RFC 1918, which allocates address space in the three primary classes of address space for private organizations to utilize for their internal networks.

IP addresses are divided into five distinct classes, with three of the classes being predominant. The classes are labeled by the alphabet, so the classes are A, B, C, D, and E. Figure 1.8 illustrates the different classes.

Figure 1.8 IP Address Classes

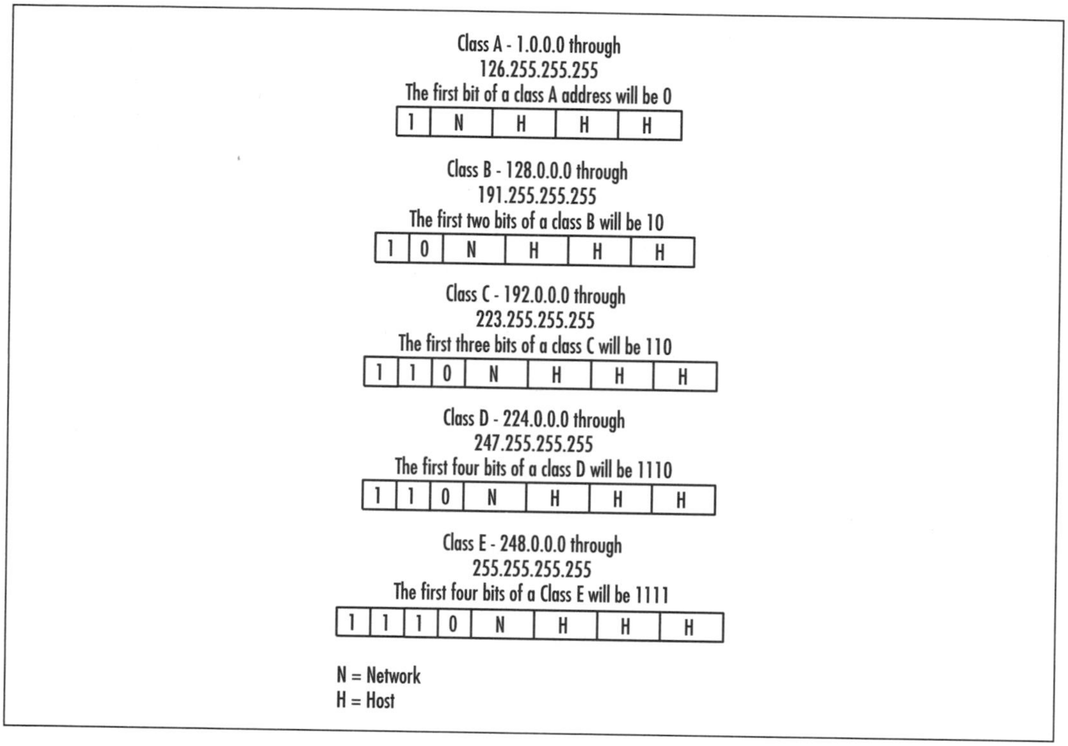

As you can see, each class of address allows for a varying number of hosts. For example, in each class A address, there is the possibility of 16,777,214 hosts, while a class C address has the possibility of 254 hosts. The class of address employed in an organization usually depends on the number of devices to be addressed.

To determine the class of address you are dealing with, there are two primary mechanisms. One, the simplest, is memorization; the other is to examine the high order, or first bits of the IP address. The high-order bits will always dictate the class of address space used without fail, whereas memorization is susceptible to human error. In Figure 1.9, you can see the high-order bits and the number of addresses possible per class.

One of the more difficult tasks for a TCP/IP network administrator is that of *subnetting*. TCP/IP addresses can be broken down into smaller networks called subnets. Subnetting can be very beneficial because it allows for effective address allocation and broadcast domain control. Subnets are created by the network administrator and can be concealed by address summarization for efficient communications to the outside world, or to maintain stability in the network.

Figure 1.9 High-Order Bits and Number of Hosts Per Classful Address

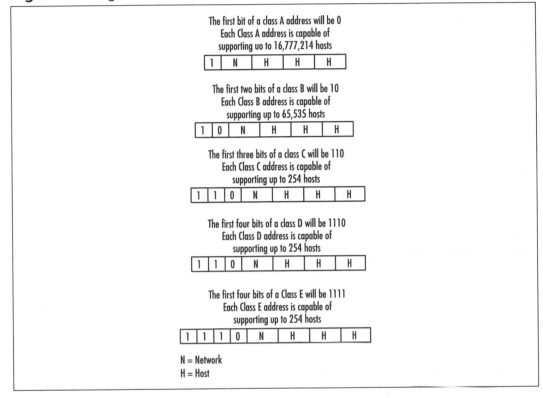

Subnetting is accomplished by borrowing bits from the host portion of the TCP/IP address and designating them as subnet mask bits. Every IP address has a subnet mask. The subnet mask has the same format as an IP address in that it is a 32-bit value represented by four groups of decimal addresses separated by periods. However, subnet masks contain all binary 1's in the fields signifying the network address and binary 0's in the fields signifying the host address. There are two main flavors of subnet masks: classful and classless. Classful, as their name implies, are based on the class of IP address. For example, a Class B network of 172.16.0.0 using a classful subnet mask would have a subnet mask of 255.255.0.0. The 255.255 portion of the subnet mask signifies the network portion; the 0.0 signifies the host portion of the address. TCP/IP protocol stacks perform a logical AND on the IP address and subnet mask to determine the broadcast and network address for a given address.

Classful subnet masks are easy to remember as they follow the class of address being used. Things get a bit more complicated with classless subnet masking. Classless subnet masking takes place when the subnet mask is anything other than the natural classful subnet mask. Back to the example of the 172.16.0.0 network: If you apply a subnet mask of 255.255.255.0, you are breaking the larger network, 172.16.0.0, into a smaller network, 172.16.0.0 with a class C mask, meaning that you will have only 254 addresses on the network. A result of the logical AND done using the 172.16.0.0 with the 255.255.255.0 mask is illustrated in Figure 1.10.

Figure 1.10 Logical AND Operation

```
172.016.000.000 = 10101100.00010000.00000000.00000000
255.255.255.000 = 11111111.11111111.11111111.00000000

– – – – – – – – – – – – – – – – – – – – – – – – – – – – – – – – –

Logical AND


172.016.000.000 = 11111111.11111111.11111111.00000000
```

Designing & Planning…

Common Practice for Subnetting TCP/IP Address Space

A common practice in many organizations is to assign TCP/IP address space from RFC 1918. This practice serves many purposes:

- It does not use registered IP space for wireless devices; which typically do not include servers.

- It enables the organization to subnet the address space without any restrictions.

- It allows for easy identification of WLAN traffic on the network because it is not sharing address space with the wired network.

In many organizations, registered IP address space is a premium commodity. By using RFC 1918 address space, precious registered address space is not consumed by WLAN devices.

Subnetting can be taken to further extremes by using other masks that move the 1 further right from the original high-order bit placement. There are fixed values for subnet masks because you are restricted to having the high-order bits be consecutive 1's. Table 1.2 shows the possible values for a subnet mask.

Table 1.2 Subnet Mask Values

Class A Addresses	Class B Addresses	Class C Addresses
255.0.0.0	255.255.0.0	255.255.255.0
255.128.0.0	255.255.128.0	255.255.255.128
255.192.0.0	255.255.192.0	255.255.255.192
255.224.0.0	255.255.224.0	255.255.255.224
255.240.0.0	255.255.240.0	255.255.255.240
255.248.0.0	255.255.248.0	255.255.255.248
255.252.0.0	255.255.252.0	255.255.255.252
255.254.0.0	255.255.254.0	255.255.255.254

TCP

Transmission Control Protocol (TCP) is one of the protocols in the TCP/IP protocol suite. TCP is a Layer four, Transport layer protocol that is responsible for establishing and maintaining reliable communications in a TCP/IP network. TCP also provides stream data transfer, efficient flow control, multiplexing, full-duplex communication, and reliability on the network at Layer four.

TCP is considered a reliable protocol in that every packet sent between nodes on a network is acknowledged before the next packet is sent. This might sound like high overhead to you—it is. TCP was developed to be used on networks that were less reliable than the networks we are used to working with in 2002. To accommodate for less reliable communication, TCP utilizes flow control and sequencing to ensure proper data flow.

As networks have stabilized, TCP has remained and is still in wide use today. On most IP networks, TCP is the most prevalent protocol because so many applications use TCP. Some of the more common applications include SMTP, FTP, HTTP, and Telnet.

UDP

UDP is one of the protocols in the TCP/IP protocol suite. UDP is a Layer four, Transport layer protocol that is used for applications that are not considered mission-critical, require low overhead, or are streamlined for speed. Unlike TCP, UDP is not considered a reliable protocol. Rather UDP attempts to send packets on a "best-effort" service. It is connectionless and as such does not have the same overhead as TCP.

Some of the more common applications include SNMP, Network Time Protocol (NTP), Domain Name Service (DNS), and some Voice over IP (VoIP) implementations.

Summary

In this chapter, you have formed a solid foundation in basic networking to delve more deeply into WLANs. The chapter has reviewed some basics of networking including defining bus, star, ring, and mesh topologies. The most common deployment model for fully meshed networks would be in the WAN arena.

Two of the different access methods networks use include Carrier Sense Multiple Access with Collision Detection (CSMA/CD) and deterministic access.

The OSI system model plays an important role in developing networking standards. The model is comprised of seven layers:

- Physical layer
- Data-link layer
- Network layer
- Transport layer
- Session layer
- Presentation layer
- Application layer

The Physical layer of the OSI system model is responsible for defining the electrical and mechanical aspects of networking. The Data-link layer defines the protocols that control the Physical layer, determining such issues as how the medium is accessed and shared, how devices or stations on the medium are addressed and how data is framed before transmission on the medium. The Network layer is where protocols such as Transmission Control Protocol/Internet Protocol (TCP/IP) are addressed, as well as where routing functions are performed. The Transport layer specifies a higher level of flow control, error detection, and correction. The Session layer is responsible for establishing, managing and terminating communication sessions between Presentation layer entities and the Transport layer. The Presentation layer is responsible for ensuring that data sent from the Application layer of one device is comprehensible by the Application layer of another device. The Application layer is responsible for providing network services to applications such as e-mail, word processing, and file transfer that are not implicitly defined in the OSI system model.

After the OSI review, we applied the OSI system model to WLANs and discussed the frame format the MAC layer uses in the 802.11 standard. We compared the familiar Ethernet frame format with a 802.11 frame to reveal differences such as the Frame Control (FC) field as well as the four address fields. Moving up the OSI system model, we touched on how the other five layers of the OSI system model apply to WLANs.

Next, we covered some basics with TCP/IP including addressing and subnetting. There are five classes of TCP/IP addresses with classes A, B, and C being the predominant addresses. Class D addresses are reserved for multicast, and class E address space is reserved for future use by the IETF. Within the classes of addresses, you can more effectively utilize the address space by subnetting. We covered the seven basic subnet mask values that you will encounter in the real world as well.

Finally, we wrapped up the chapter with a quick review of TCP and UDP as part of the TCP/IP protocol suite. TCP is the reliable protocol with flow control and connection-oriented applications such as HTTP, FTP, and Telnet. UDP is considered "unreliable" and makes a best effort to deliver data. Many applications use UDP such as SNMP, NTP, and DNS.

Solutions Fast Track

Review of Networking

- ☑ There are four main topologies a network can use: bus, ring, star, and mesh.

- ☑ Wireless local area networks (WLANs) use Carrier Sense Multiple Access with Collision Detection (CSMA/CD) for their access method.

- ☑ There are many different types of cabling for networks, including copper and fiber, each with their own subtypes.

Review of OSI System Model

- ☑ The Open Systems Interconnection (OSI) reference model provides a "road map" for network standards.

- ☑ WLAN standards are defined at Layers 1 and 2 of the OSI system model.

- ☑ The Media Access Control (MAC) header in a 802.11 frame has more options and flags than a typical Ethernet frame.

Review of TCP/IP Basics

- ☑ There are five classes of Internet Protocol (IP) address, A, B, C, D, and E with A through C in predominant use with D being used by multicast and E reserved.

- ☑ Transmission Control Protocol (TCP) is a connection-oriented protocol that is reliable. Common applications using TCP are the File Transfer Protocol (FTP), Hypertext Transfer Protocol (HTTP), Simple Mail Transfer Protocol (SMTP), and Telnet.

- ☑ The User Datagram Protocol (UDP) is a connectionless protocol that is considered unreliable. Common applications using UDP include Simple Network Management Protocol (SNMP), Network Time Protocol (NTP), Domain Name System (DNS), and some Voice over IP (VoIP).

Frequently Asked Questions

The following Frequently Asked Questions, answered by the authors of this book, are designed to both measure your understanding of the concepts presented in this chapter and to assist you with real-life implementation of these concepts. To have your questions about this chapter answered by the author, browse to **www.syngress.com/solutions** and click on the **"Ask the Author"** form.

Q: Does a wireless network require a wired network to work properly?

A: A wireless network does not require a wired network to operate, according to the standards. However, if you require devices on your wireless network to communicate with devices on the wired network, the WLAN must connect to the wired network at some point.

Q: Why would I want to subnet my address space?

A: Subnetting can be a very tricky proposition, from both a technical aspect as well as an operational aspect. Some organizations are interested in wasting as little address space as possible and therefore subnet. Other organizations may or may not subnet for political reasons. It is up to the individual organization to determine their subnetting policy.

Q: Does an 802.11 frame header offer an equivalent to the IP Precedence bits available in a standard Ethernet frame?

A: No, 802.11 does not incorporate any sort of Quality of Service (QoS) in the frame header like Ethernet does.

Q: Why wouldn't I want to use a mesh topology for my network?

A: Actually it is quite common to once again, have a "best of both worlds" design in a network. Your Frame Relay WAN may be a meshed network to provide additional redundancy or connectivity between offices. Your network may also feature a meshed environment in the data centers for additional bandwidth and redundancy. So categorically stating that you would not want to use a meshed network is not appropriate.

Chapter 2

Wireless LAN Overview

Solutions in this chapter:

- **Understanding the Fundamentals of Radio Frequency**

- **Communicating with Wireless LAN Technologies**

- **Implementing a Wireless LAN Architecture**

- **Keeping Pace with Wireless Networking Standards**

☑ **Summary**

☑ **Solutions Fast Track**

☑ **Frequently Asked Questions**

31

Introduction

The primary advantage of wireless local area networks (WLANs) is their ability to communicate to the wired network or to other WLAN devices. Integrating both wired network and wireless LAN technologies into a single device allows you to have the best of both worlds. In addition to the radio technologies enabling WLANs, other technologies are employed to provide security, efficiency, and stability of the WLAN. Because WLAN radio devices use various aspects of radio technology, we first review radio frequency (RF) fundamentals. We define and explain the various RF apparatus as it pertains to the functionality of WLANs. This chapter provides an overview of WLANs to provide a knowledge base for more detailed wireless networking topics. We provide information concerning the underlying concepts and technologies used in wireless systems in order to enhance your ability to design, implement, and troubleshoot the various processes of a wireless system. You will be given the practical information necessary to understand the functionality of any WLAN radio device to include Cisco Aironet products. Because this subject matter represents such a broad range of topics and technologies, discussing them all in the course of one chapter is difficult at best. Instead, we give focus to the fundamentals and standards as they directly relate to WLANs. Next, we discuss current wireless technologies and the advantages and disadvantages of various wireless technology implementations, with greater attention given to the technology used by Cisco Aironet devices. Finally, we turn our attention to standards with respect to wireless standards from the major standards organizations worldwide. In doing so, we examine where wireless radio devices fit into the International Organization for Standardization (ISO) Open Systems Interconnect (OSI) reference model.

Understanding the Fundamentals of Radio Frequency

A fundamental understanding of RF is necessary in order to fully understand the world of wireless networking. RF in wireless communications is typically used to describe devices or equipment that use radio waves to transmit images and sounds from one transmission point to one or more reception points. In computer networking, RF is used to describe network devices (access points [APs], bridges, and so on.) that use radio waves to transmit or receive data instead of using traditional wired data cabling or telephone lines. Wireless systems utilize components of radio technology to prepare, transmit, and receive the digital data used in WLANs. In the next few sections, we provide a brief history of radio, the RF concepts and terms used, and their place in the technology of WLANs.

It has taken the work of some of the best minds in science history to produce what is known today as radio. In 1886, Heinrich Hertz developed a device called a spark gap coil, for generating and detecting electromagnetic waves. This spark gap coil would not have been possible if it were not for the mathematical theory of electromagnetic waves formulated by Scottish physicist James Clerk Maxwell in 1865. In 1895, Guglielmo Marconi, recognizing the possibility of using these electromagnetic waves for a wireless communication system, gave a demonstration of the first wireless telegraph, using Hertz's spark coil as a transmitter, and a radio detector called a "coherer," which was developed by a scientist by the name of Edouard Branly, as the first radio receiver. The effective operating distance of this system increased as the equipment was improved, and in 1901, Marconi succeeded in sending the letter "S" across the Atlantic Ocean using Samuel Morse's dot-dash communication coding technique, commonly referred to today as Morse code. The first vacuum electron tube capable of detecting radio waves electronically was invented (by Sir John Fleming) in 1904. Two years later, Lee de Forest invented a type of triode (a three-element vacuum tube) called an audion, which not only detected radio waves but also amplified them.

The beginning of RF, in terms of the transmission of music and speech, began in 1906 with the work of Reginald Fessiden and Ernst F. W. Alexanderson. However, it was not until 1913 when Edwin H. Armstrong patented the circuit for the regenerative receiver that long-range radio reception became a practical reality. The major developments in radio initially were for ship-to-shore communications. Following the 1920 establishment of station KDKA as the first commercial broadcasting station in the United States (located in Pittsburgh, PA), technical improvements in the industry increased, as did radio's popularity. Particularly in the United States, the radio receiver became so popular that it could be found in nearly every home. Since the early days of radio, countless improvements and research has brought us such applications as television, radar, wireless phones, and eventually wireless radio devices for LANs.

In order to understand the concepts that are detailed here, we must start with a common frame of reference. We use a common transmission and reception example to look at the RF communication process in a simplified manner and then drill down into each part of the process. We start with a common analogy that most of you can relate to, your car radio communication process.

In order for you to listen to music from your car radio, a specific transmission and reception process must take place. Initially, the radio station impresses (encodes) some information, like voice or speech, on a radio wave. This information encoding on a radio wave is known as *modulation*. The radio station broadcasts this radio wave with the encoded data (music) on a certain frequency from a large antenna. Your car radio antenna picks up the broadcast based on the frequency to which your radio dial is tuned. Your car radio then decodes the music from the radio wave and plays that information through the speakers as sound. See Figure 2.1.

Figure 2.1 Car Radio Transmission and Reception Process

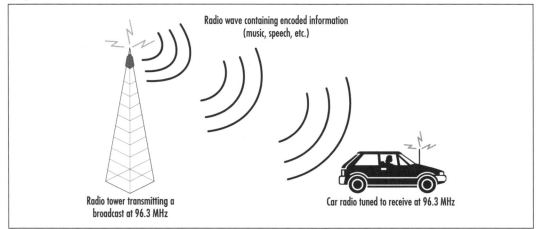

Radio wave containing encoded information
(music, speech, etc.)

Radio tower transmitting a
broadcast at 96.3 MHz

Car radio tuned to receive at 96.3 MHz

Wireless Radio Signal Transmission and Reception

Radio frequency (RF) is a specific type of electric current known as *alternating current* (AC) that generates an electromagnetic (EM) field when applied to an antenna. The resulting electromagnetic field (sometimes called an *RF field*) and subsequent electromagnetic radiation is then used for wireless broadcasting and/or communications. When an electric current flows through a wire, a magnetic field is generated around the wire. When alternating current flows through a wire, the magnetic field alternately expands and collapses. This expansion and collapse is a result of the electrical current reversing its direction. In the United States, AC reverses direction or alternates at a frequency of 60 Hertz (Hz), or 60 cycles per second. In South America and Europe, AC typically alternates at a frequency of 50 Hz or 50 cycles per second. This is one reason why electrical devices, such as hair dryers and shavers, require special converters in order to work properly outside North America. Conventional AC power is produced by rotating machines, called alternators, that produce a smooth alternation, like that of a pendulum. This alternating current and subsequent frequency changes are described mathematically as a "sine wave" (see Figure 2.2). It is the ideal waveform for the transfer of AC power and consequently radio transmission.

Figure 2.2 Sine Wave

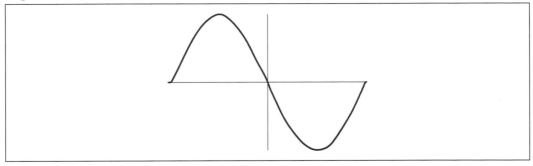

As you have seen in the car radio analogy, a radio wave is broadcast from the radio station antenna. To broadcast the radio wave, AC is applied to the antenna, giving rise to an electromagnetic field that moves and spreads through space, like the ripples caused by dropping a pebble into a pond. When we say *electromagnetic field*, you need to make the distinction between field and radiation. A *field* is a physics term for an area of space or region that is under the influence of some force that can act on matter within the area or region. A good example of this is a comet passing close to Earth: The gravitational field produced by Earth attracts the comet and therefore influences the comet's trajectory. In the car radio example, the radio transmitter and antenna generate a moving electric charge. Nonmoving or static electric charges produce electric fields around them. Moving electric charges produce both electric and magnetic fields, or an electromagnetic field. An electromagnetic field is generated when charged particles, such as electrons, are accelerated. Electric fields surround all electrically charged particles. When these charged particles are in motion, they produce magnetic fields. When the speed of the charged particle changes, an electromagnetic field is produced. In the 19th century, scientists discovered that arcs or sparks of electrical energy (in the form of an electromagnetic field) could travel between two perpendicular conductive rods without the aid of wires between them. They learned to reproduce this effect over varying distances and led them to believe that it was possible to communicate wirelessly over long distances. These electric arcs were used in the first radio transmitters.

As you have seen, electrically charged particles in motion produce electromagnetic fields. When the motion of these charged particles regularly repeats or changes, they produce what we call *electromagnetic radiation*. Electromagnetic radiation moves energy from one point to another. This is somewhat like a small ball moving the same way over and over, against the inside of a larger ball causing the larger ball to move in a certain direction. The larger ball represents the electromagnetic radiation and the smaller ball inside the larger ball represents an electrically charged particle in motion. Radio waves are not the only form of electromagnetic radiation. Light is also electromagnetic radiation, and both radio waves and light have many similarities. The most significant of these similarities, for our purposes, is the speed at which both travel. Both are moving through space in approximately straight lines at a speed of about 299,792 km per second or 186,000 miles per second. In other words, a radio wave as electromagnetic radiation travels at the speed of light.

As the distance from the energy source of electromagnetic radiation increases, the area over which the electromagnetic radiation is spread is increased, so that the available energy from the electromagnetic radiation in a given area is decreased. Radio signal intensity (amplitude), like light intensity, decreases as the distance from the source increases. The signal gets weaker as you move farther away from the source of the transmission. A transmitting antenna is a device that projects electromagnetic radiation, as RF energy, into space by a transmitter (the electromagnetic radiation energy source). The antenna can be designed to concentrate the RF energy into a beam and increase its effectiveness in a given direction.

Radio is commonly used for the transmission of voice, music, and pictures, as in broadcast radio and television. The sounds and images used in radio and television are converted into electrical signals by some input device such as a microphone or video camera, amplified, and used to encode (modulate) a carrier wave that has been generated by an oscillator circuit (a circuit used to produce alternating current) in a transmitter. A carrier wave is the form of the radio wave prior to modulation or transmission. The modulated carrier wave is also amplified and then applied to an antenna that converts the electrical signals to electromagnetic waves for radiation into space. Electromagnetic waves are transmitted by line of sight and by deflection from a specific layer of the upper atmosphere, called the ionosphere. This is the layer of the upper atmosphere that ranges from approximately 30 to 250 miles high. Ionization of nitrogen and oxygen molecules from ultraviolet radiation and X-rays from the sun produces a layer of charged particles, which allows radio waves to be reflected around the world.

Receiving antennas do not actively search for a radio wave from any source. The electromagnetic radiation from the originating antenna passes across the passive, receiving antenna. Receiving antennas intercept part of this electromagnetic radiation and change it back to the form of an electrical signal. The receiving antennas then feed this signal to a receiver, which in turn, takes the incoming signals mixed with a signal from a local oscillator in the receiver, to produce intermediate frequencies that are equal to the mathematical sum and difference of the incoming and local frequencies. In other words, the oscillator acts as a type of filter to weed out all frequencies other than the intended frequency. The oscillator then sends this intended frequency through an amplifier. Because the amplifier operates at the previously determined intermediate frequency (a single frequency), it is designed for optimum selectivity and gain. The tuning control on a radio receiver adjusts the local oscillator frequency. In order for the receiver to amplify the signal and feed it to circuits that demodulate it to separate the signal wave from the carrier wave, the incoming signals must be above the threshold of sensitivity of the receiver and tuned to the frequency of the signal.

Some radio devices act as both transmitter and receiver for radio signals. These devices are known as transceivers. When a responding signal is sent back to the originating radio, the radio transceiver changes modes from reception to transmission and back again. Cisco Aironet Access Points and bridges, as transceivers, have this characteristic. Transceivers change modes from transmission to reception over and over again. They will do this many thousands of times per second. Though transceivers allow you to transmit and receive with the same device, thus reducing the size and cost of radios; in wireless networking, this capability introduces *latency*, a delay in communications. It is idiosyncratic to radio communications and negatively affects data throughput, albeit minimally.

Frequency

AC is the type of electric current generally used to produce electromagnetic fields. As you have seen (in Figure 2.2), AC alternates, or cycles over time. This cycling over a period of time is referred to as *amplitude*. The amplitude oscillates from zero to some maximum and back again. The number of times the cycle is repeated in one second is called the frequency. AC frequencies can range from a single cycle in thousands of years to quadrillions of cycles per second. Remember Heinrich Hertz, he is the one who invented the spark coil for generating and detecting radio waves. The unit of measurement for frequency is called a Hertz, after Heinrich. In fact, radio waves were originally called Hertzian waves. A Hertz is usually defined as one cycle per second, or one wave per second. The frequency unit or Hertz is normally abbreviated Hz. Because frequencies can be very large, the standard units of quantities used in science and commonly seen in the data world are used to annotate them. For example, 1000 Hz equals 1 KHz (kilohertz), 1000 KHz equals 1 MHz (megahertz), 1000 MHz equals 1 GHz (gigahertz), and so on.

At any given instance, a radio wave will have an amplitude variation similar to that of its time variation. Picture the waves produced by a pebble dropped into a still pond. One of the waves traveling on the pond represents a radio wave, the height of that wave represents the amplitude and the speed at which that wave travels represents the time variation. The distance from the top of one wave to the next is known as the wavelength. The frequency of an electromagnetic field (RF field) is directly related to its wavelength. By specifying the frequency of a radio wave (f) in megahertz and the wavelength (w) in meters, the two are inter-related mathematically, according to the following formula:

w = 300/f

In the car radio example, the radio is tuned to 96.3 MHz. This is the signal frequency of the radio station transmitter we want to "listen to." At 96.3 MHz, the signal has a wavelength of about 3 meters, or about 10 feet. This same formula applies if the wavelength is specified in millimeters (mm) and the frequency is given in gigahertz. Therefore a Cisco Aironet AP that transmits a signal at 2.4 GHz would have an approximate wavelength of 120 mm, or a little less than 5 inches. Remember, all radio waves travel at the speed of light, so a radio wave with a shorter wavelength will cross a specific point in space (like an antenna) more times than a radio wave with a long wavelength.

In general, as the frequency of a radio gets higher the corresponding wavelength of the electromagnetic field gets shorter. At 9 KHz, the free space wavelength is approximately 33 kilometers (km) or 21 miles (mi). At the highest radio frequencies, the electromagnetic wavelengths measure approximately one millimeter (1 mm). As the frequency is increased beyond that of the RF spectrum, electromagnetic energy takes the form of various types of light and energy such as infrared light (IR), visible light, ultraviolet light (UV), X-rays, and gamma rays.

Electromagnetic radiation, as radio waves, can be generated and used at frequencies higher than 10 KHz. A considerable segment of the electromagnetic radiation spectrum is available for use, extending from about 9 KHz, the lowest allocated wireless communications frequency, to thousands of gigahertz, with the upper ends of the frequency spectrum consisting of gamma and cosmic rays.

Many types of wireless devices make use of radio waves. Radio and television broadcast stations, cordless and cellular telephone, two-way radio systems and satellite communications are but a few. Other wireless devices make use of the visible light and infrared portions of the frequency spectrum. These areas of the spectrum have electromagnetic wavelengths that are shorter than those in RF fields. Examples include most television remote controls, some cordless computer keyboards and mice, and many laptop computers. Table 2.1 depicts the eight bands of the frequency spectrum used in the United States Frequency Allocation, displaying frequency and bandwidth ranges. These frequency allocations vary slightly from country to country.

Table 2.1 The United States Frequency Allocation Chart

Designation	Frequencies	Free-Space Wavelengths
Very Low Frequency (VLF)	9 KHz–30 KHz	33 km–10 km
Low Frequency (LF)	30 KHz–300 KHz	10 km–1 km
Medium Frequency (MF)	300 KHz–3 MHz	1 km–100 m
High Frequency (HF)	3 MHz–30 MHz	100 m–10 m
Very High Frequency (VHF)	30 MHz–300 MHz	10 m–1 m
Ultra High Frequency (UHF)	300 MHz–3 GHz	1 m–100 mm
Super High Frequency (SHF)	3 GHz–30 GHz	100 mm–10 mm
Extremely High Frequency (EHF)	30 GHz–300 GHz	10 mm–1 mm

The radio frequency (RF) spectrum is divided into several ranges, or bands. Most bands represent an increase of frequency corresponding to an order of magnitude of a power of 10. The exception to this is the extreme low end of the frequency spectrum. Table 2.2 shows examples of the classes of devices assigned to each frequency.

Table 2.2 Example Device Classes by Frequency Allocation

Designation	Examples
Very Low Frequency	Radio navigation devices for marine vessels, military communication with nuclear submarines (maritime mobile)
Low Frequency	Marine and aeronautical radio navigation and location devices

Continued

Table 2.2 Continued

Designation	Examples
Medium Frequency	Marine and aeronautical radio beacons, distress beacons, AM radio broadcasting, and maritime radio voice communications
High Frequency	Amateur radio and satellite communications, radio astronomy, and space research
Very High Frequency	Amateur radio and satellite, FM radio broadcasting, TV broadcasting (Channels 2–13), radio astronomy, mobile satellite communications
Ultra High Frequency	Fixed satellite communications, meteorological satellite communications, amateur radio, TV broadcasting (Channels 14–36 and 38–69), WLANs, land mobile communications (cell phones, cordless phones, etc.), radio astronomy, and aeronautical radio navigation
Super High Frequency	Inter-satellite communications, WLANs, weather radars, land mobile communications
Extremely High Frequency	Space research, Earth exploration satellites, amateur radio and satellite communications, radio astronomy, fixed and mobile satellite communications

Bandwidth

Traditionally, bandwidth is the amount of information that can be carried through a phone line, cable line, satellite feed, and so on. The greater the bandwidth, the greater the speed of your connection and the more your Internet experience approaches a more instant-download, TV-style experience.

Bandwidth, in the computer world, is defined as how much data you can send through a connection usually measured in bits per second. A full page of English text is about 16,000 bits And a fast modem can move about 15,000 bits in one second. Full-motion full-screen video would require roughly 10,000,000 bits per second, depending on compression.

In the radio world, bandwidth is defined in a little more complicated manner. Bandwidth is the difference between limiting frequencies within which performance of a radio device, in respect to some characteristic, falls within specified limits or the difference between the limiting frequencies of a continuous frequency band. In the 2.4 GHz unlicensed frequency-band, which is used in Cisco

Aironet products, the band begins at 2.4 GHz and ends at 2.4835 GHz. The difference between the beginning point and the end point is the bandwidth. Therefore the total available bandwidth available for use by wireless devices in this band is .0835 GHz or 83.5 MHz.

WLAN Frequency Bands

In order to prevent interference from radio signals in the United States, the Federal Communications Commission (FCC) is charged with assigning small sections of the RF spectrum for specific uses called *licensed frequencies*. In order to broadcast radio signals at these frequencies you must apply to the FCC for a license. The FCC allocated separate bands of radio frequencies as public bands, allowing use of some of the radio spectrum for devices that would not require a license. No license is required to use equipment transmitting at these frequencies. These are called the ISM bands, short for industrial, scientific, and medical bands.

There are three unlicensed bands within the industrial, scientific, and medical frequency range. They are the 900 MHz, 2.4 GHz, and 5.8 GHz frequencies (see Figure 2.3). Cisco Aironet products currently use the 2.4 GHz frequency range, which adheres to the Institute of Electrical and Electronic Engineers (IEEE) 802.11b standard. Recently, the FCC also opened up the 5.2 GHz band, known as the UNII (Unlicensed National Information Infrastructure) bands, for unlicensed use by high-speed data communications devices. 5.2 GHz is the same band that is used for the European Telecommunications Standards Institute ETSI HiperLAN specification in Europe.

Figure 2.3 ISM Unlicensed Frequency Bands

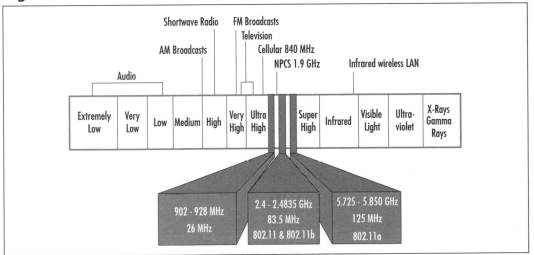

Table 2.3 lists additional 802.11b RF bands by geographic area.

Table 2.3 802.11b Radio Frequency Bands by Geography

Channel Number	Frequency GHz	North America	Europe	Spain	France	Japan
1	2.412	X	X			
2	2.417	X	X			
3	2.422	X	X			
4	2.427	X	X			
5	2.432	X	X			
6	2.437	X	X			
7	2.442	X	X			
8	2.447	X	X			
9	2.452	X	X			
10	2.457	X	X	X	X	
11	2.462	X	X	X	X	
12	2.467		X		X	
13	2.472		X		X	
14	2.483					X

Of significant importance is the total number of channels allocated in a given geographical area. The same IEEE 802.11 standard can be more versatile in areas where additional channels (bandwidth) are allocated. The advantage is due to the greater number of channels that can be potentially deployed. By allowing more channels to be deployed in a given area, the possibility of interference from other wireless devices is reduced or eliminated.

Modulation

An example of how modulation benefits us is the advances in modem technology over the years. The first modems communicated at 300 baud. Changes in modulation schemes allowed modem speeds to increase even though the physical medium (phone lines) did not change. 56K modems are today's current standard. They obtain much higher speeds over the same channel as the earlier modems. This increase in speed is due to utilizing more complex modulation techniques.

For the propagation and interception of radio waves, a transmitter and receiver are employed. A radio wave "carries" information-bearing signals through space, this carrier wave may have information encoded directly on it by periodically interrupting its transmission, as in Morse code telegraphy, or encoded on it by what is known as a modulation technique.

The actual information in a modulated signal is contained in its sidebands, or frequency components added to the carrier wave. It is important to note that the information is not contained in the carrier wave itself. Those frequency components that are higher than the carrier frequency are called *upper sidebands*. Frequency components that are lower than the carrier frequency are called *lower sidebands*. Usually only one of these sidebands needs to be transmitted because they typically contain equivalent information. Most common types of modulation techniques are analog, such as frequency and amplitude modulation (FM and AM). All WLAN radio devices including Cisco Aironet bridges and APs, must have the capability to encode digital information on an analog signal to prepare it for transmission and a reverse of the process for reception, much like the functionality of a modem. The conversion process requires modulation techniques that can efficiently convey digital information in analog form. Cisco Aironet devices use a family of modulation techniques, called *phase modulation*, to perform this efficient encoding.

Designing & Planning…

Signal to Noise Ratios and Modulation

Noise on a channel, whether wired or wireless, reduces the line speed and throughput normally available. Noise, speed, and distance are all interrelated. The importance of the signal to noise ratio of a RF system is made much clearer by investigating Shannon's Law, a fundamental mathematical equation used to calculate the channel capacity of communications systems. Claude Shannon was a Bell Laboratories engineer in the 1940s whose research resulted in the creation of the following equation:

$C = BW\log2(1+S/N)$

where C is the channel capacity, *BW* is the available bandwidth, and *S/N* is the signal-to-noise ratio within the bandwidth.

In order to be received correctly, complex modulation schemes require optimal signal-to-noise ratios (more signal with less noise). The

Continued

same is true in RF. As a receiver moves farther from a transmitter, the signal gets weaker, and the difference between the signal and the noise becomes less. At some point the signal cannot be distinguished from the noise, and loss of communication occurs. The amount of compression (or modulation scheme) at which the signal is transmitted determines the amount of signal that is required in order to be heard through the noise. As transmission or modulation schemes (compression) become more complex and data rates increase, immunity to noise becomes less; therefore the distance is reduced.

Phase Modulation

Phase modulation is the current modulation technique of choice for efficiently converting digital signals in a WLAN. Signal strength is used in amplitude modulation (AM) to modify the carrier wave to send information. Frequency modulation (FM) converts the originating signal into cycles to bear information. Phase modulation takes advantage of a signal wave's shape. It is ideal for sending digital information. Cisco Aironet radios use several forms of phase shifting for transmitting digital signals. We examine a digital signal and review current Cisco phase modulation techniques.

A digital signal means an ongoing stream of bits. These bits are usually used to communicate information in the form of data for devices capable of receiving and decoding them. These "data bits" are mathematically represented as 0's and 1's and correspond to off and on pulses electrical energy typically in the form of alternating current. Because a radio wave is an analog waveform, we must modulate the off-on-off-on beat of digital electrical signals in order to transmit them on a carrier wave.

You can send a digital signal without a carrier wave, like the earliest wireless telegraphs, but your results would be less than spectacular. If you ever have had someone turn on a hair dryer or vacuum sweeper while listening to an AM radio you know how bad interference on the signal can be and therefore how inefficient it is. Digital signals without a carrier wave are wideband, extremely inefficient, and would have extremely limited data rate capacity.

A radio wave, represented as a sine wave, is a continuous wave produced to transmit analog or digital information. The many phases or angles of the sine wave give rise to different ways of sending information. Simple phase modulation schemes begin by encoding a digital stream of bits onto an unchanging analog waveform. You now have a rising and falling pattern, in tune with the 0's and 1's.

This pattern is sometimes referred to as on and off amplitudes. A digital bit "0" might be marked by anything above some baseline value on the analog waveform, and a digital bit "1" might be marked by anything below the same baseline value. Simple enough, but it gives you just two states to send information. Binary Phase Shift Keying (BPSK) is an example of this type of modulation. Phase modulation techniques have become more complex to accommodate the need to carry greater amounts of information in the waveform. The following modulation techniques are used in Cisco Aironet radios (we describe each in the sections that follow):

- Binary Phase Shift Keying (BPSK)
- Quadrature Phase Shift Keying (QPSK)
- Complimentary Code Keying (CCK)

Binary Phase Shift Keying (BPSK)

In Binary Phase Shift Keying modulation, digital on and offs (1's and 0's) are represented by the various phases of an alternating current waveform or sine wave. BPSK uses one phase to represent a binary 1 and another phase to represent a binary 0 for a total of two bits of binary data (see Figure 2.4). This is utilized to transmit data at 1 Mbps.

Figure 2.4 Binary Phase Shift Keying

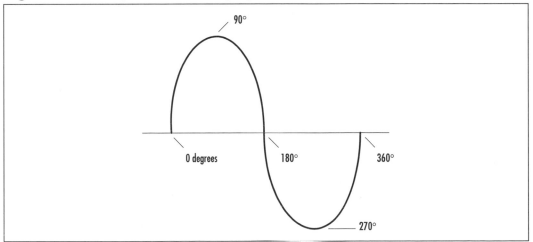

Quadrature Phase Shift Keying (QPSK)

With Quadrature Phase Shift Keying, the carrier undergoes four changes in phase and can therefore represent four binary bits of data. This scheme, used by most high speed modems, increases the speed and amount of data transferred by doubling the two states BPSK offers to at least four states to send information. QPSK manipulates or changes a sine wave's normal pattern by shifting its alternation and forcing the wave to fall to its baseline resting point. This fall to the wave's baseline is represented in the example by a premature drop to zero degrees (our baseline) before the wave would naturally drop on its own (see Figure 2.5). By forcing this abrupt drop, we are able to increase the amount of information conveyed in the wave.

Figure 2.5 Quadrature Phase Shift Keying

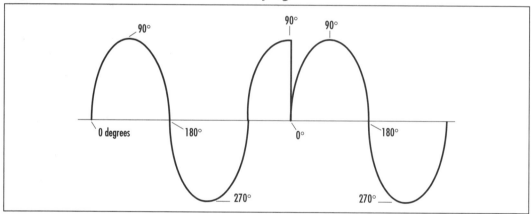

As with BPSK, we must represent digital bits using various phases of the analog waveform. In our QPSK example, the portion of the phase from 0 degrees to 90 degrees might represent binary digit 0, 90 degrees to 180 degrees could represent binary digit 1, 180 to 270 degrees and 270 back to 0 degrees might be represented by binary digits 10 and 11 respectively. The wireless radio configured for QPSK arranges a forced shift in the sine wave at each point that a bit or set of bits is transmitted. The receiving wireless radio expects these shifts and decodes them in the proper sequence. QPSK is utilized to transmit data at 2 Mbps.

Complimentary Code Keying (CCK)

Complimentary Code Keying is a newer modulation standard originally based on another modulation technique called Mary Orthogonal Keying (MOK). It was not a defined modulation technique in the original IEEE 802.11 standard for

WLANs, unlike BPSK and QPSK. CCK was designed as a new, modified modulation technique by industry leaders to overcome the limitations of the rate barrier of 2 Mbps within the original standard. It was adopted in the newer IEEE 802.11b standard that is currently employed by most vendors.

CCK is a coded QPSK modulation, where the original data bits are mapped to a corresponding modified data symbol, 8 bits for one 8-bit symbol. The data symbol is then applied to the various phases of the analog waveform as in phase shift keying modulations. The resulting waveform is the same as the original 2 Mbps QPSK modulation, however, the resulting data rate is 11 Mbps. CCK uses a complex set of functions known as *complementary codes* to send additional data in the waveform. Complimentary Code Keying provides an additional bit to each I (In-phase) and Q (Quadrature) channel by inverting or rotating the waveform 90 degrees and utilizing unmodified versions of the spreading function. There is a code set as well as a cover sequence defining the waveform. This new symbol type carries six bits and can be QPSK modulated to carry two more bits. The result is that 8 bits are transmitted with each symbol, resulting in a waveform that contains 16 bits of complexity. This is why the data rate for a Direct Sequence Spread Spectrum (DSSS) system employing CCK modulation is capable of 11 Mbps throughput rather than 2 Mbps. CCK supports both 5.5 Mbps and 11 Mbps modulation, and it is backward compatible with the 1–2 Mbps scheme. The data bit structure per codeword for BPSK, QPSK, and CCK is outlined in Figure 2.6. One of the advantages of CCK over similar modulation techniques is that it suffers less from multipath interference than systems based only on QPSK and BPSK.

Figure 2.6 Modulation Techniques

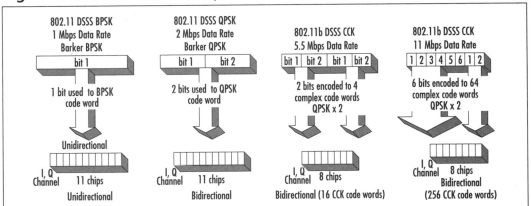

A digital signal produced using any of these techniques modulates the current carrying the signal within the radio. In other words, modulation gets wireless digital information ready for transmission. Once completed, the digital signal can then be actually transmitted over the air with another modulation technique, like direct sequence or frequency hopping spread spectrum.

Communicating with Wireless LAN Technologies

The most effective forms of wireless communications today are produced by using radio and microwave technologies. Because of licensing and cost issues, we have chosen to focus on the wireless technology used in Cisco Aironet wireless products, however, brief descriptions of other wireless technologies will be presented. In the remainder of this chapter we will discuss the core aspects of various WLAN technologies and the advantages and disadvantages of each.

The technologies available for use in WLANs include infrared, microwave, and spread spectrum radios. Two spread spectrum techniques are currently prevalent: frequency hopping and direct sequence. In the following section, we discuss the reasons for the popularity of spread spectrum technologies over infrared and microwave. In the United States, the radio bandwidth used for spread spectrum communications falls in three bands (900 MHz, 2.4 GHz, and 5.7 GHz), which the FCC approved for local area commercial communications in the late 1980s. In Europe, ETSI, the European Telecommunications Standards Institute, introduced regulations for 2.4 GHz in 1994, and HiperLAN is a family of standards in the 5.15–5.7 GHz and 19.3 GHz frequency bands. We begin by reviewing the most common forms of WLAN technologies: Microwave, infrared, and spread spectrum communications.

Microwave Technology

The complete electromagnetic spectrum includes many types of wavelengths we have become familiar with, at least in name. First among these is visible light. Two other types of wavelengths, just at either end of the visible spectrum, are infrared and ultraviolet light. These are the wavelengths that bring us "night vision" technology and tanning booths, respectively. Another portion of the electromagnetic spectrum we are becoming familiar with are frequencies called microwaves. These exist below infrared frequencies, but above normal radio frequencies.

Microwave technology is not really a LAN technology. Its main use in WLAN capacity is to interconnect LANs between buildings requiring microwave dishes on both ends of the link. The dishes must be in line-of-sight to transmit and collect the microwave signals. Microwave is used to bypass the telephone company when connecting LANs between buildings or as a backup path in the event of a telecommunications infrastructure outage. As a WAN technology, microwave is used to replace traditional wired technologies, such as dedicated circuits offered by the telephone company, with a network of microwave dishes to accomplish connectivity between businesses, cities and states. For example, Alaska has one of the largest microwave WANs at its disposal. Microwave communication satisfied the WAN requirements in the geographical area due to the limited availability of dedicated circuits for data transmission and environmental constraints in the state.

Many of the data communications services offered by major telecommunications companies are supported by microwave technology. Although it is a viable alternative even in private communications, it has two drawbacks. First, microwave communication requires FCC licensing. Once a license is granted for a particular location, that frequency band cannot be licensed to anyone else, for any purpose, within a 17.5 mile radius. Second, the cost of implementing microwave technology (tower/dish infrastructure) is higher than other options. On the other hand, microwave communication is extremely resistant to interference.

Infrared Technology

The infrared spectrum has long been used for such items as television and VCR remote controls. Over the past 10 years, infrared devices for home computers have become extremely popular. Input devices such as wireless keyboards and mice have introduced us to the freedom of working and playing without being tethered to the computer. Typically, an infrared receiver is attached to the keyboard or mouse connector on a computer. The wireless keyboard or mouse has an infrared transmitter built in. Because each wireless component manufacturer designs their own transmitters, the keyboard or mouse operates at a proprietary frequency. Keystroke or mouse movement signals are translated into an infrared signal and are sent to the receiver. Many laptop computers now come with an infrared port, which allows information from another laptop or infrared device to be transferred to each other via infrared transmission.

Just like the infrared connection between the laptops, infrared LANs use infrared signals to transmit data. These LANs can be set up using either a point-to-point configuration (line of sight) or a diffused configuration where the signals are reflected off some type of surface. The line of sight configuration generally offers the faster data rate of the two.

The advantages and disadvantages of infrared are few, however, the severity of the disadvantages are high in a WLAN scenario. Infrared's best advantage is its capability to carry a high bandwidth. The major disadvantage is its capability to be blocked. Because infrared energy is a form of light, it can easily be obstructed. Like light, it cannot pass through solid objects. Because infrared provides high-speed connectivity it is sometimes used for point-to-point connectivity, but infrared communication solutions are very expensive to implement. Because of infrared distance and coverage limitations, many more infrared devices are necessary to provide the same coverage area as radio wireless APs.

Spread Spectrum Technology

Most communication technologies we are familiar with—radio, television, two-way radios—use what is called *narrowband communications*. Each station or channel operates over a very thin slice of the radio spectrum. Because the station is assigned that particular band, and the FCC ensures that no other broadcasters in the local area use that same band through licensing, there is no interference. The range of each station is limited, so the same frequency can be reused a great distance away without interference.

Because many devices might use the ISM bands in a local area, additional technology is required to keep the various signals from interfering with each other. Fortunately, a technology has been developed over the past fifty years, which permits such bandwidth "sharing." This technology provides a way to spread the radio signal over a wide "spectrum" of radio frequencies, minimizing the impact of narrowband interference. In most cases, only small parts of the transmission are corrupted by any interference, and coding techniques allow that data to be recaptured. This technology is now generally known as *spread spectrum*.

Spread spectrum is a coding technique for digital transmission. It was developed for the military in the 1950s by engineers from the Sylvania Electronics System Division under a veil of secrecy to avoid jamming and eavesdropping of signals. Though developed and implemented by the U.S. military, the technique was first addressed by Hedy Lamarr and George Antheil. Lamarr, a famous actress of Austrian descent in the 1930s and 1940s, and Antheil, a music composer, patented the idea in 1940. Of course at the time it was not called spread spectrum. The original patent was called the Secret Communication System. The system was designed to allow the Allies to have an extremely fast and secure communication system during World War II. The idea was driven by Hedy Lamarr's personal experiences in World War II and fueled by her extreme desire to contribute to the task of defeating Hitler. She engaged the help of close friend and musician, George Antheil. Antheil assisted Lamarr with the solution to the problem of synchronization and soon the patent for their Secret Communication System was granted. Lamarr and Antheil never convinced the U.S. government to use the idea, and soon it was all but forgotten. The patent license expired before government and commercial implementation of the concepts occurred. In the mid-1980s, the U.S. military declassified spread-spectrum technology, and the commercial sector began to develop it for consumer electronics. Today, it's an increasingly important component of WLANs.

The military purpose of spread spectrum coding was to transform an information signal so that it looked more like noise. Noise has a flat uniform spectrum with no coherent peaks and can be reduced or eliminated by filtering. This made interception of radio signals extremely difficult.

The spread spectrum transmission technique modifies the signal spectrum to spread it out over a range of frequencies and increase its bandwidth. In other words, instead of transmitting a signal continuously over one narrow frequency band, the several parts are transmitted separately over a wide spectrum of radio frequencies.

The new "spread" signal has a lower power density, but the same total power. The expanded transmitter bandwidth minimizes interference to others because of its low power density. A defined, but random-appearing pattern of non-sequential bands is used, with successive parts being transmitted over the next frequency band in the pattern. On the other end, a receiver is configured to receive the signals in the same pattern. The radio receiver then reassembles the pieces into the original signal. Because many distinct patterns can be developed, it is possible to have multiple radios transmitting at the same time, but never at the same frequency at the same time. In the receiver, the incoming signal is decoded, and the decoding operation provides resistance to interference and multipath distortion. The frequencies used consist of the ISM bands of the electromagnetic spectrum. The ISM bands include the frequency ranges at 902 MHz to 928 MHz and at 2.4 GHz to 2.484 GHz, which do not require a FCC license. Spread spectrum is currently the most widely used transmission technique for WLANs.

Two different spreading techniques are currently used, both using a coded pattern of communication. A receiving unit is synchronized to use the same pattern and successfully receive the transmission. Any other radio unit hears the signal as noise because it is not programmed with the appropriate coding. The two techniques are called frequency hopping spread spectrum and direct sequence spread spectrum. All Cisco Aironet products use DSSS.

Synchronization

An extremely important and difficult part of designing a spread spectrum radio is to ensure fast and reliable synchronization in the receiver. The receiver must correlate the incoming signal and then demodulate it. The correlator removes the spreading code and the demodulator recovers the information at baseband. Both must be synchronous with the transmitted signal and usually lock up to the incoming signal and track it. Acquisition time is the period taken to lock up the receiver from a cold start and is an important measure of the receiver's performance. Other measures include the capability to synchronize in the presence of interference and/or thermal noise and to remain synchronized over long periods.

Frequency Hopping

The first type of spread spectrum developed is known as frequency hopping spread spectrum (FHSS). Simply put, frequency hopping is the process of jumping quickly from one frequency to another. A communications signal (voice or data) is split into separate parts. This technique broadcasts the signal over a seemingly random series of radio frequencies. A receiver, hopping between frequencies in synchronization with the transmitter, receives the message. The message can be fully received only if the series of frequencies is known. Because only the intended receiver knows the transmitter's hopping sequence, only that receiver can successfully receive all of the data. Most vendors develop their own hopping-sequence algorithms, which all but guarantees that two transmitters will not hop to the same frequency at the same time.

Frequency hopping has two benefits. Electrical noise as random electromagnetic signals, which are not part of any communications signal, will affect only a small part of the signal. Also, the effects of any other forms of radio communications operating in narrow bands of the spectrum will be minimized. Any such interference that occurs will result in only a slightly reduced quality of transmission, or a small loss of data. Because data networks acknowledge successful receipt of data, any missing pieces will trigger a request to transmit the lost data.

The FCC has made some rules for FHSS technologies. The FCC dictates that the transmitters must not spend more than 0.4 seconds on any one channel every 20 seconds in the 902 MHz band and every 30 seconds in the 2.4 GHz band. Also, the transmitters must hop through at least 50 channels in the 902 MHz band and 75 channels in the 2.4 GHz band (Figure 2.7 illustrates this relationship between frequency, power, and time for FHSS). A channel consists of a frequency width, which is determined by the FCC. The IEEE 802.11 committee has drafted a standard that limits FHSS transmitters to the 2.4 GHz band.

Figure 2.7 FHSS Frequency versus Power versus Time

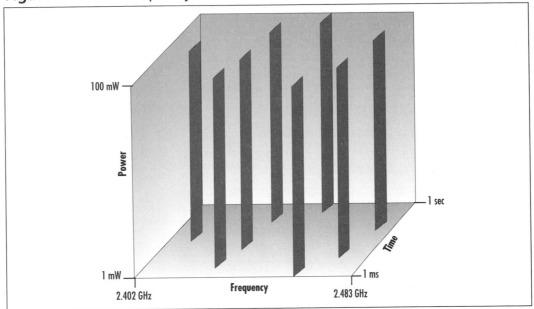

Direct Sequence Spread Spectrum (DSSS)

The other type of spread spectrum communication is called DSSS. This is currently the most common method used in WLANs. A direct sequence transmitter spreads its transmissions by adding redundant data bits called *chips* to them. DSSS adds at least ten chips to each data bit to protect the receiver from data loss. DSSS does not split a data signal into pieces, instead, it encodes each data bit into these chips. In other words, the transmitter sends the same piece of data attached to several chips to provide redundancy. Usually, 11 to 20 bits are used for the chip, depending on the application. An 11-bit chip is illustrated here:

> 0=10010010110
>
> 1=01101101001

After a fixed number of chips are sent, they repeat themselves precisely. This fixed number of chips is also referred to as the *chipping sequence*, or *Barker sequence*. A good spread spectrum code has low cross-correlation. In other words, very few sequences of chips will be in common to other spread spectrum codes issued by other radios in the same area. This results in minimum interference between users, because a code receiver, using one particular code, can be reached only by a transmitter sending the exact same code.

Similar to a frequency hopping receiver, a direct sequence receiver must know a transmitter's spreading code in order to properly decode the data stream. This spreading code is what allows multiple direct sequence transmitters to operate in the same area without interference. Once the receiver has received a transmission, it removes all the extraneous chips to produce the original length of the signal and completes the demodulation process.

As you can see in Figure 2.8, the number of chips and the frequency used is directly related to a signal's capability to avoid interference. The raw data throughput of direct sequence transmitters in the 2.4 GHz band is 11 Mbps. In addition to other factors, areas of high interference can significantly slow throughput when using DSSS.

Figure 2.8 DSSS Frequency versus Power versus Time

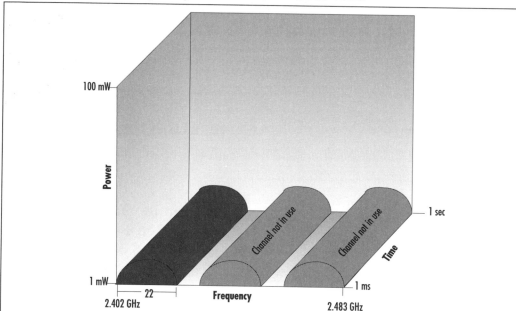

DSSS Channel Setup

For direct sequence WLANs, eleven total channels can be used for RF transmission (see Figure 2.9). Each channel is 22 MHz wide, and all channels combined equal the entire spectrum that can be used for 802.11 WLANs—in this case, the 2.4 GHz range of the ISM bands. When designing WLANs, multiple channels become an issue only when overlapping coverage is required, and this will be the case in most designs. When two APs have overlapping coverage, each AP must be using a different channel so that the client can distinguish the difference the between the RF for each AP. Figure 2.9 illustrates that only three channels do not overlap concurrently: Channels 1, 6, and 11.

Figure 2.9 DSSS Channels

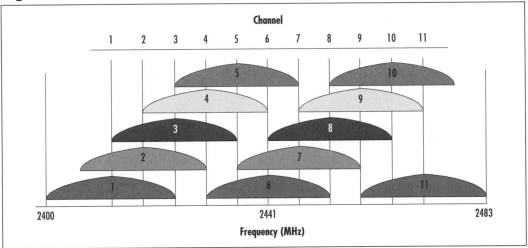

Spectrum Technology Comparisons: Frequency Hopping versus Direct Sequence

Frequency hopping radios currently use less power than direct sequence radios and generally cost less. Direct sequence radios have a practical raw data rate of 8 Mbps and frequency hopping radios have a practical limit of 2 Mbps. So if high performance is key and interference is not a problem, go with direct sequencing. But if a small, inexpensive portable wireless adapter for a notebook or PDA is needed the frequency hopping method should be good enough. With either method of spread spectrum the end result is a system that is extremely difficult to detect, does not interfere with other services, and provides large bandwidth for data.

Implementing a Wireless LAN Architecture

A complete WLAN architecture consists of several key devices and structures, not completely defined by IEEE 802.11 standards. In order to satisfy application and user requirements, other components are necessary. Figure 2.10 depicts a wireless system and the additional components that may be needed to complete it. Some of the components may already be in place for your particular implementation. In general, most sites already have Distribution Systems (DS). These DSs may be Ethernet, Token Ring, and so on, and may include WAN connectivity as well as LAN.

Figure 2.10 WLAN System

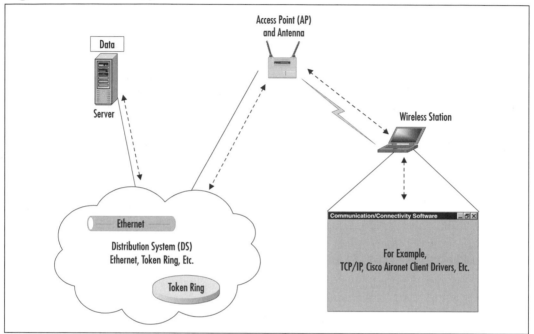

A good way to depict these functions is to specify the network's architecture. This architecture describes the protocols, major hardware, and software elements that constitute the network. A network architecture, whether wireless or wired, may be viewed in two ways, physically and logically.

As you see from the graphic, wireless systems contain both logical and physical components, many of which are not specified in the IEEE 802.11 standards. Some of the components not addressed by the 802.11 standard are distribution systems, connectivity software, such as wireless client drivers and utilities, and communications protocols (for example, TCP/IP, IPX, and so on).

The OSI Reference Model

The physical and logical components of a wireless system implement the Physical, Data Link, and Network layer functions of the OSI reference model to satisfy the functionality needed within LANs, WANs, and MANs.

The OSI reference model provides an overview of computer networking. Defined by the ISO, the OSI reference model divides the concept of computer networking into seven layers. Each layer performs a different function required to exchange data between two systems. Each individual layer supports the operations of the layers above it. Table 2.4 breaks out the layers, their names, and their functions.

Table 2.4 The Open Systems Interconnect Reference Model

Layer Number	Layer Name	Description
Layer 7	Application layer	The Application layer defines the networking applications that are visible to the computer user.
Layer 6	Presentation layer	The Presentation layer simplifies the format of data for the application. It performs such tasks as compressing text and converting images into bit streams.
Layer 5	Session layer	The Session layer creates, controls, and terminates sessions between networking applications.
Layer 4	Transport layer	The Transport layer establishes reliable, end-to-end communication between two network devices. It uses acknowledgements and data retransmissions to ensure the reliable exchange of data. The Transmission Control Protocol (TCP) is an example of a protocol that operates at this layer.
Layer 3	Network layer	The Network layer provides routing of data across a network. The Internet Protocol (IP) is an example of a protocol that operates at this layer.
Layer 2	Data-Link layer	The Data-Link layer specifies how data travels between two networking devices. It provides synchronization between devices and error detection to ensure that the data reaches its destination uncorrupted. Ethernet functions at the Data-Link layer.

Continued

Table 2.4 Continued

Layer Number	Layer Name	Description
Layer 1	Physical layer	The Physical layer defines the actual physical connection between two devices. For example, Ethernet cabling and the electrical signals that are transmitted along the wire correspond to Physical layer operation.

The Data–Link layer of the OSI model is divided into two parts: the Media Access Control (MAC) sublayer and the Logical Link Control (LLC) sublayer. The IEEE 802.2 LLC standard defines LLC activity for most networking products. The LLC provides link control between devices and is independent of the transmission medium or MAC technique implemented by a particular network. Wireless systems utilize the first two layers of the OSI reference model (see Figure 2.11).

Figure 2.11 802.11 Wireless Systems and the OSI

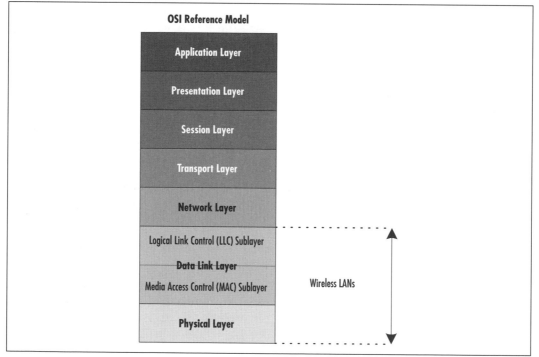

Logical Wireless System Components

Logical wireless system components are the functions and subsystems required to perform networking in a wireless system. Not to be confused with the actual hardware used in such environments, typical logical components are software-based. In general, many of the logical functions required of wired networks, such as Ethernet and Token Ring are also needed in a wireless system. Much of this has to do with the standards upon which wired networks are built. The wireless systems must comply with these standards in order to integrate with the wired networks.

Distribution System

The distribution system, also known as the DS, refers to the topology of the wired network that you may connect to, to access services and applications. Obviously, if all the network services and applications you require reside on directly accessible wireless systems, there is no need for a DS. An example of a wireless system that does not require a DS would be an ad-hoc network where wireless stations communicate directly and mutually access services and applications. A network distribution system is absolutely necessary if such things as databases, applications, and print services reside on systems accessible only from a wired network. Designers of the 802.11 standard purposely avoided the definition of a particular distribution system for connecting APs, allowing system designers the freedom to implement 802.11-compliant networks based on the unique requirements of each implementation. This gives us the ability to design the most effective and efficient wireless system for our scenarios. As a result, you need to decide what technologies and products will constitute the distribution system if multiple APs are necessary to extend the range of the complete wireless system.

In most cases, you can specify a wired LAN backbone to act as the distribution system. Typically, vendors sell APs capable of connecting to either IEEE-compliant Ethernet or Token Ring LANs. In addition, WAN components may be necessary to connect LANs separated by longer distances. The following are the logical components of a wireless system and brief descriptions of each. Because the logical components are part of current wireless standards, details of these components can be found in the section entitled "Keeping Pace with Wireless Networking Standards."

Medium Access Technique

Medium access techniques facilitate the sharing of a common medium. This component is specified in the IEEE 802.11 standard.

Synchronization and Error Control

Synchronization and error control mechanisms ensure that each link transfers the data intact. The Data Link layer of the OSI reference model is used to handle this function of the logical wireless system. IEEE 802.11 specifies the MAC to be used for WLANs.

Routing Mechanisms

Routing mechanisms move the data from the originating source to the intended destination. These mechanisms work at the Network layer of the OSI reference model.

Application Interface

The application interface connects a device, such as a laptop computer or bar-code scanner, to application software hosted on a server. An e-mail program on a wireless laptop is an example of an application interface. These interfaces also include your communication and connectivity software, such as TCP/IP and wireless client drivers.

Physical Wireless System Components

To further your understanding of wireless architecture, you need to identify the physical wireless system components used in various wireless implementations. In this section, we list the general terms for the physical components in the WLAN architecture and give a brief description of each. In addition, we give an overview of each component's place in the overall wireless scheme.

Medium

The *medium* is the physical component of the wired LAN backbone. This is part of the wireless system's DS. For example, copper cabling, coax cabling, and fiber-optic cabling are all physical components of logical topologies which are, in turn, defined as the DS.

Access Point (AP)

An AP is a wireless radio. They are the center points in an all-wireless network, or a connection point between a wired and wireless network. Multiple APs can be placed throughout a facility to provide users equipped with WLAN adapters the ability to move freely throughout an extended area while maintaining uninterrupted access to all network resources.

Antenna

The antenna, along with air, can be thought of as the medium for wireless networking, outside the DS. It is the physical component that radiates the modulated signal through the air so that the destination can receive it. Types of antennas are differentiated by their propagation patterns, gain, and transmission power.

Wireless Station

This is any appliance that interfaces with wireless medium and operates as an end user device. The wireless station is the user's interface to the wireless system. Examples of wireless stations are laptop computers, desktop computers, and PDAs with wireless network interface cards (radio cards) installed, radio bar code readers, and wireless hubs (like Cisco's Workgroup Bridge product). The wireless hub allows the addition of wired network devices such as print servers or computers with traditional wired network cards to attach to the wireless hub from which the devices gain access to the wireless network.

Server

Though not necessarily directly attached to a wireless network, servers are nonetheless a typical component in a wireless system. In many cases, wireless stations need to access servers for such things as print and e-mail services, file sharing, and application access.

Keeping Pace with Wireless Networking Standards

As you have seen in previous sections, coordination of wireless technology and its functions are key to the reliability and success of a wireless system. Many vendors contributed and coordinated with standards organizations to create the hardware and technology of today's WLANs. Because of the resulting standards put forth by this cooperation, we are able to provide inexpensive, efficient, and reliable wireless systems.

Standards organizations are groups of people interested in promoting and coordinating rules for the measure of quantity, weight, extent, value, or quality of a given technology or idea giving rise to a model or example of the idea or technology. This, in turn, allows others to build on the model or example and improve the existing idea or technology, or in some cases, foster new ideas or technologies. In the wireless networking world, standards organizations have had the welcome impact of allowing new wireless technologies to get from conception to consumer with unprecedented speed. Because the standards are used as a base for the wireless technology most vendors employ, consumers reap the benefits of interoperability, reliability, and efficient technology.

Wireless standards have been developed both in the United States and abroad and the advances made using these standards are shaping the wireless industry constantly. In order to fully understand wireless fundamentals, architecture, and design considerations, you need to understand what the current standards are for WLANs and who created those standards. We review the major standards organizations that have contributed to the wireless technology employed today, with a focus on the standard used in Cisco Aironet devices, and look at forthcoming wireless standards that are in progress. In addition, we review some organizations that influence the wireless market by providing interoperability and compliance testing.

Institute of Electrical and Electronic Engineers (IEEE)

IEEE is an association that develops standards for almost anything electronic and/or electric. Far from being limited to computer-related topics, IEEE societies cover just about any technical practice, from automobiles to maritime, from neural networks to superconductors. With 36 Technical Societies covering broad interest areas, more specific topics are handled by special committees that focus on a particular technology or technologies to develop standards that will be used to promote technological advancement.

The IEEE 802 LAN/MAN Standards Committee develops LAN standards and MAN standards. The most widely used standards are for the Ethernet family, token ring, WLAN, Bridging, and Virtual Bridged LANs. All standards created by this committee are designated 802. *Note:* The "80" in 802 refers to the year the committee was formed and the "2" refers to the month in which the committee was formed. Working groups and technical advisory groups within the committee are designated by a dot-number (.#), to define the subtechnology for which they are responsible. For example, standards listed 802.11 designate the WLAN Working Group within the LAN/MAN Standards Committee. Letters after the designations represent revisions or changes to the original standards for the working group. These groups meet several times a year to discuss new trends within their industry or to continue the process of refining a current standard.

Prior to the adoption of the 802.11 standard, wireless data-networking vendors made equipment that was based on proprietary technology. Wary of being locked into a relationship with a specific vendor, potential wireless customers instead turned to more standards-based wired technologies. As a result, deployment of wireless networks did not happen on a large scale, and remained a luxury item for large companies with large budgets.

Designing & Planning...

Additional Initiatives of the 802 Standards Committee

802.1 LAN/MAN Bridging and Management 802.1 is the base standard for LAN/MAN Bridging, LAN architecture, LAN management, and protocol layers above the MAC and LLC layers. Some examples include 802.1q, the standard for virtual LANs, and 802.1d, the Spanning Tree Protocol.

802.2 Logical Link Control Because Logical Link Control is now a part of all 802 standards, this Working Group is currently in hibernation (inactive) with no ongoing projects.

802.3 CSMA/CD Access Method (Ethernet) 802.3 defines that an Ethernet network can operate at 10 Mbps, 100 Mbps, 1 Gbps, or even 10 Gbps. It also defines that category 5 twisted pair cabling and fiber optic cabling are valid cable types. This group identifies how to make vendors' equipment interoperate despite the various speeds and cable types.

802.4 Token-Passing Bus This Working Group is also in hibernation with no ongoing projects.

802.5 Token Ring Token Ring networks operate at 4 mps or 16 Mbps. Currently, there are Working Groups proposing 100 Mb Token Ring (802.5t) and Gigabit Token Ring (802.5v). Examples of other 802.5 specs would be 802.5c, Dual Ring Wrapping, and 802.5j, fiber optic station attachment.

802.6 Metropolitan Area Network (MAN) Because MANs are created and managed with current internetworking standards, the 802.6 Working Group is in hibernation.

802.7 Broadband LAN In 1989, this Working Group recommended practices for Broadband LANs, which were reaffirmed

Continued

in 1997. This group is inactive with no ongoing projects. The maintenance effort for 802.7 is now supported by 802.14.

802.8 Fiber Optics Many of this Working Group's recommended practices for fiber optics get wrapped into other standards at the Physical layer.

802.9 Isochronous Services LAN (ISLAN) Isochronous Services refer to processes where data must be delivered within certain time constraints. Streaming media and voice calls are examples of traffic that requires an isochronous transport system.

802.10 Standard for Interoperable LAN Security (SILS)
This Working Group provided some standards for Data Security in the form of 802.10a, Security Architecture Framework, and 802.10c, Key Management. This Working Group is currently in hibernation with no ongoing projects.

802.11 Wireless LAN (WLAN) This Working Group is developing standards for Wireless data delivery in the 2.4 GHz and 5.1 GHz radio spectrum.

802.12 Demand Priority Access Method This Working Group provided two Physical layer and Repeater specifications for the development of 100 Mbps Demand Priority MACs. Although they were accepted as ISO standards and patents were received for their operation, widespread acceptance was overshadowed by Ethernet. 802.12 is currently in the process of being withdrawn.

802.13 This standard was intentionally left blank.

802.14 Cable-TV Based Broadband Comm Network This Working Group developed specifications for the Physical and Media Access Control layers for cable televisions and cable modems. Believing their work to be done, this Working Group has no ongoing projects.

802.15 Wireless Personal Area Network (WPAN) The vision of Personal Area Networks is to create a wireless interconnection between portable and mobile computing devices such as PCs, peripherals, cell phones, PDAs, pagers, and consumer electronics, allowing these devices to communicate and interoperate with one another without interfering with other wireless communications.

Continued

802.16 Broadband Wireless Access The goal of the 802.16 Working Group is to develop standards for fixed broadband wireless access systems. These standards are key to solving "last-mile" local-loop issues. 802.16 is similar to 802.11a in that it uses unlicensed frequencies in the unlicensed national information infrastructure (U-NII) spectrum. 802.16 is different from 802.11a in that Quality of Service for voice/video/data issues are being addressed from the start in order to present a standard that will support true wireless network backhauling.

The only way WLANs would be generally accepted would be if the wireless hardware involved had a low cost and had become commodity items such as routers and switches. Recognizing that the only way for this to happen would be if there were a wireless data-networking standard, the IEEE's 802 Group took on their eleventh challenge. Because many of the members of the 802.11 Working Group were employees of vendors making wireless technologies, there were many pushes to include certain functions in the final specification. Although this slowed down the progress of finalizing 802.11, it also provided momentum for delivery of a feature-rich standard left open for future expansion.

On June 26, 1997, the IEEE announced the ratification of the 802.11 standard for wireless local area networks. Because that time, costs associated with deploying an 802.11-based network have dropped, and WLANs rapidly are being deployed in schools, businesses, and homes.

As mentioned earlier, the primary reason wireless LANs were not widely accepted was the lack of standardization. It is logical to question whether vendors would accept a nonproprietary operating standard, because vendors compete to make unique and distinguishing products. Although 802.11 standardized the physical (PHY) media access control (MAC) layers, the frequencies to send/receive on, transmission rates and more, it did not absolutely guarantee that differing vendors' products would be 100 percent compatible. In fact, some vendors built in backward-compatibility features into their 802.11 products in order to support their legacy customers. Other vendors have introduced proprietary extensions (for example, bit-rate adaptation and stronger encryption) to their 802.11 offerings.

802.11

As in all 802.*x* standards, the 802.11 specification covers the operation of the MAC and PHY layers. As you can see in Figure 2.12, 802.11 defines a MAC sublayer, MAC services and protocols, and three physical layers.

Figure 2.12 802.11 Frame Format

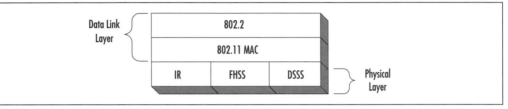

The three physical layer options for 802.11 are infrared (IR) baseband PHY and two RF PHYs. Due to line-of-sight limitations, very little development has occurred with the Infrared PHY. The RF physical layer is composed of FHSS and DSSS in the 2.4 GHz band. All three physical layers operate at either 1 or 2 Mbps. The majority of 802.11 implementations utilize the DSSS method.

FHSS works by sending bursts of data over numerous frequencies. As the name implies, it hops between frequencies. Typically, the devices use up to four frequencies simultaneously to send information and only for a short period of time before hopping to new frequencies. The devices using FHSS agree upon the frequencies being used. In fact, due to the short time period of frequency use and device agreement of these frequencies, many autonomous networks can coexist in the same physical space.

DSSS functions by dividing the data into several pieces and simultaneously sending the pieces on as many different frequencies as possible, unlike FHSS, which sends on a limited number of frequencies. This process allows for greater transmission rates than FHSS, but is vulnerable to greater occurrences of interference. This is because the data is spanning a larger portion of the spectrum at any given time than FHSS. In essence, DHSS floods the spectrum all at one time, whereas FHSS selectively transmits over certain frequencies.

The 1997 completion of the IEEE 802.11 standard for WLANs was a first important step in the evolutionary development of wireless networking technologies. The standard was developed to maximize interoperability between differing brands of WLANs as well as to introduce a variety of performance improvements and benefits.

The initial 802.11 PAR (Project Authorization Request) states, "...the scope of the proposed [wireless LAN] standard is to develop a specification for wireless connectivity for fixed, portable, and moving stations within a local area." The PAR further says, "...the purpose of the standard is to provide wireless connectivity to automatic machinery and equipment or stations that require rapid deployment, which may be portable, handheld, or which may be mounted on moving vehicles within a local area."

The resulting standard, which is officially called IEEE Standard for Wireless LAN Medium Access (MAC) and Physical Layer (PHY) Specifications, defines over-the-air protocols necessary to support networking in local area.

802.11 Topologies

The topology of a wireless network is dynamic; therefore, the destination address does not always correspond to the destination's location. This raises a problem when forwarding frames through the network to the intended destination.

The IEEE 802.11 topology consists of components, called "sets", to provide a WLAN that allows transparent station mobility. The 802.11 standard supports the following three topology sets:

- **Basic Service Set (BSS) networks** The basic topology set of 802.11 systems is the basic service set (BSS). The BSS consists of at least one AP connected to the wired network infrastructure and a set of wireless end stations (see Figure 2.13). BSS configurations rely on an AP that acts as the logical server for a single wireless LAN cell or channel. Communications between two end stations actually flows from one station to the AP and from the AP to the other station.

Figure 2.13 Basic Service Set (BSS) Network

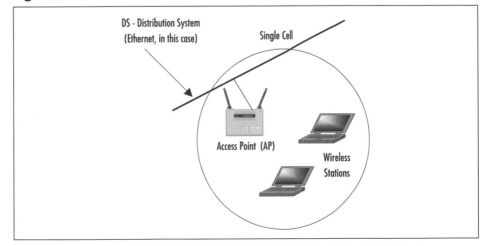

■ **Independent Basic Service Set (IBSS) networks** IBSS networks
are also referred to as an independent configuration or ad-hoc network.
Logically, an IBSS configuration is very similar to a peer-to-peer home
or office network in which no single node is required to function as a
server (see Figure 2.14). IBSS topology sets include a number of wireless
end stations that communicate directly with one another, with no inter-
vening AP or any connection to a wired network. It is useful for quickly
and easily setting up a wireless network anyplace where a wireless infrastructure does not exist or is not required for services, such as meeting
rooms in hotels, airports, or trade shows, or where access to the wired
network is barred (such as for consultants at a client site). Generally, ad-
hoc implementations cover a small (limited) area and are not connected
to any network.

Figure 2.14 Independent Basic Service Set (IBSS) Network

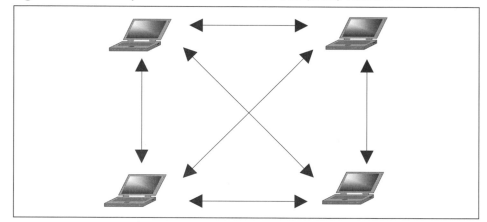

■ **Extended Service Set (ESS) networks** Extended Service Set (ESS)
topologies consist of a series of overlapping BSS sets (each containing an
AP), commonly referred to as cells. These cells are usually connected
together by some wired medium, what we referred to in our wireless
architecture section as a DS (see Figure 2.15). Although the DS could be
any type of network, it is almost invariably an Ethernet LAN. Mobile
end stations can roam between the APs, making seamless ESS–wide coverage possible. Because most corporate WLANs require access to the
wired LAN for services (file servers, printers, Internet links) they will
operate in a BSS/ESS topology.

Figure 2.15 Extended Service Set (ESS) Network

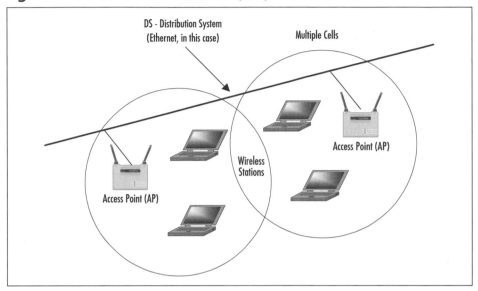

These networks utilize a basic building block: The 802.11 standard referred to as a BSS, providing a coverage area whereby stations of the BSS (or ESS) remain fully connected. A station is free to move within the BSS, but it can no longer communicate directly with other stations if it leaves the BSS/ESS.

The compelling force behind WLAN deployment is that with 802.11, users are free to move about without having to worry about switching network connections manually. If we were operating with a single infrastructure BSS, this moving about would be limited to the signal range of our one AP. Through the ESS, the IEEE 802.11 architecture allows users to move between multiple infrastructure BSSs. In an ESS, the APs talk amongst themselves forwarding traffic from one BSS to another, as well as switch the roaming devices from one BSS to another.

What makes the WLAN so unique, though, are the invisible interactions between the various parts of the extended service set. Pieces of equipment on the wired network have no idea they are communicating with a mobile wireless LAN device, nor do they see the switching that occurs when the wireless device changes from one AP to another. To the wired network, all it sees is a consistent MAC address to talk to, just as if the MAC was another node on the wire.

Because multiple APs exist in this model, the wireless devices no longer communicate in a peer-to-peer fashion. Instead, all traffic from one device destined for another device is relayed through the AP. Even though it would look like this would double the amount of traffic on the WLAN, this also provides for traffic buffering on the AP when a device is operating in a low-power mode.

802.11 Services

Nine different services provide behind-the-scenes support to the 802.11 architecture. Of these nine, four belong to the *station services* group and the remaining five to the *distribution services* group.

The four station services (*authentication*, *de-authentication*, *data delivery*, and *privacy*) provide functionality equal to what standard 802.3 wired networks would have.

The authentication service defines the identity of the wireless device. Without this distinct identity, the device is not allowed access to the WLAN. Authentication can also be made against a list of MACs allowed to use the network. This list of allowable MAC addresses may be on the AP or on a database somewhere on the wired network. A wireless device can authenticate itself to more than one AP at a time. This sort of "pre-authentication" allows the device to prepare other APs for its entry into their airspace.

The de-authentication service is used to destroy a previously known station identity. Once the de-authentication service has been started, the wireless device can no longer access the WLAN. This service is invoked when a wireless device shuts down, or when it is roaming out of the range of the AP. This frees up resources on the AP for other devices.

Just like its wired counterparts, the 802.11 standard specifies a data delivery service to ensure that data frames are transferred reliably from one MAC to another. We discuss this data delivery in greater detail in following sections.

The privacy service is used to protect the data as it crosses the WLAN. Even though the service utilizes an RC4-based encryption scheme, it is not intended for end-to-end encryption or as a sole method of securing data. Its design was to provide a level of protection equivalent to that provided on a wired network— hence its moniker Wired Equivalent Protocol (WEP).

Between the LLC sublayer and the MAC, five distribution services make the decisions as to where the 802.11 data frames should be sent. As you will see, these distribution services make the roaming handoffs when the wireless device is in motion. The five services are *association*, *re-association*, *disassociation*, *integration*, and *distribution*.

The wireless device uses the association service as soon as it connects to an AP. This service establishes a logical connection between the devices, and determines the path the DS needs to take in order to reach the wireless device. If the wireless device does not have an association made with an AP, the DS will not know where that device is or how to get data frames to it. As you can see in Figure 2.16, the wireless device can be authenticated to more than one AP at a time, but it will never be associated with more than one AP.

Figure 2.16 802.11 Authentication, Association, and Re-Association

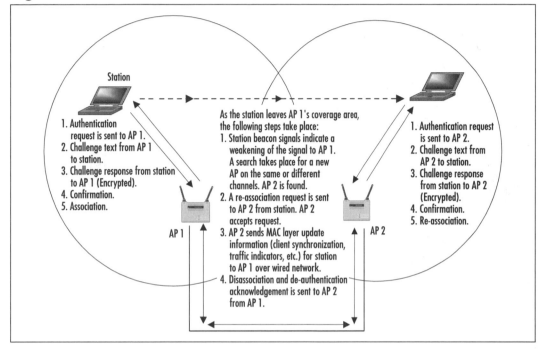

As you will see in later sections dealing with roaming and low–power situations, sometimes the wireless device will not be linked continuously to the same AP. To keep from losing whatever network session information the wireless device has, the re-association service is used. This service is similar to the association service, but includes current information about the wireless device. In the case of roaming, this information tells the current AP the previous AP the wireless devices was associated to. This allows the current AP to contact the previous AP to pick up any data frames waiting for the wireless device and forward them to their destination.

The disassociation service is used to tear down the association between the AP and the wireless device. This could be because the device is roaming out of the AP's area, the AP is shutting down, or any one of a number of other reasons. To keep communicating to the network, the wireless device will have to use the association service to find a new AP.

The distribution service is used by APs to determine whether to send the data frame to another AP and possibly another wireless device, or if the frame is destined to head out of the WLAN into the wired network.

The integration service resides on the APs as well. This service does the data translation from the 802.11 frame format into the framing format of the wired network. It also does the reverse, taking data destined for the WLAN, and framing it within the 802.11 frame format.

CSMA-CA Mechanism

The basic access mechanism for 802.11 is Carrier Sense Multiple Access Collision Avoidance (CSMA/CA) with binary exponential backoff. This is very similar to the Carrier Sense Multiple Access Collision Detection (CSMA/CD) that we are familiar with when dealing with standard 802.3 (Ethernet), but with a couple of major differences.

Unlike Ethernet, which sends out a signal until a collision is detected, CSMA/CA takes great care to not transmit unless it has the attention of the receiving unit, and no other unit is talking. This is called *listening before talking* (LBT).

Before a packet is transmitted, the wireless device will listen to hear if any other device is transmitting. If a transmission is occurring, the device will wait for a randomly determined period of time, and then listen again. If no one else is using the medium, the device will begin transmitting. Otherwise, it will wait again for a random time before listening once more.

802.11 DCF/PCF and RTC/CTS Mechanisms

To minimize the risk of a wireless device transmitting at the same time as another wireless device (and thus causing a collision), the 802.11 working group designed two functions known as DCF and PCF, employing a mechanism called Request To Send/Clear To Send (RTS/CTS).

Distributed Coordination Function (DCF) is used by any of the component topologies to determine when a station can transmit during periods of contention on the network and is a best effort delivery system. If the channel being used is sensed to be in an idle state, a specified "wait" period is initiated before transmission actually occurs.

In PCF (Point Coordination Function), a single point in the network (usually a network AP) acts as a centralized "traffic cop," telling individual stations when they may place a packet on the network. In other words, the AP periodically "beacons" each of its associated end stations, polling them to see if they have anything to transmit. Time-sensitive applications, such as voice and video, use this to permit fixed, dependable rate transmissions.

In both DCF and PCF, RTS/CTS is used as the mechanism to perform these functions. For example, if data arrived at the AP destined for a wireless node, the AP would send an RTS frame to the wireless node requesting a certain amount of time to deliver data to it. The wireless node would respond with a CTS frame saying that it would hold off any other communications until the AP had completed sending the data. Other wireless nodes would hear the transaction taking place, and delay their transmissions for that period of time as well. In this manner, data is passed between nodes with a minimal possibility of a device causing a collision on the medium.

This also gets rid of a well-documented WLAN issue called *the hidden node*. In a network with multiple devices, the possibility exists that one wireless node might not know all the other nodes that are out on the WLAN. Thanks to RTS/CTS, each node hears the requests to transmit data to the other nodes, and thus learns what other devices are operating in that BSS.

802.11 Data Acknowledgment

When sending data across a radio signal with the inherent risk of interference, the odds of a packet getting lost between the transmitting radio and the destination unit are much greater than in a wired network model. To make sure that data transmissions would not get lost in the ether, *acknowledgment* (ACK) was introduced. The acknowledgement portion of CSMA/CA means that when a destination host receives a packet, it sends back a notification to the sending unit. If the sender does not receive an ACK, it will know that this packet was not received and will transmit it again.

All this takes place at the MAC layer. Noticing that an ACK has not been received, the sending unit is able to grab the radio medium before any other unit can and it resends the packet. This allows recovery from interference without the end user being aware that a communications error has occurred.

802.11 Fragmentation

In an environment prone to interference, the possibility exists that one or more bits in a packet will get corrupted during transmission. No matter the number of corrupted bits, the packet will need to be re-sent.

When operating in an area where interference is not a possibility, but a reality, it makes sense to transmit smaller packets than those traditionally found in wired networks. This allows for a faster retransmission of the packet to be accomplished.

The disadvantage to doing this is that in the case of no corrupted packets, the cost of sending many short packets is greater than the cost of sending the same information in a couple of large packets. Thankfully, the 802.11 standard has made this a configurable feature. This way, a network administrator can specify short packets in some areas and longer packets in more open, non-interfering areas.

802.11 Power Management

Because the whole premise of wireless LANs is mobility, having sufficient battery power in the mobile device (such as a laptop or PDA) to power the communications channel is of prime concern. The IEEE recognized this and included a power management service that allows the mobile client to go into a sleep mode to save power without losing connectivity to the wireless infrastructure.

Utilizing a 20-byte Power Save Poll (PS-Poll) frame, the wireless device sends a message to its AP letting it know that it is going into power-save mode, and the AP needs to buffer all packets destined for the device until it comes back online. Periodically, the wireless device will wake up and see if there are any packets waiting for it on the AP. If there aren't, another PS-Poll frame is sent, and the unit goes into a sleep mode again. The real benefit here is that the mobile user is able to use the WLAN for longer periods of time without severely impacting the battery life of their mobile device.

802.11 Multicell Roaming

Another benefit to wireless LANs is being able to move from wireless cell to cell as you go around the office, campus, or home without the need to modify your network services. Roaming between APs in your ESS is a very important portion of the 802.11 standard. Roaming is based on the capability of the wireless device to determine the quality of the wireless signal to any AP within reach, and decide to switch communications to a different AP if it has a stronger or cleaner signal. This is based primarily upon an entity called the signal-to-noise (S/N) ratio. In order for wireless devices to determine the S/N ratio for each AP in the network, APs send out *beacon* messages that contain information about the AP as well as link measurement data. The wireless device listens to these beacons and determines which AP has the clearest and cleanest signal. After making this determination, the wireless device sends authentication information and attempts to reassociate with the new AP. The reassociation process tells the new AP which AP the device just came from. The new AP picks up whatever data frames that might be left at the old AP, and notifies the old AP that it no longer needs to accept messages for that wireless device. This frees up resources on the old AP for its other clients.

Even though the 802.11 standard covers the concepts behind the communications between the AP and the DS, it doesn't define exactly how this communication should take place. This is because there are many different ways this communication can be implemented. Although this gives a vendor a good deal of flexibility in AP/DS design, there could be situations where APs from different vendors might not be able to interoperate across a distribution system due to the differences in how those vendors implemented the AP/DS interaction. Currently, there is an 802.11 Working Group (802.11f) developing an Inter-Access Point Protocol. This protocol will be of great help in the future as companies who have invested in one vendor's products can integrate APs and devices from other vendors into their ESSs.

802.11 Security

One of the biggest concerns facing network administrators when implementing a WLAN is data security. In a wired environment, the lack of access to the physical wire can prevent someone from wandering into your building and connecting to your internal network. In a WLAN scenario, it is impossible for the AP to know if the person operating the wireless device is sitting inside your building, passing time in your lobby, or if they are seated in a parked car just outside your office. Acknowledging that passing data across an unreliable radio link could lead to possible snooping, the IEEE 802.11 standard provides three ways to provide a greater amount of security for the data that travels over the WLAN. Adopting any (or all three) of these mechanisms will decrease the likelihood of an accidental security exposure.

The first method makes use of the 802.11 Service Set Identifier (SSID). This SSID can be associated with one or more APs to create multiple WLAN segments within the infrastructure BSS. These segments can be related to floors of a building, business units, or other data-definition sets. Because the SSID is presented during the authentication process, it acts as a crude password. Because most end-users set up their wireless devices, these SSIDs could be shared among users, thus limiting their effectiveness. Another downside to using SSIDs as a sole form of authentication is that if the SSID were to be changed (due to an employee termination or other event), all wireless devices and APs would have to reflect this change. On a medium-sized WLAN, rotating SSIDs on even a biannual basis could prove to be a daunting and time-consuming task.

As mentioned earlier in the station services section, the AP also can authenticate a wireless device against a list of MAC addresses. This list could reside locally on the AP, or the authentication could be checked against a database of allowed

MACs located on the wired network. This typically provides a good level of security, and is best used with small WLAN networks. With larger WLAN networks, administering the list of allowable MAC addresses will require some back-end services to reduce the amount of time needed to make an addition or subtraction from the list.

Designing & Planning…

Limitations of WEP

Recently, researchers at the University of California, at Berkeley, published a document identifying security flaws in the 802.11 security protocol (WEP) that "seriously undermine the security claims of the system" and state that WEP is insufficient for WLAN security. Articles about the researchers' findings have appeared in *The Wall Street Journal* and other publications.

Specifically, WEP is susceptible to the following types of attacks:

- Passive attacks to decrypt traffic based on statistical analysis
- Active attack to inject new traffic from unauthorized mobile stations, based on known plaintext
- Active attacks to decrypt traffic, based on tricking the AP
- Dictionary-building attack that, after analysis of about a day's worth of traffic, allows real-time automated decryption of all traffic

In general, the extent of vulnerability depends on whether static or dynamic WEP is used. Unfortunately, many WLAN deployments use static WEP keys that significantly compromise security, as many users in a given WLAN share the same key. Cisco has addressed these security concerns through augmentation of 802.11b WEP by creating a per-user, per-session, dynamic WEP key tied to the network logon, thereby addressing the limitations of static WEP keys while maintaining ease of administration. The Cisco recommended security solution for Aironet implementations is covered in depth in Chapter 9.

The third mechanism 802.11 offers to protect data traversing the WLAN was also mentioned earlier in the section on station services. The *privacy* service uses a

RC-4 based encryption scheme to encapsulate the payload of the 802.11 data frames, called Wired Equivalent Protocol (WEP). WEP specifies a 40-bit encryption key, although some vendors have implemented a 104-bit key. As mentioned previously, WEP is not meant to be an end-to-end encryption solution. WEP keys on the APs and wireless devices can be rotated, but because the 802.11 standard does not specify a key-management protocol, all key rotation must be done manually. Like the SSID, rotating the WEP key would affect all APs and wireless users and take significant effort from the network administrator.

Some network designers consider WLANs to be in the same crowd as Remote Access Service (RAS) devices, and they claim that the best protection is to place the WLAN architecture behind a firewall or a Virtual Private Network (VPN) device. This would make the wireless client authenticate to the VPN or firewall using third-party software (on top of WEP). The benefit here is that the bulk of the authenticating would be up to a non-WLAN device and would not require additional AP maintenance.

The uses of 802.11 networks can range from homes to public areas (such as schools and libraries) to businesses and corporate campuses. The ability to deploy a low-cost network without the need to have wires everywhere is allowing wireless networks to spring up in areas where wired networks would be cost prohibitive. The 802.11 services allow the wireless device the same kind of functionality as a wired network, yet giving the user the ability to roam throughout the WLAN.

802.11b

On September 16, 1999, the IEEE ratified a revision of the 802.11 standard, called 802.11 High Rate (HR/DSSS) or 802.11b, that provides much higher data rates, while maintaining the 802.11 protocol. The basic architecture, features, and services of 802.11b are defined by the original 802.11 standard as the revised specification affects only the physical layer, adding higher data rates and more robust connectivity.

The key contribution of the 802.11b addition to the WLAN standard was to standardize the physical layer support of two new speeds, 5.5 Mbps and 11 Mbps. To accomplish this, DSSS had to be selected as the sole physical layer technique for the standard because frequency hopping cannot support the higher speeds without violating current FCC regulations. The implication is that 802.11b systems will interoperate with 1 Mbps and 2 Mbps 802.11 DSSS systems, but will not work with 1 Mbps and 2 Mbps 802.11 FHSS systems. Because the 802.11b standard has no provision for FHSS, most vendors chose to implement DSSS, as the ratified 802.11b (11 Mbps) standard. This makes migration from a 2 Mbps 802.11 DSSS system to an 11 Mbps 802.11b system very easy as the underlying modulation scheme is very similar. 2 Mbps 802.11 DSSS systems will be able to coexist with 11 Mbps 802.11b systems, enabling a smooth transition to the higher data rate technology. This is similar to migrating from 10 Mbps Ethernet to 100 Mbps Ethernet, enabling a large performance improvement while maintaining the same protocol. However, there is no easy migration path from 1 and 2 Mbps FHSS systems to the 11 Mbps DSSS system. To migrate from FHSS systems to DSSS will require wholesale replacement of radios in areas where the currently used FHSS is either no longer functional or productivity requirements outweigh conversion costs.

802.11b WLANs use dynamic rate shifting, allowing data rates to be automatically adjusted to compensate for interference or range issues on the radio channel. Ideally, users connect at the full 11 Mbps rate. However when devices move beyond the optimal range for 11 Mbps operation, or if substantial interference is present, 802.11b devices will transmit at lower speeds, falling back to 5.5, 2, and 1 Mbps. Likewise, if the device moves back within the range of a higher-speed transmission, the connection will automatically speed up again. Rate shifting is a physical-layer mechanism transparent to the user and the upper layers of the protocol stack.

There are many different devices competing for airspace in the 2.4 GHz radio spectrum. Unfortunately, most of the devices that cause interference are especially common in the home environment, such as microwaves and cordless phones. As you can imagine, the viability of an 802.11b network depends on how many of these products are near the network devices.

One of the more recent entrants to the 802.11b airspace comes in the form of the emerging Bluetooth wireless standard. Though designed for short-range transmissions, Bluetooth devices utilize FHSS to communicate with each other. Cycling through thousands of frequencies a second, this looks as if it poses the greatest chance of creating interference for 802.11. Further research will determine exactly what—if any—interference Bluetooth will cause to 802.11b networks.

These forms of interference will directly impact the home user who wishes to set up a wireless LAN, especially if neighbors operate interfering devices. Only time will tell if 802.11b will be able to stand up against these adversaries and hold on to the marketplace.

802.11a

802.11a is one of the physical layer extensions to the 802.11 standard. Abandoning spread spectrum completely, 802.11a uses an encoding technique called Orthogonal Frequency Division Multiplexing (OFDM). Although this encoding technique is similar to the European 5 GHz HiperLAN physical layer specification, which will be explained in greater detail later in the chapter, 802.11a currently is specific to the United States.

802.11a equipment will operate at 5 GHz and support up to a 54 Mbps data rate. The FCC has allocated 300 MHz of RF spectrum for unlicensed operation in the 5 GHz block, 200 MHz of which is at 5.15 MHz to 5.35 MHz (UNII), with the other 100 MHz at 5.725 MHz to 5.825 MHz (ISM). In addition to the frequency and bandwidth allocation, one key parameter that is regulated by the various authorities is the allowable transmit output power. The transmit output power is directly related with the range of coverage that a particular radio can achieve. The 5 GHz spectrum is split into three working "domains." The first 100 MHz in the lower section is restricted to a maximum power output of 50 mW. The second 100 MHz has a more generous 250 mW power budget, while the top 100 MHz is delegated for outdoor applications, with a maximum of 1W power output.

In contrast, 802.11b client cards can radiate as much as 1 watt in the United States. However, most modern cards radiate only a fraction (30 mW) of the maximum available power. This is due mainly for reasons of battery conservation and heat dissipation. Although segmented, the total bandwidth available for IEEE 802.11a applications is almost four times that of the ISM band's 83 MHz of spectrum in the 2.4 GHz range, while the UNII and 5GHz ISM bands offer 300 MHz.

When the IEEE ratified the 802.11a and 802.11b wireless networking communications standards in 1999, its goal was to create a standards-based technology that could span multiple physical encoding types, frequencies, and applications in the same way the 802.3 Ethernet standard has been successfully applied to 10 Mbps, 100 Mbps, and 1 Gbps technology over fiber and various kinds of copper.

Like Ethernet and Fast Ethernet, 802.11b and 802.11a use an identical MAC. However, whereas Fast Ethernet uses the same physical-layer encoding scheme as Ethernet (only faster), 802.11a uses an entirely different encoding scheme, called OFDM.

A drawback to using the 802.11b MAC is that 802.11a will inherit the same inefficiencies resident in 802.11b wireless implementations. The 802.11b MAC is only about 70 percent efficient. Currently your maximum throughput on an

11 Mbps 802.11b wireless implementations are between 5.5 and 6 Mbps. So even at 802.11a's 54 Mbps, maximum throughput is closer to 30 to 35 Mbps when factoring in driver inefficiencies and some additional overhead at the physical layer. Unlike 802.11b, 802.11a does not have to transmit its headers at 1 Mbps, so 802.11a will gain some efficiency (about 5 percent) over 802.11b.

Because 802.11a and 802.11b operate in different frequencies, interoperability is impossible. You have a clear migration path when you need more bandwidth, but extensive redesign is necessary to move from 802.11b to 802.11a. Coexistence of the two standards in a single environment is possible because there is no signal overlap. As bandwidth needs increase, you can begin to deploy 802.11a gear right alongside your 802.11b installation, the range and coverage will probably require that you install additional APs if you want to achieve the 54 Mbps data rate.

Other Related Working Groups

Since the first 802.11 standard was approved in 1997, several initiatives have taken place to make improvements. Each task group, outlined next, is endeavoring to improve the 802.11 standard, making it globally accessible, efficient, and secure, without having to reinvent the MAC layer of 802.11:

- **The 802.11d Working Group** Concentrating on the development of 802.11 WLAN equipment to operate in markets not served by the current standard (the current 802.11 standard defines WLAN operation in only a few countries).

- **The IEEE 802.11e Working Group** Providing enhancements to the 802.11 standard while retaining compatibility with 802.11b and 802.11a. The enhancements include multimedia capability made possible with the adoption of quality of service (QoS) functionality as well as security improvements. What does this mean for a service provider? It means the ability to offer video on demand, audio on demand, high-speed Internet access, and Voice over IP (VoIP) services. What does this mean for the home or business user? It allows high-fidelity multimedia in the form of MPEG2 video and CD quality sound, and redefinition of the traditional phone use with VoIP. QoS is the key to the added functionality with 802.11e. It provides the functionality required to accommodate time-sensitive applications such as video and audio. QoS includes queuing, traffic shaping tools, and scheduling. These characteristics allow priority of traffic. For example, data traffic is not time-sensitive and therefore has a lower priority than applications such as streaming video. With these enhancements, wireless networking has evolved to meet the demands of today's users.

- **The 802.11f Working Group** Developing an Inter-Access Point Protocol, due to the current limitation prohibiting roaming between APs made by different vendors. This protocol would allow wireless devices to roam across APs made by competing vendors.

- **The 802.11g Working Group** Working on furthering higher data rates in the 2.4 GHz radio band.

- **The 802.11h Working Group** Developing Spectrum and Power Management Extensions for the IEEE 802.11a standard for use in Europe.

European Telecommunications Standards Institute (ETSI)[1]

The European counterpart to IEEE; ETSI (the European Telecommunications Standards Institute) was formed in 1988 by the European Commission. The European Commission, formed of telecommunications vendors and operators, wanted to define standards for the European market that would allow telecommunications to function as a single entity. In the beginning, ETSI focused its standards primarily on the benefit it would provide European citizens. Later, standards benefiting all markets were introduced. ETSI is a nonprofit organization whose mission is to produce the telecommunications standards that will be used throughout Europe.

ETSI has its headquarters based in the south of France. The institute unites 789 members from 52 countries inside and outside Europe, and represents administrations, network operators, manufacturers, service providers, research bodies, and users. Any European organization proving an interest in promoting European telecommunications standards has the right to represent that interest in ETSI and thus to directly influence the standards-making process.

---

[1] © ETSI 2002. Further use, modification, redistribution is strictly prohibited. ETSI standards are available from http://pda.etsi.org/pda/ and http://www.etsi.org/eds/.

ETSI's approach to standards making is similar to IEEE's in many ways. It is ETSI members that fix the standards to function based on market drivers and needs. Accordingly, ETSI produces voluntary standards, some of these may go on to be adopted by the European Commission as the technical base for directives or regulations, but voluntary standards are requested by those who subsequently implement them, which means that the standards remain practical rather than abstract.

Similar to IEEE's model, ETSI's organizational model is broken down into various committees and working groups. It consists of a General Assembly, a Board, a Technical Organization (a.k.a, Technical Bodies), and a Secretariat. The Technical Organization produces and approves technical standards. It encompasses ETSI Projects (EPs), Technical Committees (TCs), and Special Committees. More than 3,500 experts are at present working for ETSI in over 200 groups.

The central Secretariat of ETSI has about 110 staff members. In order to promote and accelerate standardization, additional experts work on a full time basis at the ETSI Headquarters. There are about 25 Specialist Task Forces (STFs) with around 60 experts total. To date, over 5,000 ETSI deliverables have been published.

ETSI promotes the worldwide standardization process whenever possible. Its Work Program is based on, and coordinated with, the activities of international standardization bodies, mainly two groups within the International Telecommunication Union (ITU), the ITU-T and the ITU-R. The ITU is headquartered in Geneva, Switzerland, and it is an international organization within which governments and the private sector coordinate global telecom networks and services. Recently ETSI has coordinated it's efforts in the WLAN arena with the IEEE. ETSI's project Broadband Radio Access Networks (BRAN) is being coordinated with IEEE to further technological advancement by producing specifications for high capacity WLANs for both mobile and fixed wireless implementations.

In response to growing market pressure for low-cost, high capacity radio links, ETSI established a standardization project for BRAN in Spring 1997. ETSI BRAN is the successor of the former Sub-Technical Committee, RES10, which developed the HiperLAN1 specifications.

The project prepares standards for equipment providing broadband (25 Mbit/s or more) wireless access to wire-based networks in both private and public environments, operating in either licensed or license-exempt spectrum. These systems address both business and residential applications. Fixed wireless access systems are intended as high performance, quick to set up, competitive alternatives for wire-based access systems. The specifications address the physical (PHY) layer as well as the DLC layer (with medium access and logical data link control sublayers as appropriate). Internetworking specifications that allow broadband radio systems to interface to existing wired networks, notably those based on ATM, TCP/IP protocol suites, and UMTS, are or will be developed.

ETSI BRAN assists regulatory bodies with issues such as the requirements for spectrum and the radio conformance specifications that will be required to implement the new broadband radio networks.

To ensure overall coherence with other existing and emerging technologies, close relationships have been or are being established with the ATM Forum, the HiperLAN2 Global Forum, the IEEE Wireless LAN Committees 802.11a and IEEE 802.16, the Internet Engineering Task Force, the MMAC-PC High Speed Wireless Access Systems Group, the International Telecommunication Union Radio sector (ITU-R), and a number of internal ETSI Technical Bodies.

ETSI BRAN currently produces specifications for four major wireless standard Areas, HiperLAN, and HiperLAN/2, which is a mobile broadband short-range access network and HiperAccess, which is a fixed wireless broadband access network and HiperLink, which will provide short-range very high-speed interconnection of WLANs (see Table 2.5).

Table 2.5 HiperLAN Family of Standards

	HiperLAN Type 1	HiperLAN Type 2	HiperAccess	HiperLink
Application	Wireless Ethernet (LAN)	Wireless ATM	Wireless Local Loop	Wireless Point-to-Point
Frequency Range	5 GHz	5 GHz	5 GHz	17 GHz
Data Rate	23.5 Mbps	~20 Mbps	~20 Mbps	~155 Mbps

HiperLAN

HiperLAN or High Performance Radio LAN, is a radio LAN standard designed to provide high-speed communications (20 Mbps) between portable devices in the 5 GHz range. It is intended to allow flexible wireless data networks to be created, without the need for an existing wired infrastructure. In addition, it can be used as an extension of a wired LAN. The support of multimedia applications is possible due to the higher bandwidth that this standard supports over IEEE's 802.11 standard.

HiperLAN/2

HiperLAN/2 is the next generation of HiperLAN WLAN technology that is currently being developed by ETSI. It is an ATM-based wireless system, and the new set of standards is incorporating many new features such as QoS, Connection Oriented, Automatic Frequency Allocation, and High Speed (exceeds 50 Mbps), which are new to HiperLAN.

HiperLAN/2 will give consumers in corporate, public, and home environments wireless access to the Internet and future multimedia, as well as real-time video services at speeds of up to 54 Mbit/s. The system will be quick and easy to install and provide internetworking with several core networks including the Ethernet, RFC 1394, and ATM. HiperLAN/2 is able to operate at a speed up to 54 Mbps in the 5 GHz RF band. HiperLAN/2, in nature, is connection-oriented, hence it is able to support to implement/support for QoS.

Another difference between HiperLAN/2 and HiperLAN/1 is the frequency modulation scheme. HiperLAN/2 employs OFDM to modulate its data. The advantages over OFDM over CSMA/CA, include higher data rate, less susceptible to multiple path interference and co-channel interference.

The standard can support multibeam antennas (sectors) to improve the link budget and to reduce interference in the radio network. It also defines a set of protocols (measurements and signaling) to provide support for a number of radio network functions, such as Dynamic Frequency Selection (DFS), link adaptation, handover, multibeam antennas, and power control, where the algorithms are vendor-specific. The supported radio network functions allow cellular deployment of HiperLAN/2 systems with full coverage and high data rates in a wide range of environments. The system shall automatically allocate frequencies to each AP for communications. This is performed by the DFS, which allows several operators to share the available spectrum by avoiding the use of interfered frequencies.

To cope with the varying radio link quality (interference and propagation conditions), a link adaptation scheme is used. It aims at keeping up a communications link at low signal-to-interference ratios in order to maintain the QoS, and to trade off between communications range and data rate. Based on link quality measurements, the physical layer data rate is adapted to the current link quality. Transmitter power control is supported in both the mobile terminal (uplink) and the AP (downlink). The uplink power control is mainly used to simplify the design of the AP receiver by avoiding automatic gain control at AP. The main goal of downlink power control is to fulfill the regulatory requirements in Europe to decrease interference to other systems using the same 5 GHz band. The 5 GHz band is open in Europe, the United States, and Japan. The current spectrum allocation at 5 GHz comprises 455 MHz in Europe, 300 MHz in the U.S., and 100 MHz in Japan.

In parallel to the HiperLAN/2 standardization work, the Multimedia Mobile Access Communications (MMAC) Association in Japan started to develop different high-speed radio access systems for business and home applications at 5 GHz. One of these systems for business applications in corporate and public networks is aligned with HiperLAN/2 at both physical layer and DLC layer. In addition, the PHY layer of IEEE 802.11 standard in the 5 GHz band is harmonized with that of HiperLAN/2. With these alignments, the three communities succeeded to specify a unique radio platform at 5 GHz, which supports the development of cost-efficient multimode terminals for world-wide high-speed communications. The ETSI HiperLAN/2 functional specifications encompass the PHY layer, the DLC layer, and the Convergence layers (CL) that perform service specific functions between the DLC layer and the network layer. In other words, Specific Convergence sub-layers are used on top of the HiperLAN/2 PHY and DLC layers to provide access to networks such as IP, ATM, or UMTS. This makes HiperLAN/2 a multinetwork air interface.

HiperAccess

The HiperAccess Standard Area produces standards for broadband multimedia fixed wireless access. The HiperAccess specifications will allow for a flexible and competitive alternative to wired access networks. It will be an interoperable standard, in order to promote a mass market and thereby low cost products. During 1999, significant progress was made in the standardization process, for example, it was decided that HiperAccess will be a point-to-multipoint system. HiperAccess is targeting high frequency bands, especially it will be optimized for the 40.5 to 43.5 GHz band. For these frequency bands, TDMA will be used as multiple access scheme, and a single carrier modulation scheme will be used. The creation of specifications for frequencies below 11 GHz is currently under consideration.

ETSI BRAN, also known as ETSI Project BRAN or EP BRAN, is cooperating closely with IEEE-SA (Working Group 802.16) to coordinate the interoperability standards for broadband multimedia fixed wireless access networks. The groups have appointed liaison officers to each other, where the liaison officer from either party could attend all group meetings of the other and is provided all group notices, and in addition, is eligible to provide input documents and to recommend document changes with the same privileges of a member. Furthermore, copies of relevant working documents and drafts from either group will be made available royalty-free to the other upon request.

HiperLink

This modification of HiperAccess will provide short-range very high-speed interconnection of HiperLANs and HiperAccess, e.g. up to 155 Mbps over distances up to 150 m. Spectrum for HiperLink is available in the 17 GHz range. As of this writing, the work on this standard has not yet begun.

Wireless Ethernet Compatibility Alliance (WECA)

To ensure that consumers can build interoperating 802.11 wireless networks, an organization called the Wireless Ethernet Compatibility Alliance (WECA) tests and certifies 802.11 devices. Their symbol of approval means that the consumer can be assured that the particular device has passed a thorough test of interoperations with devices from other vendors. This is important when considering devices to be implemented into your existing network, because if the devices cannot communicate, it complicates the management of the network—in fact, essentially you will have to deal with two autonomous networks. It is also important when building a new network because you may be limited to a single vendor.

They have announced the "wireless fidelity" standard that is an awarded "seal of approval" for those WLAN products that have successfully completed prescribed interoperability testing. The Wi-Fi seal (see Figure 2.17) is to provide customers the assurance that products bearing this logo will work together. The WECA group members include a growing number of the industry's leading WLAN manufacturers, including Cisco Systems. Wi-Fi has become synonymous with 802.11 wireless technology in many articles related to the subject. However, Wi-Fi is not a technology standard, it merely assures interoperability between member manufacturers. In other words, you can have 802.11-compliant hardware and still not be considered Wi-Fi.

Figure 2.17 Wi-Fi Seal of Approval

WLAN Interoperability Forum (WLIF)

Extremely similar to WECA, the WLAN Interoperability Forum's (WLIF) mission is to promote the use of WLANs through the delivery of interoperable products and services, at all levels of the market. The WLI Forum also bases its interoperability testing on IEEE's 802.11 standard. The popularity of WECA's standard has had significant impact on the WLI Forum and its influence on the wireless market has diminished rapidly.

Infrared Data Association

The Infrared Data Association (IrDA) is a standards organization comprised of a consortium of leading U.S. and Japanese manufacturers of computers, communications equipment, and semiconductors, focused on developing standards for infrared-based attachments for infrared wireless communication. Today, nearly all consumer electronic devices that use infrared as a method of wireless communication are IrDA compliant. Most laptops sold are equipped with an IrDA-compliant infrared transceiver, which enables you to communicate with devices such as printers, modems, fax, LAN, and other laptops. Typical infrared devices use a transmission method known as *diffused infrared transmission* whereby the receiver and transmitter do not have to be aimed at each other and do not need a clear line-of-sight. Range is up to about ten meters only (in-building) and speeds are anywhere from 2400 bps to 4 Mbps.

Summary

Radio technology is the basis for Cisco Aironet wireless LANs. It consists of electromagnetic fields, radiation, frequency, and modulation to move information carrying radio signals through space.

An electromagnetic field is generated by applying alternating electric current (AC) to a conductive material such as a wire or antenna. The number of times per second that the electromagnetic field cycles or alternates is called frequency, and it is measured in units known as Hertz. For example, if an electromagnetic field alternates 9,000 times per second, it would be measured as 9 KHz. Frequency and wavelength are interrelated. As the frequency increases, the wavelength of the signal decreases. The movement of the electromagnetic field through space is called electromagnetic radiation. Electromagnetic radiation allows radio signals to travel from a transmitting antenna to a receiving antenna. Electromagnetic radiation travels at the speed of light or 186,000 miles per second. This radiation becomes weaker or less powerful as the distance increases from its source. Because all radio signals move at the speed, regardless of frequency, the wavelength of a signal with a higher frequency passes a receiving antenna more frequently.

Receiving antennas are typically passive, they intercept part of the electromagnetic radiation as it passes the antenna. The part of the signal that is intercepted is filtered of unwanted signals to isolate the intended signal for that receiver. The intended signal is the signal transmitted at a predetermined frequency from a transmitting antenna and received on that same frequency on a receiving antenna. Once the isolated signal is received, it must be demodulated to access the information or data being sent from the transmitting antenna that modulated the signal to begin with. Modulation is the technique used to impress information (data) onto the signal and determines the amount of information that can be contained within it. In general, the more complex the modulation technique is, the more information that can be carried in the signal. However, the more complex a modulation technique is, the more time or latency is introduced to de-modulate the signal. Complimentary Code Keying (CCK) is a phase modulation technique used by most 802.11b wireless devices, including Cisco Aironet devices.

The wireless LAN technology used in most current WLAN devices is called spread spectrum. There are two types of spread spectrum technology: direct sequence and frequency hopping. Cisco Aironet devices use Direct Sequence Spread Spectrum (DSSS), which uses a range of frequencies to "spread" the signal out and a unique spread spectrum code from device to device to ensure that no conflicts arise from multiple devices transmitting in the same area. The receiving device must know the transmitting device's spread spectrum code in order to decode the transmission.

Wireless LAN architecture consists of both physical and logical wireless system components. The logical components are the distribution system (DS), medium access technology, synchronization and error control, routing mechanisms, and application interface. The physical components are the medium, access point (AP), antenna, wireless station, and server.

Cisco Aironet wireless LAN devices are designed based on industry standards created by the Institute of Electrical and Electronic Engineers (IEEE). Specifically the 802.11 working group of the IEEE is responsible for generating the standards to encompass all aspects of wireless local area networking. IEEE 802.11b is a ratified standard added to the original 802.11 standard to address a physical layer change that supports higher speeds of 5.5 Mbps and 11 Mbps. The 802.11 standard defines the physical and data link components of a wireless local area network. The standard also addresses WLAN security, power management, multicell roaming capabilities, and other integral components of the WLAN. The European community has similar wireless standards, developed by the European Telecommunications Standards Institute (ETSI). Some of ETSI's standards were developed independently, whereas others were developed cooperatively with the IEEE. ETSI's standards encompass many of the same components addressed in the IEEE's standard.

Solutions Fast Track

Understanding the Fundamentals of Radio Frequency

- ☑ Radio waves are electromagnetic energy traveling at the speed of light.

- ☑ Frequency equals the number of waves that pass a specific point in one second. The measure of frequency is Hertz.

- ☑ Three license-free RF bands are used in RF wireless networking. These are called the ISM bands (for industrial, scientific, and medical).

- ☑ Modulation is the technique used to encode data in preparation for transmission.

Communicating with Wireless LAN Technologies

☑ Three popular technologies are used for WLANs: microwave, infrared, and spread spectrum.

☑ The two spread spectrum techniques are called frequency hopping spread spectrum (FHSS)and Direct Sequence Spread Spectrum (DSSS).

☑ Spread spectrum transmission enables multiple wireless transmissions over the same frequency bands without interference.

Implementing a Wireless LAN Architecture

☑ Other components beyond the wireless standards are needed to complete a wireless system.

☑ Wireless radios function in only the first two layers of the OSI reference model.

☑ Both physical and logical components make up a complete wireless system.

☑ Distribution Systems are the underlying logical topology used in a wired network environment.

Keeping Pace with Wireless Networking Standards

☑ IEEE 802.11 is the wireless standard of choice for North America.

☑ IEEE 802.11 specifies the Physical and Media Access Layer technology used in WLANs.

☑ IEEE 802.11 specifies three WLAN topologies: the BSS, IBSS, and ESS.

☑ IEEE 802.11b is an addendum to the original 802.11, which eliminates FHSS as a PHY layer choice and increases the data rates available for DSSS to 5.5 and 11 Mbps.

☑ IEEE 802.11a is a forthcoming IEEE revision to the 802.11 standard designed to increase data rates to 54 Mbps using a new PHY layer specification, Orthogonal Frequency Division Multiplexing (OFDM).

☑ ETSI is the standards organization responsible for wireless standards in the European community.

Frequently Asked Questions

The following Frequently Asked Questions, answered by the authors of this book, are designed to both measure your understanding of the concepts presented in this chapter and to assist you with real-life implementation of these concepts. To have your questions about this chapter answered by the author, browse to **www.syngress.com/solutions** and click on the **"Ask the Author"** form.

Q: The clear benefit of WLANs will be the ability to roam physically around an area, as well as logically from one AP to another. What is the specified standard for how this is done, and does it integrate with existing login mechanisms?

A: The IEEE standards working groups are developing a roaming model that will provide the means to support the roaming of users from one wireless AP to another. At present, most solutions require re-authentication when moving from one wireless AP to another. Vendors who provide a managed roaming capability have developed their own roaming management, which may or may not interface with other WLAN vendor solutions.

Q: When will wireless speeds catch up to current wired speed technologies?

A: Formation of the newer 802.11a standard is driving increased wireless speeds to the 50 Mbit range and are currently becoming available to the consumer. Though this speed increase is welcome, it still is not up to the current 100 Mbit wired speed prevalent in today's networks. Many factors, such as market drivers, frequency allocations, and technology development, will be key to bringing wireless speeds up to wired speeds.

Q: Why would I use fiber for my wired network in place of copper?

A: Fiber is commonly used in high-speed backbone connections and emerging technologies such as Gigabit Ethernet and Dense Wave Division Multiplexing (DWDM). Most networks have a "best of both worlds" approach where the backbone of the network may be fiber-based and user connections are copper-based.

Chapter 3

Cisco Wireless LAN Product Line

Solutions in this chapter:

- Overview of Cisco Wireless Systems
- Cisco Aironet 3X0 Series APs and Bridges
- Cisco Aironet Wireless NICs
- Cisco Aironet Antennas

☑ Summary

☑ Solutions Fast Track

☑ Frequently Asked Questions

Introduction

As you saw in Chapter 2, the wireless local area network (WLAN) is exactly what it sounds like, a network that is connected primarily through wireless technology. It provides all of the features of a conventional wired LAN (such as Ethernet) without the need to have wired connections to each device. But that is only half of the story; WLANs have the potential to revolutionize how network connectivity is viewed. Using wireless technologies, individual users can connect to the network without the need for cabling to be pulled to their desks. This not only gives the users the ability to move around with their laptops and personal digital assistants (PDAs), it also allows for easy migration of desktop machines during the inevitable office "reorganization." Beyond the local user level, wireless technologies also offer the capability to connect a remote workgroup without the need to trench and install cabling or order carrier services such as a T1. If conditions are correct, the Cisco WLAN technology set can connect this remote workgroup at speeds up to 11 Mbps even if they are located miles away.

In addition to the potential of providing long-term infrastructure benefits and cost savings, you can also use WLANs to quickly bring up connectivity in the event of a disaster or unexpected move. For example, if your company's office space was flooded, but the warehouse was spared, you can install Cisco's WLAN technologies in the warehouse and move the PCs into this space, thus giving access to the network to all PCs within range. This alleviates the need to run new cabling to support this temporary configuration until the office space is repaired. This solution also allows for easy addition or relocation of machines as the needs in this temporary office space changes.

Once considered cost-prohibitive, sluggish, and proprietary, today's WLAN products are now reasonably high-speed (currently 11 Mbps but moving forward), working toward a standards based, and priced for many businesses to consider its use. Cisco Systems built itself on the fact that in modern offices every worker needs to be connected to the LAN, and more often than not, to the Internet. Cisco also realized that there are some issues with the traditional wired network, such as distance limitations, or cost effectiveness where it may not be possible or practical to cable the entire workspace for intermittent connectivity. This is especially common in warehouses, public places, and in conference rooms. In these instances, it makes a lot of sense to install a wireless network that can support connectivity to all areas of your business. Cisco WLANs will allow you to cover every inch of your site and allow users to be more productive.

WLANs have been available for several years now, but they were relatively slow, most were unable to exceed the 1.5 Mbps throughput barrier. As such, wireless was used only for small bandwidth applications, such as inventory-scanning systems most warehouses and retailers use. This began to change when the Wireless Ethernet Compatibility Alliance (WECA) committee was formed. The main goal of WECA was to create new products that were faster, more compatible, and cheaper to deploy and maintain. They wanted to make wireless networking more practical for use in the modern technology world, and allow users that were unable to connect before the chance to use this new technology.

One of the first things WECA did was create a standard they called Wi-Fi, an interoperability certification, to verify interoperability and ease of deployment. This, in conjunction with the "global" acceptance of the 802.11b standard, helped reassure users that wireless equipment would function within their existing infrastructure and be supported for the long term.

Cisco is one of the vendors that embraced this standard and worked on making the Cisco Aironet series compliant with WECA standards. Though two primary mediums exist for wireless data transport, infrared light (IR) or radio frequency (RF), the one we focus on is RF. RF is more prevalent, can handle a wider coverage area, is capable of higher bandwidth, and has a longer range. In addition, the Aironet line of devices support a RF signal; specifically a signal in the 2.4 GHz range. The 2.4 GHz frequency is the only range of the RF spectrum that is available (worldwide) for the use of unlicensed devices.

Overview of Cisco Wireless Systems

In November, 1999, Cisco purchased one of the leading companies in the field of wireless technology (Aironet Wireless Communications, Inc.) in an effort to catch up to other vendors who already had a head start in the field. Aironet was a leading developer of high-speed WLAN products and played an important role on the IEEE 802.11 working group.

Cisco WLAN Product Line

In this section, we discuss the various products in the Cisco WLAN product line. Cisco makes a varied offering in the wireless arena. We talk about the differences between product lines and what role each plays in your network. We discuss the Cisco Aironet 340, 350, and several other products that are necessary to make your WLAN function properly.

You can manage Cisco devices remotely, with Web browsers, Telnet sessions, and Simple Network Management Protocol (SNMP). Through these connections, you can also monitor statistics from the devices. You can also map the wireless access points (AP) to their associated clients, and monitor those clients. The APs also allow you to control the throughput of traffic through the WLAN using Media Access Control (MAC) and protocol-based filters. If you have multiple APs deployed in your network, you can also configure these devices at a central location and manage them through the network. This allows you to maintain a consistent policy throughout the network.

One of Cisco's driving objectives is to create a seamless environment where users can utilize their network while moving from office to office and from the office to the conference room. Users are able to use their mobile devices (PDAs, handheld PCs, and notebooks) anywhere within range of the wireless network without connecting via a cable of any sort. In addition, Cisco wanted to create a solution for connecting a campus environment or even a metropolitan area together in a reliable and relatively inexpensive manner. The result of this evolution is two different solution sets. One geared toward the individual user and an office space environment and one geared toward building-to-building connectivity.

There are two main types of devices on a WLAN: the AP and the bridge. The AP is a device that connects the wired LAN to the WLAN, and allows the data to go from one media to the other. The APs connect to the wired LAN through a hub or a switch and contain encryption and communication software, as well as the radio transceiver. A second device is needed to operate with the AP: The LAN adapter that is used by the client device. This NIC is usually a PC card that works in your portable device or a card that is installed in your desktop PC. The client device normally has some type of antenna that can interact with the AP.

The second wireless device type is a wireless bridge. Much like its wired namesake, a wireless bridge is a WLAN device that connects two or more remote networks into a single LAN. The Aironet wireless Ethernet bridge is designed to support three connection types: 10Base2 (Thinnet), 10Base5 (Thicknet), or 10BaseT (twisted pair). As you will see, the Aironet 340 series bridges have 10Base-T, AUI and coaxial connection, but the Aironet 350 series devices have only an RJ-45 connection.

Using WLANs for Individual User Connectivity

Seeing WLANs implemented in place of the conventional wired network is more common today than ever before. In most cases, this transition is not all or nothing. Usually, the WLANs are used in conjunction with the wired network. To allow devices access to the wireless network, Cisco makes Personal Computer Memory Card International Association (PCMCIA) cards, Personal Computer Interface (PCI) cards, and Industry Standard Architecture (ISA) client adapters. These cards have the capability to talk directly to each other or can be used with an AP. In this scenario, APs perform the same function a hub would perform in a wired network.

As was mentioned before, this configuration allows users the freedom to remain connected to the network even when moving from place to place. In addition, this configuration allows for PCs to be placed in locations that are difficult to get cable run to, such as a factory floor, or an open space. Finally, the APs allow for the use of pass-through DHCP services to allow existing DHCP servers to handle requests, or in some cases can act as the DHCP server itself.

As with any new technology, you need to consider certain issues when using a WLAN in an office environment. First and foremost among these issues is security. With a conventional wired network, you really did not have to worry about someone walking into your office, going to your Intermediate Distribution Frame (IDF) and plugging his or her laptop into your network. However, in a wireless environment, if you do not address security up front, someone can essentially do just that. You can find more detail on how to secure your WLAN in Chapter 8. The second concern in using wireless systems is interoperability between vendors. If you are just using a basic setup, interoperability between vendors should not be an issue. However, many vendors provide proprietary solutions to "enhance" their products. Therefore, be sure to do an appropriate amount of research if you plan to implement a multivendor wireless solution. In addition to these issues, the range and signal strength of the AP as well as each individual station needs to be taken into account.

Using WLANs to Connect Campuses

As was stated earlier, the WLAN can be an effective alternative to traditional copper and fiber configurations for connecting two buildings together or for connecting to remote facilities in the same building. This is especially true if you need to connect two locations that would require you to traverse an area that cannot be easily accessed, such as a river or lake, a railroad right of way, or a highway. A wireless bridge is an upfront investment that you can install in a small amount of time and use almost immediately. Depending upon distance, the bandwidth could be anywhere from about equal to a T1 to a little more than seven times (11 Mbps) faster. Theoretically, using Cisco Wireless technology you can span a distance of up to 25 miles. In reality, this distance is probably less than that, and before attempting any wireless connection, you should test to ensure that the signal strength is appropriate.

Because you are using a LAN technology, you have the same set of alternatives when making connections between remote locations as you would in a conventional LAN environment. That is you can either directly bridge two parts of a subnet together to put the user devices in a single broadcast domain, or you can connect the wireless bridges directly into router ports to create a point-to-point Ethernet connection.

As was the case with the APs, using the bridges to connect campus buildings can be a security risk, and you need to take appropriate steps to ensure that "passers-by" cannot see your network traffic or connect to the network. In addition to this concern, environmental issues can create more of a problem in a building-to-building installation. Weather and other obstacles can affect the overall signal quality, thus creating the potential for outages.

Designing & Planning…

Third Generation Networks and Mobile Users

What are third generation (3G) networks? 3G networks are those that are based on open standards that utilize Internet Protocol (IP). Cisco has created a group that was specifically targeted to work with mobile users, the Mobile Wireless Group (MWG). The MWG interfaces with clients in an effort to address concerns that can arise from the deployment of wireless technologies. Mainly the MWG works on helping to streamline the wireless network for optimal data traffic transfer and integrating the system with existing core technologies that are already in place.

3G is also supported by the Mobile Wireless Internet Forum (MWIF) and several other standards organizations. By using a common IP core as the basis of 3G, it is able to scale efficiently and can be used by standard company implementations while transitioning from second generation networks. Second generation networks were considered voice-centric, whereas 3G networks are considered to be more a multi-service network that can support not only voice and data, but can also carry multimedia through the deployment of a multivendor-based packet infrastructure.

Cisco Aironet 3X0 Series APs and Bridges

Three main pieces of hardware go into a successful wireless installation: a base unit (AP or bridge), NIC cards (if you are using an AP), and an antenna. The base units that Cisco offers are detailed in this section, and the NIC cards and antennas are detailed in later sections.

Cisco Aironet 3X0 series APs and bridges consist of the Cisco Aironet 350 and Cisco Aironet 340 series. In this section, we discuss several of the features that are inherent in both and several of the differences between these two platforms. We also discuss the usage of Direct Sequence Spread Spectrum (DSSS) for frequency bands and the authentication such as Remote Authentication Dial-In User Service (RADIUS), which you can use so that your wireless network is secure from outsiders. We also begin to discuss the Aironet series client software in this section. For more information on the client software that is available for APs and wireless bridges, see Chapters 5 and 6.

The Cisco Aironet 350 Series

The first of the product line that we look at is the 350 series. Cisco has designed the Aironet 350 series to meet the needs of mobile users and satellite offices so that they can maintain connectivity and have the freedom to move around and the flexibility to grow. In this section of the chapter, we first discuss the features that are common to all of the 350 series product line and then discuss the individual product types that are available.

Features Common to All 350 Series Devices

As previously stated, the 350 is designed to support a wide array of wireless devices, such as PCs, PDAs, handheld PCs, printers, point of sale devices, management and monitoring equipment, and just about anything else. Some of the items that make the 350 so popular are that it has the highest transmit power (100 milliwatt) in its class, is highly sensitive for receiving transmissions from other units, can be powered inline, and allows for centralized security.

The Cisco Aironet 350 is IEEE 802.11b–compliant so that it will interoperate with other vendor devices within your range of coverage. Because it is part of Cisco's offering, they have worked hard on integrating the wireless devices into their network devices. One nice feature of the 350 platforms is that it comes bundled with software that installs on a laptop, and you can use it to map out the strength of the wireless signal in your environment.

The 350 can support a variety of features depending on the version of bridge or access point (AP) firmware that you have installed, such as the following:

- **Accounting** This feature allows for collection of data from wireless devices that are located on your network. You can also establish a collection center for this data and enable accounting on the bridge or AP by using RADIUS servers located on the network. This feature is available in firmware version 11.10T and above.

- **Protection for Wired Equivalent Protocol (WEP) keys** This feature allows for the capability to add WEP keys for greater security. Three advanced security features can enable you to enhance the security of your wireless network that are built into these devices. They are WEP key hashing, Broadcast WEP key rotation, and Message Integrity Check (MIC). These features are available in firmware version 11.10T and above. This is also covered more in-depth in Chapter 8.

- **LEAP (Lightweight Extensible Authentication Protocol) to authenticate nonroot bridges** This feature will allow the nonroot bridges to authenticate to the network so that they can receive and use dynamic WEP keys. This feature is available in firmware version 11.10T and above. This is also covered more in depth in Chapter 8.

- **Software Image Management (SWIM) tool** If you are also using CiscoWorks 2000, you can also have advanced software management—you can use this tool to enhance the level of management on your wireless network. The SWIM tool is located within the Resource Management Essentials (RME) section of CiscoWorks 2000. The SWIM allows you to manage AP and bridge firmware from a centralized location. This feature is available in firmware version 11.08 and above.

- **Publicly Secure Packet Forwarding (PSPF) to block inter-client communication** PSPF enables you to prevent devices that are located on the wireless network from unintentionally sharing data with other devices that are located on the same network. PSPF will allow you to give Internet access to the devices and disallow them from the network, if you wish. When PSPF is configured, it will not allow client devices to transmit directly to other clients that are located on the WLAN in a peer-to-peer manner. You will most often see this feature enabled in campus environments, such as college campuses, airport terminals, and coffee houses. This feature is available in firmware version 11.08 and above.

There are also some features that are not dependant on the firmware revision that you are using; the client software will also allow you to have the following:

- **Observation of the activity on the radio transmitter**   This is accomplished through the carrier test tool, which measures the amount of radio activity (not radioactivity, as in nuclear fallout) on each frequency that is used by the bridge or AP. Using this tool will allow you to configure the bridge or AP to use the most efficient frequency available.

- **Antenna alignment tool**   This tool will assist you in the alignment of your antenna so that you can receive the best signal quality between your bridge or AP and other wireless devices.

- **Port Assignment**   You can assign ports for specific use, so that you can maintain consistency throughout your network environment.

- **Bridge location detection**   This tool will assist you in finding the location of a specific bridge that is located within the wireless network.

- **Bridge association limits**   This allows you to limit the number of devices that the bridge will accept.

- **Integrated network management**   Cisco wireless devices can utilize Cisco Discovery Protocol (CDP) to improve the efficiency of your network monitoring. CDP will also allow you to browse other Cisco (and miscellaneous) network equipment located on the network.

- **Security**   You can configure your wireless bridge or AP to restrict access to a group of users. You could encrypt the data with WEP. You can also use EAP/LEAP with MAC-based authentication and use a RADIUS server to control access to the network (you could then add a backup RADIUS server for redundancy).

- **Filtering**   You can create filters that will allow or prevent specific protocols to be used through the bridge or AP. You can also control the forwarding of traffic from the bridge or AP with unicast and multicast filtering.

- **Hot standby**   You can assign a bridge to be the backup rugged AP, so that you can provide redundancy and reliability in case of AP failure.

- **World mode**   This setting allows for the connection of wireless devices to occur no matter where in the world you are located (as long as there is wireless coverage in that area). What this means is that a visitor from Europe could travel to America, and the wireless device could associate itself with a wireless bridge or AP and configure itself to work with the correct channel settings.

- **Automatic load balancing** The bridge will automatically direct client devices to an AP that will allow them the best connection. This is accomplished through a number of factors, such as the transmission rate, the signal strength, and the number of currently connected users.

- **Rugged APs** This allows you to configure the bridge as a rugged AP for coverage purposes.

Configuring & Implementing...

Cisco Aironet AP Safety

The FCC has adopted a safety standard for human exposure to radio frequency (RF) electromagnetic energy that is emitted by FCC certified equipment. The Cisco Aironet WLAN products are considered to be within the uncontrolled environmental limits for these safety standards. The proper operation for this radio device is outlined in the instructions that you'll find in the manual included with the device and in the hardware installation guide located on the Cisco Aironet AP and Bridge CD. This guide recommends the following:

- You should not touch or move the antenna(s) while the unit is transmitting or receiving data.

- You should not hold any component of the radio devices so that the antenna is very close to or touching any exposed parts of your body, especially the face or eyes, when transmitting.

- You should not operate the radio device near unshielded blasting caps or in an explosive environment.

- You should not operate the radio or attempt to transmit data unless the antenna is connected. If you try do use this device without the antenna, the radio may be damaged.

- Be sure to adjust the antenna so that it is at least 8 inches (20 centimeters) away from your body at all times.

The Cisco Aironet 350 APs are powered *inline*. This means that they receive their power through Ethernet cables. This Ethernet cable can be up to 300 feet in length. Therefore, you do not need a power cord for the unit. You can power the 350 in three ways:

- A powered patch panel
- A switch that is capable of inline power (the Cisco Catalyst 3524, 4000, and the 6500)
- A Cisco Aironet power injector (designed for the Aironet 350 line)

NOTE

The Cisco Aironet power injector is for use only with the 350 series bridges and APs. If you use the injector with other Ethernet devices, you could cause damage to them. Also, the injector is not rated for use in places within a buildings environmental air space, like above a suspended ceiling.

Individual 350 Series Device Features

The 350 series product line has three base models: *APs*, *wireless bridges*, and *workgroup bridges*. In general, you use APs to connect any wireless PCs, PDAs, or like devices to the network. In most instances, the AP is used in combination with existing wired infrastructure. The wireless bridges are used to connect disparate parts of the network together. Whether that is to connect two different office spaces in the same building or to connect two buildings together, the concept is still the same. Finally, the workgroup bridges are used to connect smaller remote offices back to a central location. The workgroup bridge will allow for up to eight Ethernet-connected (wired not wireless) devices to be connected via wireless to the central wired network. It should be noted that the workgroup bridge only has one 10BaseT port, so if more than one device needs to connect to it; an intermediary hub or switch will be needed. You would then connect this hub or switch the port on the bridge allowing up to eight stations to access the wireless connection.

350 Series AP

As was mentioned before, the 350 series AP is designed to connect individual users using some format of wireless NIC card to the network. The AP then allows this traffic to be converted to travel across the wired LAN or to another wireless segment. In addition, by using multiple APs together, users are able to seamlessly travel between coverage areas.

The 350 series APs come in a normal plastic case model and a sturdier metal case or "rugged" model. The rugged model is designed to be used in environmental airspace or areas that require plenum-rated equipment. As such, the rugged model has a wider range of operating temperatures, –4 to 131 degrees Fahrenheit (–20 to 55 degrees Celsius), compared to the plastic case models, 32 to 122 degrees Fahrenheit (0 to 50 degrees Celsius). Also, if an inline power injector is used, it is not plenum-rated and has an even smaller operating range, 32 to 104 degrees Fahrenheit (0 to 40 degrees Celsius). Therefore, you will need to ensure the location of the power injector meets these requirements. In addition to the regular or rugged versions, you can also get APs with two nonremovable 2.2 dBi diversity dipole antennas or two external, removable 2.2 dBi dipole antennas with RP-TNC connectors if you plan on installing you own antenna. (Chapter 9 provides more information on RP-TNC connectors.)

In order to ensure that the uplink connection is not a bottleneck in the configuration, the 350 series APs are equipped with an auto-sensing 10/100BaseT Ethernet uplink port. This uses standard RJ-45 connectors and UTP cabling. For connecting to the wireless clients, the AP will communicate at either 1, 2, 5.5, or 11 Mbps depending on signal strength and quality. Depending on the speed of the connection, the AP will use different modulation settings. These settings are shown in Table 3.1, but in general, these modulation techniques are optimized to fit the signal characteristics that are present in their operating speed. As such, the Differential Binary Phase Shift Keying (DBPSK) and the Differential Quadrature Phase Shift Keying (DQPSK) modulation techniques are similar in structure and are quite different from the Complementary Code Keying (CCK) technique that is used for the 5.5 and 11 Mbps transmission. No matter which modulation technique is used, the wireless transmission with the APs; the methodology used for the transmission is Direct Sequence Spread Spectrum. DSSS uses the entire frequency band for transmission of the data, thus allowing for higher throughput than if just one of the frequencies was used. As is the case with most wireless systems, the AP acts as a hub, and as such must deal with collisions. To do this, the AP uses Carrier Sense Multiple Access with Collision Avoidance (CSMA/CA) as the MAC protocol. For more information on the 350 AP, see Table 3.1.

Table 3.1 350 Series AP Features

Description	Specifications
Supported data rates	1, 2, 5.5, 11Mbps
Supported standard	IEEE 802.11b
Indoor range	11 Mbps at 150 ft; 1 Mbps at 350 ft
Outdoor range	11 Mbps at 800 ft; 1 Mbps at 2000 ft
Encryption support	128-bit
Authentication?	Yes
Wireless medium	DSSS
Media Access Control (MAC)	CSMA/CA
Modulation	DBPSK @ 1 Mbps; DQPSK @ 2 Mbps; CCK @5.5 and 11 Mbps
Frequency band	2.4 to 2.497 GHz
Operating systems supported	Windows 95/98/2000/NT/CE, LINUX Netware 4.x
Remote configuration support	Telnet; HTTP; FTP; TFTP; and SNMP
AP acts as DHCP client?	Yes
Antenna options	Two external removable 2.2 dBi Dipole with RP-TNC connectors; integrated (non-removable) diversity dipoles
Uplink	Auto-sensing 10/100BaseT Ethernet
Operating temperature range	Plastic case AP: 32 to 122° F (0 to 50° C); Rugged AP: −4 to 131° F (−20 to 55° C); Power injector: 32 to 104° F (0 to 40° C)

Designing & Planning...

CSMA/CD versus CSMA/CA

In an Ethernet environment, it is just a matter of fact that collisions occur on a regular basis, and you need a way to deal with them. As you are already aware, in a wired Ethernet environment, you can address collisions by moving to a device that supports full duplex communication, or if that is not a feasible option, by allowing the standard collision

Continued

control mechanism, Carrier Sense Multiple Access with Collision Detection (CSMA/CD) standard to take care of the collision.

In a Cisco wireless setting, there is no option for full duplex communication to eliminate the possibility of collisions, so that leaves a manner of dealing with collisions to a separate methodology. The methodology employed in a wired Ethernet setting, CSMA/CD, relies on the fact that every station on segment can hear every other station on the segment to determine if there is a collision. In a wireless setting the AP is usually the only station that can hear and communicate to every station on the wireless network. As you can see in Figure 3.1, Workstation A can send and receive directly from the AP, as can Workstation B. However, Workstation A does not have the signal strength to send or receive any data directly from Workstation B. As a result, using CSMA/CD in this instance would not work because Workstation A could not tell if there was a collision with Workstation B traffic and vice versa.

Figure 3.1 Hidden Node Problem

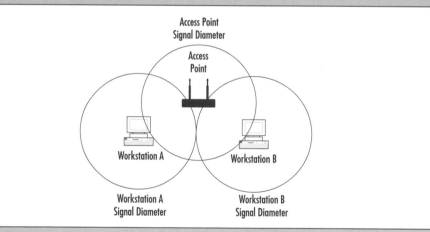

To solve this problem, Carrier Sense Multiple Access with Collision Avoidance (CSMA/CA) is used in the wireless environment. With CSMA/CA the workstation that wants to transmit first listens to see if another station is transmitting. If the workstation senses that there is no one transmitting it begins sending its packet. It is the receiver's responsibility to send back an ACK packet to the transmitter stating that the packet was received. If the transmitting workstation does not receive an ACK it assumes there was a collision (or error) and retransmits the packet.

Continued

If the workstation senses another workstation already transmitting, it waits until that transmission is complete, then waits a set amount of time to allow for the transmission of the ACK packet, and then waits a random amount of time longer before beginning its transmission.

350 Series Bridge

Unlike the AP, the 350 series bridge comes only in the rugged, metal case, version. As a result, all of the 350 series bridges are plenum-rated and as such can be installed in environmental air space. They also inherit the larger operating temperature range, −4 to 131 degrees Fahrenheit (−20 to 55 degrees Celsius). This extended range also allows you to install them in appropriate National Electrical Manufacturers Association (NEMA) enclosures outdoors. (You can find more information on NEMA enclosures in Chapter 9.) Note that because the 350 series bridges are powered by inline power through the Ethernet cable, the power supply used in most cases will not be plenum-rated nor have the same operating temperature range. Because the power supply can be up to 300 feet away; in most installations this is not an issue.

In most cases, the bridges are used in a point-to-point configuration, however they do have the capability for point-to-multipoint configurations as well. No antennas are supplied with the bridge; instead it comes with two RP-TNC connectors that can be attached to an existing antenna. As was the case with the AP, the only uplink port on the 350 series bridge is an auto-sensing 10/100BaseT Ethernet port. Also similar to the 350 AP, the bridge uses DSSS as the wireless medium, and can transmit at 1, 2, 5.5, or 11 Mbps depending on signal strength and quality. CSMA/CA is used for the MAC protocol. Finally, the maximum range (depending on antenna and environmental conditions) is up to 25 miles at 2 Mbps, or 18 miles at 11 Mbps. See Table 3.2 for more information about the 350 series bridge.

Table 3.2 350 Series Bridge Features

Description	Specifications
Supported data rates	1, 2, 5.5, 11 Mbps
Supported standard	IEEE 802.11b
Range	25 miles at 2 Mbps; 18 miles at 11 Mbps
Encryption support	128-bit
Bridging protocol	Spanning tree

Continued

Table 3.2 Continued

Description	Specifications
Wireless medium	DSSS
MAC	CSMA/CA
Modulation	DBPSK @ 1 Mbps; DQPSK @ 2 Mbps; CCK @5.5 and 11 Mbps
Frequency band	2.4 to 2.497 GHz
Remote configuration support	Telnet; HTTP; FTP; TFTP; and SNMP
Antenna options	2 RP-TNC connectors (no antenna ships with bridge)
Uplink	Auto-sensing 10/100BaseT Ethernet
Operating temperature range	Bridge: –4 to 131° F (–20 to 55° C); Power injector: 32 to 104° F (0 to 40° C)

350 Series Workgroup Bridge

The 350 series workgroup bridge is specifically designed to connect a small number (up to eight) of hard-wired attached Ethernet stations to an AP. Because the 350 series workgroup bridge has only one uplink port; if you need to connect more than one device through it, you need to use an external hub or switch. Though the wireless connection usually takes place within a building, it can also be done between buildings. Figure 3.2 shows a typical workgroup bridge configuration.

Figure 3.2 350 Workgroup Bridge

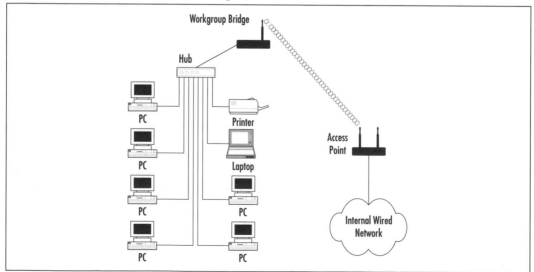

In many respects, the workgroup bridge is very similar to the other members of the 350 series family. It uses DSSS as the wireless medium, uses CSMA/CA as the MAC protocol, and can communicate at 1, 2, 5.5, or 11 Mbps. However, there are a couple differences as well. The 350 series workgroup bridge does not use inline power. The uplink port on the workgroup bridge is only a 10BaseT uplink, not a 10/100BaseT uplink. This design characteristic was chosen due to the limited number of workstations that it can support. In addition, because it is in general designed for indoor use, the workgroup bridge comes only in a plastic case model, therefore, it is not plenum-rated. Also, its operating temperature matches that of the plastic case AP, 32 to 122 degrees Fahrenheit (0 to 50 degrees Celsius). Two antenna options are available for the 350 workgroup bridge, a single nonremovable 2.2 dBi dipole antenna, or two RP-TNC connectors with no supplied antennas. For more information on the 350 series workgroup bridge, see Table 3.3.

Table 3.3 350 Series Workgroup Bridge Features

Description	Specifications
Supported data rates	1, 2, 5.5, 11 Mbps
Supported standard	IEEE 802.11b
Range	Indoor: 130 ft @ 11 Mbps; 350 ft @ 1Mbps Outdoor: 800 ft @ 11 Mbps; 2000 ft @ 1Mbps
Encryption support	128-bit
Maximum number of users supported	8
Inline power?	No
Wireless medium	DSSS
MAC	CSMA/CA
Modulation	DBPSK @ 1 Mbps; DQPSK @ 2 Mbps; CCK @5.5 and 11 Mbps
Frequency band	2.4 to 2.4897 GHz
Remote configuration support	Telnet; HTTP; FTP; TFTP; and SNMP
Antenna options	One nonremovable 2.2 dBi dipole antenna or 2 RP-TNC connectors (no antenna ships with bridge)
Uplink	10BaseT Ethernet
Operating temperature range	Bridge: 32 to 122° F (0 to 50° C)

Features of the Cisco Aironet 340 Series

The 340 series of wireless devices closely resemble that of the 350 series. Because the feature set that is available with the 340 series line is essentially the same, please refer to the list in the earlier section "Features Common to all 350 Series Devices." One if the differences between the two product lines are that the 340 line has an additional device not included in the 350 product line. Called a base station, this component is described in greater detail later in the section "The Cisco Aironet 340 Series Base Station." In addition, none of the 340 series products support the inline power that the 350 series products support. Other differences are covered in the sections detailing each product.

Individual 340 Series Device Features

All of the product groups for the 340 series products are detailed in the following sections. The products that are available in the 340 line are APs, wireless bridges, workgroup bridges, and base stations. The information on the NIC cards available, as well as the antenna options, are covered in subsequent sections.

The Cisco Aironet 340 Series AP

The design of the 340 series AP allows individual users to connect to the network using some format of wireless NIC. The AP then converts this traffic into a format that allows it to travel across the wired LAN or to another wireless segment. In addition, by using multiple APs together, users are able to seamlessly travel between coverage areas.

Like the 350 series APs, the 340 series AP use CSMA/CA as the MAC protocol for the wireless connection. It also uses DSSS as the wireless medium. Transmission speeds are also the same at 1, 2, 5.5, or 11 Mbps using DBPSK, DQPSK, and CCK modulation based on transmission speed. In addition, the 340 series AP comes with an auto-sensing 10/100BaseT Ethernet port for connecting to the wired network.

There is no rugged version of the 340 series AP, and none of these APs are plenum-rated. In addition, the operating temperature range matches that of the plastic case 350 series AP at 32 to 122 degrees Fahrenheit (0 to 50 degrees Celsius). All of the 340 series line of APs can be connected to 110-volt power source, and a couple models also support 220-volts. Another difference between the 340 series APs and the 350 series is that the 340 series does not support TFTP for management purposes. It supports only Telnet, HTTP, FTP, and SNMP. Three antenna choices are available for the 340 series AP. You can get a single nonremovable 2.2 dBi diversity dipole antenna, two redundant nonremovable 2.2 dBi diversity dipole antennas, or two RP-TNC connectors with no antenna supplied, if you plan to install you own antenna. Finally, though most of the 340 line supports 128-bit, a few models support only 40-bit encryption, so if security is important in your installation, be sure to verify the encryption level and other security features before ordering. For more information on the 340 series APs, see Table 3.4.

Table 3.4 350 Series AP Features

Description	Specifications
Supported data rates	1, 2, 5.5, 11 Mbps
Supported standard	IEEE 802.11b
Indoor range	11 Mbps at 80 ft; 1 Mbps at 250 ft
Outdoor range	11 Mbps at 300 ft; 1 Mbps at 1300 ft
Encryption support	40-bit or 128-bit
Authentication?	Yes
Wireless medium	DSSS
MAC	CSMA/CA
Modulation	DBPSK @ 1 Mbps; DQPSK @ 2 Mbps; CCK @5.5 and 11 Mbps
Frequency band	2.4 to 2.4834 GHz
Operating systems supported	Windows 95/98/2000/NT/CE, Linux
Remote configuration support	Telnet; HTTP; FTP; and SNMP
AP acts as DHCP client?	Yes
Antenna options	2 RP-TNC connectors (no antenna ships with AP); Single Integrated (nonremovable) diversity dipoles; 2 Integrated (nonremovable) diversity dipoles
Uplink	Auto-sensing 10/100BaseT Ethernet
Operating temperature range	32 to 122° F (0 to 50° C)

The Cisco Aironet 340 Series Wireless Bridge

As was the case with the 350 series bridge, the 340 series bridge is designed to either connect multiple buildings in a campus or metropolitan area together or to connect two LANs together that are in the same building. In most cases, you would also install an external antenna to boost the signal that bridge sends and receives.

Most of the features of the 340 series bridge are the same as the 340 series AP. Therefore, items such as data rates, wireless medium, MAC protocol, modulation, and power are shown in Table 3.5 but not specifically discussed here. One item that is different between the 340 AP and bridge is the uplink port. The 340 series bridge has support for 10Base2, 10Base5, and 10BaseT wired connections. This allows you to easily integrate the 340 bridge into an older network that has not been upgraded to 10/100BaseT Ethernet. You will also notice that that the operating temperature range of the 340 series bridge, –4 to 122 degrees Fahrenheit (–20 to 50 degrees Celsius), is close to that of the rugged version of the 350 series bridge. This gives you the flexibility to install the bridge in a location that has higher temperature variations. The rest of the information regarding the bridge is detailed in Table 3.5.

Table 3.5 340 Series Bridge Features

Description	Specifications
Supported data rates	1, 2, 5.5, 11 Mbps
Supported standard	IEEE 802.11b
Range	18 miles at 11 Mbps
Encryption support	128-bit
Bridging protocol	Spanning tree
Wireless medium	DSSS
MAC	CSMA/CA
Modulation	DBPSK @ 1 Mbps; DQPSK @ 2 Mbps; CCK @5.5 and 11 Mbps
Frequency band	2.4 to 2.4835 GHz
Remote configuration support	Telnet; HTTP; FTP; and SNMP
Antenna options	2 RP-TNC connectors (no antenna ships with bridge)
Uplink	10Base2, 10Base5, and 10BaseT
Operating temperature range	–4 to 122° F (–20 to 50° C)

The Cisco Aironet 340 Series Workgroup Bridge

The 340 Series workgroup bridge is designed to address the same niche that the 350 series workgroup bridge services—that being a small (up to eight) user community that has hard-wired Ethernet devices that need to be connected back to the main wired LAN. The 340 series workgroup bridge comes with a single 10BaseT RJ-45 connector, so if you want to use it to connect multiple devices, you will need to also use a hub or switch as a concentrator for these devices. (This concept is illustrated in Figure 3.2 in the 350 series section). The remaining details about the setup of the 340 series workgroup bridge are detailed in Table 3.6.

Table 3.6 340 Series Workgroup Bridge Features

Description	Specifications
Supported data rates	1, 2, 5.5, 11 Mbps
Supported standard	IEEE 802.11b
Range	Indoor: 100 ft @ 11 Mbps; 300 ft @ 1Mbps Outdoor: 400 ft @ 11 Mbps; 1500 ft @ 1Mbps Outdoor with antenna: 10 Miles
Encryption support	40-bit or 128-bit
Wireless medium	DSSS
MAC	CSMA/CA
Modulation	DBPSK @ 1 Mbps; DQPSK @ 2 Mbps; CCK @5.5 and 11 Mbps
Frequency band	2.4 to 2.497 GHz
Remote configuration support	Telnet; HTTP; FTP; and SNMP
Antenna options	One nonremovable 2.2 dBi dipole antenna or 2 RP-TNC connectors (no antenna ships with bridge)
Uplink	10BaseT Ethernet
Operating temperature range	32 to 122° F (0 to 50° C)

The Cisco Aironet 340 Series Base Station

The Cisco Aironet 340 Series Base Station is designed to provide wireless connectivity to the Internet for telecommuters and small offices. If you install a wireless client into a device, it can connect to a home or small office wired network through the Cisco Aironet 340 Series Base Station.

The base station can be connected to the Internet through a cable modem or Digital Subscriber Line (DSL) connection with an Ethernet RJ-45 port (see Figure 3.3). The unit can support a recommended limit of approximately 10 simultaneous devices (but could be more or less, it depends entirely on bandwidth requirements for your applications). This device is used to connect multiple office users so that they can share computer peripherals and access the Internet with the least amount of equipment. There is also a base station that has a 56K v.90 dialup modem integrated within it.

Figure 3.3 340 Series Base Station

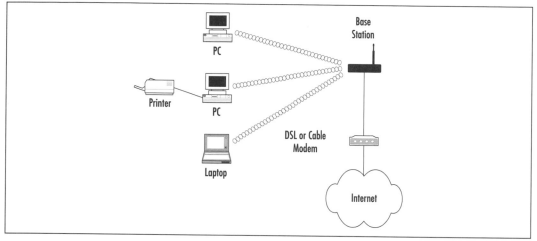

The unit is also capable of performing Network Access Translation (NAT) and Dynamic Host Configuration Protocol (DHCP) so that you can automatically configure an IP address range for multiple users. This will allow all users of the wireless network to share a single Internet connection and allow additional users to be added without the complication and expense of readdressing the network. However, the roaming feature that is available with APs is not available in the base station. Complete details are shown in Table 3.7.

Table 3.7 340 Series Base Station Features

Description	Specifications
Supported data rates	1, 2, 5.5, 11Mbps
Supported standard	IEEE 802.11b
Range	Indoor: 100 ft @ 11 Mbps; 300 ft @ 1Mbps Outdoor: 400 ft @ 11 Mbps; 1500 ft @ 1Mbps
Encryption support	128-bit
Wireless medium	DSSS
MAC	CSMA/CA

Continued

Table 3.7 Continued

Description	Specifications
Modulation	DBPSK @ 1 Mbps; DQPSK @ 2 Mbps; CCK @5.5 and 11 Mbps
Frequency band	2.4 to 2.497 GHz
Remote configuration support	Telnet; HTTP
Antenna options	One nonremovable 2.2 dBi antenna
Uplink	10BaseT Ethernet or RJ-11 line connector for versions with built-in modems
Operating temperature range	32 to 122° F (0 to 50° C)

Cisco Aironet Wireless NICs

You would normally find network interface cards, or adapters, installed inside your desktop computer or server. In the case of portable and notebook computers, the NIC is, more often than not a credit card-sized PCMCIA card that is connected through a PCMCIA slot. Cisco makes NICs that support wireless networking, using radio technology to transmit a signal through the air, instead of over a wired connection. These NICs offer the same functionality as a traditional wired NIC, preparing data for transmissions from your PC to the network. There are three major types of network cards:

- Industry-Standard Architecture (ISA)

- PCMCIA (also called PC Cards) for laptops and notebooks

- Peripheral Component Interconnect (PCI)

With the PCI and ISA adapters, you can connect desktops to the network without the need to run cables to each station. As your number of users grow, or change locations within the network, you will be able to maintain connectivity and therefore productivity. The users will not sacrifice performance, because the 11 Mbps should be sufficient to handle many of the data-intensive applications that the users need.

The PC adapters have dual internal antennas that will automatically select the strongest signal so that it can maintain the most efficient connection. The external antenna is designed for transmission from a fixed system, and it is designed to take up a small amount of space. The Cisco Aironet Client Adapter is a fixed solution that works in conjunction with 11 Mbps Cisco Aironet Series APs and bridges. These adapters are designed for DSSS technology and operate at 2.4 GHz. All Cisco wireless client adapters comply with the IEEE 802.11b standard, so that they can ensure that your devices with work correctly with other WLAN products using this standard.

In addition, many Cisco adaptors support a feature called world mode. When an adapter is configured for this mode, it will automatically inherit channel configuration properties directly from the Cisco Aironet AP to which they associate. This allows your user's client adapter to work around the world while still meeting local or regional standards without the need for any reconfiguration.

Key features of the ISA NIC include the following:

- IEEE 802.11b standard compliance
- Supports the highest range and throughput performance
- Transmits at up to 100mW
- Supports 128-bit WEP RC4 encryption for data security
- Offers 802.1x security support via EAP and LEAP
- Offers World mode (roaming) for international mobility
- Dual antenna connectors allow for the support of multipath compensation
- Support for popular operating systems
- Full-featured utilities for easy configuration and management

Key features of the PCMICA NIC include the following:

- IEEE 802.11b standard compliance
- Supports the highest range and throughput performance
- Transmits at up to 100mW
- Supports 128-bit WEP RC4 encryption for data security
- Offers 802.1x security support via EAP and LEAP
- Offers World mode (roaming) for international mobility
- Dual antenna connectors allow for the support of multipath compensation
- Support for popular operating systems
- Automatically inherits channel configuration settings directly from Cisco Aironet APs

- Full-featured utilities for easy configuration and management

Key features of the PCI Wireless NIC include the following:

- Based on the Type IIIa Mini-PCI form factor
- Utilizes True PCI bus interface
- IEEE 802.11b standard compliance
- Supports the highest range and throughput performance
- Transmits at up to 100mW
- Supports 128-bit WEP RC4 encryption for data security
- Offers 802.1x security support via EAP and LEAP
- Offers World mode (roaming) for international mobility
- Dual antenna connectors allow for the support of multipath compensation
- Support for popular operating systems
- Full-featured utilities for easy configuration and management

Cisco Aironet Antennas

Because every wireless deployment is going to have different considerations for data transmission, you want to be sure that you have the maximum network coverage and efficiency for your environment. Some of the considerations include the construction of the campus, structure sizes, and inside partitions of office spaces. To accommodate these needs, many of the Cisco wireless products have the capability to use an external antenna. Before going through the antenna choices that are available, we need to examine a few terms to better explain the terminology used:

- **Decibel (dB)** A decibel is the unit of measure for power ratios describing loss or gain, normally expressed in watts. A decibel is not an absolute value—it is the measurement of power gained or lost between two communicating devices. These units are normally given in terms of the logarithm to Base 10 of a ratio.

- **dBi value** This is the ratio of the gain of an antenna as compared to an *isotropic* antenna. The greater the dBi value, the higher the gain. If the gain is high, the angle of coverage will be more acute.

- **Isotropic antenna** An isotropic antenna is a theoretical construct that describes an antenna that will radiate its signal 360 degrees to cover the area in a perfect sphere. It is used as a basis by which to describe the *gain* of a real antenna.

- **Line of sight** Line of sight is an unobstructed straight line between two transmitting devices. You will most often see the need for a line-of-sight path for long-range directional radio transmissions. Due to the curvature of the earth, the line of sight for devices not mounted on towers is limited to 6 miles (9.65 km).

- **Signal attenuation (multipath fading)** This is the reduction of signal strength based on one of several factors: absorption, diffraction, reflection, and refraction.

  - Absorption occurs when an obstruction (such as trees) soaks up the signal so that it is unable to reach the receiver that it is trying to communicate with.

  - Diffraction is when a signal bends around an obstruction that has a reflective quality (such as glass).

  - Reflection is when the signal bounces off a surface (such as a body of water) causing distortion, and sometimes cancellation, of the signal.

  - Refraction is the bending of the signal based on atmospheric variations (such as fog).

A number of different antennas are described in this chapter. Each was designed to fit specific needs and as such has differing characteristics that better allow it to serve these needs. In addition to the antenna itself, a major factor in the performance of the overall wireless system is the cabling and connectors that attach the antenna to the AP or bridge. For more information on cabling and connector choices, see Chapter 9. Each antenna is discussed in the following sections, with a summary provided in Table 3.8.

The sections that follow reference horizontal and vertical coverage of an antenna. This refers to the transmission area of the antenna on the horizontal and vertical axis. See Figure 3.4 for a diagram of horizontal coverage and Figure 3.5 for a diagram depicting vertical coverage.

Figure 3.4 Horizontal Coverage Area

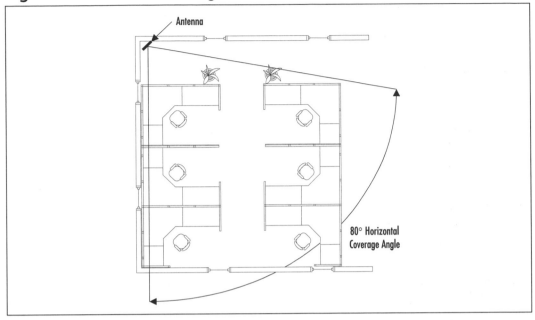

Figure 3.5 Vertical Coverage Area

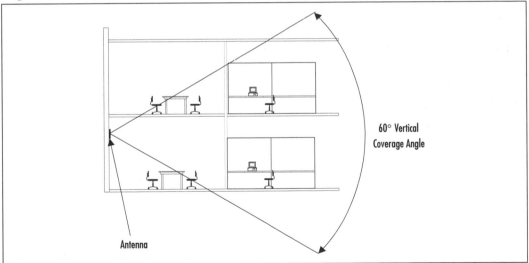

Ceiling Mount Omni-Directional Antenna

This indoor medium range antenna is designed to provide 360-degree coverage in an office space environment. Specifically, the antenna has a 360-degree horizontal coverage and a 38-degree vertical coverage. It is cylindrically shaped and is 9 inches long with a 1-inch diameter. It is light enough, 4.6 oz. (131 g), to be hung from a drop ceiling and comes with a mounting bracket specifically for this purpose. It has a three-foot pigtail of coaxial cable at one end that terminates in a RP-TNC connector. The approximate range provided by the antenna is 500 feet at 1 Mbps and 145 feet at 11 Mbps.

Mast Mount Omni-Directional Antenna

The mast mount is primarily a short-range outdoor antenna. Much like the ceiling mount omni-directional antenna, the mast mount omni-directional antenna has a 360-degree horizontal coverage and a 38-degree vertical coverage. Though it is specifically designed for outdoor short-range point-to-multipoint applications, it can also be used indoors if needed providing similar performance to the ceiling mount omni-directional antenna. The mast mount antenna is cylindrical in design, 11.5 inches long and 1.125 inches in diameter. It has a three-foot pigtail of coaxial cable at the end that terminates in a RP-TNC connector. The approximate range provided by the antenna for an outdoor bridge configuration is 5,000 feet at 2 Mbps and 1,580 feet at 11 Mbps.

High-Gain Mast Mount Omni-Directional Antenna

This antenna is much like the mast mount omni-directional antenna described in the preceding section. It is a medium range outdoor antenna that has a 360-degree horizontal coverage and is designed to be fastened to a mast and used for point-to-multipoint applications. However, the major performance difference comes in the vertical coverage. The high-gain antenna has a vertical coverage of only 7 degrees compared to a 38-degree vertical coverage for the normal mast mount antenna. Because it transmits the signal at a smaller angle, more of the energy of the signal is concentrated thus giving the antenna better range. Specifically, the range of this antenna is 4.6 miles at 2 Mbps and 1.4 miles at 11 Mbps. This mast mount antenna is also cylindrical in design, like the previous mast mount antenna, however at 40 inches in length it is about four times longer. The diameter of the high-gain mast mount antenna is also slightly larger at 1.3

inches. The cable used as a pigtail on the antennas is a 1-foot RG-8 cable with an RP-TNC connector on the end.

Pillar Mount Diversity Omni-Directional Antenna

This antenna is specifically designed to provide omni-directional service while being unobtrusive. For indoor use, this medium range antenna has two RP-TNC connectors on the end of a 3-foot Siamese coaxial cable. The two inputs allow for the transmission of diverse signals in the event that there is a failure of one of the transmissions. The exterior of the antenna is covered with a tan cloth and when mounted with the mounting brackets that ship with it, it will sit approximately 6 inches from the wall. It has a rectangular shape and is 1 foot tall by 5 inches wide and 1 inch thick. The antenna has a 360-degree horizontal coverage and a 30-degree vertical coverage. The approximate range provided by the antenna is 500 feet at 1 Mbps and 145 feet at 11 Mbps.

POS Diversity Dipole Omni-Directional Antenna

All of the other antennas discussed in this section are specifically designed to work with the APs or bridges, however, this one is designed to work with special client adapters. Specifically, this antenna works with LMC adapters that have dual MMCX connectors. These connectors attach to the antenna's 3-foot pigtails (also with MMCX style connectors) and allow for better signal transmission from the workstation. The antenna provides 360-degree horizontal coverage, a 75-degree vertical coverage, and a range of 350 feet at 1 Mbps and 100 feet at 11 Mbps. Though somewhat irregularly shaped, the diversity dipole antenna has dimensions of 7 inches long, 2.25 inches wide, and 6.5 inches tall.

Diversity Ceiling Mount Omni-Directional Patch Antenna

This small, 5.5 inches long by 3 inches wide by 1 inch thick rectangular antenna was specifically designed to be unobtrusive in a normal office environment. It comes with a mounting bracket that allows it mount to a drop ceiling, thus allowing for maximum coverage in a cubicle environment. In addition, it has roughly the same range—350 feet at 1 Mbps and 130 feet at 11 Mbps—as the standard dipole antenna that comes with some of the APs. It has two diverse transmitting elements accessed via two 3-foot pigtails each with their own RP-TNC connector.

Directional Wall Mount Patch Antenna

As opposed to all of the other antennas discussed up to this point, the wall mount patch antenna is not omni-directional. The horizontal and vertical coverage area for this antenna is 60 degrees. The main difference in installation between and omni-directional and directional antennas is that an omni-directional antenna is meant to be installed in the center of the area that you wish to cover while a directional antenna is installed at the edge. The wall mount patch antenna is a long-range (700/200 feet at 1/11 Mbps) indoor antenna for use with the AP products, or can also be installed as a medium-range (2 miles/3,390 feet at 1/11 Mbps) outdoor bridge antenna. Specifically, this particular antenna is small, 5 inches square by .5 inches thick, and lightly colored so that it will blend in easily to an office environment. Mounting this antenna requires nothing more than four screws to attach it to a wall. In addition, it has a 3-foot pigtail that terminates in an RP-TNC connector for connecting the antenna to you AP or bridge.

In addition to the patch antenna, another version of this antenna available from Cisco. This version has a larger vertical and horizontal angle (75-degree horizontal and 60-degree vertical) for transmission and as such has a lower overall gain. It is also appropriate for indoor or outdoor applications, and it has a range of 540 feet at 1 Mbps and 150 feet at 11 Mbps if used with an AP, or 1.1 miles at 1 Mbps and 1,900 feet at 11 Mbps if used with a bridge. The final difference between the two is that this antenna is slightly smaller being 1 inch narrower in width.

Diversity Directional Wall Mount Patch Antenna

As was the case with the previous patch antenna, this one also is a directional-based antenna. It is designed primarily for indoor use and has a medium range (550/170 feet at 1/11 Mbps). However it has the advantage of having two radiating elements that each have their own 3-foot pigtail attached to them. This allows you to take advantage of the dual RP-TNC connectors that are supplied on many of the APs. Due to its compact size (rectangular 4.75 inches by 6.75 inches by 1 inch thick), it can easily blend into the surroundings when attached to a wall in an office environment.

Yagi Antenna

The last two antennas we discuss in this chapter are specifically designed for outdoor use in a point-to-point configuration. The first of these is the yagi antenna. Cylindrical in shape and relatively compact in size (18 inches long with a 3-inch diameter), the signal from the yagi antenna comes out the end of the cylinder. The yagi antenna is able to get its gain though limiting the horizontal and vertical radiation pattern. With a 30-degree horizontal and 25-degree vertical pattern, the yagi antenna is able to obtain a maximum range of 6.5 miles at 2 Mbps and 2.0 miles at 11 Mbps. As was the case with most of the other antennas discussed here, the yagi antenna comes with a 3-foot pigtail with an RP-TNC connector on the end.

Dish Antenna

Finally, the last antenna we discuss is the dish antenna. Similar in size (2-foot diameter) and function to the small satellite dishes that are used for television transmission, the dish antenna provides that longest range of any of the Cisco antennas. Specifically, it has a maximum range of 25 miles at 2 Mbps and 11.5 miles at 11 Mbps. As is the case with any antenna, the dish antenna was able to get its longer range by reducing the radiation angle. In this case, both the vertical and horizontal radiation angles are the same at 12.4 degrees. This small area can make aligning two dish antennas over a large distance a difficult task if not done with care. As is implied by the previous statement, the dish antenna is specifically designed for point-to-point applications. Finally, you can connect the dish antenna to your bridge via the attached 2-foot pigtail with RP-TNC connector.

Table 3.8 Summary of Antenna Features

Antenna	Indoor/ Outdoor	Gain (dBi)	Radiation Pattern	Range (Adapter/AP/Bridge)
Ceiling Mount Omni	Indoor	5.2	360° H 38° V	AP: 500 ft @ 1 Mbps AP: 145 ft @ 11 Mbps
Mast Mount Omni	Indoor/ Outdoor	5.2	360° H 38° V	Bridge: 5000 ft @ 2 Mbps Bridge: 1580 ft @ 11 Mbps
High-Gain Mast Mount Omni	Outdoor	12.0	360° H 7° V	Bridge: 4.6 miles @ 2 Mbps Bridge: 1.4 miles @ 11 Mbps

Continued

Table 3.8 Continued

Antenna	Indoor/ Outdoor	Gain (dBi)	Radiation Pattern	Range (Adapter/AP/Bridge)
Pillar Mount Diversity Omni	Indoor	5.2	360° H 30° V	AP: 500 ft @ 1 Mbps AP: 145 ft @ 11 Mbps
POS Diversity Dipole (for use with LMC cards)	Indoor	2.2	360° H 75° V	Adapter: 350 ft @ 1 Mbps Adapter: 100 ft @ 11 Mbps
Ceiling Patch Omni	Indoor	2.0	360° H 80° V	AP: 350 ft @ 1 Mbps AP: 130 ft @ 11 Mbps
Directional Wall Patch	Indoor/ Outdoor	9.0	60° H 60° V	AP: 700 ft @ 1 Mbps AP: 200 ft @ 11 Mbps Bridge: 2 miles @ 1 Mbps Bridge: 3390 ft @ 11 Mbps
Directional Wall Patch (lower gain)	Indoor/ Outdoor	6.0	75° H 65° V	AP: 540 ft @ 1 Mbps AP: 150 ft @ 11 Mbps Bridge: 1.1 miles @ 1 Mbps Bridge: 1900 ft @ 11 Mbps
Diversity Directional Wall Patch	Indoor	6.5	80° H 55° V	AP: 550 ft @ 1 Mbps AP: 170 ft @ 11 Mbps
Yagi	Outdoor	13.5	30° H 25° V	Bridge: 6.5 miles @ 2 Mbps Bridge: 2.0 miles @ 11 Mbps
Dish	Outdoor	21	12.4° H 12.4° V	Bridge: 25 miles @ 2 Mbps Bridge: 11.5 miles @ 11 Mbps

Summary

The WLAN will and has redefined the way people are connecting to the network. It has allowed users to go outside of the normal boundaries of the office and allows you to be more dynamic with the deployment of your network. Go to many of your local Starbucks coffee houses and you will find that many of them now support wireless networking, as do many of the major airports and hotel chains. Soon you will not only be able to roam anywhere within you office or campus, but anywhere within your city, state, and country and still maintain your connection to the network and to the Internet.

Wireless technology and its growth is very similar to Ethernet's move to prevalence in the network world. The Institute of Electrical and Electronic Engineers (IEEE) originally defined Ethernet as the 802.3 standard to provide a platform that was widely available, interoperable, and allowed for high-speed data transfer, and as time passed it has evolved into the technology that we know today. Because the 802.3 standard is an open standard, users can choose from a wide range of suppliers and vendors and still be certain that the equipment will play well with other equipment. The same can happen with wireless—a tremendous opportunity for growth exists if vendors want to continue on this path.

The IEEE 802.11b standard defines that wireless devices will operates at 11 Mbps at 2.4 GHz, which is used worldwide for unlicensed radio based traffic. The frequency band also allows for more growth within the band, so there should be plenty of potential for growth with minor changes to the standard (not like IP numbering needing classes that are defined for nonroutable networks). You can also use an optional modulation procedure that will allow you to double the data throughput rate, as discussed in Chapter 2. To show that there is mobility (no pun intended), you need only to see that the original wireless vendors worked with the 900 MHz band frequency, but migrated to the 2.4 GHz band so that they could improve the throughput of data.

In fact, the next step is the utilization of the 5 GHz frequency band that is capable of support transmission speeds of 54 Mbps. A standard is now in place (IEEE 802.11a) for equipment specifications so as to support this higher data transmission rate. But it does not stop there; the next step is to utilize the 5.7 GHz band, which should handle 100 Mbps throughput for data transmission. As you know, in the field of technology, something faster is always going to be on the horizon as users becomes more used to current data rates, and in time users and applications will require more and more (speed, power, and so on). So you can see that there is the expectation for more growth.

Because Cisco wireless devices function like hubs and switches, converging data and transmitting it to other areas, the clients that are attached to the WLAN APs and share the LAN (like a hub) can also be tracked as they move through (roams) the LAN. This will allow you an added bit of security because you can deny traffic or clients from accessing the network, allowing for greater manageability.

The WLAN consists of two main parts: the AP and the bridge. In general, the AP is used to connect individual wireless users to the network. Whereas the bridges are used to connect two or more portions of the network together, whether inside a single building or between two buildings miles apart. Cisco's 340 and 350 Series product lines contain both APs and bridges to accommodate either of these needs. In addition these product also include some specialized devices that allow for the connection of smaller groups or offices. These products provide a myriad of services and features that allow you to get the most out of your wireless installation. They allow for remote management as well as a centralized security policy. Most also support WEP, LEAP, and EAP to allow you to better secure your network. If you are going to want coverage of a wide-area nature, you will need to deploy more than one AP. As you will see in Chapter 4, you will also need to do a site survey to see what you will need to support to get the coverage you want. This site survey will usually take into account what the building is composed of, what the layout of the space is, what is considered line of sight, whether the signal will need to go through ceilings and floors, where users are going to be, and so on. What you want to be sure of is that users will be connected, even if they move from office to office, or anywhere on the campus. This feature is called roaming. Roaming allows users to move through the coverage zones, maintaining their connection as the transceiver transfers from one AP to another.

The client adapter is then able to connect to the wireless AP so that it can negotiate a connection speed that can maintain the highest level of signal quality at whatever distance it can support. The Cisco series of devices includes a line of client adapters (PCMCIA, ISA, and PCI), for connecting your desktop or notebook to the WLAN. All client adapters are high-speed, long range, secure, and compliant with 802.11b standards, and they offer a full set of tools for management.

The final section of the chapter dealt with the antenna options available from Cisco. Numerous types of antennas are available, each designed to fit specific purposes. Omni-directional antennas are designed to be placed in the center of the desired coverage area and come in models to support both indoor and outdoor functionality. Patch antennas are directionally based and are designed to be placed at the edge of the coverage area. In general, patch antennas are small in size and unobtrusive in design so that they can go unnoticed in a normal office environment. Finally, yagi and dish antennas are used for long-range, outdoor connectivity. These antennas allow for two buildings to be connected even if they are miles apart.

Solutions Fast Track

Overview of Cisco Wireless Systems

☑ The use of wireless systems is continuing to grow. They are being used to connect users on a LAN in an office environment as well as being used to replace terrestrial carrier services such as T1 lines.

☑ Today, not only can PCs and laptops be connected to the WLAN, many other devices such as PDAs, printers, point-of-sale terminals, and scanners are also being connected.

☑ Cisco has a complete system for wireless connectivity. This includes APs, bridges, client adapters, antennas, and related accessories.

Cisco Aironet 3X0 Series APs and Bridges

☑ Cisco has two main product lines for wireless connectivity the 340 and 350 series. Both have all the components that are needed to create a successful WLAN installation.

☑ The 340 series product line includes, APs, bridges, workgroup bridges, and base stations. Each of these products has design features that make it better suited for one environment over another.

☑ The 350 series product line includes APs, bridges, and workgroup bridges. Like the 340 series, each of these products has differing features that make it better suited for a particular task, however, one advantage the 350 series of products has over the 340 series is that most of the 350 series products support inline power over the Ethernet cable that is used to uplink the device.

Cisco Aironet Wireless NICs

- ☑ PCMCIA NICs are designed specifically to allow laptop and small mobile devices access to the wireless network.

- ☑ ISA NICs are designed to allow desktop machines access to the wireless network. In general, ISA cards are used in older machines as most newer model desktops are using PCI slots.

- ☑ PCI NICs are also designed to allow desktop machines access to the wireless network. As computer manufacturers migrate more and more to the PCI slot in their machines, this card will be used more often.

Cisco Aironet Antennas

- ☑ Omni-directional antennas transmit a signal 360 degrees, and as such, should be placed in the center of the desired coverage area. You can use these antennas to connect users to your APs or connect two or more buildings together using wireless bridges.

- ☑ Because patch antennas are directional in nature, you should install them at the edge of your coverage area. As was the case with the omni-directional antennas, patch antennas come in configurations that allow for indoor and outdoor functionality.

- ☑ Yagi and dish antennas are specifically designed to connect two building together. They have the longest range of any Cisco antenna.

Frequently Asked Questions

The following Frequently Asked Questions, answered by the authors of this book, are designed to both measure your understanding of the concepts presented in this chapter and to assist you with real-life implementation of these concepts. To have your questions about this chapter answered by the author, browse to **www.syngress.com/solutions** and click on the **"Ask the Author"** form.

Q: The devices are only 300 meters apart, but trees are located in-between the two buildings where the APs reside. Can Cisco Aironet wireless APs connect through trees?

A: Yes, the signal will pass through trees, but you will need to calculate your db losses correctly and take the trees into account.

Issues that will affect your loss calculation include the following:

- The type of antennas on the units
- The radios' transmit power
- The radios' receive sensitivity
- The distance between your antennas (known as free-space loss)
- The "objects" in-between your antennas (trees, buildings, and so on)
- An amplifier, if you are using one
- The cabling to the antenna
- The connectors or splitters used from the radio to the cables or from the cables to the antenna

After you have used these points to calculate your signal loss and have a positive db left over, you will be able to use your wireless device.

Q: How far can a wireless client communicate to an AP?

A: Client adapters can support 11 Mbps at a range of 400 feet (120m) in open environments and 100 feet (30m) in typical closed/indoor environments. Client adapters can support 1 Mbps at a range of up to 1,500 feet (460m) in open environments and 300 feet (90m) in closed/indoor environments.

Q: How many users can a Cisco wireless AP support?

A: Depending on the available bandwidth and the applications you are using, a Cisco wireless AP can theoretically support up to 20,000 addresses for filtering wireless clients. For example, a Cisco Aironet 340 Series wireless network is equivalent to a shared 10 Mbps Ethernet LANs in the number of users that it can sustain. If you are using typical applications, the number of users per segment that would normally be used on a 10 Mbps wired segment could also be implemented on an 11 Mbps wireless segment. You could also add additional APs so that you can create additional network segments. However, if you are using a Cisco network that operates at lower data rates, less bandwidth is available. This means that fewer wireless clients can be supported. In an average environment, a Cisco AP can support 25–50 clients.

Chapter 4

Wireless Network Design

Introduction

The design of your wireless system encompasses three specific stages or phases: planning, designing, and site surveying. In addition to these phases, you must combine a certain amount of knowledge, creativity, and skill to overcome design obstacles. You must have knowledge and understanding of your organization's requirements for an implementation, infrastructure, wireless technology, and environment. You will also need creativity to overcome business, political, and physical barriers. Finally, you need skill to properly test and deploy your wireless design. This chapter provides you with the information necessary to execute the different phases of a wireless network design, raise awareness of the various obstacles you may encounter throughout all stages of your design effort, and provide examples of designs for common scenarios.

The first phase in your wireless design is the *planning* phase. This phase represents the initial possibilities of a wireless solution for a given business issue or scenario. Wireless system feasibility testing begins in this phase and will continue throughout all stages of your design.

Next, in the *rough design* phase you must apply the knowledge gained in the planning stage to create a "blind" design. A blind design is your initial, untested wireless system design. You will use the information gathered in the planning stage to apply to this rough design.

The third and final phase is the preparation and execution of a *wireless site survey*. This phase allows you to eliminate any remaining variables in your design, permits you to test the feasibility of the rough design you created in phase two, and make revisions as necessary to present a complete, efficient, and reliable wireless system design for implementation or approval.

Wireless Planning Considerations

The planning phase requires knowledge of the benefits and limitations of wireless networks, requirements for a wireless implementation in your business, and the ability to analyze the feasibility of a wireless local area network (WLAN).

In order to properly plan a wireless system, you must first identify the goal of the potential system. We use a fictitious company, Andromeda Manufacturing, to help you understand what is required throughout all phases of the wireless system design process.

Andromeda is a manufacturer of a tool destined for the retail market. Their campus is located in a rural area, and the facilities that are farthest away are approximately one mile from each other (see Figure 4.1). The president of the company has asked you to provide solutions for three business requirements the company has issued.

Figure 4.1 Andromeda Manufacturing Campus

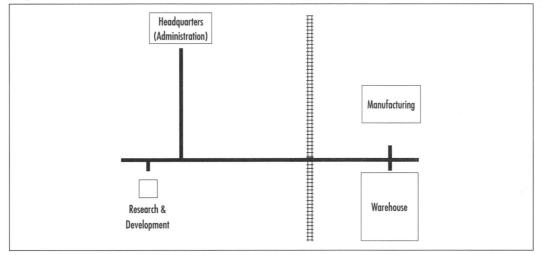

The first of the three requirements is to provide data connectivity from the administration facility to the manufacturing and warehouse facilities. This will allow management at headquarters to gather production and shipping information and to provide e-mail for the supervisors in the remote facilities.

The second of the three requirements is to provide a better solution to the slow inventory process at the warehouse. The president has heard of a "wireless way" to perform inventories more efficiently and would like you to investigate this further.

Due to the poor quality of the telephone lines in the company's locality, frequent outages of the only data circuit the company owns is negatively affecting production and the "bottom line." This circuit is from the headquarters facility to Research and Development (R&D). As the final requirement issued, the president would like an alternate solution to the existing unreliable circuit.

The three mandates from the president of Andromeda Manufacturing clearly outline the goals and requirements of the business. You will need to investigate possible solutions to achieve these goals. In the example, further investigation is necessary before a rough design can be achieved. Such information as the type and bandwidth of applications used in the facilities and the number of users in each facility will all play a part in developing the wireless system designs for this company.

In the following sections, you'll get to know the benefits and limitations of wireless LANs to aid in asking the proper questions to determine the feasibility of a wireless system.

Wireless Benefits and Limitations

Wireless LANs offer much in the way of productivity and convenience over traditional wired networks. Among these are mobility, implementation simplicity and flexibility, speed of installation and good scalability. Mobility is probably the most popular reason organizations choose wireless systems. There is much to be said for the other benefits of wireless systems. Installing a WLAN system can be fast and easy and can eliminate the need to pull cable through walls and ceilings. Wireless technology allows the network to go where wire cannot go. WLAN systems can be configured in a variety of topologies to meet the needs of specific applications and installations. Configurations are easily changed and range from peer-to-peer networks suitable for a small number of users to full infrastructure networks of thousands of users that can roam over a broad area. These advantages and others have promoted wireless networking to a point that continues to move on an upward curve.

As with any technology, wireless has its limitations. Depending on your business, aesthetic, or technological requirements, wireless may or may not best suit your needs. To determine if wireless will be an effective and successful solution in your environment, you need to answer certain questions.

What Type of Data Will Be Traversing the Wireless Network?

The first thing you should understand about wireless networks is the limitations to speed and throughput inherent to the technology. Wireless networks are not wired networks and as such technology has not sufficiently advanced to meet the speeds and throughput we expect from wired networks. Because of this, you must give consideration to the type of data being transmitted across the WLAN. Current wireless technology supports 11 Mbps speed and approximately 5.5MB throughput. For example, a wireless network may not be a good solution if the implementation is meant to replace a FastEthernet network (100 Mbps network) where 50 or more users are consistently sending and receiving large graphics files (20–30MB+). Because of the large size of the files and the amount of traffic, you may wish to consider the wireless LAN implementation as a redundancy solution and not a replacement solution in this scenario. As a redundancy solution, you still have to deal with less performance, but the expectation set for a backup connection would be that slow, inexpensive, and functional is better than hours or days of downtime because a single link failed.

Application traffic that is typically suited for WLANs includes any low- or medium-bandwidth applications, such as e-mail, Web-based applications, network printing, and file sharing. Of course, there are always exceptions to this guideline. If the number of users in the previous scenario had been much fewer, say five users, the impact of consistently sending those large graphics files would have been acceptable on the wireless LAN. Conversely, if the number of users is extremely high and the frequency in which the application sends network traffic is extremely high, even a low-bandwidth application, such as Web browsing, can significantly impact wireless LAN performance. You need to evaluate each wireless cell implementation individually.

NOTE

When gauging application traffic for use on a WLAN, you need to take a number of considerations into account:

- How many users will be associated to a single cell at any given time?
- How frequently will the application produce network traffic?
- Will the application traffic that those same users will be utilizing exceed the typical throughput per cell?
- What types of applications will those users be expected to use on the wireless LAN?

How Much Data Will Be Traversing the Wireless Network?

The amount of data traveling across your wired network can be prohibitive to a WLAN implementation. Existing traffic on a network may be more than the wireless network can handle. If all the traffic is necessary to the requirements of the users on the wireless segment, you may to consider other alternatives for connectivity, such as traditional wired technology. An evaluation of your current traffic as compared to the application and connectivity requirements of the potential wireless users will be necessary. You can utilize a number of tools to gather the traffic information necessary for evaluation. Protocol and network analyzers, commonly called *sniffers*, will give you network traffic information by protocol, Media Access Control (MAC) address, and network address. A good sniffer will allow you to rank your traffic in various ways and can allow you to capture network information for detailed analysis. Other tools, such as Remote Monitor (RMON) probes and Simple Network Management Protocol (SNMP) traps, can assist you in gathering traffic information as well.

What Is the Return On Investment for Your Wireless Implementation?

Calculating return on investment (ROI) can be extremely easy or extremely difficult depending on your business and the intended use of the proposed wireless system. ROI is the financial point where the wireless system pays for itself and over time saves money for your business over traditional methods of installation and deployment. This point and the savings associated with it are highly variable and contingent upon what is used to calculate it. We discuss ROI in detail in the "Cost and Return on Investment" section later in this chapter. Suffice to say, you will need to know your current business model very well in order to answer this question and in most cases, you will need to calculate this to get approval for your implementation. Should the ROI be less than expected or accepted, a wireless system in your business may be financially impractical.

How Does Mobility Factor into Determining if Wireless Is Right for Your Business?

Mobility is a great leveraging tool to gaining approval for a wireless system in your business. Depending on how great the need for users to be mobile is in your business, your design requirements must reflect it. Some organizations may want a wireless system simply to allow their users the freedom to move about while working, as a benefit to working there or to reduce lost production due to employee morale. This is not a high factoring mobility requirement. The organization may not be committed to this way of improving morale, because a wireless implementation could have nominal or unproven benefits. However, in the case of a warehouse facility, paying either another company or its own employees after-hours rates to perform inventories, mobility would be an enormous factor in the requirements of the business. If mobility is one of the greater requirements for your business, a wireless system may be just what the doctor ordered. We cover mobility in more detail in the following section.

Does Your Business or Corporation Have Any Restrictions That Would Prohibit You from Implementing a Wireless LAN Solution?

Another key question you need to answer to determine if wireless is the way to go in your environment is how important are such things as aesthetics? Pleasing to the eye may not be a primary concern to a manufacturing facility, but a financial institution that serves the public may not be happy with antennas hanging from the ceiling of their lobby. If restrictions are placed on the aesthetics to the point that it affects the performance and functionality of the technology, wireless will not be suitable for that environment. An example of this is a clothing manufacturer I once worked with that was constructing a new campus of buildings. The client wanted wireless coverage in the entire interior of a building constructed with an open ceiling (no drop ceiling, just rafters and heating/cooling ductwork). They restricted the placement of the antennas for the facility to a 6-inch space between two metal heating ducts that ran the length of the building. Needless to say, wireless coverage was less than optimal due to the interference caused by the metal. Eventually they agreed to move the antennas to more suitable locations after convincing them antennas could be painted (without using lead-based paint) to match the ceiling.

These are but a few of the most common questions you may need to answer in determining the feasibility, up front, for a wireless system in your business or organization. Due to the unique nature of every business and organization there may, and likely will, be more questions to answer.

Asking these questions and several others pertaining to the business processes of our fictional company, Andromeda Manufacturing, revealed that the R&D users produce very large CAD drawings that are electronically transferred daily to the headquarters facility for approval and revisions. The files range in size from approximately 40MB to over 100MB each, and up to 20 to 30 transfers take place to and from the facility daily. It is not expected that the CAD files will be sent to the manufacturing or warehouse facilities when they are added to the network. In addition, the Headquarters facility has four Apple Macintosh computers networked into the LAN. They are used to design, create, and share marketing literature. This literature will not be shared with manufacturing or the warehouse. Although 60 people are employed in the manufacturing facility, only the supervisors and managers will have access to the network. The total number of users and network printers to be added to the network in manufacturing will be approximately 10.

The manufacturing facility currently runs two shifts daily starting at 6 A.M. and ending at 11 P.M. All other facilities run first shift only (8 A.M. to 5 P.M.). Total number of users and network printers for the warehouse will be approximately 5 to 10. None of the facilities have any aesthetic restrictions. The information obtained is noted and retained for use during the design process.

Mobility

Mobility is typically the primary purpose and one of the key benefits of implementing a wireless LAN. Wireless LAN systems can provide users with access to real-time information anywhere in their organization. This mobility supports productivity and service opportunities not possible with wired networks. Wireless gives users the freedom to move about while performing their tasks without being forced to go to, or remain at, a wired station. An example of this would be small item inventory. The usual process requires users to count items in a small bin and write the quantity down. The written quantity is then brought to some device for input into the data system. This adds a lot of time and therefore, loss of productivity, into the process. If the bins to be inventoried were within a wireless coverage area, users could input the quantities directly into the system from the site of the bin, therefore increasing productivity substantially.

There are limitations to the mobility of a wireless system. If a user strays to the outside range of the wireless coverage area, he may have degraded performance and reliability or worse, he may lose data. A good design will consider the mobility of the users and try to compensate for user error. Training and setting user expectations are the best ways to handle issues such as straying. In addition, a design for mobility should include thorough testing to ensure that data rates are acceptable at typical production speeds for highly mobile users. What are highly mobile users? There are actually two types of users when discussing mobility: mobile users and highly mobile users.

A *mobile user* is defined as a user that moves within a wireless coverage area but stop moving to input or retrieve data. They require portability for their data input devices, such as a laptop on a cart or handheld bar code reader. A police officer, whose job is to check parking meters for violations, is a good example of this type of user. If you were to apply their position to a wireless coverage area, they could walk from meter to meter using data collection devices and portable printers. Stopping at a meter that requires processing a violation, the police officer can input the violator's automobile information and print the ticket, sending the information directly into the police department's data processing system. Once completed with this task, the police officer moves on to the next meter.

A highly mobile user is a user that moves within a wireless coverage area and continue to move while data input or retrieval takes place. A good example of this: A data collection device is mounted to a forklift that moves throughout a warehouse. A driver may scan a barcode and then enter the quantity as she is driving away.

Determining if your users will mobile or highly mobile is important to your design. Take the time to work with your customer to determine exactly what mobility needs exist, and just as important, what the customer's expectations are for the mobility of their users.

Questions regarding the mobility of the users in the Andromeda Manufacturing facilities revealed a dire need for mobility in the warehouse. All other facilities did not have this requirement.

Designing & Planning…

Operating Systems and Data Throughput

Different operating systems also affect the data throughput you can expect to achieve in your wireless system. Whereas Microsoft operating systems typically achieve 5.5 to 6 Mbps of throughput on an 11 Mbps wireless network, Linux operating systems—using the same Cisco wireless hardware, the same client hardware, and positioned the same distance from the access point (AP), on the same wireless network—are able to yield a typical throughput of 7 Mbps. This is due to the way each of the operating systems handle network functionality, especially in terms of network client drivers.

Throughput versus Data Rate and Load

Throughput and data rates do not equal each other in either a wireless or wired network. Typical data throughput on an Ethernet network is about 60 percent of the nominal capacity. Therefore, a 10 Mbps Ethernet network under typical load would yield a throughput of 6 Mbps. Factors that affect nominal throughput on a network include overhead, number of users, operating systems and so forth. A wireless link has slightly greater overhead associated with it than a wired link and therefore typically yields approximately 5.5 Mbps of throughput on an 11 Mbps network (based on the use of Cisco wireless gear).

The load on an AP (the total number of potential clients) should be considered in any design. For design purposes, an 11 Mbps wireless network roughly equates to a 10 Mbps Ethernet network in terms of the number of users the wireless LAN can handle. One potential problem with wireless LANs is that the number of clients is very dynamic because the freedom of a wireless system allows any number of people to converge within an area. The actual number of clients is limited by a table within the AP, Cisco APs have a table that will theoretically allow 2,048 clients. Although this is the maximum, it is not practical. Keep in mind that wireless LANs are a shared infrastructure, and the more clients on the AP, the less overall available bandwidth there is for each individual user. Therefore the distribution of the clients among more APs in congested areas may be required. The number of clients that can be handled by a single AP is a function of the applications supported, the data rate of the AP, and the desired performance of the application by the customer. I have found that the number of users per AP should not exceed 20 to 30 to maintain acceptable performance levels in the average environment. This number will of course be higher or lower depending on the applications, operating systems, and simultaneous usage of the users on the network.

Cisco APs give you the ability to load balance users across APs to further enhance performance in your wireless network. By placing two APs in the same coverage area you have the ability to "balance" the load on any single AP in a coverage area. This increases performance in your wireless system.

Expectations are everything in a wireless implementation. If the correct expectation is set and accepted, your wireless implementation will be a great success, and you will reap the benefits of that success. One of the most important expectations to set will be that of throughput in your wireless system. If your environment has, for example, FastEthernet already in place, users are accustomed to those speeds on their network and will notice the difference in performance from the wired 100 Mbps network to the wireless 11 Mbps network. If you set the expectation that throughput will not be at the accustomed speed, but will be more like a 10 Mbps network, usually there is no problem when the wireless network "goes live" in regards to performance. I like to compare speeds to T-1 wired circuits, especially where Internet access over wireless will take place. When my customer hears that they will have the same speed as their wired network Internet access (typically my customers have a full T-1 or fractional T-1 to the Internet) and that their wireless connection equates to about six T-1s. The expectation is set and the client walks away feeling confident in their decision to go wireless.

Cost and Return on Investment

Although the initial investment required for WLAN hardware can be higher than the cost of wired LAN hardware, overall installation expenses and life-cycle costs can be significantly lower. Long-term cost benefits are greatest in dynamic environments requiring frequent moves and changes or in interconnections of LANs where recurring circuit costs are eliminated.

We use the Andromeda Manufacturing scenario as an example of the process involved to determine ROI for a wireless implementation over a wired solution.

In order to accurately determine whether a wireless solution for any one of the Andromeda Manufacturing mandates will offer any significant cost savings over a wired solution, we must gather current costs used by the company to achieve these goals and just as important, the cost to *not* achieve them.

Currently Andromeda spends $400 a month on the unreliable circuit that is being used between their headquarters and the research and development facility. Research indicates the company is losing approximately $15,000 a month because of connectivity issues. This amount is based on lost man hours resending information over the circuit as well as lost business due to the inability to get new schematics approved, sent to manufacturing, and shipped to Andromeda Manufacturing's clients in a timely manner.

Company losses due to exceptionally long inventory processes at the warehouse facility have been estimated between $3,000 and $5,000 a month. This is based on information gathered from several competitors' average inventory process times, overtime paid, and production losses incurred for the average duration of the inventory.

Savings in the estimated amount of $2,000 a month will be gained based on a recent study of the methods of intercompany communications. These savings are a result of minimizing supplies costs and ensuring accurate communications to manufacturing and warehouse supervisors. This is to be accomplished by some solution to reduce production and shipping flaws from faulty "word-of-mouth" directives and eliminate hard copy memos and reports. This gave rise to the requirement for an e-mail solution from Andromeda's president.

An additional $5,000 a month is estimated to be saved by the ability to quickly identify and make production changes based on "real-time" information being provided to management, instead of the weekly hard copy reports currently used. This is related to the connectivity request from Andromeda's president.

At this point, we must consider the possible solutions for each of the issues. Keeping in mind the information previously gathered, we can consider rough wireless designs and compare them to other, more conventional, solutions with a focus on monetary considerations. Because we do not have the precise requirements to implement any solution we are merely speculating to eliminate grossly inefficient solutions.

Adding additional recurring costs in the form of additional circuits to each facility eliminates this as a possible connectivity solution, especially in light of the circuit stability issues experienced by Andromeda Manufacturing. This leaves us with basically two other connectivity alternatives: fiber or wireless. Because fiber does not satisfy the mobility requirements of the warehouse, it is eliminated as a possible solution to the inventory problem. However, at this point it is still a viable solution for connectivity of all facilities, including the warehouse.

We must now compare the costs associated with using wireless versus fiber in each remaining solution. Costs associated with a fiber installation depend greatly on the type of fiber required. Single mode fiber and the hardware needed for it, is usually much more expensive than multimode fiber. The main difference in the two fiber types is the distances each can be used. Single mode fiber is used for distances up to 14 kilometers (a little over 8.5 miles) and requires laser hardware to provide the light through the fiber, where multimode fiber can only be used to distances not exceeding 2 kilometers (1.2 miles) and typically uses light-emitting diodes (LEDs) to provide the light necessary for functionality. In addition to the type of fiber, installation costs can be steep for fiber as well. Fiber is usually installed underground, requiring trenching services. Termination of fiber lines usually is not a cost issue because it is not much more expensive than termination of traditional copper connections.

After considering the distances of the warehouse and manufacturing from the headquarters facility, multimode fiber will be sufficient if it is chosen as the connectivity solution. The numbers of expected users at each of the facilities, the applications to be used, and network traffic expected does not justify the added cost of a fiber solution over wireless for the warehouse and manufacturing facilities. In addition, the railroad owns a section of track running between the warehouse, manufacturing facility, and the headquarters facility and will not grant permission to run fiber either over or under the tracks. This eliminates fiber as a connectivity solution for these two facilities.

The research and development facility is another story. Fiber is the best solution for their requirements even though the number of users is not significant. The main reason for this is the type, size, and transfer frequency of the files traversing the network. Because fiber offers much higher bandwidth than wireless, it proves to be the solution of choice in this scenario and can be easily cost justified. Fiber eliminates the recurring costs associated with the circuit, improves reliability, and provides more than adequate bandwidth for future growth.

We now know that to satisfy the requirements of our solutions in the most efficient and cost effective manner, we will likely implement a fiber solution to the research and development facility, a point-to-multipoint wireless solution for the warehouse and manufacturing facilities and an internal wireless solution for the warehouse.

We now move on to creating the rough design for each solution. To do this, however, we will need to understand the design considerations involved. The next section in this chapter covers those design considerations.

Wireless Design Considerations

In order to create a design for a wireless system, you must consider common wireless LAN transmission and reception impairments, such as attenuation, radio frequency (RF) interference, and application and structural considerations. As you will see, many of the design considerations in this section relate to point-to-point and point-to-multipoint wireless implementations, which is mainly because wireless coverage in these implementations is not spread out over an area, but rather it is focused to a specific point. This section explains various common types of impairments and considerations that you may face in your wireless design and testing efforts.

Attenuation

Attenuation is the decrease in strength of a radio wave; the strength decreases as the distance from the antenna increases. It can be caused by the natural conductivity or resistance of all sorts of physical matter, but the greatest resistor to radio waves is the Earth. Radiated energy from the Earth, and interference from trees and buildings will cause attenuation of the signal's ground waves, as radiated energy and interference from water and dust particles in the atmosphere will affect the signal's sky waves. You must plan your design and equipment use based on these factors affecting ground and sky wave propagation, such as transmitter height, distance between transmitters, and solar radiation factors. Low-frequency radio wave propagation utilizes propagation of both ground and sky wave transmissions and can be used at varying distances; high-frequency wave propagation (3,000 kHz to 30 Mhz) relay more upon sky waves for transmission and may be used at long distances (like 12,000 miles); and very high frequency wave propagation (above 30 MHz) is reliant upon line-of-sight direct wave transmission.

Attenuation Due to Antenna Cabling

Loss due to antenna cable length must always be considered when designing your wireless system. Cisco cabling produces 6.7 dBi of loss per 100 feet of cabling. The reason for this is that the radio wave actually starts at the radio device. The radiated energy traveling through the cabling from the radio device to the antenna induces a voltage in the cabling, decreasing the strength of the wave as the distance from the radio device to the antenna becomes greater.

Attenuation Due to Exterior Considerations

If you plan on coverage outdoors that is point-to-point or point-to-multipoint, you will need to pay particular attention to considerations that are distance-related. For example, Earth bulge will come into play only if you are implementing a point-to-point or point-to-multipoint WLAN, whereas weather is a consideration for any outdoor implementation.

As we have seen, all matter produces attenuation (loss) to some degree. Because weather can produce rain, snow, or fog, all of which are matter, you also need to consider weather in your wireless LAN design.

Researching any unusual weather conditions that are common to the site location is important. These conditions can include excessive amounts of rain or fog, wind velocity, or extreme temperature ranges. If extreme conditions exist that may affect the integrity of the radio link, you should take these conditions into consideration early in the planning process.

Rain, Snow, and Fog

Except in extreme conditions, attenuation (weakening of the signal) due to rain does not require serious consideration for frequencies up to the range of 6 or 8 GHz. When microwave frequencies are at 11 or 12 GHz or above, attenuation due to rain becomes much more of a concern, especially in areas where rainfall is of high density and long duration.

The attenuation rate for snow is generally higher, due in large part to the size of the particles of snow, or for that matter rain and fog as well, in comparison to the wavelength of the signal. For example, a 2.4 GHz signal will have a wavelength of approximately 125 millimeters, or 4.9 inches. A 23 GHz signal will have a wavelength of approximately 0.5 inches. A raindrop approaches 0.25 of an inch. At 2.4 GHz, rain or snow, even heavy rain or snow, should not have much of an impact on your wireless system, however in a 23 GHz system, the wavelength is reduced to half by this rain. At this size, the rain or snow becomes a reflective surface and disperses the 23 GHz signal.

In most cases, the effects of fog are considered to be much the same as rain. However, fog can adversely affect the radio link when it is accompanied by atmospheric conditions such as temperature inversion, or very still air accompanied by stratification (layers of significantly differing air temperatures). Temperature inversion can negate clearances, and still air along with stratification can cause severe refractive or reflective conditions, with unpredictable results. Temperature inversions and stratification can also cause ducting, which may increase the potential for interference between systems that do not normally interfere with each other. Where these conditions exist, use shorter paths and adequate clearances.

Atmospheric Absorption

A relatively small effect on the wireless link is from gases and moisture in the atmosphere. It is usually significant only on longer paths and particular frequencies. Attenuation (loss) in the 2–14 GHz frequency range is approximately 0.01 dB/mile. You may have to include atmospheric absorption in your design consideration if you are planning on implementing a wireless system above 10 GHz where atmospheric absorption is prevalent. There are some wireless systems on the market today, licensed in the 23 GHz band that are significantly impacted by this type of loss. Antenna height has some impact on loss related to atmospheric absorption because the density of the air decreases as altitude increases. Thus, a 23 GHz system with an antenna significantly elevated over a similar implementation at a lower elevation will suffer less from attenuation due to atmospheric absorption. Table 4.1 depicts attenuation due to atmospheric absorption versus path distance. Attenuation is listed as negative decibels, or −dB.

Table 4.1 Attenuation (Absorption) over Distance

Path Distance (In Miles)	2–6 GHz	8 GHz	10 GHz	12 GHz	14 GHz
20	−0.20 dB	−0.26 dB	−0.32 dB	−0.38 dB	−0.48 dB
40	−0.40 dB	−0.52 dB	−0.64 dB	−0.76 dB	−0.96 dB
60	−0.60 dB	−0.78 dB	−0.96 dB	−1.14 dB	−1.44 dB
80	−0.80 dB	−1.04 dB	−1.28 dB	−1.52 dB	−1.92 dB
100	−1.00 dB	−1.30 dB	−1.60 dB	−1.90 dB	−2.40 dB

Multipath Distortion

Multipath distortion is caused, as the name implies, by the transmitted signal traveling to the receiver via more than one path: A common cause of this is reflection of the signal from bodies of water, hills, or tall buildings. Figure 4.2 shows an example of multipath distortion caused by reflection. The antennas are the same height. In the worst case, the reflected signal arrives at the receiving antenna at the same time as the intended signal, but out of phase with the intended signal, both signals will cancel each other out, resulting in complete loss of data. Best case, the reflected signal arrives a moment later than the intended signal causing distortion and therefore reduced performance. Examples of reflective surfaces include water, asphalt, fields, metal roofs, or any smooth, relatively flat surface. Dispersing extraneous radio waves is better than reflecting them. Examples of dispersal surfaces include rough rocky surfaces, shrubbery, trees, and so on. In a big city, more people receive an echoed distortion of the wireless signal than receive the actual signal, because the original signal bounces off buildings and the like.

Figure 4.2 Multipath Distortion Diagram

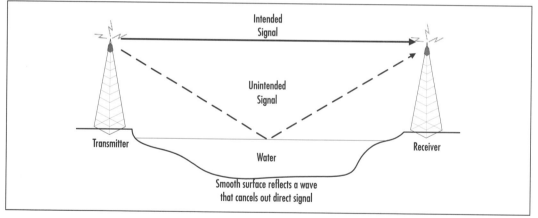

The best way to reduce multipath distortion is to use a directional rooftop antenna. For example, a directional antenna that will only pick up signals coming from the direction of the transmitter and will reject reflections that arrive at its sides or its back. A Yagi antenna is one example of a directional antenna that will help you reduce or eliminate multipath distortion (see Figure 4.3).

It is also sometimes possible to mount the antenna so that the mounting structure screens it from the reflections but not from the wanted signal. By changing the antenna height you can effectively reduce or eliminate the multipath signals by dispersing the signals away from the receiving antenna (see Figure 4.4).

Figure 4.3 Directional Antenna to Reduce or Eliminate Multipath Distortion (Birds-Eye View)

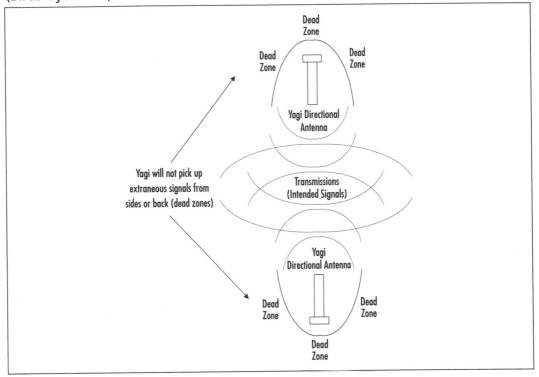

Figure 4.4 Dispersing Multipath Reflections

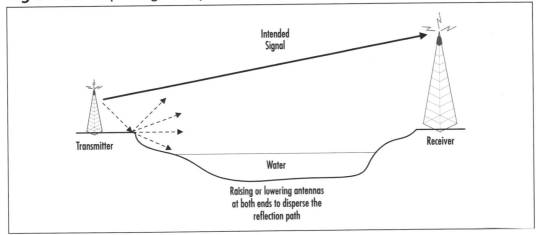

Refraction

When a radio wave travels between two substances of different densities, the wave will bend or refract because electromagnetic signals move slower through substances of greater density. This phenomena impacts a radio wave as it travels through the atmosphere. The density of the Earth's atmosphere decreases as altitude increases. Therefore, the bottom of the radio wave travels through a denser atmosphere than the top of the wave. This means the bottom of the wave will move slower than the top of the wave, causing the signal to bend towards the Earth's surface and follow the curvature of the Earth, but at an arc radius approximately 1.33 times greater than the Earth's arc radius (see Figure 4.5).

Figure 4.5 Refraction

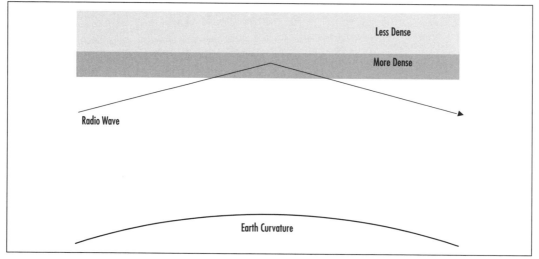

At night, the air cools, and much of the moisture in the air moves closer to the Earth's surface. The cool, wet air near the Earth is denser than the air higher in the atmosphere, so radio signals can bend farther than they do in the daylight hours. This is known as *super refraction*.

Other refraction phenomena, such as ducting or bending can also occur, which you should be aware of for design purposes. *Ducting* happens when radio waves are trapped in a high-density duct between two areas of lower density.

Bending is similar to super refraction, but it is not caused by atmospheric conditions related to day or night. Instead, differences in air density in a horizontal plane, like cooler air over a lake or field and warmer air over a shore or highway cause the radio waves to bend in the direction of the cooler, denser air over the lake or field.

Refraction is one reason why radio line-of-sight is not necessarily the same as optical line-of-sight. Refraction is minimal for paths under 10 miles, with the exception of hot, humid areas like the Southeastern United States.

Accounting for the Fresnel Zone and Earth Bulge

A main consideration of any point-to-point design is the Fresnel zone. An electromagnetic signal traveling between two antennas does not travel in a straight line. The wave spreads out as it propagates. The individual waves that make up the signal do not travel at a constant velocity. A pair of antennas define a three-dimensional elliptical path for the radio waves that propagate between them. This elliptical path is divided into several zones based on the phase and speed of the propagating waves. These zones are referred to as Fresnel zones, pronounced "Fre Nel" (the "s" is silent). Each Fresnel zone differs in phase by up to half a wavelength, or 180 degrees. We think of this Fresnel zone commonly as line-of-sight (see Figure 4.6). Radio line-of-sight is not the same as visual line-of-sight. In visual line of sight, a direct line exists between two points, it is easy to think this way between two antennas in a point-to-point design. However, radio line of sight is not a straight line between the antennas, it is more of an ellipse. In a good point-to-point design, this ellipse should be calculated to determine its size and clear of obstacles to provide a good signal.

Figure 4.6 Fresnel Zone (Radio Line of Sight)

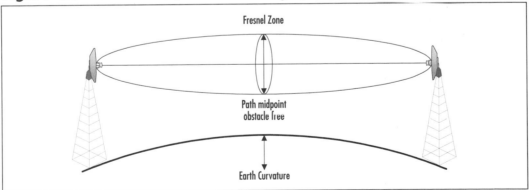

Because of the elliptical shape of the Fresnel zone, the antennas used in a point-to-point design must be high enough to provide clearance of the Fresnel zone's radius at the midpoint. As the distance increases, you must concern yourself with other factors, such as the curvature of the Earth, where line of sight becomes difficult at 6 miles (for a 6-foot tall person) and disappears altogether at 16 miles (for two structures at 10 feet) because your clearance from the Earth at the horizon point will have minimum clearance (see Figure 4.7). Paths over 20 miles are extremely difficult to align and install, so take caution when recommending these types of configurations.

Figure 4.7 Minimum Clearance for Long Distances

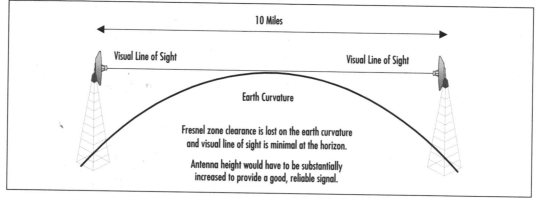

Radio Frequency Interference

Radio frequency interference is extraneous energy that impedes the reception of signals. It can be caused by a radio emission from another transmitter at approximately the same frequency.

When we talk about the frequency that an AP radio operates on, we really mean its "center frequency," because both the transmitter and receiver operate within a band of frequencies that is several megahertz (MHz) wide. AP transmitters will transmit strongest at frequencies very close to its center frequency, with a decrease in signal strength as you move away from the center frequency. Similarly the wireless AP receiver will be most sensitive to frequencies very close to its center frequency, with a decrease in sensitivity as you move away from the center frequency. Note that the center frequency of the receiver can be slightly different than the center frequency of the transmitter and things will still seem to work okay, but because power decreases as you move out from the center frequency, range will be reduced.

The width of this band of frequencies around the center frequency is a major factor in determining the effects of radio interference. If your receiver encounters a second signal that is too close to its center frequency, and the two bandwidths end up overlapping too much, interference will result. The closer the interfering signal is to the receiver's center frequency, the less power is needed to cause inter-ference. In the extreme case, if somebody turns on their microwave oven and its emanations are on exactly the same frequency as yours, you may drop down in speed even if the signal is very weak. Conversely, if something is operating on a frequency that is quite far away from the center frequency of your AP's receiver, it can still interfere if its signal is strong enough.

Interference from Radio Transmitters

Interference usually occurs when radio transmitters and electronic equipment are operated within close range of each other. Interference is caused by the following:

- Incorrectly installed radio transmitting equipment

- An intense radio signal from a nearby transmitter

- Unwanted signals generated by the transmitting equipment and not enough shielding or filtering in the electronic equipment to prevent it from picking up those unwanted signals

Any signal other than the desired signal is called an unwanted signal, or *spurious radiation*. Spurious radiation includes harmonic radiation, usually in the form of standing or traveling waves. Use a spectrum analyzer, a calibrated field intensity meter, or a frequency-selective voltmeter to measure unwanted radiation. A spectrum analyzer is a device that measures the frequency components of a radio signal. It provides a visual image of how the amplitude of a radio signal varies in relation to its frequency. If adjusting the channel does not solve the problem completely, you should permanently install a low-pass band filter in the transmitter antenna feed line after all the other accessories.

Standing waves are a form of spurious radiation causing undesired effects that occur when two or more waves of the same frequency are present at the same time and do not travel away from their source. This may happen, for example, when the transmitter, transmission line (antenna cabling), or antenna are not properly matched to each other. Incorrectly terminated or damaged antenna cabling is a typical source of standing waves. When this happens, the transmitted signal to the antenna is reduced because the damaged cable is transmitting unwanted signals.

Harmonics

Harmonics occur when signals are produced at two or three times the station's operating frequency in addition to the desired signals (see Figure 4.8). If the harmonics fall on another locally used frequency, such as an AP channel, they are likely to cause interference. Figure 4.8 shows how a signal from some radio device may interfere with an AP set to channel 1.

Figure 4.8 Harmonics

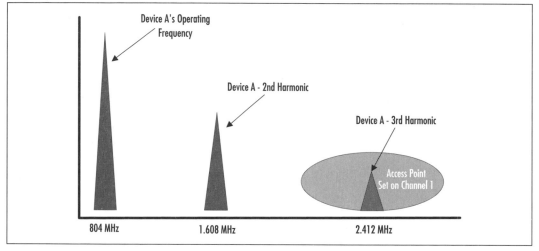

These undesired transmissions occur at multiples of the original frequency. In the example, harmonics of Device A, which is transmitting at 804 MHz, may occur at 1.608 MHz (frequency × 2) or 2.412 MHz (frequency × 3). In addition, Device A's second harmonic is reduced in power by roughly half of the originating signal's power. The third harmonic's power is roughly half of the second harmonic and so on.

As you can see in Figure 4.8, the harmonic frequencies of some device (Device A) could present a potential problem in your wireless design. Although Device A's second harmonic does not interfere with your AP's frequency channel, the third harmonic, although weaker in strength, can affect your transmission and reception for your channel 1 AP.

Application Considerations

Applications play a significant role in the determination of a wireless implementation. Due to the high bandwidth utilization of some applications, you may need to modify or completely remove a wireless design as an infrastructure solution. If the high bandwidth and/or high traffic application is not necessary on the wireless system you intend to deploy, you should filter that application's traffic from the wireless network by installing a router between the wireless segment and the wired segment.

Graphics-intensive applications, such as desktop publishing and CAD programs, can have significant impact on your wireless design depending on how the applications are used on the network. For example, if these files are stored on a shared network device such as a file server, there will be some network impact each time a user stores or retrieves a file. Typically these files are large (20 MB or more), if the number of users is large and/or they store or retrieve files frequently, the impact on the network becomes greater. The same is true for file transfer applications. To determine if the impact on the network is significant enough to justify changing or removing your wireless design, you should perform a baseline of network utilization for the existing network. A device or program known as a protocol analyzer can give you this information by monitoring the number, type, and size of packets traversing the network over a period of time. Network management programs, such as Ciscoworks and HP Openview, will also give you this type of information.

Structural Considerations

Physical considerations are classified into two major groups of issues that can affect wireless connectivity and performance. These issues are path fading and propagation losses. Below these two groups are specific causes that produce either propagation loss or path fading. We explain propagation losses and path fading and then we explore common causes for each, keeping in mind their affect on wireless design.

As we have discussed in Chapter 2, radio waves are propagated through space at the speed of light. This speed is attained assuming that there are no obstructions for the electromagnetic wave to pass through. The reason for this is because electromagnetic waves pass through different substances at different speeds. The greater the density of the substance, the slower the wave propagates through it. As an example, a radio wave will travel faster through the air than it will water and faster through water than a concrete building.

Under normal circumstances, as the signal radiates out from an antenna and it encounters objects within the environment, it will exhibit one or more of the following reactions: The signal may penetrate the object, reflect off the object, or be absorbed by the object.

In most cases, all of these reactions will occur to varying degrees, depending on the density and type of object encountered. This is the *propagation* of the signal. The strength of the signal decreases as it propagates. Penetration, reflection, and absorption all factor into the signal as it travels, each taking with it some amount of signal strength. These actions not only weaken the signal, but they may affect the direction in which the electromagnetic wave travels and the speed at which it travels.

As the radio wave propagates through the Earth's atmosphere and encounters objects within the environment, the strength of the signal will decrease. Any distortion of a wave's amplitude, phase, or direction can affect the strength of the received signal. This is known as *path fading*. The strength of the received signal is equal to the strength of the transmitted signal minus path fading.

As you can see propagation loss and path fading are very similar. The difference is really a matter of perspective. Receivers can suffer from path fading and transmitters suffer from propagation losses. Ideally, because most wireless LAN radios both send and receive, elimination or minimization of propagation losses and path fading are extremely desirable.

Differing environments can have substantial structural considerations to work around or overcome to successfully implement a wireless LAN solution. The following list takes a look at some of the common problems encountered in various environments and the solutions or alternatives available for each.

- **Hospitals** The most obvious issue that comes to mind in any medical environment is compatibility of wireless networks with existing medical equipment and, more importantly, medical diagnostic devices.

    Another consideration is the need for many healthcare providers to meet federal regulations in terms of their information systems. HIPAA (Health Insurance Portability and Accountability Act of 1996) is causing a major reassessment regarding privacy and related issues in healthcare information systems. Because of the lack of security in previously implemented wireless LANs used in these organizations, data encryption is a must for compliance in these facilities.

    Structurally, hospitals offer a variety of radio frequency obstacles. You should be aware of X-ray areas in particular, because most hospitals have lead-lined or extremely thick walls surrounding these areas to prevent X-ray bleed-through. Consider these areas "dead zones" to radio frequency. If coverage is necessary in these areas, you will have to install your antenna directly in each room requiring coverage. Full site surveys are recommended for all areas of a hospital, and all equipment normally used in the hospital should be on during the survey.

■ **Warehouses** Warehouses generally contain stock and rows of shelving. This presents coverage problems due to the density of the stock items and the metal construction of the shelving. Be sure to find out what the current stock levels are when performing your site survey. If the stock levels are high, you will get a much more accurate picture of coverage in your wireless implementation. The type of product that is stored in the warehouse makes a difference as well. For example, a fully stocked warehouse that contains only cases of empty plastic water jugs will have better coverage with fewer APs than the same warehouse containing cases of full plastic water jugs.

■ **Metal construction** In general, wireless LAN radio devices do not penetrate metal construction very well, if at all. Keep this in mind when designing your wireless LAN. In most cases, you will need to place antennas in each area that is contained by metal construction. Your site survey will aid you in verifying this requirement.

■ **Other construction** The materials used in construction of walls, pillars, and supports can also cause radio frequency impairments and impair coverage in a given area. Exterior walls tend to be thicker and contain more reinforcement materials than interior walls and partitions. Rebar (metal rods used to increase the strength of concrete construction) reinforced cinder block, or concrete walls and pillars can present a design issue in most facilities that use them. In general, the denser the material, the more difficult it will be for radio waves to penetrate.

■ **RF-producing devices** In addition to the construction and application considerations in your site survey and wireless design, you should constantly be on the lookout for potential interference from other electronic devices. There many devices that can potentially cause interference and require you to change your AP channel assignments. The most common culprits are 2.4 GHz cordless phones and microwave ovens. Be sure to have someone use these devices if they are inside a coverage area in your design. This will help you to determine the best channel to use on your AP.

Other potential interfering devices can be arc welding and telemetry equipment, 2.4 GHz lighting systems, and Spectralink phone systems.

Spectralink phone systems are used to provide cellular phone coverage within a company and is based on the IEEE 802.11b standard—the same standard used for wireless LANs.

Andromeda Manufacturing Rough Design

Armed with the knowledge gained from this and previous sections, you are now able to produce a rough design for the fictitious company, Andromeda Manufacturing. We number the prospective rough wireless designs for ease of identification. The following numbers will represent the following wireless designs (also see Figure 4.9):

1. Point-to-multipoint wireless implementation from the headquarters facility to the warehouse and manufacturing facilities.

2. Interior wireless implementation for the manufacturing facility.

Figure 4.9 Wireless Rough Designs

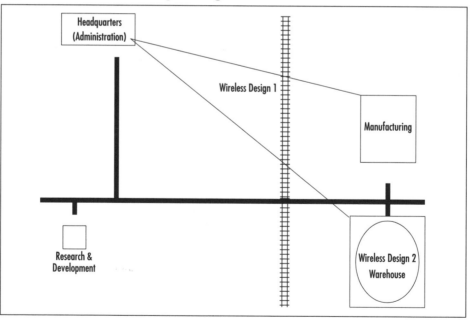

The site survey will provide the details to placement and any conditions affecting rough designs. It will verify the designs and provide all the detailed information required to install the wireless equipment, finalizing the designs for implementation.

Wireless Design 1

The goal of this rough design is to provide data connectivity back to the headquarters facility, allowing users in the manufacturing and warehouse facilities to send and receive e-mail from all facilities and send "live" information of manufacturing production runs and warehouse shipping and receiving information.

To accomplish these goals a point-to-multipoint wireless implementation is proposed. Based on information provided by Andromeda Manufacturing, the rough design for this implementation will consist of one Cisco wireless bridge at each of the three facilities. In addition, an exterior omni-directional antenna will be placed at the headquarters facility and one directional antenna will be placed on each of the two remote facilities. The remote facilities will send their radio signals in a tight beam into the circular radio coverage (provided by the omni-directional antenna) at the headquarters facility. This should provide reliable and efficient connectivity between the facilities.

Wireless Design 2

The goal of this rough design is to provide interior mobile coverage for inventory users in the warehouse facility. This will allow users performing inventories to input data directly into the data entry system as they inventory without having to wait until they can access a fixed terminal.

Interior wireless coverage is required throughout the warehouse, specifically in the aisles between the rows of shelving. The warehouse manager has restricted hardware placement to each far end of the facility (see Figure 4.10), therefore the rough design calls for seven Cisco APs, four at one end of the warehouse and three at the opposite end with directional antennas providing narrow coverage between the racks and shelves, down each aisle. This will meet the requirement for complete warehouse coverage while staying within the limitations mandated by the warehouse manager.

Now that you have the rough designs created, you will need to verify those designs, and in doing so, determine what changes, if any, will be required to make the designs feasible. The wireless site survey will provide you with this information. It will allow you to determine the antenna types required, cabling requirements for the APs, bridges and antennas, power requirements, and installation locations of all hardware. In a nutshell, the site survey will give you the details required for your designs.

Figure 4.10 Warehouse Facility Design

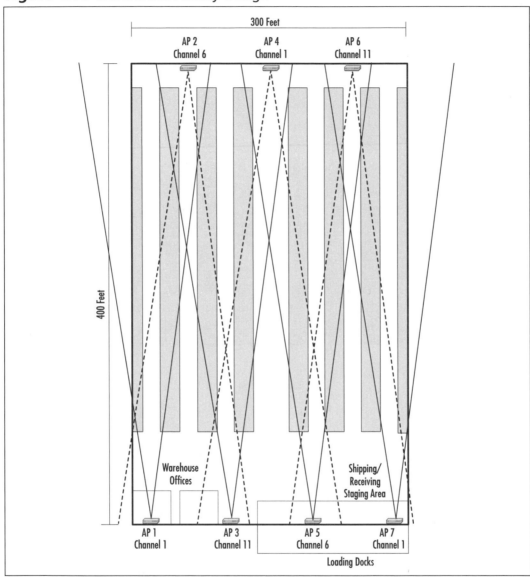

Performing a Wireless Site Survey

Wireless site surveys are critical to the successful implementation of a wireless LAN. There are as many ways to perform a wireless site survey as there are differing environments and businesses. As the person performing the survey, you must be able to creatively address all the unique issues of the business and/or environment while staying within the best practices of the wireless technology. This is not always an easy task. As you have seen in previous sections, wireless may not be the answer to your business needs, or the cost to work around some business issue may outweigh the practicality of the installation. You will have to be knowledgeable on the wireless equipment you are installing and the wired equipment with which you may be interfacing, the physical environment, the application considerations and the structural environment.

A site survey performed by you or a certified wireless professional, will verify the feasibility of the initial (rough) design in the face of obstacles such as wired connectivity limitations, radio hazards, and application requirements. The survey will help you determine the number of APs needed throughout a facility to provide the desired coverage, and it will determine the placement of those APs, detailing the necessary information for placement. Point-to-point surveys will also provide you with detailed information for placement of both the bridge units and antennas as well as determine feasibility of the link desired. With the information gathered from a site survey, a site survey report can be generated to assist you in "selling" the productivity and return-on-investment benefits of wireless LANs to the decision makers in your company. For those who already understand the benefits of wireless, the successful wireless site survey will allow you to properly install the wireless LAN and have efficient, reliable wireless access.

In your site survey, whether interior or exterior, try to identify potential problems up front and discuss how these issues will be handled. This can potentially save you a lot of time and trouble during the installation. You don't want to discover these issues during the installation or the "go live" period. A faulty or incomplete wireless site survey can be detrimental to your business for a very long time.

In this chapter, we have covered many design considerations. Keeping those design considerations in mind, we now discuss what is needed to prepare and perform a site survey and the differences in performing exterior versus interior surveys. Best practices for surveying are integrated into this section, in addition to examples of creative approaches to specific issues.

Preparation

Preparation for your wireless site survey will provide you important information needed to perform the survey and will guide you in your design process. In general, find out as much about the facility and business environment as you can before the performing your survey. You will have enough to keep you busy without having to worry about whether you are allowed in an area without escort or interviewing to find out what possible RF interference is in or around the coverage areas. To this end, the pre-site survey questionnaire was created and indeed, it will become your friend. The following section contains a sample questionnaire form; as you use this form, you may find it useful to change or add sections to tailor this to your specific requirements.

Sample Pre-Site Survey Form

Filling out a pre-site survey form helps us in our preparation prior to our arrival at your site and helps us ensure that we design a Wireless LAN (WLAN) that will meet your needs and requirements. Please fill in the form and e-mail to <Surveyor's e-mail address> or fax to <Department or Business Name> attention: <Surveyor's Name> at <Surveyor's Phone Number>.

Customer:		Contact:		
Site Address:				
Department:		E-mail:		
Phone:		Fax:		
Mobile:		Pager:		
• Total Number of Sites (Please fill out one form for each site)				
Site No.:	of	No. Buildings at site:		
Require 802.11 Compliance: ☐YES ☐NO		Require Redundant WLAN?: ☐YES ☐NO		
Hours of Operation:		Approximate sq. footage:		
Hours during which site survey may be performed:				
Total No. users:	Minimum		Maximum	
Packet Size:	Average		Maximum	
PC and/or Terminal type(s):				
• RF Coverage				
☐ Complete Inside ☐ Selective Inside (Provide diagram of facility indicating desired coverage)				
☐ Complete Outside ☐ Selective Outside (Provide diagram of facility indicating coverage)				
Using WEP Encryption: ☐YES ☐NO				
Desired Link Speed(s): ☐ 11Mb ☐ 5.5Mb ☐ 2Mb ☐ 1Mb				
Utilize Rate Shifting: ☐YES ☐NO (Please indicate where desired link speed will be needed)				
• Existing Network				
Existing Network Topology: ☐Ethernet ☐Token Ring ☐Other				
All sites use the same topology? ☐YES ☐NO				
Explain:				
Application type(s) to be used on WLAN: ☐Client/Server ☐Emulation ☐Other				
If emulation, what type?				
If Other, explain				
Protocol(s):				
Host Environment:				
WAN Connectivity:				
LAN Connectivity: (Check all that apply)	☐10Mbps ☐Switches	☐100Mbps ☐Routers	☐Hubs ☐Bridges	
Media: (Check all that apply)	☐Coax ☐Cat 5	☐Copper ☐Cat 7	☐Fiber ☐Gigabit	
Existing Wireless LAN? ☐YES ☐NO				
If Yes, explain:				

Continued

- **Site Information**

Ceiling Height:	☐8-10ft.	☐10-20ft	☐20-30ft.	☐30+ft.

Is lift available?　☐YES　☐NO　If No, will customer provide?　☐YES　☐NO

In-Building Roof Access? ☐YES　☐NO

Racking/Shelving?　☐YES　☐NO　If Yes, please describe construction:

Clearance above storage level:　☐<4ft.　☐4-8ft.　☐8+ft.

Any Hazardous areas?　☐YES (Please indicate Hazardous areas on diagram)　☐NO

If Yes, please describe:

Temperature range inside facility:　Temperature range outside facility (if applicable):

Any Freezers?　☐YES (Please indicate freezer area(s) on diagram)　☐NO

Temperature (Check all that apply)　☐30°+　☐15°-30°　☐0°-15°　☐-5°--10°　☐<-10°

Special Safety Rquirements:　☐Steel Toed Boots　☐Hard Hat　☐Safety Glasses　☐Other:

Other Non-WLAN RF Equipment installed at facility?
☐YES (Please indicate on diagram where installed)　☐NO

If Yes, please describe and provide frequency used for the device.
Device:	Frequency:
Device:	Frequency:
Device:	Frequency:

Materials Stored at Site:

Do stock levels fluctuate?　☐YES　☐NO

Explain:

Current Stock Levels:　☐High　☐Average　☐Low

Any Conveyors?　☐YES (Please indicate location on site diagram)　☐NO

Continued

Available Power:	☐110VAC	☐220VAC

Does site experience power problems?	☐YES	☐NO

If Yes, please describe:

Site Construction (Please provide a brief description of each)

Building:

Ceiling:

Walls:

Floor:

Other Preparations

In order to perform a successful and complete wireless site survey, the following items and/or services should be made available where applicable.

- In-building surveys will require blueprints, CAD drawings, or if those are not available, fire escape drawings of the facility. These should detail the location of office spaces, cubicles, and equipment to scale.

- Point-to-point surveys will require topographical maps of the area to include all the facilities involved in the survey.

- Provide a dedicated escort, if required, to allow full access to the facilities being surveyed.

- Provide facility identification or badges, if necessary for full access.

- Provide any facility guidelines or restrictions concerning equipment mounting.

- If the facility is a union facility, please provide a declaration of operating equipment limitations, if any.

- Provide information regarding asbestos construction, if applicable.

- If the facility has been designated a historical site, please provide any limitations or specifications for modifying the interior or exterior of the building.

- Be prepared to provide an Occupational Safety and Health Administration (OSHA) representative where regulations prohibit non-OSHA certified personnel from access or installation.

- Be prepared to provide qualified personnel to access facility rooftops for the duration of any point-to-point survey.

If you do not fill out the pre-site survey form yourself and plan on giving the pre-site survey form to a customer or client, as is the case with larger organizations where Information Systems performs requests for other departments or divisions, do not be surprised if many of the more technical questions go unanswered. Remember, your customer is not likely to know what Wired Equivalent Protocol (WEP), rate shifting, or even what LAN or WAN is, so it will be difficult for them to know if they have it or need it. You will need to be prepared to explain to the customer, in layman's terms, what some of the various technical questions are asking for. You will be in a much better position to survey and produce a survey report if you already have these questions answered.

It is not uncommon for a client to request 11Mbps coverage in all areas in the questionnaire, but after your survey, they find out how many APs are required to provide that coverage and your customer then decides that 5.5 or 2 Mbps is sufficient for several of the areas. If you do not follow-up the questionnaire with a meeting or phone call to discuss the answers you received, you may find yourself spending additional time to resurvey your coverage areas for the lower speeds. By asking why your customer needs 11 Mbps coverage everywhere, for example, you can ensure that you will survey an area only once.

Depending on your local laws and regulations, you may have other inquiries that you will want to add to this questionnaire. In the United States, such things as safety requirements and regulations may impede or hinder your site survey, so you should be aware of these regulations and plan accordingly. OSHA will sometimes require you, through the business, to complete paperwork verifying your understanding and compliance of specific or unique work safety requirements in a given area. An example would be, surveys performed in a biohazard or chemical manufacturing area, requiring body suits and/or masks.

During your installation, fire codes for office, manufacturing, healthcare, and other facilities will need to be adhered to. Prior to your survey, you will need to find out if the facility contains firewalls. No, we are not talking about the firewalls used in your business to keep out Internet intruders, we are talking about firewalls used in building construction. In building construction, a firewall keeps a fire from spreading from one building or part of a building to another. Firewalls are used to divide overall structures into allowable areas permitted by building code. Building codes vary by locality and country. Firewalls can be difficult to spot if you are not looking for them, thus we have added them to the list of questions to be answered prior to performing the survey. Because firewalls typically extend to the roof of most buildings, it is important to determine during the survey, if you will need to penetrate a firewall for any reason. During the survey, it is unlikely you will have need to penetrate the firewall, but you may discover this need for your implementation. In the event that you must penetrate a firewall, procedures exist in your locality for this. In the U.S., most of these procedures must be compliant with the National Electric Code (NEC). You can usually obtain copies of the NEC from local electrical suppliers. In my locality, penetration of a firewall requires a special fire-stop caulking to be applied around the penetration point and an inspection of the work by local fire authorities afterwards.

In addition to firewalls, another typical fire code related question commonly encountered is whether plenum cable is required for this facility. *Plenum cable* is cable that is coated with a fire-retardant coating (usually Teflon) so that in case of a fire, it does not give off toxic gasses and smoke as it burns. Twisted-pair and coaxial cable are made in plenum versions. In building construction, the plenum is the space that is used for air circulation in heating and air conditioning systems, typically between the structural ceiling and the suspended ceiling or under a raised floor. The plenum space is typically used to house the communication cables for the building's computer and telephone network(s). This impacts your installation and design only if you must have either your antenna cabling or your data cabling running through plenum areas of a facility to get to your APs and/or bridges, and the facility requires plenum cabling. Knowledge of plenum cabling requirements in your facility prior to the survey will help you determine how you may have to cable your wireless gear for your design and implementation.

You do not want to cause undue strife by performing certain functions during the site survey that union personnel are required to perform, such as running a man-lift to get to the ceiling of a facility. The questionnaire will help you determine what coordination with other parties, if any, will be necessary to complete the survey.

Another preparation to consider is the need for permits to work in and on historical sites. Due to the nature of these sites, you must use extreme care to ensure that you make little or no changes to the facility or site. You should consider the differences required in surveying these sites as opposed to installing. Permission from one or more authorities may be needed to allow the installation, and even the survey, to occur.

Based on the preliminary information obtained from your questionnaire, you should be able to form one or more rough designs that may accomplish the desired coverage. You will use these rough designs to test during your site survey. The last section of your questionnaire contains some very important requests. The first of these is the request to have blueprints, CAD drawings, or fire escape drawings of the facility and any obstacles, such as offices, cubicles, and equipment, to be diagramed to scale. This is important for your preparation because without it you cannot create any rough designs for anticipated coverage. To do this while surveying takes a significant amount of time and will force you to start your testing with no predetermined designs to guide you through the creative aspect of the survey.

The other extremely important request in the last section of the questionnaire pertains to escorts, badges, Ids, and in general, access to facilities or areas needed to survey or areas you must go through to get to the survey areas. I know there is nothing more frustrating than to wait 20 or 30 minutes to start surveying a particular area because the security guard doesn't know who you are and will not let you into an area or facility, especially when you have just toted 50 pounds of gear up three flights of stairs (no elevator). Do this for several areas or facilities and you may have blown several hours just to get into the place. Even if the person with whom you deal with is aware that you are going to be surveying, verify this ahead of time by speaking to the manager or security company in charge of the actual areas you intend on visiting. If an escort is needed, confirm that they are actually at the location prior to going to the site. They may have called in sick, or an emergency is preventing them from being there, in which case the area or facility may not have someone else to escort you. In the case of badges and IDs, this is usually a little easier provided that your company doesn't require "special" badges to get you into certain areas. If this is the case, you should request the appropriate badge(s) as far ahead of time as possible and confirm that the badge is ready before you go to the area or facility requiring it.

One more thought on preparation: Understand that surveys are typically less intrusive than the actual implementations of a wireless system. As you prepare to survey, always keep in mind what it will take to actually take to install your system and how this will affect production of services or goods in the particular environment. Is the business a 24/7 shop? Does the business have a weekly or monthly business cycle that is critical? When and where can you install the wireless system so that it will have minimal impact on the business? These are but a few of the keys to the success of your implementation.

Infrastructure Awareness

In order to properly perform a site survey, you should make yourself aware of the environment you are surveying. What types of media and infrastructure devices are used in this environment? Will bleed-through of radio waves affect any sensitive equipment in the area you are in? What about floors above and below you in multifloor facilities? Will you receive interference from or transmit interference to any devices? Is there adequate power and network connectivity for your APs? These questions are a good starting point for making yourself aware of the environment in which you are surveying and in which you intend to install a wireless system.

In the next section, we describe the common infrastructure items you should aware of while preparing and performing a wireless site survey.

What Types of Network Media Are Used?

Be aware of the media types that encompass the network. Most networks likely use some type of copper cabling, and many use fiber optic cabling for backbone or longer runs. As you are surveying a facility and deciding on locations for your APs or bridges, you should also be looking for ways to connect them to the network.

The most frequently used cabling in today's networks are Category 5 (Cat5) or Category 5e (Cat5e) unshielded twisted pair (UTP). It consists of eight strands of solid copper wires, grouped into four pairs. Each pair is twisted, at a specific rate per inch, to create magnetic "shielding" when current is applied. This helps UTP to avoid cross-talk or interference from the other strands.

In Category 5e UTP cabling, the four already twisted pairs of cable (as in Cat5) are twisted together inside the cable sheath to provide additional (though not complete) shielding from outside interference. This is why it is called Category 5 enhanced. Cat5 and Cat5e are typically terminated with RJ-45 connectors or punched down to a patch panel or wall jack. In an Ethernet topology, Cat5 or Cat5e can be run a maximum of 100 meters or 328 feet.

The typical sheathing on UTP cabling is made of polyvinyl chloride (PVC). PVC can melt, smoke, and give off toxic fumes in the event of a fire. As we have discussed in the preparation section, the alternative to PVC sheathing is plenum cabling. Upon first observation, plenum is exactly the same as normal UTP, except the cable is much stiffer and harder to work with. In addition, the cable will be marked with a code, for example "CMP", which indicates a plenum rated, unshielded cable.

The following are some common sheath (jacket) types and their ratings:

- **Teflon** Plenum rated

- **FR-PVC** Flame-retardant PVC

- **PVC** Non-plenum PVC

The following are some common copper wire types for UTP:

- **CM** Communications cables

- **CMP** Communications plenum cable

- **CMR** Communications riser cables that passes the UL1666 test

- **CM** Communications cables that passes the UL15812 test

When calculating cable runs for either your wired network connection or your antenna connection, always measure what the actual cable path will be, do not measure a straight line from end to end because bends or turns in the cable path can add significantly to the cable length. In your design, this could mean cable runs that are too long for your topology causing loss of data or bad performance and will also throw off any estimates you may obtain from wiring contractors or unnecessarily increase the cost of the implementation if you are installing the wiring.

Do not run cabling at an angle; instead, try to run cabling as straight as possible using 90-degree turns where necessary to avoid obstacles. Avoid running cable on top of ballasts in fluorescent light fixtures, because this will wreak havoc by interfering in your data transmission through the cable.

Always calculate for service loops at both ends of your cable run. Service loops give you or your wiring contractor some "play" in the cable in the event the cable has to run around some unforeseen object or in case the cable must be terminated numerous times. Service loops are usually an additional 10–15 percent of the estimated cable length. For example, on a 200-foot run, an additional 20 feet to act as a service loop is typical. This would work out to 10 feet on each end of the cable.

If your design calls for fiber connectivity to the APs or bridges, you will require a media transceiver because Cisco radios only interface the wired media via an RJ-45 connection.

What Operating Systems, Protocols, and Drivers Are Used?

Different operating systems can use different protocols on the local area network. These protocols have different overhead and bandwidth requirements. Some are more efficient than others. Ask about the operating systems that are being used for the clients and servers and find out specifically what protocols are being used in the current LAN and which ones will be required to traverse the wireless LAN. The reason for this is to determine what protocols, if any, can be filtered from accessing the wireless LAN and thus increase performance.

Some drivers are not yet available or supported from Cisco. For example, Cisco provides drivers for Macintosh operating system 9.*x* only. In addition, Cisco PCI client adapters are not supported for use with Apple computers.

What Hubs Are Used?

Hubs may be 10,100 or 10/100 hubs. The Cisco APs have 10/100 auto-sensing ports, and they will try to work on either port, but whenever possible you should try to connect via a 100 Mbps–capable port.

What Switches Are Used?

Access points communicate with each other on Layer 2 of the OSI model. Access points communicate with each other only if they're going to have clients roaming from one AP to another, in this situation those two APs would need to be on the same broadcast domain. If for some reason two APs that are going to have clients roaming between them cannot be on the same broadcast domain, the Layer 3 devices must be configured to pass required packets for the APs to communicate with each other.

It is the client that determines if it will change APs, and, of course, the prerequisite is that the client has an encryption key for the new AP and a matching service set ID (SSID) as well. The client uses three criteria to make this determination: signal strength, packet error rate, and AP load.

Switches have the capability for each port to be seen as a "virtual" LAN (VLAN). VLANs may be grouped together to form larger VLANs. Switches are designed for wired networks with stationary users. They were not designed to handle mobile users. If the switch sees each port as a VLAN, and there are APs on each port, the switch is not set up to handle users moving from one VLAN to another.

Cisco APs are set up to work with these switch features. When a client roams from AP1 to AP2, AP2 sends a multicast packet with the source address of the roaming client. This packet is sent by the AP on behalf of the client and updates the switch's addressable memory. AP1 can then forward any packets that it has for the client to AP2.

Your application may not be set up to handle a switched network. The application may send out broadcast packets. If the client is connected to an AP that is not on the same virtual LAN as the server(s), the broadcast may never reach their destination(s)

A potential solution to this problem is to group the ports with the APs connected to them with the ports the host is using to form a VLAN. This may or may not work for you depending on requirements of the host to your wired clients.

Another solution is to network all the APs to the same hub the host uses. Cable distance limitations may make this impossible. Still another solution may be to network all of your APs together via hubs and have them connect to the same hub the host uses. This is not a viable solution if the host is remote. This solution may present problems for some people. Under the 802.3 standard, when using a switch, you should not extend beyond two hops when using a 100 Mbps network. Although the wireless link between the client and the AP is not considered a hop, a remote host may be well past the two hop limit.

The ideal solution for switching across VLANs connected to APs is to install a router or Layer 3 switch between the VLANs to perform routing across the VLANs, thus providing the ability to deny or allow the appropriate traffic between VLANs.

What Routers Are Used?

Routers present problems similar to switches in that they stop broadcast packets and may present a problem for the application or for clients trying to use DHCP. Static routes configured in the router may be necessary if the users on the wireless segment intend to use a remote host.

What Bridges Are Used?

Bridges can also present challenges because of their tables. Most bridges used today build dynamic tables. Some facilities may need to build their tables manually, sometimes by choice or sometimes because they are using older bridges.

Because most IT personnel are not eager to work with these tables, you may need to configure them in order for wireless LAN applications to work properly, especially if they will be accessing a remote host.

How Is Power Supplied?

Cisco APs and bridges require power to function. The 340 series APs and bridges use traditional power inputs; the 350 series APs and bridges utilize inline power. Inline power consists of sending DC power over standard Category 5 UTP cable up to 100 meters. Instead of requiring wall power, APs and bridge devices can utilize power provided from Cisco line power-enabled devices, such as Cisco Catalyst Switches and line power patch panels. You can also use a line power injector, included with the Cisco 350 series APs and bridges, to provide the inline power required from a traditional wall outlet.

During the site survey, you will need to look for methods of power for your AP and/or bridge devices for the locations in your design requirements. Take note of any areas that do not have power available and consider how you will provide the power—traditionally or via inline power. A note on inline power; if your design requires the wireless network to stay up in the event of a power outage, inline power is much more efficient than traditional power because you can place an uninterruptible power supply (UPS) on the switch or line power patch panel that is providing the power to the AP. Otherwise, UPS will be necessary for each and every one of your AP or bridge devices, as well as the switches or hubs they are connected to, to maintain connectivity to the network during the power outage.

Preparing a Site Survey Kit

A site survey kit contains all the equipment necessary to evaluate, test, and record the possible wireless designs and their implementation ramifications for a given site. We discuss the different types of equipment you should have to perform a site survey, when and where they are used, and we provide you with sources for some of the more difficult equipment to obtain.

Although not specifically listed in the following sections, note that you will need a device, preferably a portable device, capable of running a Cisco wireless client adapter and the Cisco client software and utilities in order to perform a wireless site survey. I use a lightweight laptop computer with plenty of battery life (I actually have two batteries). I use Windows 2000 as my operating system, but you can equally use Linux, Windows 95, 98, or NT to run the client software.

Many of the sections list additional or optimal tools and equipment for a specific task. Your need for this additional or optimal equipment has much to do with your role in wireless site surveys. Differentiation is made between a one-time or limited site surveyor, for example, an information systems employee at a company intending to implement wireless for themselves, and a surveyor who intends to perform multiple surveys over time, as with a wireless consultant or engineer.

NOTE

Your site survey kit should definitely be a portable unit. If you intend to perform multiple surveys, as is the case with wireless engineers and consultants, invest in foam equipment cases to protect your survey equipment from damage due to weather and the various bumps and bangs of moving your equipment around.

Often, site surveys are requested on very short notice, and the ability to carry the carry the case in the trunk or backseat of a car, or check it as luggage allows you to travel with your equipment and solves the problem of your kit being lost or detained during shipping.

Using Client Adapters in the Survey

Cisco recommends that you survey with the wireless network adapter you intend to use in your rough design. Therefore, if you intend to have desktop computers act as wireless workstations in your design, you should use the PCI or ISA client adapter to perform your site survey. This is not always practical, especially if the intended workstations are large and bulky and are not located where they will be located under the actual implementation. A combination of creativity and skill are required in this scenario. Different client adapters can have differing types of antenna connections, giving you a variable in the spread pattern of the antennas between different client adapters. Receive sensitivity, maximum transmit power, and typical indoor and outdoor ranges vary from the Cisco 340 series to 350 series client adapters producing several other variables to consider.

The best way to handle the desktop workstation scenario is to either provide or request from your client a cart that has a desktop workstation with the client adapter card you intend to use for the implementation. This gives you the flexibility to move about during your survey and eliminates from consideration many of the variables related to using a client adapter that is not intended for the design.

You can find more information regarding client adapters and their specifications in Chapter 8.

Surveying with LEAP as a Requirement

In order to conduct a proper wireless site survey that takes into account Cisco's Lightweight Extensible Authentication Protocol (LEAP) or standards-based EAP, you must have an authenticator capable of supporting it on the network you are surveying. If you perform or expect to perform multiple wireless site surveys, you should outfit your survey laptop with Windows 2000 Professional Server and install IAS services configured for Remote Authentication Dial-in User Service (RADIUS) and EAP to allow you test authentication against your design. Typically, LEAP and EAP do not add significant performance degradation, however, you should survey with this configured and tested to ensure design functionality.

The following bullets list Cisco's requirements for LEAP or EAP with their equipment:

- The minimum Cisco client adapter firmware version required for LEAP support is 4.13.

- Cisco AP firmware release 11.00 is the minimum version required to support LEAP or EAP. Release 11.00 is the first version of firmware that enables the AP to be configured as an EAP or LEAP authenticator.

- The AP requires an EAP authenticator. The RADIUS server must support the type of authentication you are using (either EAP or LEAP).

Using APs and Bridges in the Survey

Obviously the most critical component needed to perform a wireless site survey is the radio devices themselves. You typically need only one AP for interior surveys and two bridges for exterior surveys. Be sure to have your AP or bridge console cable with you to allow you to configure the devices directly. The console cable for the AP and bridge is a straight-through cable with 9-pin male to 9-pin female connectors. Previously, these console cables did not come with the

APs or bridges, but are now being supplied. If you really prefer using the browser-based configuration tool over the console, set the IP address of your devices and laptop to a network other than the subnet you are on to allow you to move from subnet to subnet without reconfiguring your laptop and radio devices each time. For example, if the network in the facility you are surveying is 192.168.0.0, set your laptop and APs for network 172.16.0.0 to prevent conflicts and allow you to go to any subnetwork without reconfiguring your laptop and AP.

Some configuration will have to take place on your APs or bridges prior to surveying. You should configure the devices exactly as they will be used in a potential implementation. So if your design requires a wireless network that is optimally 11 Mbps with rate shifting to 5.5 Mbps, WEP encryption, LEAP authentication, and mandatory service set identifiers, configure your AP with these parameters. All of these configuration parameters are explained in detail in Chapter 5.

You should always carry more than one AP with you when surveying. This allows you to continue to survey in the event your AP fails for any reason. In a previous survey, I dropped an AP from a ladder and had I not had a backup AP, I would have had to reschedule the site survey while I waited for my spare AP to be shipped.

Choosing Antennas for the Survey

There is no single antenna that is perfect for all wireless design applications. A variety of antennas are offered by Cisco because the variety of wireless design applications possible requires them. Your choice and placement of an antenna is in many cases, dictated by your customer. Your customer may not want the antenna to be visible; or it may be located in a high traffic area requiring a low profile antenna. By carrying a variety of antennas, you will be prepared for any situation.

The minimum collection of antennas should include, but not be limited to, the following:

- 2.2 dBi "Rubber Duckies" These are the rubber antennas that come with your Cisco AP or bridge
- 5.2 dBi Ceiling Mount
- 5.2 dBi Mast Mount
- 5.2 dBi Ground Plane
- 5.2 dBi Diversity Pillar Mount

- 6.0 dBi Patch
- 8.5 dBi Patch
- 13.5 dBi Yagi

If you will be performing site surveys where you are aware that you will be using an antenna that is not in your kit, carry that antenna as well. Always survey with the antenna you intend to use. Do not use a different antenna and attempt to guess what the coverage will be. The reason you are performing the site survey is to take the guesswork out of the installation.

Antenna coverage is one of the most critical factors in a wireless system deployment because it applies directly to a client's ability to roam and communicate with the wired network. A large selection of antennas is required to handle a variety of potential networks from warehouses, retail floors, outdoors, and offices.

Although you choose among a variety of antennas, only two versions exist:

- **Omni-directional** Provide a coverage pattern that is mostly circular and is usually used for indoor implementations. The signal is strongest at the center (nearest to the antenna) and gets weaker as the signal radiates outward. Mast mount antennas are examples of omni-directional antennas.

- **Directional** Frequently installed outdoors. The coverage area is similar to a triangle, and it gets weaker as the signal extends outward. The coverage area varies from antenna to antenna, and coverage can range from 12 to 65 degrees. Yagi and solid dish antennas are examples of directional antennas.

Providing Battery Packs and Inverters for the Survey

When you perform your survey, you will need to provide power for your APs and/or bridges. You will not be able to count on the site having the appropriate power in the proper locations for every survey or part of a survey performed. Therefore, you will need to provide some type of portable power. Because most wireless radios, including Cisco APs and bridges, utilize AC power, you will need, in addition to a battery pack, an inverter to convert the DC power of the battery pack to AC. You should ensure that the battery pack provides you with enough power for about eight hours or a days worth of surveying. It would not do to have to reschedule your survey because your battery packs lost power in the middle of your survey.

I have also had to use the battery pack to supply power to my laptop computer during site surveys that extended beyond my laptop battery's capacity. As you can see, choosing the right number and capacity of your battery packs can be crucial to your site survey.

There are several approaches to providing power for your APs for the purposes of surveying. The most common approach is to purchase commercially available battery packs and inverters. The downside to this is that you will have two pieces of extra equipment to carry with you and hook up for each AP you are surveying with, in addition to the cost of the equipment. If you are performing a survey for your company, and you are fairly sure this will be the only wireless implementation for some time, you may want to just rent several battery packs and inverters for the period of the survey.

Some commercially available battery packs have inverters built in to them, thus reducing the amount of equipment to carry. A company called Statpower produces a line of mobile battery packs with inverters built in to them, called xPower. The 21-amp-hour rated xPower300 will power one Cisco 350 series AP for well over 12 hours, a larger 40-amp-hour version on wheels is also available. Keep in mind that most inverters have only two outlets on them, so if you plan on powering several devices, you should purchase some inexpensive five- or six-outlet power strips to plug into the inverter outlets.

Remember, you are going to be carrying this equipment around, so weight plays a factor in choosing your battery packs as well. The xPower300 battery pack/inverter combination weighs about 18 pounds. Most of this weight is due to the lead in the batteries themselves. The carrying handle, however, makes this relatively easy to move about.

Another alternative for portable power is to build your own battery pack and inverter combination. This requires good knowledge of electronics, but can be affordably done and can accommodate not only the power components but also the AP or bridge in one unit.

Providing Tools for the Survey

There are many other tools you should have in your site survey kit to aid you in the successful completion of your wireless site survey. Some of the tools listed in this section should be considered needs, whereas others can be considered "nice to have" or wants. This section provides you with the extra items you will need to perform your site survey and provide an explanation of their uses.

NOTE

In addition to the tools and equipment needed for your site survey kit, you need some specific tools for installation. Among these are a cordless drill with a drill bit set containing both hole saw bits and dry core bits to makes holes in masonry block and brick, in sizes up to two inches. These are needed to penetrate interior and exterior walls for running antenna cabling.

You will also require a caulk gun and clear silicone caulking to seal the area around the cabling on the exterior holes. I sometimes use expanding foam sealant for this.

You may also need to provide some quarter-inch plywood to serve as backing for wall mounting APs and bridges.

- **Graph paper, ruler, pencil and sticky notes** These simple, inexpensive tools will probably be the most valuable tools you can have in your site survey kit. Even if your client has provided you with scaled diagrams of the survey area(s), you may still need to write down installation and/or design notes during the survey or draw an area to scale on your graph paper that is not on the client-provided diagram. Post-It or sticky notes are also invaluable when you need to make notes on a diagram that your customer may need back (and does not want changes written on it); this allows you to copy the diagram with your notes on it.

- **Markers** Once your AP, bridge, and/or antenna placement is determined in your site survey, you will need to mark their location for ease of installation later. Location markers should be very bright, resistant to dust, grease, and water, and be easy to remove when necessary. They should be sturdy but temporary.

- **Surveyor's tape** This is probably the best solution for temporary markers. It comes in a variety of colors and is inexpensive. You can tie, tape, or pin it to just about any surface. I prefer the fluorescent colored surveyor's tape. It is much easier to see when marking locations, especially in areas that are not well lighted. I usually carry two colors of this tape at a minimum. One color is used to mark the location of the AP, or bridge and the other is used as an antenna placement marker.

- **Measuring devices** In order for you or your customer to get accurate installation costs, you will have to provide many measurements in the site survey report. And these measurements need to be as accurate as possible. If you guess the Cat5 run to be 300 feet, and it turns out to be 380 feet, the cost for this portion of the installation could be more than anticipated.

  Your kit should include a measuring wheel to allow you to accurately measure cable distances. Of course, you can use more advanced measurement devices, such as laser and ultrasonic range finders, but a measuring wheel will give you the measurement detail you will need.

  Vertical measurements, such as floor to ceiling distances, can be best accomplished with a simple rope marked in ten-foot increments.

  Note that counting structural features such as floor tiles, ceiling tiles, or cinder blocks typically does not give accurate measurements of distance. This is because much of the time these structural elements are cut or shortened to accommodate the site architecture and are therefore unreliable for measurement.

- **Ladders, man–lifts, and safety harnesses** In wireless site surveys and installations, you will frequently need gain access to ceilings and roofs of buildings. A ladder in most buildings will get you to the ceiling. However, in warehouses where the ceilings are typically very high (20–30 feet) and to reach rooftops that do not have interior access, you will need some type of powered equipment such as a forklift with a personnel basket or a man–lift to give you access to these areas. This equipment can be rented for a day or two or perhaps your customer may already have this type of equipment for their facility.

  In addition, you should purchase a safety harness for working in these areas. Several different types of safety harnesses are available with differing levels of protection. I recommend a full body harness and some type of compatible lifeline or lanyard, preferably self-retracting to allow ease of movement. For insurance reasons, some organizations do not permit this type of work by anyone other than their own employees.

- **Digital camera** A digital camera is a very useful tool in your site survey kit. It will allow you to take pictures during your survey of the coverage areas, antenna, and radio device placements, and it will allow you to insert these directly into your site survey report after the survey.

- **Laser** Laser pointers are used for point-to-point wireless site surveys to determine precise line of site. This is one of the items I mentioned as "nice to have." The green lasers are the best to use because they are easier to see than the red lasers. The highest power for a green laser allowed by U.S. law is 5 milliwatts. Lasers are especially handy for aligning antennas that are more than 1 mile away. The downside to using these lasers however, is in direct sun they are very difficult to see. They work much better during overcast or cloudy days and obviously very well at night.

- **Global Positioning System (GPS)** Another "nice to have" item is a GPS device. Although you can use the odometer in your car to get fairly accurate distances between antennas in a point-to-point survey, a GPS will give extremely accurate readings as well as altitude. A GPS can also aid you in determining vehicle speeds in a highly mobile wireless installation and survey.

- **Spectrum analyzer** A spectrum analyzer as used in a wireless site survey is a device that allows you to monitor a specific portion of the radio frequency spectrum to determine what interference, if any, is present in the band of frequencies you intend to use for your wireless implementation.

    Though considered by some to be a necessary component in a wireless site survey, I consider the spectrum analyzer as a component to use if you suspect interference from other sources, such as neighboring facilities.

    Spectrum analyzers are very expensive and can range in price from $5,000 to over $30,000. This a lot of money to invest for a one-time survey; you can rent them instead from many companies. If I feel a spectrum analysis is warranted for a particular survey, I will rent the equipment as necessary.

Bringing Temporary Mounting Equipment for the Survey

Your APs and/or bridges will need to be temporarily mounted in the survey area(s). Because you will move them frequently, you should take care to mount them as securely as possible without damaging the site. You may not be installing an AP or bridge in the location you are surveying, so you do not want to unnecessarily damage a drop ceiling or I-beam by drilling holes in them. To this end, you will need a variety of tools and equipment to "soft" mount the APs.

If you are a wireless consultant or engineer, carrying both AP and bridge mounts in your survey kit is advisable to allow you to get the best ideas, during you survey, for installation mounting of these devices. You should also carry antenna mounts, for this same reason.

Both wireless consultants and one-time surveyors should also have in their survey kits various alternative mounting solutions for equipment. You must again be creative. Beam clamps, C-clamps, bar clamps, tie wraps, and Velcro are common components in a good site survey kit.

During a wireless site survey, there is no bad mounting technique with the exception of a mounting technique that does not properly secure the AP/bridge, battery pack, and antenna. For safety and prudence, you should definitely double- or triple-check the temporary mounting of all your equipment during the survey. This protects your equipment from possible damage, but also eliminates the risk of injury to you or others from falling APs and antennas. As an added incentive, failure to ensure secure mounting of equipment, at a minimum, can result in a loss of confidence in you (the wireless professional), as your customer or peers watch your expensive equipment shatter to pieces, after dropping 30 feet to the floor of the facility. The following pieces of equipment will be essential for safely mounting your equipment:

- **Tools and miscellaneous equipment** A good socket set and driver and bit set are invaluable for your site survey kit. These are used for another piece of equipment I recommend: U-bolts. I use these to attach to antennas to aid in the temporary mounting that is required for the site survey. I have various U-bolt sizes ranging from one and one-half inches to six inches to accommodate various antennas. Another good tool for mounting antennas is a modified camera tripod for mounting exterior antennas on roofs for exterior surveys.

- **Velcro** Velcro is a good choice for strapping an AP to a beam or post as long as the only weight the Velcro must bear is the radio device itself. I typically use this for APs and antennas that do not have low-loss cable connected to them. The cabling can add substantial weight to an AP or antenna hanging from an I-beam 30 feet in the air. Velcro is typically not strong enough to hold the additional weight. Also, replace your Velcro regularly, because it tends to "wear out" over time and heavy usage.

- **Tape and other adhesive-based products** I typically try to avoid adhesive products of any sort when soft mounting equipment. It is frequently difficult to remove the adhesive "leftovers" when moving the equipment from place to place and solvents can remove paint and other finishes as well as the adhesive. The only adhesive I carry is a removable adhesive putty-like substance. This reusable adhesive has many brand names, but it is usually blue or green in color. It is typically used to attach pictures or posters to walls without damaging the wall finish. I use only this removable adhesive to attach my location markers during site surveys. This type of adhesive product does not leave glue residue when removing the markers.

- **Tie wraps** Tie wraps are a good, strong alternative to Velcro for soft mounting your survey equipment. The only downside to tie wrap use is that you normally must cut the tie wraps to free your equipment. This is not too much of an obstacle because they are relatively inexpensive, especially in bulk if you plan to perform many surveys.

- **Clamps** My personal choice for soft mounting APs, bridges, and antenna are clamps. They are easy to use and reuse, do not wear out easily, and can be low cost. If you plan to perform surveys in many different environments, you will need a range of sizes to accommodate whatever type mounting structure you may encounter. Beam clamps and C-clamps are the most inexpensive, but they typically require both hands to manipulate when mounting your equipment. I prefer the grip action bar clamps that have become increasingly popular. You can generally hold your AP or antenna in one hand and secure the clamp around them using the other hand. Grip action bar clamps are very quick to install and remove, fasten securely to even the most difficult structures, and because they usually have foam rubber grips on them, they do not damage anything.

Performing an Interior Wireless Site Survey

There are specific methodologies for performing wireless site surveys, and these methodologies differ depending on the type of survey you need to perform. There are two main styles of surveys: the interior site survey, sometimes referred to as an in-building survey, and the exterior or point-to-point /point-to-multi-point survey.

You should complete certain steps regardless of the type of site survey you are going to perform. You will want make sure your equipment is operational and preconfigured prior to arriving at the site. You should ensure that your battery packs and laptop batteries are all fully charged. If your customer is providing a man-lift (from the pre-site survey questionnaire), call to be sure it is already on site, available, and can reach the ceiling of the area you are about to survey.

The interior site survey requires you to understand cellular architecture, roaming, and rate shifting. The following sections first explain these interior site survey components and conclude with the actual interior survey method.

Designing for Coverage

Each AP and antenna combination produces a single area of coverage. Each of these single areas is referred to as a cell. Multiple overlapping cells are used to provide wireless coverage for areas larger than a single cell alone can produce. This is cellular architecture.

DSSS wireless LANs have 11 total channels that can be used for RF transmission. Each channel is 22 MHz wide, and all channels combined equal the entire spectrum that can be used for 802.11b wireless LANs. When designing wireless LANs multiple channels become an issue only when overlapping coverage (multiple cells) is required, and this is usually the case in most designs.

When two APs have overlapping coverage (they have a cellular architecture), each AP must use a different channel so that the client can distinguish the difference the between the RF for each AP. The only three channels that do not overlap concurrently are channels 1, 6, and 11.

Rate requirements also factor into the cellular architecture of a wireless coverage area because the distance from an AP affects the data rate. The data rate decreases as the coverage area increases until of course, you have no coverage at all.

Depending on the coverage rate required for a given area, you may need more or less APs to fulfill the coverage requirements. As you can see in Figure 4.11, it will require many more APs configured at the 11 Mbps rate to cover a specific area than to cover the same area with APs configured at the 2 Mbps rate. Bandwidth is sacrificed for distance.

You can extend the coverage for a client by using an AP in repeater mode to extend the coverage of an existing AP. The repeater AP does not have a wired connection the network, instead, the client associates to the wired, root AP *through* the AP acting as a repeater. This solution can provide additional coverage when the wiring infrastructure is not available for another AP. There are limitations to the use of repeaters to extend coverage. You cannot continuously add APs in repeater mode to gain extremely long coverage areas. Repeater cells need 50 percent overlap with a wired AP cell. Each repeater loses approximately half its normal coverage distance as they are added farther away from the wired root AP.

For example, you may have about 200 feet of 11 Mbps coverage from a wired, root AP. You add one repeater, and you gain an additional 100 feet of 11 Mbps coverage. The next repeater you add will give you approximately 50 feet of additional coverage and so on. Eventually, adding an AP in repeater mode will give you only nominal additional coverage at 11 Mbps.

Figure 4.11 Cellular Architecture

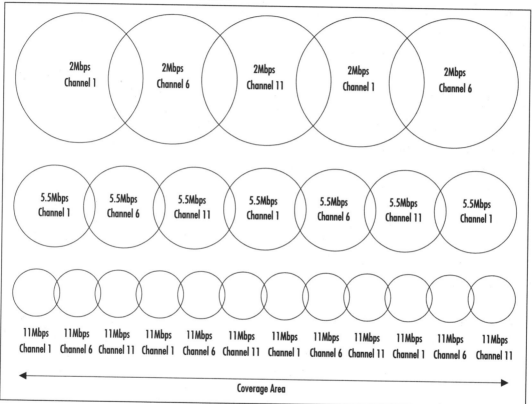

Generally within buildings, the availability of Ethernet connections is fairly predominant. Repeaters are typically used to extend APs from the building edge to the surrounding outdoor portions or additional rooms of a building as a temporary measure. As an example, the owner of a retail store may use APs in repeater mode to extended coverage into the parking lot of their facility during an outdoor tent sale.

Designing Seamless Roaming

When a client travels throughout a wireless cell (one AP coverage area), this is called *roaming*. The *smooth* transition from one wireless cell to another (one AP coverage area to another) is called *seamless roaming*. A large factor when designing a wireless system is determining whether clients require seamless roaming. All devices that require seamless roaming must be turned on when moving from location to location. Seamless roaming is not required for devices that are turned off before being moved. Several factors are involved when designing and surveying for a wireless LAN that requires seamless roaming. You must ensure overlapping coverage for the entire roaming path, you must maintain a consistent client IP address, and you must stay on the same subnetwork.

If a client is going to travel between more than one AP, coverage must exist for the entire path. The IP address must be consistent within the coverage area because the client will acquire its IP address at its starting point and use that address throughout the path. If the IP subnet for each AP is located on separate switches, and the switch is a Layer 3 switch or is separated from the other switch by Layer 3 devices, such as a router, you should consider using switch trunking, such as Inter-Switch Link (ISL) or 802.1Q to span the VLANs to ensure that a single broadcast domain is used for all APs.

As we have discussed previously, multipath distortion can be a problem in RF. The transmission between a client and an AP travels on radio frequency. Those signals interact with the surrounding environment and can be deflected while in transit to the AP. Under optimal conditions, the RF signals arrive at their destination in the same order in which they were sent. There is a good possibility that some of the RF signals will reflect off surrounding objects and arrive out of phase at the antenna, which causes the signals to cancel each other out and result in inoperability. This scenario is very similar to TCP packets arriving out of order within a wired LAN infrastructure.

If the RF between the two devices is strong, it can sometimes give the misperception of good connectivity. Even if the signal strength is good, the signal quality might be poor, thus causing traffic performance to suffer. By adding a second antenna to the AP, you can increase the area in which signals are received and thus minimize, if not eliminate, the "dead path" and increase the signal quality and performance. Using antennas in this way, with APs, is called *antenna diversity*. The AP chooses the best antenna and uses that antenna to receive signals. Only one antenna at a time is active; the active one is selected on a per-client basis for the optimal signal. It applies only to a specific client. The AP can jump back and forth between the antennas when talking to different clients.

Cisco wireless network cards (client interfaces) can also use antenna diversity because they have a diversified antenna built in to them or have diversified antennas available externally. Whether using an AP or a client card, you can turn off the diversity through the configuration menu of both devices. Antenna diversity is used to overcome multipath issues, not to increase the coverage area of an AP.

When configuring APs for cellular coverage, the amount of overlap required to allow a mobile client to seamlessly roam throughout the coverage area is approximately 15 percent. The amount of this overlap depends upon how mobile the users will be. In a highly mobile environment, the amount of overlap required to allow the users to seamlessly roam may be higher than would normally be required. Your site survey will allow you to determine how much overlap will be necessary in your environment. Be sure to test this roaming capability in your environment and especially in highly mobile user environments by performing the roaming yourself as closely as possible to the actual use the wireless system will see when in production.

Considering Rate Shifting

Rate shifting refers to the capability of the wireless client to negotiate the data rate at which it sends and receives at any given distance from the AP. This is also referred to as *auto rate negotiation*. As an example, a client negotiates the best speed of 11 Mbps while in close proximity to an AP. As the client moves away from the AP and the distance increases, the speed (rate) is renegotiated to allow for the best possible signal quality. These rates shift down from 11 Mbps to 5.5 Mbps to 2 Mbps to finally 1 Mbps if the AP is configured to allow this rate shifting function. Cisco APs give you the ability to specify the rates that they will "shift to." For example, you may configure your AP to only allow rate shifting from 11 Mbps to 5.5 Mbps. This will have the effect that a client roaming away from an AP will renegotiate its speed to 5.5 Mbps from 11 Mbps, but will lose its association (and therefore connectivity) to the AP if they roam out of range of the 5.5 Mbps coverage instead of shifting down to 2 Mbps.

Performing the Interior Survey

In your interior wireless site survey, you will need to determine the coverage area produced by the AP/antenna combination you chose in your rough design and intend to use in your implementation. This is done by temporarily installing your AP and antenna, then using your Cisco Aironet Client Utility (ACU) application installed on a laptop computer with a wireless network card to verify the signal rate (11, 5.5, 2, or 1 Mbps) in the area. If your customer has specified that they require 11 Mbps coverage throughout the coverage area, you move your laptop to the point where the 11 Mbps rate drops to 5.5 Mbps. This point where the rate drops is the outer edge of your 11 Mbps coverage area and should be annotated on a scaled drawing of the room or area. The scaled drawing of the room or area may have been provided by your customer, or if it has not been provided, you will need to draw this coverage on your graph paper in your site survey kit. Typically, you will start by placing your AP/antenna combination in the corner of the room or area (see Figure 4.12, A) and survey the coverage of that AP, making a note of where the furthest point of coverage is from that AP. You will then move the AP/antenna combination to the annotated point and survey the coverage again. If you were to leave your AP in the corner for an implementation, you would waste as much as 75 percent of your coverage cell radiating an area outside the building or an area on the other side of a wall that does not require coverage. You may need to move the AP several times in order to find the best placement and coverage pattern.

Once you have established this first coverage cell, move to another corner of the facility (see Figure 4.12, B) and repeat the process until you have surveyed the entire area (see Figure 4.12, C and D). In larger facilities, you may need to repeat these steps from the entire perimeter and/or center of the facility in order to fill in "gaps" in the coverage area. You must overlap your coverage cells in order to have seamless roaming in the area.

Figure 4.12 Survey from Corners to Middle until You Achieve the Best Coverage Area

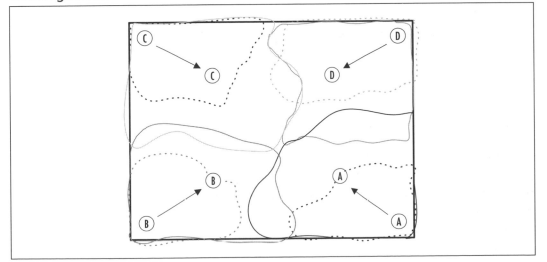

Once you have determined the best coverage for the entire area, it will be extremely important for you to both annotate the AP and antenna placement on your drawing and place markers from your site survey kit at these locations. Be sure to photograph the area (with the markers in place) with your digital camera before proceeding to a new survey area.

In addition to the locations, you should take into account that only three non-overlapping channels are available and annotate the channel your AP is using in each cell of coverage. Be sure to change the channel to the channel you intend to use during the installation for each cell. For example, cell A in your rough design may be using channel 1. In the same room, cell B is supposed to use channel 6. Be sure to change your survey AP's channel to 6 before surveying cell B. This is done to ensure the accuracy of your site survey. It would be embarrassing to install the second AP only to discover that channel 6 has severe interference on it, drastically reducing the 11 Mbps coverage area for cell B, when you could have identified and corrected this prior to installation had you not surveyed the entire area on channel 1.

During your survey, you may discover that you have too much overlap in some of your coverage cells. One or more APs may be providing too much coverage in an area, but without them, there is too little coverage. At this point you have a few choices. You can add more APs and use smaller antennas (lower dBi rated antennas), or you may elect to use the same number of APs, but increase the coverage by using larger antennas. Still another option is to change the power levels on one or more APs, thus changing the size of the coverage cells. You may have to use some combination of these options to properly achieve your coverage goals.

Using the Cisco Aironet Client Utility for Interior Site Surveys

You may ask yourself, how will I determine the point at which my coverage ends during the survey? How can I tell if my signal strength and quality are acceptable in a given area? What speed am I currently using? Cisco has conveniently provided you with the tool you will need to answer these questions. The tool is called the Aironet Client Utility (ACU), which allows you to measure signal quality, signal strength, rates, lost packets, and more. This section covers the use of the ACU in terms of your interior site survey. You can also find more information on the ACU in Chapter 8.

Within the ACU are several screens giving you the ability to configure your wireless client for power modes, SSID, and other parameters. Among these screens is the site survey screen. You can use the site survey screen (see Figure 4.13) to help determine the best placement or coverage (overlap) for your APs. The current RF status is read from your Cisco wireless network card four times per second to provide you with a gauge of the signal strength, beacons, overall link quality, and the current AP association. The site survey screen also displays the IP address of the associated AP, the name of the AP, and the frequency channel the client is using to communicate with the AP. In addition, trends over time, in graphic representations on the site survey screen indicate signal strength, beacons received, and link speed (rate).

Figure 4.13 Passive Mode Site Survey ACU Screen

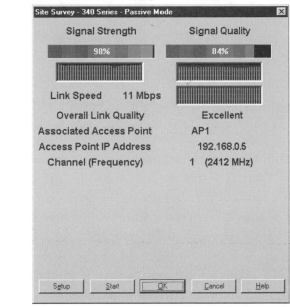

The site survey tool operates in two distinct modes: passive (the default) and active. The passive mode does not initiate any RF network traffic, it merely listens to any RF network traffic that the Cisco wireless network card hears. The active mode (see Figure 4.14) will actively send and/or receive packets to or from the associated AP, and update the Percent Complete, Percent Successful, Lost To Target, Lost To Source, and Percent Retries accordingly.

Lost To Target indicates the number of packets that were not received by the other device. Lost To Source indicates the number of packets that were lost on the way back to your wireless network card. Packets may be lost due to interference from other devices producing RF, because you are on the edge of the radio reception range, or due to multipath distortion.

Figure 4.14 Active Mode Site Survey ACU Screen

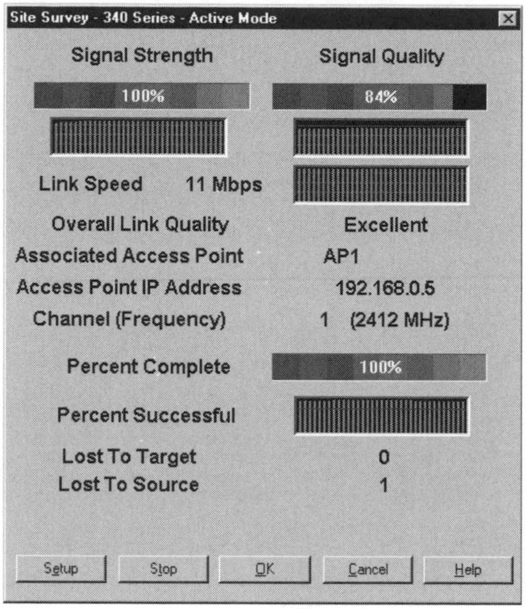

To set up the Active Mode, click **Setup** at the bottom of the page. To start the Active Mode, click **Start**. To stop the Active Mode and return to Passive Mode, click **Stop** (the Start button changes to the Stop button while the Active Mode test is running). Otherwise, Active Mode will change back to Passive Mode once the Percent Complete has reached 100 percent.

Overall Link Quality is an indication of the ability of the Cisco wireless network card to successfully communicate with an AP. Ratings are Excellent, Good, Fair, and Poor. It is derived from the current signal strength and current signal quality. A result of Excellent indicates that both values are greater than 75 percent; Good indicates that both values are greater than 40 percent, but one (or both) is less than 75 percent; Fair indicates that both values are greater than 20 percent, but one (or both) is less than 40 percent; and finally, Poor indicates that one or both values is less than 20 percent. When I perform a site survey, I have found my overall link quality should be Good or Excellent for the implementation—anything less is unacceptable.

You also have the option to display the Signal Strength in dBm, the Signal Quality as Noise Level (in dBm), and the Overall Link Quality as the Signal to Noise Ratio. You can do this from the Preferences menu.

Figure 4.15 Active Mode Setup Page

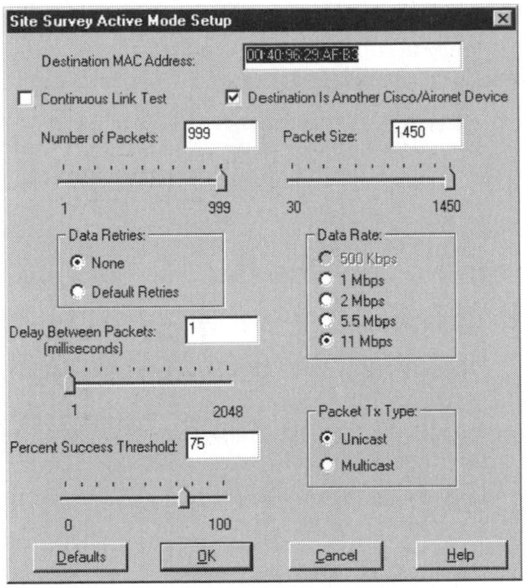

The Active Mode Site Survey Setup page (see Figure 4.15) allows you to set the parameters for the active mode. You can change the following parameters:

- **Destination MAC Address** This parameter allows you to select the AP, by MAC address, with which you will perform the active mode test. The default MAC address is the address of the AP that you are currently associated to via your wireless network card. The active mode test will not roam to other APs, allowing you to determine the size of a single cell. You should make sure the address in this field is the AP you are currently using at that moment in your survey and not another survey AP that just happens to be on in the area.

- **Number of Packets** Sets the quantity of packets that will be sent.

- **Continuous Link Test** Causes the active mode test to run repeatedly until you click **OK** or **Stop** on the Site Survey page. (The test will loop repeatedly for the number of packets that you specified). You should choose to perform this test at least once per area you survey to provide you with continuous feedback of your RF link as you survey. It will give you information on expected loss over a period of time at any given survey point.

- **Packet Size** Sets the size of the packet to be sent. The packet size should be set to the packet size that can be expected to traverse this wireless segment when it is in production.

- **Data Retries** The number of times to retry a transmission if an ACK is not received from the destination.

- **Data Rates** Sets the bit rate at which the packet will be transmitted. No rate shifting will be performed.

- **Delay Between Packets** Sets the delay (in milliseconds) between successive transmissions.

- **Packet Tx Type** Unicast—expects an ACK back from the destination and retries can occur. Multicast—No packet retries.

- **Packet Success Threshold** The percentage of packets that are not lost. This parameter controls the red line on the "Percent Successful" histogram. Percentages greater than or equal to this value will show up as green bars; percentages below this value will show up as yellow bars on the Percent Successful histogram.

Watching Your Power Consumption

When using wireless network cards, power consumption while surveying (roaming) is going to be an issue because devices within the laptop will use power, and the laptop battery has a limited life. Three modes for power are available on Cisco wireless network cards:

- **CAM—Constant Awake Mode** CAM is best for devices when power is not an issue. This would be when AC power is available to the device, and it provides the best connectivity option, and therefore, the most available wireless infrastructure from the client perspective.

- **PSP—Power Save Mode** Select PSP when power conservation is of the utmost importance. In this mode, the wireless network card will go to sleep after a period of inactivity and periodically wake to retrieve buffered data from the AP.

- **FastPSP—Fast Power Save Mode** FastPSP is a combination of CAM and PSP. This is good for clients who switch between AC and DC power.

I typically choose to use FastPSP in my site surveys because I am usually able to plug my laptop into AC power for short periods of time during the survey.

Setting Your Service Set IDs

Service set IDs (SSIDs) are required for clients to communicate to APs. You can define three possible SSIDs on the client, although you can configure only one on the AP. The most common configuration within a corporation has the SSIDs the same for all APs. SSIDs act as a password, allowing the client to gain access into the infrastructure through the APs. The default SSID for the Cisco products is "tsunami"; it is preconfigured in the shipping product. By default, the AP is configured for "Allow Broadcast SSID to Associate = YES," this means that clients do not have to have an SSID configured to associate to the AP. The recommended setting for SSIDs while surveying is to have the AP configured to "Allow Broadcast SSID to Associate = NO". If the AP and client SSIDs do not match, the association between the two will not happen, and access will not be granted. This will force you to configure your client with the matching SSID, but will give you a more accurate survey because most organizations require SSIDs in their wireless systems.

You can find more information on SSIDs, power modes, and how to configure them on your wireless client in Chapter 7.

Interior Survey Problems

Wireless site surveys are a process of trial and error. Experience is the best way to overcome many of these problems, but this may not be possible for the one-time surveyor. Most, if not all, problems encountered during your site survey are a result of unexpected design, business, or environmental issues. You may find yourself trying option after option to force a solution to a problem. This is where frustration sets in. You may find yourself working on a single thought process over and over because you don't want to start the survey over again. If you find yourself in this situation, take a break. Get a cup of coffee, go to lunch, just get away from the problem for a bit and more times than not you will find the solution to the problem presents itself upon your return. If it does not, you really may need to wipe the slate clean and start your survey over. By starting over, you will be aware of the trouble spots in your survey and will be able to factor this knowledge in when planning the layout of your APs again. Starting the survey over again and designing the wireless LAN properly is always better than trying to force or use a solution that may not provide the best coverage and performance.

Sometimes, the location of your APs may be dictated by available network connectivity. For example, copper Ethernet cabling has a length limit of 328 feet. No matter what the problem you encounter, there is almost always a way around it.

Your customer may restrict antenna and AP placement to one or two walls of a facility, as in the Andromeda Manufacturing design. We were able to work around this problem and survey the area successfully by using directional antennas to "shoot" coverage down the aisles of the warehouse.

Some business may want coverage in a large walk-in freezer in their facility. Of course they didn't tell you this until you came out to perform your site survey. How will you handle this issue? The freezer is much too cold for the AP to be placed in it without expensive heated enclosures. Is this the only solution to the problem? You could mount the AP outside the freezer and install the antenna (which can withstand the cold) inside to provide the coverage required. You could even use antenna splitters to provide coverage both inside and outside the freezer for an even more cost-efficient solution to coverage. The only caveat for your antennas is to not use both antenna connections on your Cisco AP to provide this coverage (see Figure 4.16). Remember, when using antenna diversity the AP uses one antenna or the other, never both.

Figure 4.16 Antenna Splitters

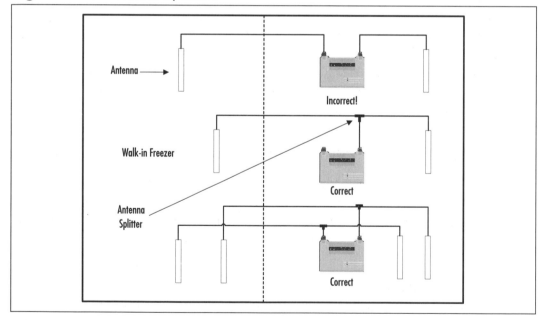

Take caution when surveying multifloor facilities because APs on different floors can cause as much interference as if they were located on the same floor. You can possibly use this bleed-through to your advantage in your design. During your site survey, you may be able to penetrate floors and ceilings with a single AP to provide coverage for floors above and below you by using a larger antenna.

Performing an Exterior Wireless Site Survey

Exterior site surveys are very different from the interior surveys. This type of survey requires drastically fewer physical survey procedures but much more thought and analysis than interior surveys. Much of this has to do with the nature of point-to-point implementations. Unlike the interior site survey, exterior site surveys are performed without the use of the ACU. This is because clients will not directly associate with the bridges as they do with APs. The bridges simply link two or more wired LANs together to provide connectivity. However, specific steps and tools allow you to perform your survey.

Because you are usually attempting to transmit a signal over some distance, signal attenuation (loss) is of significant importance during your survey. Every component used in an exterior survey produces some loss. Cabling, connectors, splitters, the environment, and weather all affect the distance you may achieve during your site survey. When performing this type of survey, signal attenuation (loss) in your survey is of the highest importance, because the signal is not spread around as in interior wireless implementations and therefore is not as forgiving of interference and multipath issues.

Point-to-point and point-to-multipoint wireless implementations use bridges rather than APs to achieve wireless connectivity. These bridges are designed to interconnect two or more wired LANs, using narrow RF transmissions or beams over distances up to 25 miles. As with the APs, the bridges will require a wired connection to the network and either conventional power (340 Series) or inline power fed directly through the RJ-45 interface on the bridge (350 Series).

The steps for performing this type of site survey consists of the following:

- **Link distance determination** You will need to determine the distance of each site to be connected. This is the distance from a transmitting antenna to a receiving antenna. If these distances are long, you may wish to use the odometer in your car or a GPS to calculate this. You may already have gathered this information to create your rough design.

- **Fresnel zone calculation** The next and most complicated step in the survey process, is to determine the radio line of sight for the wireless link. This is done by calculating the wireless link's Fresnel zone and possibly taking into account the curvature of the Earth (depending on link distances). If you already have your link distances and building or tower heights for your antennas, you can perform this step prior to arriving for the site survey.

Designing & Planning...

Calculating the Fresnel Zone

A bit of mathematics is required to calculate the size of the Fresnel zone radius at its widest point (midpoint radius). The following formula (see Figure 4.17) will allow you to calculate the radius in feet of the widest point in your Fresnel zone:

Figure 4.17 Fresnel Zone Radius Formula

$$R = 72.1 \sqrt{\frac{d_1 d_2}{F_{GHz}(d_1 + d_2)}}$$

where
d1 = the distance from the transmitting antenna (to the midpoint in the path)
d2 = the distance from the receiving antenna (to the midpoint in the path)
F = the frequency in gigahertz (GHz)
R = the radius of the first Fresnel zone (at the midpoint)
For d1 and d2, it is usually much easier to determine the entire path length and divide that by 2 to get the distance for d1 and d2. So a 7-mile path length would have d1 and d2 values of 3.5 each.

Also you can replace the 72.1 parameter with 43.3 (60 percent of 72.1) to give you your 60 percent clearance factor right off the bat, without having to calculate this later. Here is how I calculate my Fresnel zone. I have a total path distance of 7 miles. I divide my 7 miles by 2 to get my d1 and d2 values. In this case, it is 3.5. Multiplying 3.5 times 3.5 gives me 12.25. I then take my total path distance in miles (7) times 2.4 (my frequency in GHz) to produce a value of 16.8. I now divide 12.25 by 16.8 to get a value of .729. The square root of .729 is .854. I now multiply .854 times 72.1 to result in my midpoint Fresnel zone radius of 61.57 feet. I need 60 percent of this radius for a good link path, so I take my radius value (61.57) times 0.6 to get my antenna height for this link, which is approximately 36 feet.

Once you have calculated the Fresnel zone's largest radius point, you must then determine what obstructions, if any, obstruct the ellipse more than 40 percent into the Fresnel zone (see Figure 4.18). If you have

Continued

more than this percentage of path interference, you will experience transmission loss. Remember that the Fresnel zone should be clear of obstructions all year round. Many a surveyor has been tripped up by trees in their Fresnel zone. When surveyed in the fall or winter, the trees did not have any leaves and therefore did not cause much, if any, interference with the signal. Summer arrives and they have to return to correct the antenna height because the leaves in the trees in the Fresnel zone were so thick they caused noticeable interference. You should also consider a tree that may be very close to 40 percent of your zone, because it will grow and eventually hit this mark.

Figure 4.18 Fresnel Zone Clearance

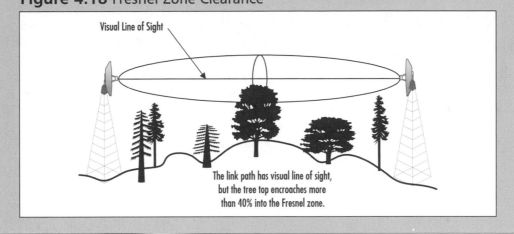

Link Setup and Testing Once you have completed the previous tasks, you will set up your wireless link based on your rough design. This will entail determining antenna alignment, identifying cable lengths required, power requirements, wired connectivity for the bridge unit, and available infrastructure hardware (such as a switch for the wired connectivity to the network). The testing portion encompasses verification of connectivity and determination of optimal performance factors such as signal quality and strength and packet loss. You will use the tools built in to your Cisco bridge to acquire this information. We cover more on these bridge tools and configurations for point-to-point and point-to-multipoint wireless implementations in detail in Chapter 6.

Link Impairment Identification and Consideration You will need to identify and consider all the design obstacles we covered earlier in the chapter (see the "Wireless Planning Considerations" section), with special attention paid to possible link impairments and taller-than-esti-mated trees, new building construction that may be in the path, and potential reflection points (such as flat, paved roads, pools, or other bodies of water). These considerations, if any, will then need to be cor-rected, and the solutions worked into your final design.

Designing & Planning...

Calculating Antenna Height

Calculating antenna height simply requires you to determine the Fresnel zone radius and plan your implementation height so that your zone clears any obstructions by no less than 60 percent. When planning for paths longer than seven miles, the curvature of the Earth might become a factor in path planning and require that the antenna be located higher off the ground. To calculate the additional height due to curvature of the Earth, use the following formula:

$$H = D^2/8$$

where
H = Additional height of the antenna (in feet)
D = Distance between antennas (in miles)

For example, we have already calculated our midpoint Fresnel zone and antenna height to be about 36 feet (for our 7-mile path). Now because we are 7 miles apart, we must consider the additional height required to compensate for the curvature of the Earth. By using the previous formula, we are able to determine that we will require approximately 6 additional feet to the antenna height to bring our total height requirement to approximately 42 feet.

Wireless Design Examples

The following examples of both interior and exterior wireless designs will help guide you through some of the more common wireless implementations.

Warehouse Design Example 1

The example in Figure 4.19 shows a design for a warehouse in which wireless coverage is the maximum concern for the customer. Automatic rate negotiation will be used because coverage is the primary concern and cabling is available to all points in the store. The warehouse has a very high ceiling and the visibility of antennas to the customers is not of concern; therefore, we chose a high-gain, mast-mount antenna for the maximum coverage.

Figure 4.19 Warehouse Example 1

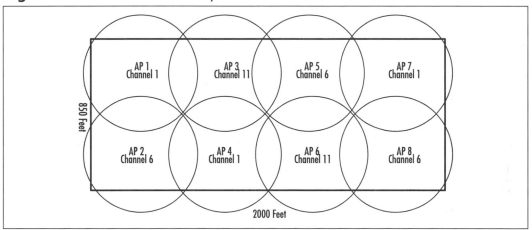

Warehouse Design Example 2

Here in Figure 4.20 is the same warehouse as described in the previous section, but instead of using the high-gain, omni-directional antenna, we used the patch antennas and one rubber dipole to provide coverage for the facility. With this design, we were able to get identical coverage using different types of antennas but with two less APs.

Figure 4.20 Warehouse Example 2

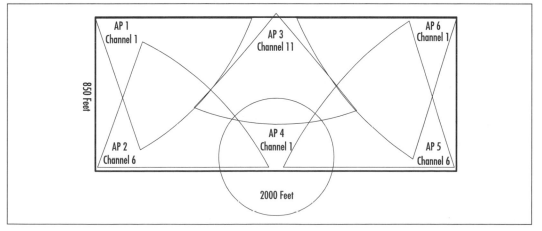

One possible reason to use the patch antennas could be that cabling for wired Ethernet is not available in the middle of the warehouse and is available only around the edges of the facility. Therefore, the patch antennas in the warehouse would increase coverage from the perimeter.

Warehouse Design Example 3

Figure 4.21 depicts the same warehouse except in this situation Ethernet wiring is available only in the front of the warehouse. Racking extends all of the way to the ceiling and runs with the aisles extending the length of the building. In addition to the changes in racking, the data closet is located near the right side of the building.

Figure 4.21 Warehouse Example 3

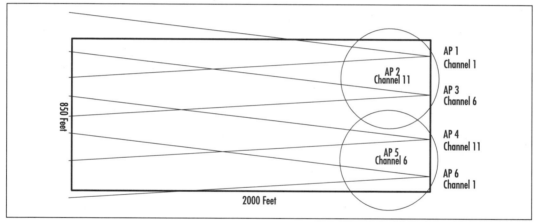

Because the forklifts will need to extend very close to the ceiling height and because the racking extends from floor to ceiling making it difficult for the RF coverage to leak through the racks, different antennas must be deployed.

We've decided to use the Yagi antenna with a small beam but long distance at the front and a couple of dipole antennas to complete the storefront coverage.

Retail Design Example

Retail implementations often involve a large number of users sending data very frequently. Stores are likely to do their inventorying at night. This can mean that there will be a limited number of users during the normal store hours, which does not tax the WLAN.

But when the inventory crew comes in at night, the customer expects that the WLAN will be able to handle the demand. You need to work with the store manager to determine how often they do inventory, how many data collection devices will be used, and what the requirements are for their particular application.

Also ask if they will require coverage on the loading docks or inside the trucks at the loading docks. Depending on the WLAN design, enough RF coverage may be bleeding through to the outside of the buildings to accommodate this, but you should not depend upon this unless you have factored it into your design.

Other concerns within the retail industry include the close proximity of the store to other RF devices. Some stores may stock and demo RF devices in their store. These may include satellite systems, baby monitors, or cordless phones. Many of these may be 900 MHz, but some may also be 2.4GHz. In any case, you shouldn't install APs next to this type of equipment. Typically these devices have a higher output than the APs. Also be aware that many stores use internal cordless phone systems. Encourage them to use a system that operates on a different frequency (900 MHz). It is far less expensive to replace a few cordless phones than to try and design a WLAN around an existing phone system that interferes.

Retail stores may also be located in malls or strip malls where there may be other users operating 2.4 GHz equipment. Examine this possibility before starting the site survey. Talk with surrounding store managers about their systems. If other systems are in the area, you will have to try and separate the stores by channel, SSID, and so on.

The design shown in Figure 4.22 represents a retail store in which the customer is concerned with maximum coverage at 2 Mbps because of third-party interoperability with bar coding products that do not support auto negotiation. Cabling is available throughout the store, but one concern is to make sure that the antennas are well hidden from the browsing shoppers. For this reason, a ground plane antenna is chosen so that it can be flatly mounted on a drop-down ceiling permitting the antenna to blend in and not be easily seen.

Education Design Example 1

The design shown in Figure 4.23 is for an educational environment that is very similar to our warehouse environment with the exception of the walls between the classrooms. We are able to provide enough coverage using the rubber dipole antennas attached to the APs. The school is concerned that the students using the APs could gain access to the production network, so the APs will be on a firewall. Connectivity for the teachers will be handled by Ethernet switches in the wiring closets and Category 5 cable pulled into the classroom teaching stations.

Figure 4.22 Retail Example

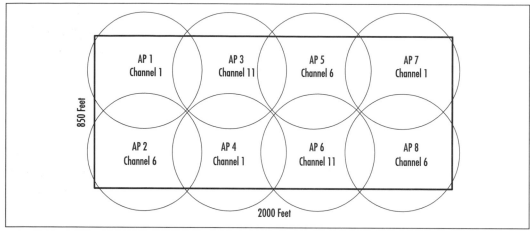

Figure 4.23 Education Example 1

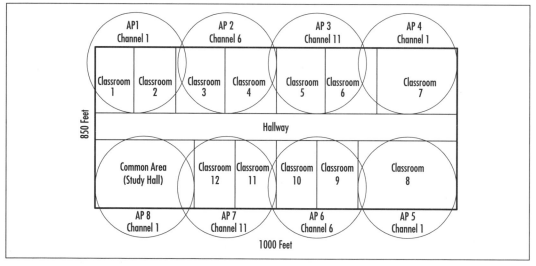

Education Design Example 2

In education solutions, wireless is popular in higher education and colleges where students require more mobile options. In the example shown in Figure 4.24, we've chosen to locate the patch antennas directly outside the building, allowing coverage in the courtyard for students who work outside.

Figure 4.24 Education Example 2

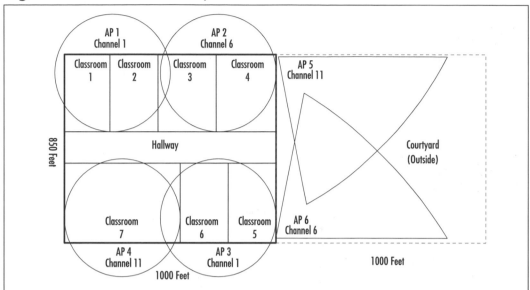

Point-to-Point Design Example 1

The site-to-site design example shown in Figure 4.25 is for a point-to-point connection where two buildings need to have a bridge link between them across a freeway. The required distance is only half a mile, therefore the antennas need to be mounted at 13 feet. This height will be exceeded because the buildings are higher than that.

The cabling from the bridge to the antenna is 20 feet in building A and 50 feet in building B. This is not a significant problem on the link because the distance is so short that it does not severely impact the design.

Patch antennas were chosen in this example because the beam is kept focused, and there will be no interference from other companies. Distances at 11 Mbps in this scenario allow you to go .81 miles; 2 Mbps rates allow you go 2.57 miles.

Point-to-Point Design Example 2

The design in Figure 4.26 shows a headquarters building within a metropolitan area where three separate point-to-point links have been implemented. It is possible that the point-to-point links are required because of interference from other companies using wireless LANs and point to multipoint is not an option. Each building will receive greater bandwidth than used with point-to-multipoint because there is no shared bandwidth here. Antenna mounting is not a concern because of the short distance and existing building heights. Possible distances at 11 Mbps in this scenario are .57 miles; 1.82 miles at 2 Mbps.

Figure 4.25 Point-to-Point Example 1

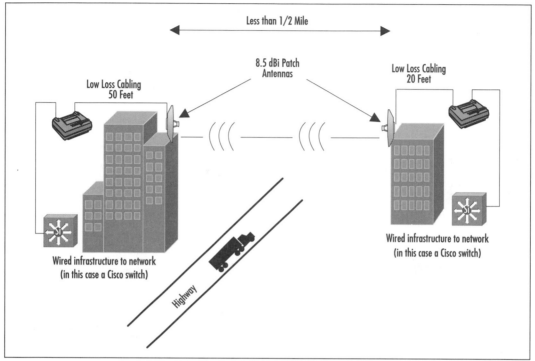

Figure 4.26 Point-to-Point Example 2

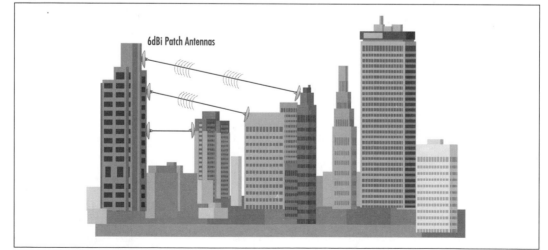

Point-to-Point Design Example 3

The design example shown in Figure 4.27 is in a rural area that requires a distance of 25 miles. Because of the long distance, parabolic dishes are chosen and cable lengths are kept to a minimum to ensure the greatest possible distance.

This distance precludes the use of 11 Mbps, therefore, 2 Mbps will be used, which is within the specification.

Even though the possible distance of 2 Mbps is 50 miles, please be sure and note that line–of–sight over 25 miles is difficult to align.

Figure 4.27 Point-to-Point Example 3

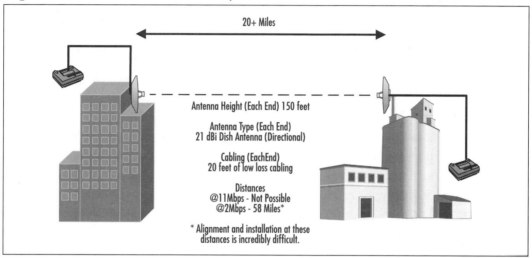

Summary

Your wireless design process has three stages or phases. They are the planning phase, rough design phase, and wireless site survey. It is imperative that you carefully evaluate the requirements of your business, users, and applications in order to determine the feasibility of a wireless solution in your environment. Be sure to evaluate the application traffic that you may expect on the wireless LAN, the types of applications used and the number of users in a given cell. User expectations should be set throughout your design and implementation processes to ensure the support and success of your final implementation. Establishing the expected performance of your wireless LAN with your users will not only help you during implementation, but also will ease support of your wireless LAN after the installation. Build a business case for your proposed wireless implementation to include return on investment, productivity benefits, and cost savings resulting from more efficient processes.

A thorough wireless site survey and test of your initial wireless LAN design is your best bet to ensure the success of your implementation. The site survey will provide you with the information necessary to turn your initial design into a completed design that is ready for implementation. It will allow you to factor in previously unknown environmental variables, such as interference from other radio frequency devices and obstructions, and it will allow you to verify coverage areas, channel settings, throughput, antenna/radio placement, wired network availability, and power requirements prior to a permanent installation. When performing your wireless site survey, be sure to configure your radio devices (APs or bridges) because they will be configured in the permanent installation. Try to use the same radio devices and antennas that you plan to use in the permanent installation where possible. Utilize a pre-site survey questionnaire to gather as much information as possible about the intended wireless location. The more information you can gather prior to your site survey, the better equipped you will be to perform it.

The right tools for the wireless site survey will make the process much more efficient. Be sure to include tools that will allow you to temporarily, but securely, attach your APs and antennas. Include measuring tools for both vertical and horizontal measurements and always bring along paper and pencil to take notes during the survey.

A good understanding of attenuation and its common causes are an integral part of your wireless LAN design and implementation. Take particular note of metal obstructions, cordless phones, and microwave ovens for interior designs, and weather, Earth curvature, and natural obstructions for exterior designs. Remember, line of sight for exterior designs is not all that is needed for a point-to-point implementation. The Fresnel zone, the elliptical path formed between two directional antennas, must be at least 60 percent clear of path obstructions to be considered for a point-to-point installation. Interior designs that require roaming, should have at least a 30 percent overlap in the cells to allow for a smooth transition from one coverage cell to another.

Every wireless LAN design and implementation will be different, based on the requirements of the business, the geography, applications, obstacles, weather, existing infrastructure and number of users. You should take this into account when designing and site surveying. Do not assume anything.

Solutions Fast Track

Wireless Planning Considerations

☑ Ask yourself the questions necessary to determine if wireless is right for your situation.

☑ Remember, throughput and data rate are not the same thing. You should determine your company's throughput requirements as a first step in planning your wireless solution.

☑ The difference between mobile and highly mobile users is of significant importance to your wireless design; be sure to identify this early in your planning process.

Wireless Design Considerations

☑ An understanding of attenuation is extremely important in exterior wireless implementations and surveys. Make sure that you understand these considerations and keep them in mind when surveying.

☑ Make sure that you list all of the potential wireless issues you could face when surveying. Multipath issues, construction materials, weather, and application considerations should top your list.

☑ Make sure that your clients expectations are set by you, and be thorough when asking questions to your organization's representatives.

Wireless Site Surveys

☑ The pre-site survey questionnaire is an invaluable tool for preparing for your site survey. Ensure you have most if not all of your questions answered before you arrive on site to survey and call ahead of time to ensure a smooth survey.

☑ The site survey kit will also serve you during installation, so make a reasonable investment in the tools you will use.

☑ Always perform your survey with all hardware and configurations settings as they will be in the potential implementation. This ensures "no surprises" when it comes to actually installing your wireless system.

Frequently Asked Questions

The following Frequently Asked Questions, answered by the authors of this book, are designed to both measure your understanding of the concepts presented in this chapter and to assist you with real-life implementation of these concepts. To have your questions about this chapter answered by the author, browse to **www.syngress.com/solutions** and click on the **"Ask the Author"** form.

Q: Can I use an amplifier to increase my power and distance?

A: Technically, you can achieve great distances with more power. However, in the U.S., federal regulations prohibit you from using an amplifier to increase your signal unless it comes as part of a licensed package.

Q: Can I have five sites at 2 Mbps to a single 11 Mbps center site for better throughput?

A: No, this will have the effect of limiting bandwidth to 2 Mbps for every client who associates to any of the five APs. The bandwidth to the client cannot be aggregated to achieve better throughput.

Q: Can I use a splitter and two antennas?

A: Yes, this will allow you to increase the reliability to receive and transmit data, but it will not substantially increase the coverage area because your power output will be split between antennas.

Q: Can I double my distance with a repeater?

A: You can increase the distance you are covering with a repeater, however, it will not double because the overlap required for repeaters is much greater than for another wired AP.

Chapter 5

Installation and Configuration of Cisco 340 and Cisco 350 Series Access Points

Solutions in this chapter:

- Installation of the Cisco 340/350 Series AP

- Initial Configuration of the Cisco 340 and 350 Series AP

- Web-Based Configuration of the Cisco 340 and 350 Series APs

- Web-Based Configuration of the Cisco 340 BSE/BSM Series AP

- ☑ Summary

- ☑ Solutions Fast Track

- ☑ Frequently Asked Questions

Introduction

The installation and configuration of the Cisco Aironet access points (APs) is relatively simple for most administrators, however, there are some complexities that arise as the installation becomes more complex or involves more APs. In addition, the configuration of the wireless "connections" between the APs and the clients is a little more difficult than following a simple 100-meter rule in wired Ethernet. Interference from cordless phones, walls, partitions, microwaves and other hindrances can quickly complicate the wireless installation.

Aside from these differences, the general steps are very consistent with wired installations. IP addresses, management, and documentation are all key to the successful deployment of a wireless network.

Other challenges that may confront the designer of the wireless network include security and management. Inclusive in this list is the need to control the WEP keys should this security model be used—note that it is no longer recommended because it may quickly be compromised, however, it is better than no security at all. Lightweight Extensible Authentication Protocol/Extensible Authentication Protocol (LEAP/EAP) management requires the use of a security server running Remote Authentication Dial In User Service (RADIUS), a protocol developed by Livingston Enterprises for transport of authentication and configuration information over the User Datagram Protocol (UDP), which exchanges the keys to the receiver. This is still a WEP-based installation, but the variance is that the key is no longer of unlimited duration. In WEP, the key is stored in the network interface card (NIC), and loss of the NIC may require an entire enterprise to change their WEP key. Please note that there are two WEP standards—the 40-bit key specified in the Wi-Fi (802.11b) interoperability standard. This key length should interoperate with all vendors. The 128-bit key length, which is only marginally more secure, is not always interoperable.

Note that although the Cisco APs can be configured as wireless bridges between buildings, the more common installation is to service a small number of mobile users in hotel, manufacturing floor, or office-to-conference room domains. This chapter, as such, focuses on the configuration of the APs as they relate to wireless 802.11b clients. It is noteworthy that the configuration of the APs as wireless bridges is quite simple once you gain a basic understanding of the client configuration process. Wireless NICs may also be configured for an ad hoc configuration. This setting is defined under the Infrastructure Mode parameter. Because this type of installation is also uncommon and very limited, it is only mentioned in this chapter here.

Designing & Planning...

Planning the Design of a Wireless Network for Today and Tomorrow

For some wireless network installations, the network administrator has little to do other than place the AP on a desk and plug it in. A few configuration changes and a small office can quickly communicate as if they were all wired on a traditional LAN.

However, it is much more likely that your installations will have to consider a number of factors because of its need to scale in the enterprise. These include the following:

- Upgrades to 802.11a
- Interference from 2.4 GHz cordless phones
- Antenna placement for range or appearance reasons
- The use of inline power in various installations
- Integration with SNMP and other management systems
- Frequency selection for capacity or interference reasons
- Security
- Secure Set Identifier (SSID) management
- Wired Equivalent Protocol (WEP) management
- Lightweight Extensible Authentication Protocol (LEAP)/EAP management
- Integration with other vendors' systems

This chapter covers the configuration of the Aironet 340 and 350 series APs, including the Cisco 340 BSE, which is a fixed-configuration Network Address Translation (NAT)-enabled AP. This section addresses those elements that are not part of the main chapter.

One of the first challenges in 802.11b is the limited bandwidth of the system. With an effective data rate of approximately 6 Mbps (depending on traffic type, frame size, operating system, and other factors), it is clear to see that users could quickly perceive the shared model of wireless networking as slow, especially if accustomed to 100 Mbps switched Ethernet. The 802.11a specification will increase throughput to over 40 Mbps (the actual rate is 52 Mbps), however, the technology is

Continued

www.syngress.com

still shared between users. The design challenge is that 802.11a networks will likely have a much shorter range than their 802.11b counterparts due to the frequencies used by the two systems. As such, placement and wiring of an 802.11b network with a single AP may lead to an entire rewire of the wireless APs when migrating to 802.11a. Designers would be better served by planning for an 802.11a installation and only installing 802.11b systems where required.

Interference from 2.4 GHz systems, including cordless phones, is another challenge. Under 802.11a the frequency space is also free for public use, so interference may remain a design concern. Today the 2.4 GHz range is becoming more popular, and conflicts with other systems is a real issue. Again, companies may address this with bans on cordless phones within their control, but this may not be sufficient to prevent a problem if another company nearby allows their use.

Many end-users may be concerned regarding the look of the antennas for wireless networks, in addition to the potential health risks that may be associated with them. For this reason, some companies may implement guidelines to increase the distance between the closest user and the antenna, and antenna selection may include directional systems that radiate power in a single direction instead of in all directions.

The Federal Communications Commission (FCC), in addition to the European Telecommunications Standard and other groups, have established minimum guidelines for the use of radio frequency equipment. Cisco has taken these guidelines (presented in the form of FCC ET docket 96-8, ETS 300.328, and CEPT recommendation T/R 10.01) and documented the safe methods for working with radio frequency equipment, including the Aironet products. These guidelines include never touching the antenna during transmission or reception, always maintaining at least eight inches between the body and the antenna, and not using the antenna near the face or eyes. You can research this further on Cisco's Web site—as of this writing the URL was located at www.cisco.com/ univercd/cc/td/doc/product/wireless/airo_350/accsspts/ap350qs .htm#xtocid271823.

Inline power can negate the need for running distinct power for each AP. In ceiling installations, the ability to run power over the Ethernet cabling is a huge advantage because the administrator does not need to provide a second connection to supply power. Please note that only the 350 series supports inline power, and that many of these installations may use the rugged chassis option.

This chapter discusses this in greater detail; however, inline power is rarely needed for non–large scale installations.

Installation of the Cisco 340/350 Series AP

The installation steps for the Cisco 340 and 350 systems are fairly straightforward and include the following:

- Determine the placement of the AP and select the antenna. Please refer to the Cisco documentation for more information on this process and the current options available.

- Determination if inline power or plenum installation is needed for your installation, noting that the 350 series provides for these needs.

- Selection of the virtual LAN (VLAN) architecture for wireless networks, as discussed later in this section.

- Selection of IP addresses within that VLAN, including the assignment methodology, including Dynamic Host Configuration Protocol (DHCP).

- Selection of the SSID values for your network.

- Determine if WEP will be used and how you will manage the keys. Key management is dependent on the use of RADIUS or static configuration, discussed in this chapter.

- The selection of using LEAP/EAP for WEP services, including the installation and configuration of a capable RADIUS server.

- Selection of a channel for the AP. Note that in the U.S., there are only three nonoverlapping channels that you may use, and you may need to refer to the Cisco documentation for country-specific instruction.

- Determination of the proper settings for management services, including SNMP and Syslog. This will be specific to your network, but this section presents how to configure the AP for interoperation.

- Deciding how to integrate with virtual private networking (VPN) services, including IPSec, to augment security. This is dependent on your installation.

- Deciding if access limitations on resources are warranted for your wireless network. This may be via router access control lists (ACL) or VLAN ACLs (VACLs). You may also choose to use Secure Sockets Layer (SSL) or other security-conscious protocols. This is dependent on your installation.

- Determining if you should use Publicly Secure Packet Forwarding (PSPF) to limit wireless device connectivity. This option is discussed in this chapter.

If the hardware is not yet selected, many administrators would likely choose the Cisco 350 APs and adapters. The differences are minor, but significant. They are outlined in the next section.

Configuring & Implementing...

Enterprise Installations of Wireless Networks

Many corporations have been slow to adopt wireless networking for two very specific reasons. The first is security, which is discussed elsewhere in this chapter. The second is management. Quite simply, few wireless solutions provide the level of network management integration that comes with wired systems. Although this is changing quickly, the likelihood is that network managers will need to manage wireless systems with a degree of manual processes for both the AP and the user's network interface.

Unlike their wired counterparts, wireless networks require a minor degree of configuration for correct operation. (Please note that Windows XP and newer operating systems can change these configuration requirements). In addition to a driver for proper operation, many installations require the configuration of the SSID at a minimum. This parameter controls the domain of the AP when more than one AP exists within the range of the receiver. An example of this would be two companies, one on the fourth floor and on one the fifth of a building, each with its own wireless network. Because the natural behavior of a radio network is to bond with the strongest signal, it is possible to have a wireless NIC in company B attempt to speak with company A's AP.

The SSID provides a simple mechanism for the administrator to control which APs bond with which NICs. It is easy to understand how early users of wireless systems could mistake this with a security measure as well. However, you will not make this error. SSIDs are transmitted in clear text by the AP, and wireless network analyzers are widely available to capture this information for misuse. In Windows XP, the operating system includes this capability as well. The use of the SSID is recommended; it can also control the installation of noncorporate APs, as

Continued

client adapters will be configured to associate with the SSID provided by the corporation. It will not prevent a noncorporate AP from entering the network, but it may prevent most users from bonding with an AP that is within range but not on the wired network—an installation that could be used to access the wireless workstations without needing physical access to the corporate network

Installations are also challenged with the first generation of key management for the security model proposed with 802.11b. The Wired Equivalent Protocol (WEP) is designed to provide a reasonable amount of security for wireless users, however, in the protocol's lifespan, security experts have easily broken the encryption mechanism used. As such, hackers can compromise a WEP installation in a fairly short amount of time, yielding its security features relatively inadequate. Enterprises are left with three options—use the protocol without augmentation; use WEP in concert with SSL, VPN technology, or with LEAP/EAP; or abandon WEP completely and use only alternatives in the wireless network. Many installations already have WEP installed, which means that administrators will need to integrate with existing systems. Of course, new installations may also have comparable issues where the administrator may have limited alternatives to WEP, and, shortcomings aside, is left to use the inadequate security afforded by WEP. Please note that LEAP/EAP does not provide data encryption—they provide a mechanism for key exchange and management. This can limit the duration when a compromised key can be used to decrypt data. A number of freeware tools are available on the Internet for allowing non-expert users to be wardrivers, or wireless LAN decoders. Simply put, if security is your concern, do not rely on WEP, even with LEAP/EAP. The use of VPN IPSec or other encryption protocols would be mandated.

Aside from this, the installation of a wireless network remains similar to wired installations. However, you should always start small, as opposed to removing all the Cat-5 in your campus, when introducing a new technology such as a wireless LAN.

Specific Differences of the Cisco 350 Series AP

Using the Cisco 350 series APs has a few advantages. First, these devices can operate at 100 millawatts (mW), which can greatly increase the range of 802.11b compared to the Cisco 340's 30 mW configuration. Second, the Cisco 350 can accept inline power, or powered Ethernet, which negates the need for a separate power cord. The 350 is also available in a rugged chassis, which may be warranted for your installation, including an in-plenum installation.

In all other regards, the configuration of the 340 and 350 is virtually identical.

Power Requirements

You can choose among three methods for powering the Cisco 350 Series APs—the 340 platform cannot accept inline power, discussed later in this section. The choice of which solution will work best for your particular installation will depend largely on the budget and complexity of your specific circumstances, in addition to the presence of legacy equipment or non-Cisco equipment.

By far the simplest installations will take advantage of the inline power options, which are available on specific modules of the Catalyst series switches, including the Catalyst 6000 (WS-X6248 with the WS-F6K-VPWR daughter card), the 4006 (with the WS-X4148-RJ45V) and 3524-PWR-XL. Each of these products supply power to the Cisco 350 series AP via the standard Ethernet pins—1, 2, 3, and 6. The physical configuration of this installation is shown in Figure 5.1. Please note that this list of modules is not complete, and it is very likely that Cisco will include this feature on new products, in addition to new modules and line cards for existing products when possible.

Figure 5.1 Inline Power

Catalyst Switch

Access Point

For installations where only Ethernet cable is available to the AP, no electrical wiring is present, and the existing hub or switch infrastructure does not support inline power, users may select the WS-PWR-PANEL patch panel. This panel connects in-between the switch or hub and the AP, and is better suited to installations that require a large number of powered Ethernet lines, such as IP telephony. When a single link solution is required, administrators may opt for the Cisco Aironet Power Injector. This is often used for in-the-ceiling installations. The physical characteristics of the powered patch panel installation is shown in Figure 5.2. Please note that all Ethernet powered solutions are limited to 300 feet, which should not present a problem for most installations within the 100-meter rule for Ethernet.

Please refer to your local building codes for the specific requirements regarding power distribution within your construction, including cable types, fire ratings, and other parameters. This is true for commonly referred to *plenum installations* in the raised ceiling, or for other enclosed areas, such as a raised floor.

Figure 5.2 Using the Powered Patch Panel

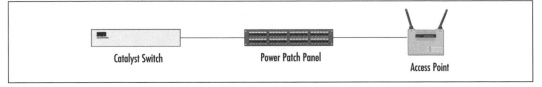

Of course, the AP may also be connected to a standard wall outlet for power. These installations use a "vampire," or AC-to-DC converter transformer, and isolate the power channel from the data path. Figure 5.3 illustrates the connections for this option; note that the Cisco 340 series is powered by this method only. Vampires are also called power packs, or AC adapters. They are commonly black boxes with prongs that enter the wall (AC power source) or a black box in the middle of two connectors—the AC plug that enters the wall and the DC connector (round, dual pole) that enters the electronic device. The term "vampire" is common in the power industry as these devices draw power even when the host device is powered off (note that they are warm to the touch), and they have two "teeth"—the AC prongs.

Figure 5.3 Using Standard Power

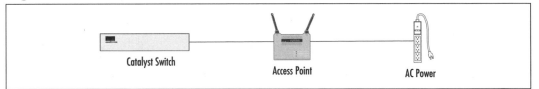

Network Connectivity

Although configuring a wireless network that never touches a traditional wired network is entirely possible, the usability of such an installation is obviously limited. At a minimum, most users expect access to e-mail and other services, if not complete connectivity to their servers and printers.

At the lower end, Cisco provides the Cisco 340 BSE/BSM APs, discussed later in this chapter, for basic network connectivity to a dial-up line, DSL, or cable Internet connections, or a small wired network. The more popular 340 and 350 APs provide much more usability for larger installations, including those most commonly found in the enterprise.

The Cisco APs support both 10 and 100 Mbps Ethernet connections, and the installation should terminate on a switch port as opposed to an Ethernet hub. This limits the collision domain to the wireless segment only and allows for better control of Media Access Control (MAC) addresses and other security and diagnostic options.

The only other challenge in network connectivity for wireless networks is the selection of the IP addresses and broadcast domain—the three common choices are as follows:

- **Place the AP on the current wired subnet** This solution is quite simple, and it allows for the quick placement of the AP on any port of the switch. This solution has a few downsides, however. One is that no easy methods exist for isolating a wireless connectivity problem from a wired one—the installation appears quite transparent to the help desk and other support staff until they ask for the user to identify the connectivity option. Another issue is roaming within the wireless domain. Frequently, until the installation of Windows 2000 and greater, changing the IP address required a reboot or DHCP renewal. Placing multiple APs within a building would potentially conflict with the address assigned to the workstation. Also, some applications cannot change IP addresses dynamically, yielding another challenge for the designer.

- **Create a second collision domain with a second subnet per AP** This solution is very good for single AP installations, but it may impact scalability. The same challenges that existed in the first solution remain— the workstation will need to change IP addresses in any roaming configuration.

- **Place an overlay network or VLAN into the campus or building that allows all APs to reside in one subnet** This third option addresses the problems mentioned in the first two solutions, but it is not without its own concerns. It eliminates the IP address swapping of the first two solutions and provides technical support with a single element to monitor, however, it often fails to scale well in very large campuses and metropolitan area networks (MANs). This is because most large networks and their administration, especially in highly redundant networks, fail to administer all of the various protocols and timers that would be needed to manage a Layer 2 topology that would scale to a large size. This is not to say that it cannot be done, but one must ask what benefits arise in trying. A single Layer 2 design, which is a VLAN construction, spreading over an entire campus will ultimately be limited by broadcast traffic, convergence, administrative control, and protocol conversions, each of which should give one pause before embarking on such a path.

Administrators may wish to address the historical limitations with spanning tree, a requirement for large Layer 2 deployments, by using 802.1w, MST, Port Fast, Uplink Fast, or other extensions or changes to the historical 802.1d Spanning Tree Protocol. This can help, but, again, it may not provide the desired benefits for a growing wireless deployment, especially when added to the complexities of router redundancy (Hot Standby Routing Protocol [HSRP]) and routing protocols (Enhanced Interior Gateway Routing Protocol [EIGRP], for example). These are indeed improvements to Radia Perlman's original spanning tree specification, which was never designed for large switched networks, but, again, the advantages may be offset by the added complexities.

The designer should evaluate each installation considering the likely growth that will inevitably occur and plan accordingly. Each solution will work, but, as presented, each is also fraught with compromises. As noted elsewhere in this chapter, there is little to differentiate wireless networks from their wired brethren, and the same rules of broadcast and collision domains, in addition to support models and administrative controls, are valid. As a designer, you ultimately need to decide what model works for you and your organization.

Initial Configuration of the Cisco 340 and 350 Series AP

The initial configuration of the AP is fairly straightforward. Most administrators prefer to use the console port to configure a starting configuration for the device. Afterwards, they may opt to use the Web-based interface to complete the work, or they may finish the configuration process from the console. However, Cisco provides an alternate methodology for the configuration. The primary solution is the use of the IP Setup Utility, which operates at the data link layer to configure a preliminary SSID and IP address. An easier alternative, depending on the installation, is to collect the IP address from the DHCP server and forgo the IP Setup Utility—the administrator would then use the Telnet or Web interfaces to connect to the AP. This section presents the IP Setup Utility and the console port solutions as provided by Cisco.

It may be warranted to note that some administrators will not configure an IP address on the AP for security reasons, however, this is generally not a good idea. The Web interface is much easier to use as a configuration tool, and the ability to monitor the AP and remotely administer it in-band should be sufficient to make the administrator want to configure an IP address on the AP. Because the AP is not a router, the actual forwarding of packets is independent of the address being configured, however, features such as LEAP and SNMP do require an address.

IP Setup Utility

In order to simplify the initial configuration of the AP, Cisco provides a network application called IPSU, or IP Setup Utility. This program allows the administrator to determine the IP address of the AP if the AP was assigned an address via a DHCP server. Otherwise, the utility is used to assign the IP address statically. Please note that the utility is usable only if the workstation and AP are on the same network. If the obtained address is 10.0.0.1, it signifies that the AP has reverted to a default setting and the DHCP request has failed.

In order to obtain an IP address, select the **Get IP addr** option on the right-hand side of the screen, then input the MAC layer address, identified on the bottom of the AP, and select the **Get IP Address** button.

To configure the IP address or SSID, the administrator will select the **Set Parameters** radio button and then enter the values. The IPSU program is shown in Figure 5.4.

Figure 5.4 The IP Setup Utility

Please note that IPSU will work only with a default AP—changes made to the AP will preclude use of IPSU. In addition, to set the SSID you must assign an IP address, even if that address is the same as the one already configured on the device. Setting the IP address does not require an SSID.

Terminal Emulator Setup

The terminal emulator setup, or console port connection, is a quick and simple method for configuring the AP. This solution is particularly convenient when there is no DHCP server on the network and the administrator wants to assign a static IP address.

The console port is a standard DB-9 with a configuration of VT-100, 9600, N, 8, 1. Most terminal emulators support the port, including Windows Hyperterminal. A straight-through connection is required.

The interface for the console port is the same as the Telnet interface, which is based tightly on the Web interface engine within the AP. The Express Setup screen is the most frequently used on the console port for configuration issues. To set the IP address of the Ethernet interface, the administrator would start typing the word **Address** into the interface, for example. The system, by default, will automatically guess the command and execute it after enough letters have been entered.

```
ap340-Padjen              Express Setup           Uptime: 6 days, 02:30:03
  System [Name              ][ap340-Padjen                      ]
 [Terminal Type             ][teletype]
  MAC Address               : 00:40:96:32:dd:d1
  Config. Server [Protocol  ][None ]
  IP [Address               ][192.168.1.5     ]
  IP [Subnet Mask           ][255.255.255.0   ]
  Default [Gateway          ][192.168.1.1     ]
 [Radio Service Set ID (SSID)][padjen                           ]
 [Role in Radio Network      ][Root Access Point            ]
 [Optimize Radio Network For ][Throughput]   [Hw Radio]
  Ensure Compatibility With:  [2Mb/sec Clients][_]   [non-Aironet
802.11][_]
 [SNMP Admin. Community       ][rpadjen                          ]
 [Apply] [OK]    [Cancel] [Restore Defaults]
-----------------------------------------------------------------


[Home] - [Network] - [Associations] - [Setup] - [Logs] - [Help]


The access point also provides a limited help screen function, as shown
in the following output.
```

```
ap340-Padjen     Brief Help For the Console Browser     Uptime: 6 days,
02:29:52


Follow a link:


    When typing the first few characters for an anchor, the browser will
go to the page as soon as it finds a unique match. If the numerical
notation for links is on, one can also go to that page by typing in the
number for that link directly.


Quick Keys:


    =                Go to the home page
    ^R               Force the screen to refresh
    ENTER            Scroll down one page
    Hitting 3 ENTER's in a row will force the screen to refresh.


Use command Line:


    Enter the command line mode by typing in ':' followed by a command
and the ENTER key. Commands are case insensitive.
Supported Commands:


    :AUTO            Turn on/off switch for the Auto-Apply feature
    :BACK            Return to the previous page
    :BOTTOM          Scroll to the bottom of the current page
    :CLEAR           Clear history list
    :CLOSE           Close the telnet session if the connection is open
    :CMD             Enter SNMP Command Line mode
    :DOWN            Scroll down one page
    :FORWARD         Return to next page
    :GOTO            Go to the page specified by the URL following the
                      goto
    :HOME            Go to the home page
    :NUMBERS_ON      Turn on the numerical notation for links
```

```
:NUMBERS_OFF    Turn off the numerical notation for links
:PING ipAddr    Send 5 IP Echo requests to "ipAddr".
:REFRESH        Force the screen to refresh
:RESETALL       Reset ENTIRE configuration to Factory Defaults,
                  including security controls.  Only available from
                  serial console for the first 2 minutes after a
                  reboot.
:TOP            Scroll to the top of the current page
:UP             Scroll up one page
:REFRESH        Refresh the screen
:=              Go to the home page
```

You should note that the automatic completion feature may be toggled on and off with the *auto* command. Some administrators find this feature to be more confusing than helpful—hence its optional status. The *resetall* command is quite powerful—note that it is used to restore the entire AP to its default configuration, but that it is available only within the first two minutes of powering the device. There is also a recessed reset button on the back of the AP.

Web-Based Configuration of the Cisco 340 and 350 Series APs

Using the Web interface is likely the most common methodology for configuring the AP. All of the system's options are available from this interface, and the menu-driven Telnet interface is difficult to navigate by comparison.

This section presents the settings that administrators will need to change in their installations, in addition to noting design and configuration recommendations.

Configuring the Cisco 340 and 350 Series APs

The configuration process is simply a matter of reaching the proper screen and altering the applicable settings. There is no IOS command structure to the AP—configurations are prepared via a menu and navigation-based interface.

Please note that different versions of the AP software will alter the placement and options available to the administrator. This section is written to present the options available within the current version and generically define the options regardless of placement.

Configuring the Web Interface

By default, the Web interface configuration is adequate for most users. However, in some instances, the administrator may want to disable the Web interface (configured with the nonconsole browsing setting). Some administrators like to change the network port for the Web interface to thwart limited network scanners that examine only port 80 for Web servers. In Figure 5.5, the HTTP port has been changed to 8000. Please note that the help interface engine is also configured from this screen and that the reference is to a Web page on the Cisco Web site. This allows Cisco to provide the latest information for the help system, or it allows a company to provide customized help information to users and administrators. The negative to this configuration is that locating needed information can be difficult without a network connection.

Figure 5.5 The Web Interface Configuration

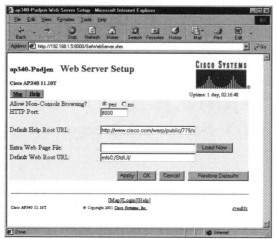

Configuring a Name Server

Most administrators will find it unnecessary to configure a name server, but the AP does provide for the option, as shown in Figure 5.6. The administrator can define up to three Domain Name System (DNS) servers, in addition to the domain information.

The Radio Hardware Setting

The AP Radio Hardware setting (shown in Figure 5.7) is one of the first setup screens that administrators will confront. This screen provides access to the SSID setting and allows for configuration of the SSID Broadcast feature. The default radio channel is also selected from this screen.

Figure 5.6 The DNS Configuration Screen

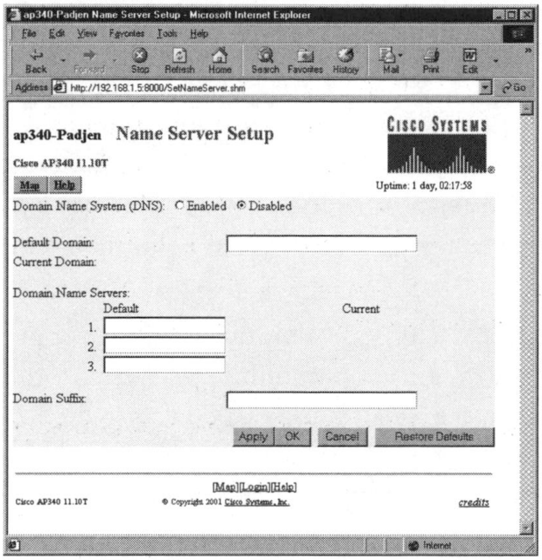

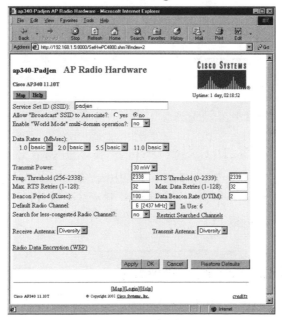

Figure 5.7 The AP Radio Hardware Setting Screen

Please note that the default is for the SSID broadcast feature to be enabled. As such, any wireless client can connect to the AP if they do not specify one. This may not be desired. The default SSID is "tsunami".

Security Alert

You need to consider the frequency selection as a radio consideration only, and not a security methodology. Each AP transmits on each channel with a broadcast message poll. This allows the clients to discover and configure the frequency setting.

The SSID is a 32-character, case-sensitive field that controls the APs and client NICs that are allowed to communicate with each other.

As noted previously, the SSID is used to control which AP a workstation client connects to. However, in some instances, the installation may benefit from having no SSID controls. These types of installations are increasingly common in airports and other public places where a wireless domain is configured for transparent public use and crossover from multiple APs is unlikely.

In addition to the SSID, this screen also allows the configuration of the channel to be used by the AP for communications to the clients or to each other, as is the case with using an AP as a repeater. A repeater is an AP used to extend the range of coverage in an area. They do not perform a load balancing function, and they are not connected to the wired network. At first appearance, one might deduce that 11 channels are available to the network. This is incorrect, because the channels' frequency ranges or spreads will overlap—the administrator technically should find only three channels available (channels 1, 6, and 11 in North America) with interference-free overlaps. This is not to say that overlap will occur with channels 2 and 9, for example, but selecting these two channels would restrict the administrator from adding a third AP within the same radio coverage. Please also note that channels are country-specific, and limitations may exist for your installation.

Note

International limitations may restrict the channels that you can use in your installation. Please refer to local regulations or the Cisco documentation for more details.

The AP Radio Port Status Screen

The AP Radio Port status screen provides a verification of the configuration selections made in the AP Radio Hardware Setting screen. Shown in Figure 5.8, the screen displays detailed receive and transmit statistics in addition to the SSID and operational radio data rates. Some installations artificially limit the acceptable data throughput rates for administrative or performance reasons—for example, allowing connections at only 11 Mbps so users do not become frustrated with wireless networking, or 2 Mbps to increase the coverage and user experience across the wireless domain. This screen is useful in determining if such policies have been implemented for both initial setup and troubleshooting.

Figure 5.8 The AP Radio Port Screen

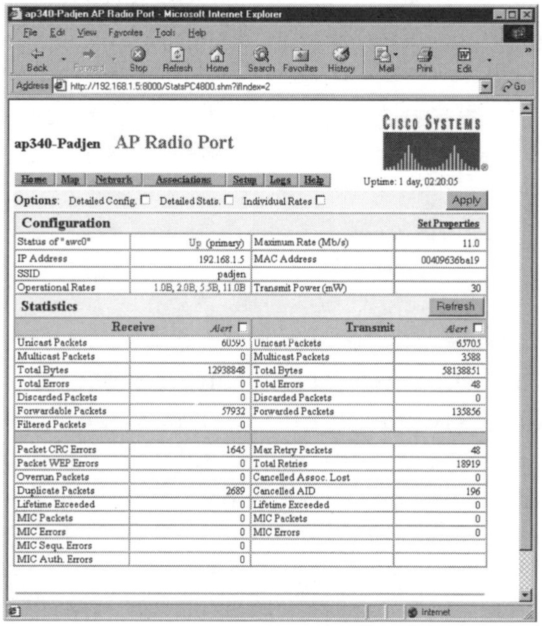

Setting the Time

The AP allows for three time-reporting methods. Accurate reporting of the time can greatly assist troubleshooting and logging efforts. The first of the three time setting methods is actually not setting the time at all—the system begins tracking the time based on the duration since startup. This is acceptable for very simple installations; however, enterprise installations will likely prefer more consistent tracking.

The second method is to set the time manually. As shown in Figure 5.9, the time, time zone, and daylight savings settings are all configurable. This method works well, however, no provisions are given for retaining the time if power is lost. If this happens, the AP will revert to the uptime method of time tracking.

Figure 5.9 Setting the AP Time

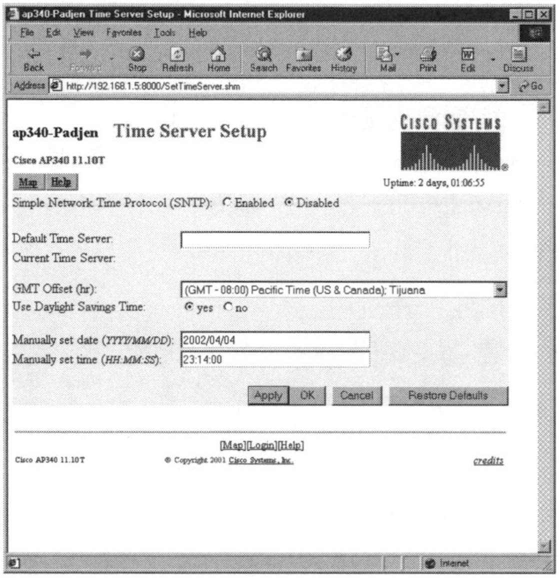

The third method of setting time on the AP may be the best in a large enterprise. The AP can learn the time over the network via the Simple Network Time Protocol (SNTP). This will be relearned upon a restart of the device, and all APs, in addition to all other network resources, will have the same time—a significant advantage for troubleshooting. Note that SNTP time can be provided by the Internet, a local time server, or a GPS (Global Positioning System) receiver.

Figure 5.10 shows the acceptance of the time set in Figure 5.9. The current time is displayed in the upper right-hand corner.

User Accounts

AP administration can be controlled through the use of user accounts. Figure 5.11 shows the user account interface, which has been configured with an account for user "rpadjen". This user has permissions for each of the available options, including writing changes to the AP, to configure the SNMP parameters, to change the identity of the AP, including the IP address and network mask. The user may also upgrade the firmware and administer other user accounts. By default there are no user accounts, and user management is disabled.

Figure 5.10 Acceptance of the Manually Set Time

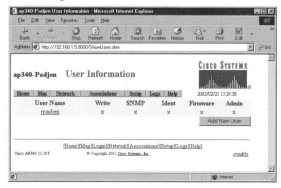

Figure 5.11 Administering User Accounts

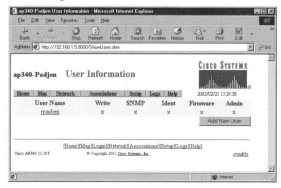

Setting the WEP Key

Cisco provides the Client Encryption Manager (CEM), which sets each of the four slots available on the client adapter with the static WEP key. As noted earlier, in the "Enterprise Installations of Wireless Networks" sidebar, use of the static WEP key is not recommended for installations where security is important—the key has been compromised by hackers in war driving case studies in as little as 15 minutes. The time to compromise the WEP key is a function of the packets captured and the software used to decode the key, as opposed to a processor-intensive effort where hardware makes a significant difference in decode time. However, use of WEP can dissuade casual hacking attempts.

Figure 5.12 shows the initialization screen for CEM. The default password is "Cisco", and it is case-sensitive. The CEM configuration password can be changed by the administrator from the Commands menu option.

Figure 5.12 The Cisco Encryption Manager

Figure 5.13 shows the Cisco Encryption Manager summary screen. This screen defines which key positions are already assigned, the length of the respective keys, and the capabilities of the hardware.

Figure 5.13 The Cisco Encryption Manager Summary Screen

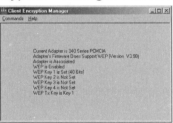

After selecting the menu option, the user or administrator can enter the static key value. Typically only the administrator in large enterprises knows this value, if they use WEP, and NICs are controlled and preconfigured for users. Determining the WEP key value from the NIC is difficult, although it is possible. Loss of a NIC can quickly require changing all WEP keys in the network. This is another reason for the interest in LEAP/EAP and 802.11i—new specifications for WLAN security.

The length of the key is determined by the number of bits involved—40-bit WEP is shown in Figure 5.14 as a 10 hexadecimal value. Enter the value and click **OK**. The software will write the value into NVRAM on the NIC.

Figure 5.14 Setting the WEP Key

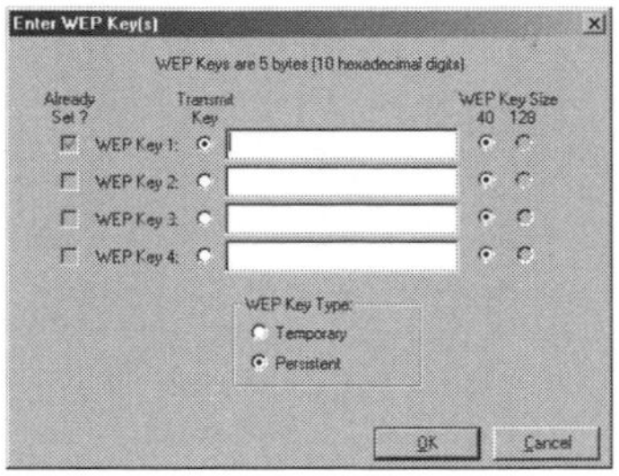

The AP must also be configured with the identical key value, as shown in Figure 5.15. These values may be 40- or 128-bit values, and the AP must be configured for full encryption.

Figure 5.15 Configuring the WEP Keys on the AP

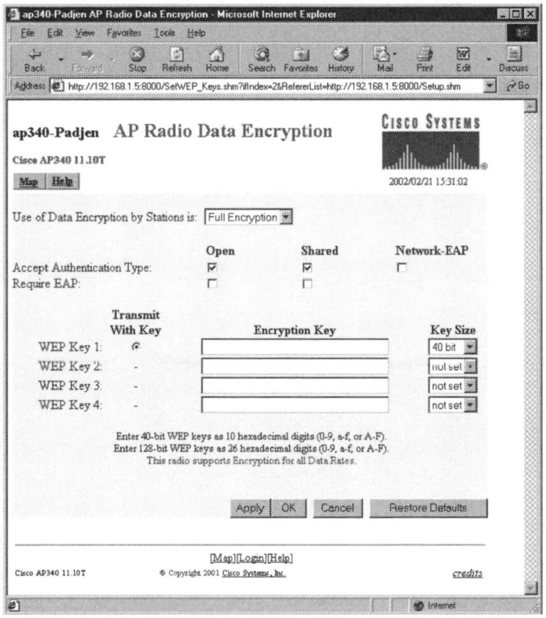

Specifically, the administrator will want to configure the key value first. This value, in the referenced figure, is a 40-bit key. Forty-bit values are 10 hexadecimal characters in length, whereas 128-bit values are 26 hexadecimal characters. Please note that the compromises of WEP-based security have rendered both key lengths insecure.

Administrators will then set the transmit option, labeled **Transmit With Key**. Although one may set four WEP keys, only one may be used at a time for transmissions. The authentication parameters are open and shared key, in addition to the Network-EAP setting, which is used for EAP/LEAP configurations. The open setting is slightly preferred to the shared key configuration because shared key transmits a clear-text query. However, either setting will allow for the use of WEP.

The encryption setting enables or disables the use of WEP, and you should use caution in enabling the security feature—many administrators accidentally disconnect themselves from the wireless network by not having the WEP key configured and enabled on their wireless adapters.

Encryption may be set to *on*, *off*, or *mixed*. The *on* and *off* settings enable and disable all WEP features. The mixed setting is to differentiate between bridge communications and devices—turning the feature on means that the bridge will communicate only with the AP via WEP, but all other resources can choose to not use WEP. Mixed off is effectively the same as setting the value to off, because WEP is not used for any communications. Note that the mixed settings are applicable only when using an AP to connect to another AP, and the value for encryption is normally set to on or off only.

Accounting Setup

The Accounting Setup screen is used to define RADIUS servers and accounting services for authentication logging (see Figure 5.16). Authentication is part of the Cisco AAA (Authentication, Authorization, and Accounting) security model.

Figure 5.16 The Accounting Setup Screen

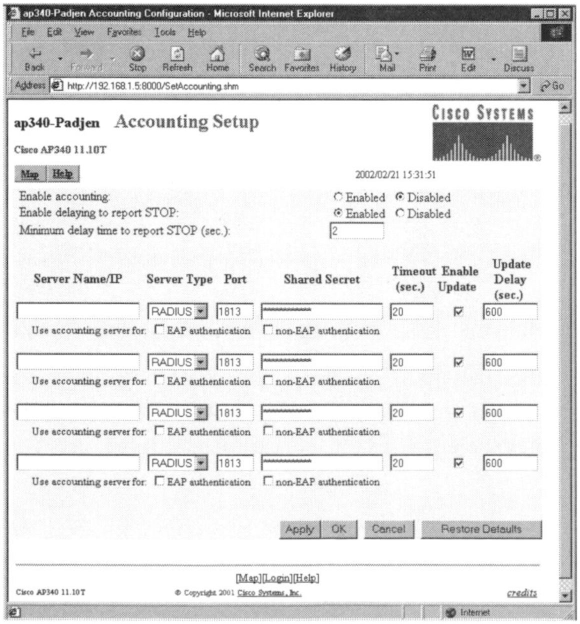

Hot Standby

Cisco provides the Hot Standby feature as a hardware redundancy system for APs. As shown in Figure 5.17, the configuration screen also provides a means for determining the status of the hot standby feature. Please note that APs are Layer 2 devices, and, as such, hot standby operates on the MAC layer address and not the IP, or network, address.

Figure 5.17 The Hot Standby Feature

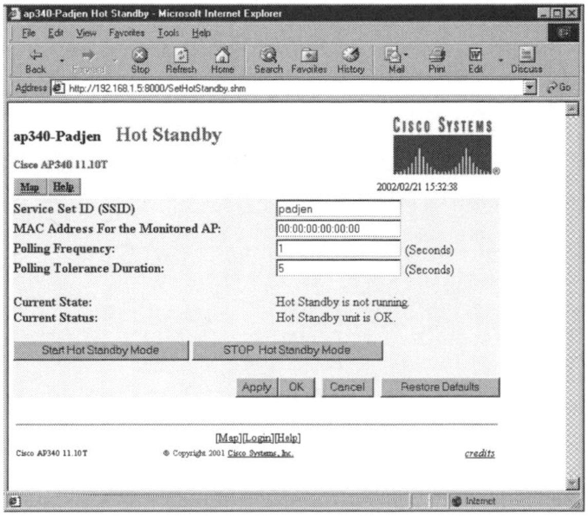

Publicly Secure Packet Forwarding

With the release of Cisco AP firmware release 11.08T, Cisco added the Publicly Secure Packet Forwarding (PSPF) feature. This setting will likely be used in airports, coffee houses, and other public use installations where the wireless network needs to ignore its shared-media characteristics and follow a more secure switched model. With this setting enabled, the wireless network works to block each wireless client from the others—thus providing a degree of security for the individual users.

Configuration of PSPF is very straightforward once running the proper version of firmware. As shown in Figure 5.18, the setting is a simple toggle switch, labeled as **Block *ALL* Inter-Client Communications ("PSPF")** on the Association Table Advanced screen. Please note that this screen also controls the timeout values for each device class in the wireless network.

Figure 5.18 Configuring Publicly Secure Packet Forwarding

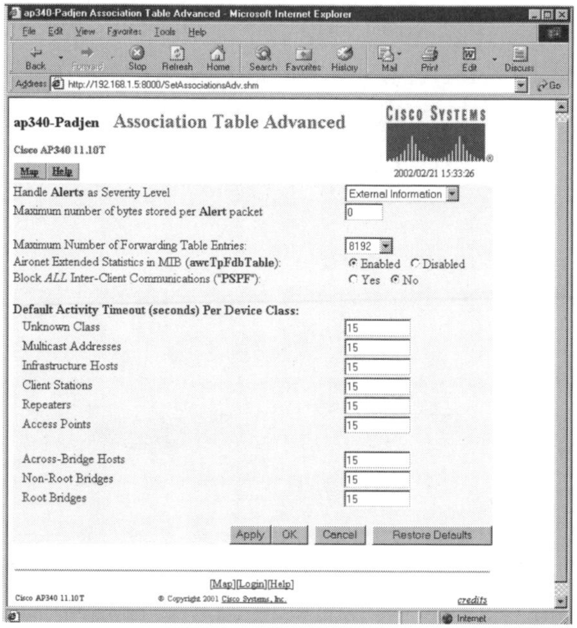

Troubleshooting the Cisco 340 and 350 Series APs

Most troubleshooting in Cisco wireless networks involves the configuration settings of the overall network, including the WEP keys, SSIDs, and nonwireless settings, including IP addresses. However, there are other elements at the physical layer of 802.11b networks that warrant concern and attention when things don't work properly.

Figure 5.19 shows the Link Status Meter, which provides an efficient means to check two wireless characteristics. The first is listed at the bottom of the application with the line, "Your Cisco Wireless Adapter is Not Associated." This line is very telling for troubleshooting, although a number of potential causes exist:

- The SSID is incorrectly set.

- The AP is not powered.

- The signal between the AP and the NIC is too weak to establish a connection.

Figure 5.19 A Non-Associated AP

Once these settings and issues have been resolved, and the NIC is placed within 10 feet unobstructed of the AP the screen should change to the relative strength of the signal, as shown in Figure 5.20.

Figure 5.20 The Link Status Meter

The figure shows an AP approximately 70 feet away from the respective note-book, and separated by three walls. This distance and the obstructions weaken the signal, but the quality of the signal is quite good. As such, this installation is acceptable and should work for the user.

Please note that the Link Status Meter is a good tool to use for site surveys and pre-installation documentation as well. Install an AP in a trial position and use the notebook as a mobile meter to see where dead zones and other problems arise.

If the Link Status Meter is not available, the PCMCIA (PC Card) NIC also has two indicator lights that you can use for basic troubleshooting. The Status light will blink at two-second intervals if the NIC is associated, and it will blink faster when trying to acquire. The Activity light will blink when traffic is present. If this light shows activity, the Status light appears correct, and the Link Status Meter verifies this information, it is appropriate to examine the IP connectivity settings.

A common installation for WLANs is the use of DHCP. DHCP automatically assigns the IP address of the host, which can greatly simplify workstation management. As with wired networks, it is possible to have the host connect to the network but not connect to the DHCP server for an address. In most Windows systems, the IP address can be viewed with either the WINIPCFG or the IPCONFIG command (Windows 95, 98 and Windows NT, 2000 and XP, respectively). When the workstation cannot obtain an IP address, it may retain a previously assigned address, announce a clear rejection of the DHCP request, or substitute a locally assigned (host-based) IP address. The locally assigned address is always in the 169.254.0.0/16 address space, and, if when troubleshooting, the administrator sees this address, it should be an indication that the DHCP process failed.

Another diagnostic tool is the Network Ports screen in the AP. Shown in Figure 5.21, this screen reports the errors and traffic volumes for both the Ethernet and wireless interfaces of the network. Remember that both interfaces are important to diagnose when researching a connectivity problem.

Figure 5.21 The Network Ports Screen

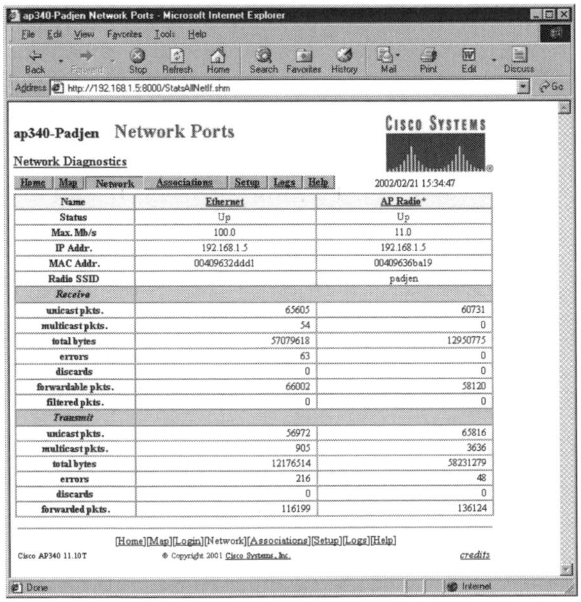

Each port also has a dedicated screen for interface statistics—the Ethernet-only port statistics are shown in Figure 5.22. Note that some statistics, such as underruns, are available only from the interface-specific screen. As with a wired network, errors and discards are both significant, as would be unusual traffic patterns based on expectations. Collisions, particularly on the Ethernet interface configured for full duplex, should not occur, and would indicate a error or duplex mismatch, just as with a wired network.

Figure 5.22 The Ethernet Statistics Screen

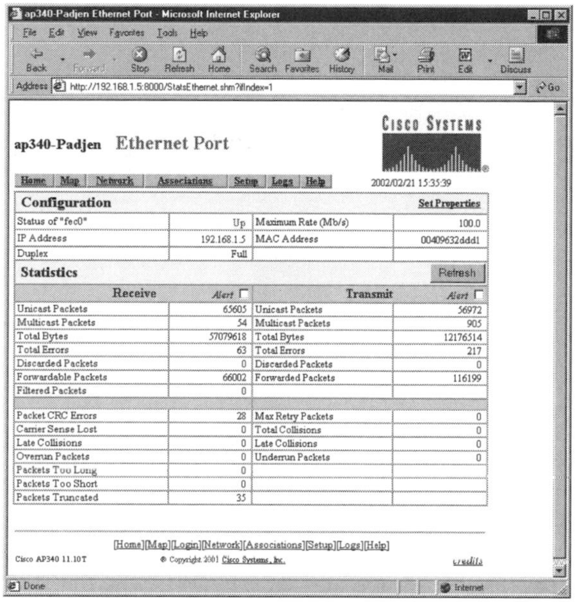

In addition to the reactive processes available in the Link Status Meter and the Network Ports screen, the AP supports SNMP alarms and traps, as well as Syslog messages. These are configured to integrate with your management system, yielding an integrated solution.

The Event Notifications screen, shown in Figure 5.23, is used to configure the SNMP and Syslog receivers.

In addition, the administrator can tune the system to provide additional information regarding specific types of error conditions. The Event Handling Setup, shown in Figure 5.24, controls this.

The event display sctup also provides management services for error messages. This is configured from the Event Display Setup screen, which is shown in Figure 5.25.

Figure 5.23 The Event Notifications Screen

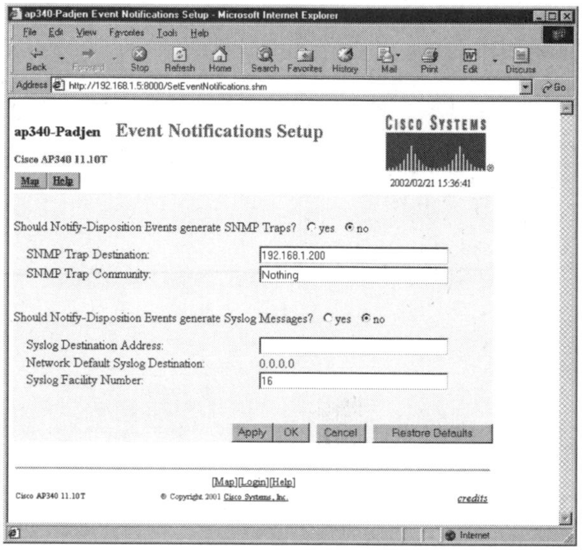

Figure 5.24 The Event Handling Setup

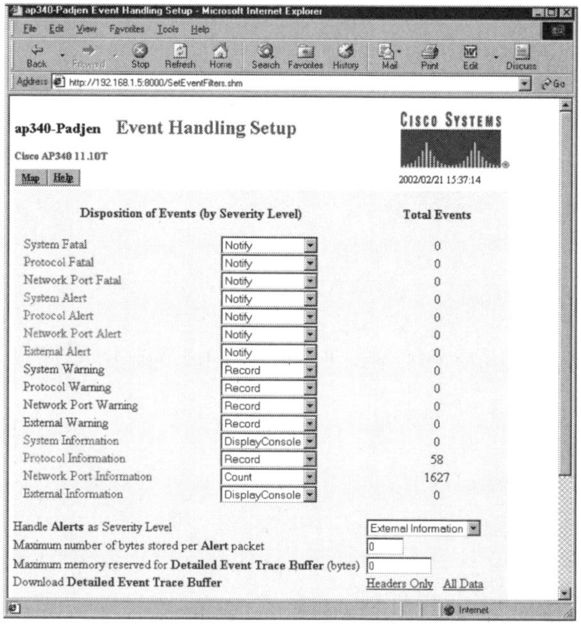

Figure 5.25 The Event Display Setup Screen

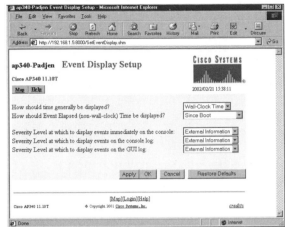

The Cisco Discovery Protocol (CDP) is a proprietary, SNAP-based protocol that advertises Cisco hardware to attached systems. The protocol is often used to verify physical layer connectivity because it is independent of Layer 3 services, such as IP. Although configuration of CDP is a fairly simple process, administrators and designers should consider the security ramifications of enabling the service. On trusted enterprise interfaces, it should always be enabled; however, on unprotected Internet or untrusted connections, this service can provide too much information that could be used in concert with other attack vectors (methodologies for compromising a system). The default settings transmit a CDP packet every 60 seconds, with a three times hold time, or 180 seconds. In Figure 5.26, the service has been disabled. Note that the wireless and Ethernet ports may be individually selected for CDP services.

Figure 5.26 Configuring CDP Services

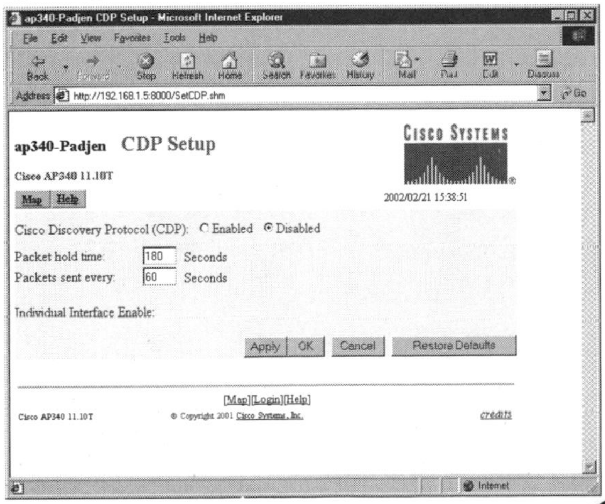

Some problems with the AP may be resolved only with the installation of a product upgrade. These files and the problems they resolve are listed on Cisco's Web site (currently www.cisco.com/kobayashi/sw-center/sw-wireless.shtml) and the presentation of the files is shown in Figures 5.27 and 5.28. Cisco Connection Online is the best source of bug listings and resolutions, and administrators should review this information prior to installation to eliminate repeating known problems with the wireless systems.

As shown in Figure 5.27, the Wireless Software page provides client drivers and AP software for users. Please note that in addition to the Aironet 340 and 350 platforms (Aironet was the original manufacturer of the APs and was acquired by Cisco Systems) the drivers and utilities include Linux, Windows, Macintosh, and DOS resources.

Figure 5.27 The Wireless Software Download Page

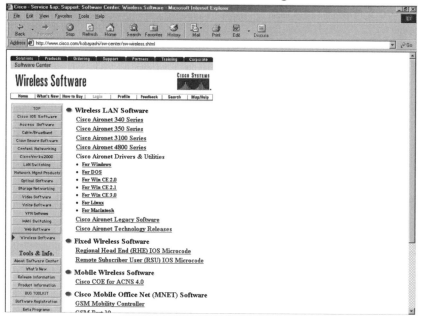

In Figure 5.28, the current and recent versions are available for download. This includes technical documentation and firmware. Please note that the firmware version numbering system is comparable to the mainline IOS. The 340's current software releases, as of this writing, are 11.06, 11.07, and 11.10T. Versions in the T train are new feature releases that may have more quality issues than mainline releases, however, Cisco realizes that some customers need the new features even with the added risk. Mainline IOS releases are generally more stable and incorporate only those features that have undergone significant production testing. These releases are the only ones that can be categorized as "GD," or general deployment. This classification is typically the most error-free of all releases.

Figure 5.28 The Software Listing Page

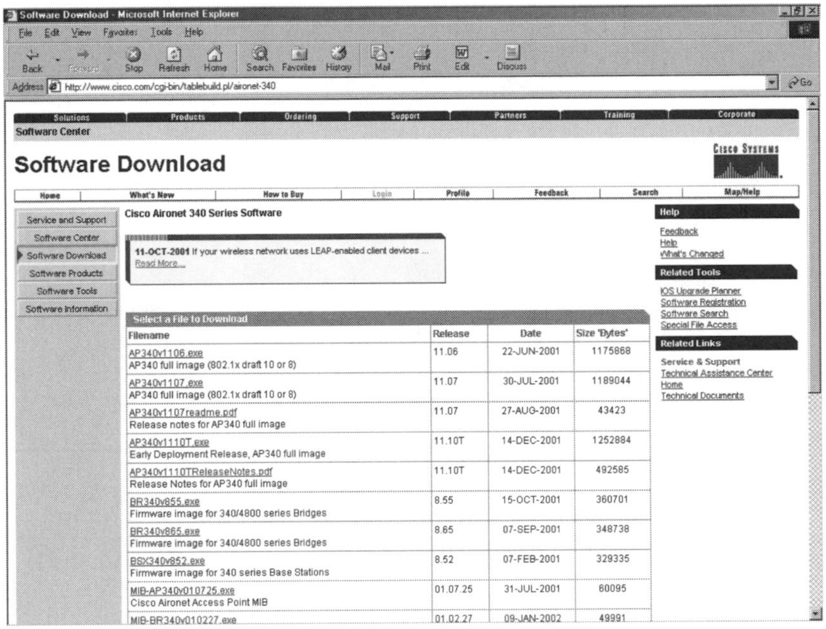

File upgrades are well accounted for by the system, and although the tools are less than ideal for upgrading hundreds of APs, they are well suited for the upgrade of multiple systems.

The AP also has a useful summary display from the Aironet Client Utility, under the **Commands | Status** menu option. As shown in Figure 5.29, this screen provides a real-time view of the AP, its current signal level to the workstation running the software, and the firmware and other characteristics of the AP.

Web-Based Configuration of the Cisco 340 BSE/BSM Series AP

The Cisco 340 BSM (Base Station AIR-BSM128) is a variant of the standard Cisco 340 AP. It is ideally suited to installations with up to 10 users, and the product features an integrated modem and fixed antenna. (The nonmodem version is the AIR-BSE128, and is suited to cable modem and DSL installations only.) The product supports WEP and incorporates a DHCP server. It is designed to provide single users or small groups with efficient networking, and the device terminates cable modems, digital subscriber line (DSL), or analog modem connections. Please note that PPP over Ethernet (PPPoE) is supported and is commonly required for DSL installations.

Figure 5.29 The Series Status Screen

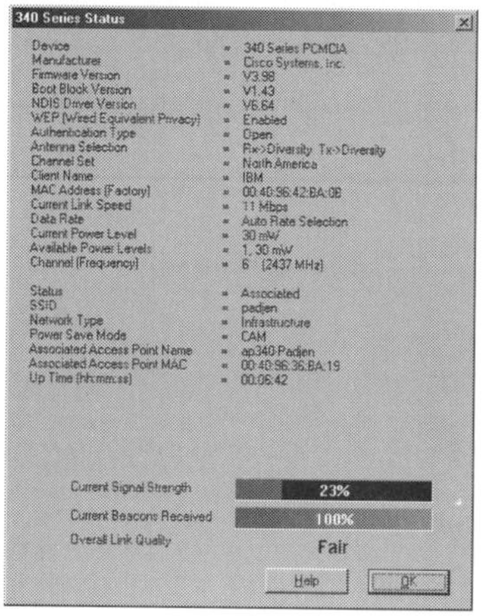

Configuring the Cisco 340 BSE/BSM Series AP

The configuration of the BSE and BSM models is somewhat different from the other Aironet models. First, the configuration of the device may be accomplished only by use of the wireless interface. This is intended to be a security measure to prevent unauthorized persons from accessing the AP from the Internet connection; however, it can lead to a more compromised system for a number of reasons. First, the installation of any connection to the Internet should include a level of firewall protection. Placing this outside of the AP is always a good idea to protect both the AP and the computers connected to the wireless side of the bridge. This, of course, is limited when using the built-in modem. The second is that many users do not change the default SSID, which is "tsunami".

Although we cannot stress enough that the SSID is not a valid security measure (it can be quickly discovered), it is recommended that this value be changed. With the BSE and BSM APs, the SSID is the only default protection to restrict access to the configuration parameters. This is unlike the other Cisco APs, which may also be configured with user accounts and passwords.

Many administrators will choose to use the Base Station Client Utility to configure the BSE/BSM. The initial screen of this tool is shown in Figure 5.30.

Figure 5.30 The Base Station Client Utility

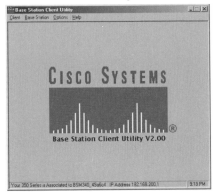

Note that the bottom line of the screen shows that the AP is associated with the workstation—both the IP address (192.168.200.1) and the MAC address are displayed. This requires that the workstation wireless adapter is configured with the default SSID of "tsunami". You can configure this without the client utility by using the Control Panel, Network option, as shown in Figure 5.31. You can also select the setting in the Client Utility.

Figure 5.31 Setting the SSID from the Network Control Panel

To modify the settings, select the **Base Station | Set Up Base Station** option, as shown in Figure 5.32.

This will take you to the Settings screen, as shown in Figure 5.33. Many of the settings are already provided from the workstation configuration, including Computer Name and Network Name. Selecting **Edit Base Station Settings** will allow modification of the configuration, including selection of the dial-out modem. Note that the BSE/BSM always uses 192.168.200.0/24 and network address translation for the wireless interface. The BSE/BSM is addressed as 192.168.200.1.

Figure 5.32 Configuring the Base Station

Figure 5.33 The Settings Screen

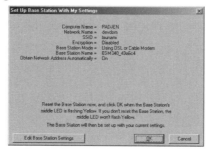

The BSE/BSM also provides Web and Telnet interfaces for configuration. No passwords exist to protect the configuration parameters, which makes the BSE/BSM ill-suited for corporate installations. The product is well suited for home installation and small office/temporary installations. The Web and Telnet screens are shown in Figures 5.34 and 5.35, respectively.

NOTE

As of version 8.52, the NAT protocol on the BSE/BSM was not compatible with VPN tunnels (IPSec).

Figure 5.34 The Web Interface of the BSE/BSM

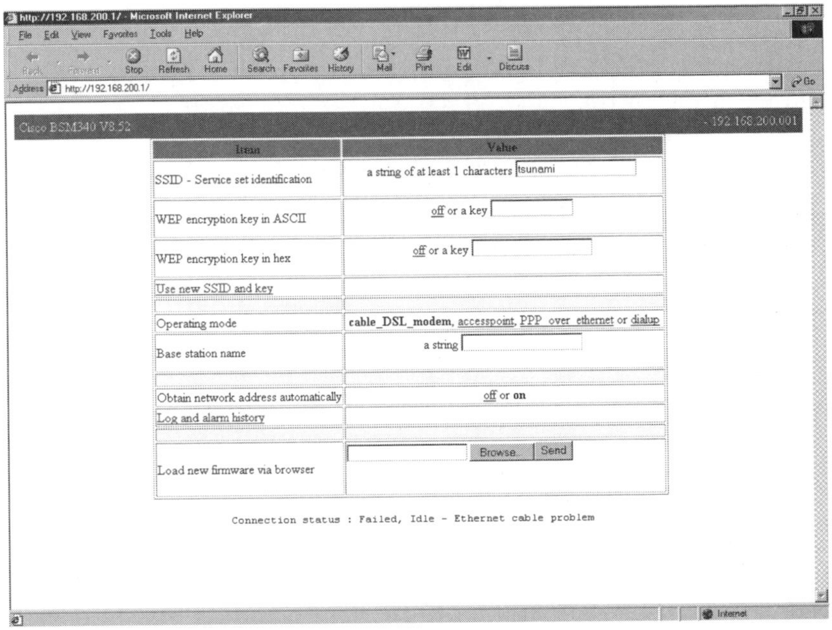

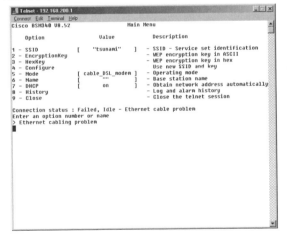

Figure 5.35 The Telnet Interface of the BSE/BSM

Troubleshooting the Cisco 340 BSE/BSM Series AP

Troubleshooting the BSE and BSM models of the Cisco Aironet APs is comparable to troubleshooting the standard AP models. Certain features are simpler to eliminate—for example, the BSE/BSM does not support roaming or antenna selection. In addition, such installations tend to be much smaller in diameter, so the overall configuration is much easier to review and isolate as it relates to problems.

Summary

Cisco provides three 802.11b APs for different user communities. The Cisco 340 is designed to provide a wide range of wireless services; the Cisco 350 adds inline power features and greater radio power for improved range. The simpler 340 BSM provides a reasonable home-office solution with integrated Port Address Translation and DHCP services. The integrated modem can greatly assist rapid, small group deployments.

Configuration of the Cisco 340 and 350 APs is a fairly straightforward process. The initial installation considerations are quite similar to those of a wired network; however, you should consider a site survey when considering deployments of more than a few APs. This will allow you to address such issues as the IP addressing schema, roaming requirements, security, coverage issues, and antenna placement. Once these considerations have been addressed, the installation of the AP is virtually identical to those of a router or switch.

Cisco provides three methods for configuring the AP. The first is the use of the IP Setup Utility to locate the IP address of the AP before configuring it. The second is the local console port, which allows configuration via the command-line interface. The third is to configure the AP via a DHCP server and determined IP address via Telnet or the Web interface. Many users find the Web interface to be easier in practice.

Configuration of the 340 BSM is much more limited, however, the product includes the option of using WEP and the SSID. The antennas are fixed on this system, however, and there is no console port. Configuration is possible only via the wireless interface, which is provided as a minor security feature. The default SSID is "tsunami", and it should be changed upon installation.

The configuration of the AP, regardless of the methodology, is facilitated with a solid documentation process. Unlike their wired counterparts, wireless networks can include many additional configuration details, including the SSID, WEP keys, channel selection, antenna aiming and range, and power options—inline or out-of-line. Each of these parameters is in addition to VLAN and IP address configuration. Also, administrators may wish to deploy VPN technologies in addition to their wireless network for additional security, or use LEAP/EAP to correct deficiencies in WEP.

Troubleshooting wireless networks requires skills in both traditional wired technologies and the presumably new skills involved with wireless systems. Common problems with wireless networks include radio interference, incorrect

SSID values, and misconfigured WEP keys. Cisco provides tools for isolating each of these problems as they occur.

In addition, the AP can integrate with the traditional wired management systems, including SNMP, Syslog, and CDP services. These tools can simplify the challenges of bringing wireless networking into the enterprise environment; however, they do not replace careful planning and training.

Solutions Fast Track

Installation of the Cisco 340/350 Series AP

☑ Document each of the changes that you intend to make, including the SSID, WEP keys, IP addresses, and other configuration parameters.

☑ Plan for upgrades to 802.11a and optimal antenna placement at the beginning of the deployment. Consider using the non-omni directional antennas where applicable.

☑ Remember that security, even with LEAP/EAP is a weak point in wireless networking. Evaluate the installation and determine if augmentation with IPSec or other security protocols is warranted.

Initial Configuration of the Cisco 340 and 350 Series AP

☑ Evaluate the power options available to you, including inline power from the switch, powered patch panel, or power adaptor.

☑ Consider the additional power output of the 350 compared to the Aironet 340 when placing antennas.

Web-Based Configuration of the Cisco 340 and 350 Series APs

☑ If the network has DHCP, you may wish to allow the AP to request an IP address and then use the DHCP server to locate the address based on the MAC address, printed on the bottom of the AP.

☑ The console port is available for simple, out-of-band configuration, including the initial configuration of the AP.

☑ Cisco provides the IPSU, or IP Setup Utility, to facilitate network configuration by allowing locally attached APs to identify their IP addresses or assign an address.

Web-Based Configuration of the Cisco 340 BSE/BSM Series AP

☑ Use of the Web-based interface is preferred for configuration of the AP.

☑ Although not a complete security solution, it is recommended that user accounts and nonstandard ports be used for the Web configuration tool

☑ The Web interface allows for firmware upgrades, log review, configuration changes, and diagnostic information.

Frequently Asked Questions

The following Frequently Asked Questions, answered by the authors of this book, are designed to both measure your understanding of the concepts presented in this chapter and to assist you with real-life implementation of these concepts. To have your questions about this chapter answered by the author, browse to **www.syngress.com/solutions** and click on the **"Ask the Author"** form.

Q: How can 802.11b installations plan for upgrades to 802.11a?

A: Remember that the 5 GHz frequency range of the 802.11a standard reduces the range of the wireless LAN compared to the 2.4 GHz 802.11b. As such, it may theoretically require up to four times the number of APs to provide the same 802.11b coverage under 802.11a.

Q: How can I secure an 802.11 installation?

A: If any single factor has limited the rate of adoption within wireless networking, it is security. WEP was defeated quite quickly and scanners rapidly located installations. Currently, a WEP key can be cracked in about 15 minutes with simple hardware and software. Other elements of the 802.11 specification, including the SSID, were thought to be security functions, however, this was not their true intention. Cisco, along with other vendors, adopted extra methods for augmenting the security of wireless LANs, including the use of MAC address control and EAP, which exchanges keys via RADIUS. The 802.11x specification further adds to the security available in wireless networks, as would unrelated solutions such as IPSec.

However, if the goal is to completely secure a wireless installation, a better recommendation would be to overlay another technology or protocol. Common considerations include the use of IPSec, or VPN technology, or SSL Web services. Both of these standards provide excellent security over both wireless and wired transports.

In the near future, new standards will be introduced. These solutions include works by the 802.11 task group I, or TGi, which is working on the 802.11i specification. The 802.11i standard may continue to use the RC4 protocol that was used in WEP v1 and WEP v2, and is, as of this writing, mired in political and technical debate. Solutions using the newer Advanced Encryption Standard (AES) and AES with Secure Remote Password (SRP) may be available within 2002, which should greatly enhance the adoption of wireless technology within a secure model.

For more information, readers may wish to read Syngress Publishing's *Hack Proofing Your Wireless Network* (ISBN: 928994-59-8) or research at the following sites:

- **AirSnort** http://airsnort.sourceforge.net/
- **Melbourne: Digital and Wireless** http://melbwireless.x.net.au/
- **RFC 2945** www.faqs.org/rfcs/rfc2945.html
- **NetStumbler** www.netstumbler.com

Q: What can be done to increase bandwidth within a wireless LAN?

A: It is true that the 802.11b shared bandwidth of 11 Mbps can quickly become a limitation of the technology. The 802.11g standard will increase this limitation within the 2.4 GHz spectrum to greater than 20 Mbps. Of course, the 802.11a standard already provides over 50 Mbps, and vendor-specific implementations have improved upon this figure substantially.

A few tricks can improve performance within an existing 802.11b network however. First, although there are 11 channels, or frequencies within the specification, only three can be used within a particular area. As such, by controlling the channels for each of three APs, one could create a combined 33

Mbps wireless domain. Careful placement of antennas, including the use of directional antennas, can further control the boundaries of a wireless network, and thus, the number of nodes and the bandwidth available to each.

In addition, network designers are again looking to application control and user demands in the design of the network. An all-PDA network, for example, will likely require little in terms of total bandwidth. In a notebook or tablet PC environment, you may need to provide additional services and higher bandwidth applications. For these installations, you should consider remote control terminal server technologies. In terms of bandwidth, these installations require very little—typically less than 30 Kbps per user, regardless of the applications in use. Although the entire cost of the network increases, the security and support models for such an installation may warrant its usage.

Q: What will be the impact of 3G cellular services and other long-distance solutions on WLANs?

A: The answer to this question will be quite interesting and is simply unknown at this time. Most likely, however, third generation cellular services will be one part of a larger solution that includes wireless LAN technology. Phones, PDAs, tablet PCs, watches, and pagers will all likely converge into various hybrids that make use of the most effective technology. For example, a PDA with cellular phone services will likely incorporate 802.11 WLAN, cellular, and Bluetooth services, and it will automatically select the fastest and cheapest available service for the needed function. It is unlikely that cellular public networks will supplant WLANs, because control, privacy, and bandwidth will remain differentiators.

Chapter 6

Installation and Configuration of Cisco Aironet Bridges

Solutions in this chapter:

- **Installation of the Cisco Aironet Bridge Unit**

- **Initial Setup of the Cisco Aironet Wireless Bridge**

- **Operational Configuration of the Cisco Aironet Wireless Bridge**

- **Event Logging**

- **Viewing Statistics**

- **Cisco Aironet Wireless Bridge Troubleshooting**

☑ **Summary**

☑ **Solutions Fast Track**

☑ **Frequently Asked Questions**

253

Introduction

Wireless bridges are used as the intermediary connection between wireless network segments. They provide a means of linking separate LAN components into a logical whole. In this chapter, we discuss the use of traditional bridges within a cabled environment, and we draw parallels to the operations of wireless bridges within the wireless network.

In subsequent sections of the chapter, we discuss the overall architecture layout of wireless bridges in point-to-point and point-to-multipoint mode and look at environmental constraints that you should take into account when bridging over a wireless connection. We take a close look at wireless bridge configuration from an operational and security perspective followed by event logging and network testing and troubleshooting.

Within the Cisco Aironet wireless LAN family, two series of wireless LAN components are available, namely the 340 series and the 350 series. All of the 340 and 350 series of components, including bridges, adapters, access points (APs), and repeaters, are all interoperable. The basic difference between the two model series relates to the power level output of the radio used.

The 350 series provides a more powerful radio transmitter that the 340 series. The 350 transmitter can operate at power signal strengths up to 100 milliwatts. The 340 transmitter is limited to power strengths up to 30 milliwatts. Depending on the deployment requirements, lower powered 340 series wireless bridges may suit the networking needs of most bridges located within short proximity to other wireless components. For longer transmission distances or in areas where radio signals are impacted by environmental factors, the more powerful 350 series wireless bridge may be better suited. Selecting the right bridge for each specific environment can be facilitated by testing the throughput of the wireless media using the radio link test menu options as described later in this chapter.

Understanding the Role of Traditional Network Bridges

Before we take a look at how wireless bridges work, you need to understand where the bridging concept came from. This understanding will help you have a better perspective regarding why bridges are used and how to better integrate their capabilities within the wireless network environment.

In traditional cabled networks, bridges are used to interconnect smaller network segments together to form a larger contiguous network segment. This provides the means for network nodes such as servers and workstations to communicate over a shared network media link In addition, to providing a link between smaller network segments, bridges are also be used to interconnect network segments that use the same base network protocol but different media or speed to create a single network. An example of this would be to interconnect a TCP/IP network segment that operates at 10 Mbps over twisted-pair cable with a TCP/IP network segment that operates at 100 Mbps using optical fiber. Although these networks use different media speeds, a bridge can be used to interlink the two segments to form a larger network capable of supporting communications between any and all of the workstations on either of the segments. This is often used to support LAN environments where a hybrid network is in use to support the higher throughput requirements of servers and lower throughput requirements of desktop stations.

Bridges operate at Layer 1 (the Physical layer) and Layer 2 (the Data Link layer) of the ISO Protocol Stack (see Figure 6.1).

Figure 6.1 Bridges and the OSI Protocol Stack

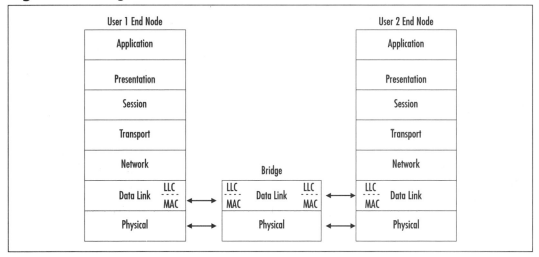

Bridges use a minimum amount of processing and are protocol transparent. They often provide a more cost effective means of interconnecting network segments. Bridges generally perform three basic functions (see Figure 6.2): learning, forwarding, and filtering.

- **Learning** Bridges can "learn" the addresses of network components and their overall location based on either static configurations that are manually entered by an administrator and/or intelligent routing proto-cols that are used by the bridge to learn the network and/or packet traffic analysis. In learning mode, bridges can determine the location of devices be it "local" for devices located on the local segment or "remote" for devices not located on the local segment. While bridges "learn" the network at a high level, they do not have a total under-standing of the true topology of the entire network. Simply speaking they know what is on the local network segment and what is not.

Figure 6.2 shows an example of a bridge learning the location of workstations on each of its interfaces. Notice that on LAN#1 it has identified two workstations (PC-L1A, PC-L1B), and on LAN#2 it has identified to other workstations (PC-L2A and PC-L2B).

- **Forwarding** Bridges have knowledge of the location of network resources (local or remote) and as such, can forward data packets intended for resources not located on the local segment on to the next LAN segment for further transmission and address resolution.

  In Figure 6.2, the first LAN layout provides an example of packet forwarding. In this example, workstation PC-L1B is sending a packet to PC-L2A. The bridge identifies that the packet destination is not on the local interface and thus forwards the packet to the remote side, which in this case is LAN#2 and where PC-L2A is located.

- **Filtering** Bridges can also filter data packets originating and destined for network resources located on the local segment. As such, the bridge discards these packets and prevents the further communication of the packets onto other LAN segments.

  In Figure 6.2, the second LAN layout provides an example of packet filtering. In this example, workstation PC-L1A is sending a packet to PC-L1B. When the bridge sees the packet, it identifies that the packet destina-tion is located on the local interface and thus does not forward the packet to the remote side, and the packet remains on the local segment only.

Types of Network Bridges

Before we take a look at wireless bridges, we take a moment to review the various types of bridges used over traditional cabled networks. As we noted earlier, bridges are used to interlink various types of network segments and as such generally fulfill one or more roles. As we describe each type of network bridge, we draw parallels between the operations of each and how they relate to wireless bridges.

Figure 6.2 Using Network Bridges

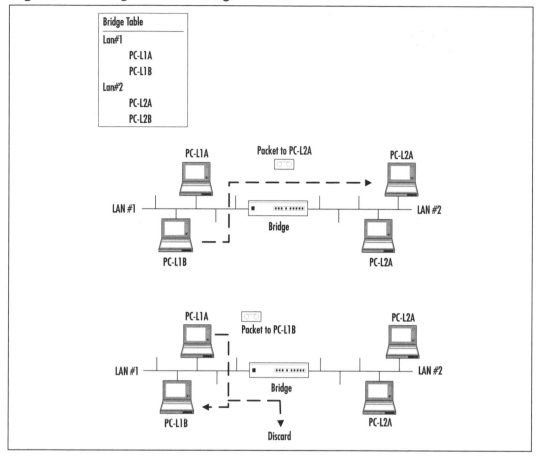

There are four major types of network bridges:

- Transparent
- Translating
- Encapsulating
- Source Route

Transparent Bridges

Transparent bridges are configured on LANs where the same physical and MAC level protocols of the datalink layer are used on both of the segment but where transmission speed may vary. Over traditional cabled LANs, an example of this would be an Ethernet LAN segment operating at 10 Mbps over twisted-pair connected using a bridge to an Ethernet LAN segment operating at 100 Mbps over twisted-pair.

Wireless bridges provide a similar functionality in that client-to-bridge and bridge-to-bridge connections can be established over Ethernet of varying throughputs (1 Mbps, 2 Mbps, 5 Mbps or 11 Mbps) depending on the type of connection and environmental factors that can impact radio transmission and reception. The wireless bridge provides the means to support connections between wireless LAN segments operating at a different throughput rates.

Translating Bridges

Translating bridges are configured for LANs where each LAN segment is using different physical and MAC level protocols. Translating bridges translate data transmissions from one format to the other by manipulating the packet data so that it corresponds to the frame structure of other media. Protocols used at the Network layer and above still need to be compatible for proper communications to occur between network devices.

An example of this would be to use a translating bridge to link an Ethernet LAN and a token ring LAN to each other. In this example, network resources located on the Ethernet LAN can exchange data with users on the token ring LAN and the reverse is also true.

A note of caution: Translation bridges generally do not provide for frame segmentation, and as such, you need to take care to ensure that the size of packets transmitted by a host on one LAN will be supported by the networking protocols of the other LAN. If you don't account for this, invalid packets can be transmitted over a LAN segment causing network issues, deterioration of network services, and availability of the transmission media.

In most cases, wireless bridges are used on Ethernet-based networks. Although the wireless LAN protocols are designed around the same 802.3 MAC layer used by Ethernet networks, wireless protocols are provided with special enhancements that are used to optimize the use of the radio network. Generally speaking, the differences between the 802.3 MAC protocols used on wireless LAN and Ethernet LANs are minimal, and wireless bridges are not required to support MAC-level protocol translation.

Wireless bridges do, however, provide physical media translation, that is bridging the cabled Ethernet LAN with the wireless Ethernet network.

Encapsulating Bridges

Encapsulating bridges are used when similar LAN segments are interconnected using a third intermediary LAN segment that is not similar to the others at either end. An example of this would be bridging two Ethernet LAN segments using a token ring LAN segment in-between. In this example, the encapsulating bridge wraps Ethernet packets destined for the remote LAN into a token ring packet and places them on the token ring. When the encapsulated packet arrives at the remote bridge, it is unwrapped of its token ring envelope and is transmitted over the Ethernet LAN segment. As with translating bridges, you need to take due care to ensure compatibility of frame sizes over different network services.

Wireless bridges generally are not required to fulfill this function.

Source Route Bridges

Some network protocols allow network resources to specify the complete routing instructions for each packet transmitted. The routing information is located within Data Link layer and not the Network layer. Source Route bridges use this routing data to determine the appropriate route for each packet.

Wireless bridges generally are not required to fulfill this function.

Comparing Traditional Bridges with Wireless Bridges

Cisco Aironet wireless bridges are similar to traditional wired network bridges in that they are standalone devices providing an interface between two types of network segments: wired network segments and wireless network segments over TCP/IP and Ethernet. As such, the wireless bridge is akin to a translating bridge, providing an interface that allows devices and resources that are located on the wired network segment to communicate and exchange data with devices and resources that are located on the wireless network segment. The opposite is also true.

The wireless bridge is protocol independent in that it does not verify, analyze, or modify packets that are to be forwarded. When the wireless bridge receives multicast packets, it processes the packet based on the packet header regardless of whether the protocol is recognized. When the wireless bridge receives packets that are intended for its own use, such as network management packets and configuration sessions, the packet is examined and the protocol header is assessed. If the protocol is recognized, the packet is processed. The wireless bridge supports TCP/IP and SNMP conforming to the MIB-I and MIB-II standards.

The Cisco Aironet 340 and 350 wireless bridges use the Direct Sequence Spread Spectrum (DSSS) radio transmission and modulation technique within the 2.4 GHz Industrial Scientific and Medical (ISM) band. It supports transmission rates of up to 11 Mbps over a half-duplex radio channel, meaning it can send or receive transmissions but not do both at the same time.

Cisco Aironet 340 and 350 wireless bridges can communicate with Cisco Aironet APs and other Cisco Aironet wireless devices but not with wireless networking devices manufactured by other vendors.

Cisco Aironet 340 and 350 wireless bridges can be used in one of three modes:

- Wireless bridge between two wired network segments (point-to-point)

- Wireless bridge between three or more wired network segments (point-to-multipoint)

- Wireless bridge used as a repeater (repeater)

Cisco Aironet Wireless Bridge—Point to Point

You can use the Cisco Aironet wireless bridges as the interconnection point between two wired network segments to form a larger contiguous network segment (point-to-point). In this mode, a Cisco Aironet wireless bridge is used to communicate with another Cisco Aironet wireless bridge that is itself connected to its own distinct wired LAN. While both units are configured with a matching system Service Set Identifier (SSID) or wireless LAN number, one of the units is configured as the Root Node while the other unit is configured as a Remote Node. The use of Root Nodes and Remote Nodes are covered in detail in the section entitled "Initial Setup of the Cisco Aironet Wireless Bridge" found later in this chapter.

Wireless radio signals broadcast and received by the Cisco Aironet wireless bridge are used to "bridge" the physical the gap between the LAN segments. Network resources located on one wired network segment can access network resources located on the other wired network segment via the wireless network bridge connection (see Figure 6.3).

This configuration is useful for interlinking two wired LAN segments located on different floors of a building or between different nearby buildings where traditional cabling solutions may not be feasible or are cost prohibitive. This amalgamation of wired LANs using wireless bridging is often referred to as a Virtual LAN. This should not be confused with Virtual LANs or VLANs identifiers used in switched network environments.

Figure 6.3 Point-to-Point Wireless Bridging

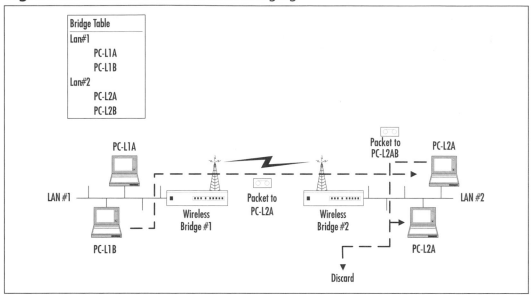

In Figure 6.3, notice how Bridge #1 is used to forward a packet from PC-L1B to PC-L2A and how Bridge #2 is used to filter a packet that is sent from PC-L2A to PC-L2B.

Cisco Aironet Wireless Bridge—Point-to-Multipoint

You can use the Cisco Aironet wireless bridge as the interconnection point between three or more network segments (point-to-multipoint). In this mode, all of the wireless bridges share the same SSID LAN number, but one of the wireless bridges is configured as the Root Node while all of the other wireless bridges are configured as Remote Node (see Figure 6.4).

In point-to-multipoint mode, the wireless radio signals transmitted by one of the Remote Nodes is acknowledged and acted upon only by its parent node or the Root Node. Signals received by Remote Nodes from the Root Node are acknowledged and acted upon. All other communications are discarded.

Cisco Wireless Bridge—Repeater

When a Cisco Aironet wireless bridge is configured as a Remote Node, it is also configured as a *repeater*. Although not a configuration by itself, it is important to note it as an operating distinction. As a repeater, it will rebroadcast any and all communications from the Root Node or from a parent that is destined to a

bridge with a child relationship or that of a wireless bridge that has a child relationship with the remote bridges' own child. This is effective in increasing the
range of the radio signals broadcast by the Root Node and for extending the
radio hop count of transmissions.

Figure 6.4 Point-to-Multipoint Wireless Bridging

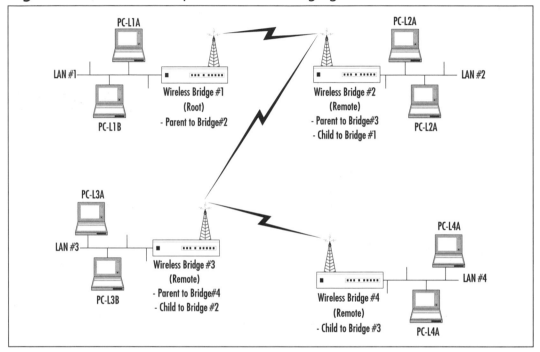

Wireless bridge repeaters can act as standard Remote Nodes with a connected local wired LAN or as standalone repeaters with no local wired LAN
connections.

Installation of the Cisco Aironet Bridge Unit

The Cisco Aironet 340 and 350 wireless bridge consists of an antenna connector,
a 10Base2 network connector, a 10Base5 network connector, a 10BaseT network
connector, a DB-9 female console port connector, an Ethernet LED, a Status
LED, and a Radio LED.

Before powering up the wireless bridge, you should make the antenna, network and console/serial port connections.

Installing the Antenna

The Cisco Aironet wireless bridge provides a connector port for an external antenna on the back of the unit. You can use a low-loss antenna cable to extend the distance between the wireless bridge and the antenna. Before deciding on which type antenna to use, you should perform a wireless site survey to assess the specific environmental factors that will impact the transmission and reception of radio signals. The wireless site survey will provide guidance for the type and placement of antennas and will help establish baseline metrics for the expected sensitivity, range, and data communication rates.

Some of the key factors that will impact the selection and position of antennas include the physical location of the wireless bridge with respect to overall physical environment, power lines, the presence of obstructions, and the types of materials through which the radio signals may have to propagate. Radio signals can also be hampered by interference from other devices operating within the 2.4 GHz frequency range, microwave ovens, electrical motors, and metal objects within the vicinity of the antenna.

DSSS (Direct Sequence Spread Spectrum)

DSSS is the acronym for Direct Sequence Spread Spectrum. In DSSS, the digital data signal is inserted in a higher data rate chipping code according to a predetermined spreading ratio. The *chipping code* is a bit sequence generally consisting of a redundant bit pattern that incorporates the original bit pattern. Figure 6.5 is a simplification of how a statistical technique is used to create the chipping code abstraction from the original bit sequence.

This technique reduces interference because if the original data pattern is compromised, the data can be recovered based on the remainder of the chipping code. The longer the chipping code, the more likely it is that the original data can be recovered. Long chipping codes have the drawback of requiring more bandwidth.

In general, a clear line of sight should be maintained between communicating antennas (see Figure 6.6). Obstructions can attenuate signals thus limiting the range of the wireless bridge. Directional antennas can also be used to focus the radio signal strength in one direction. When sending signals outside, care should be taken to ensure a clear line of sight is available between the wireless bridges. This is especially relevant to the Cisco Aironet 340 wireless bridge transmitting in the 2.4 GHz frequency. Although signals emitted at 2.4 GHz will pass thought most solid objects such as walls, they do not pass through objects with a high water content very well because 2.4 GHz signals are absorbed by water molecules and causes these molecules to become excited, otherwise known as heated. This is the same principle that makes microwave ovens work so well with "wet" food and not very well with "dry" food.

Figure 6.5 Direct Sequence Spread Spectrum

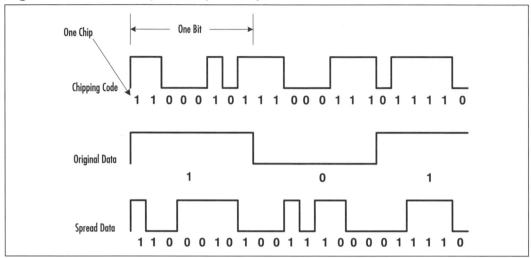
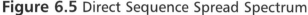

Figure 6.6 Line of Sight

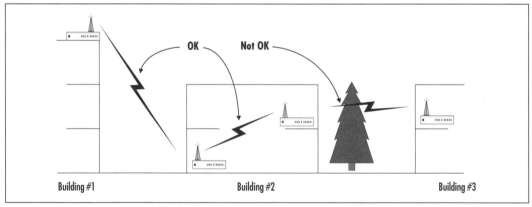

In addition to line of sight considerations, you need to consider the Fresnel zone when planning long-distance radio transmissions or transmissions that will be outside of a building. The Fresnel zone refers to an elliptical area that wraps the direct line of sight path above, below, and to either side (see Chapter 4 for more detail on line of sight and the Fresnel zone).

Lastly, you should install a lightning arrestor to the antenna connector on the wireless bridge when using antennas located outside a building. The lightening arrestor will provide protection from voltage surges resulting from a lightning discharge striking the antenna.

Additional information on the installation and use of antennas, lightening arrestors, low-loss antenna connection cables, and other optional components are covered in greater detail in Chapter 9 of this book.

Configuring the Network Port

You can connect the Cisco Aironet wireless bridge to 10Base2 (Thicknet), 10Base5 (Thicknet), or 10BaseT (twisted-pair) Ethernet LAN segments. The wireless bridge network connection can be used only by one type of network segment at any given time. Segments that are connected to the wireless bridge must conform to the IEEE 802.3 Ethernet specification. If you're connecting the wireless bridge to a network other than an Ethernet segment, you can use a third-party network bridge to interface the non-Ethernet network with one of the Ethernet ports on the wireless bridge.

The wireless bridge's 10BaseT network port can be connected to a hub. In this configuration, the wireless bridge will support up to eight devices connected to the hub. When connecting to a hub using the 10BaseT network interface on the wireless bridge using a standard straight-through twisted-pair cable, you should use the hub's cascade port to allow for the proper transmission of signals. Some hubs use a cascade switch to activate one of the ports in cascade mode; this again allows for the interconnection of two network devices using a standard straight-through twisted-pair cable. If the hub does not have a cascade port or cascade port switch, or when connecting to other end devices such as workstations and servers, you must use a cross-over twisted-pair cable.

LED indicators are provided on the back of the wireless bridge next to the network interfaces indicating which is the active network interface along with the data transmission activity in terms of when packets are being received or transmitted (see Table 6.1).

Table 6.1 LED Indicator Status

Message Type	Radio LED	Status LED	Infrastructure LED	Definition
Association status		Steady green		Connection established to the wireless LAN.

Continued

Table 6.1 Continued

Message Type	Radio LED	Status LED	Infrastructure LED	Definition
		Blinking green		Connection not established to the wireless LAN; check SSID and WEP configuration.
Operational	Blinking green	Steady green		Transmitting and receiving packets over the radio network.
		Steady green	Blinking green	Transmitting and receiving packets.
	Blinking amber	Steady green		Reached maximum retries or radio packet buffer is full. The AP being communicated with may be overloaded. Radio reception may be poor.
Error and warnings		Steady green	Blinking amber	Transmit or receive errors encountered.
			Blinking red	Ethernet cable has been disconnected.
		Blinking amber		General warning. See error logs.
Failure	Steady red	Steady red	Steady red	A firmware failure occurred. Power cycle the bridge or reload firmware.
		Steady red		Firmware upload is in progress.

Configuring the Console Port

The console/serial port connection located on the side of the wireless bridge is used to establish the baseline configurations. A standard 9-pin male to 9-pin female straight-through cable is used to connect a data terminal or a terminal emulation program operating on a PC to the console port. The terminal communications protocol is set to 9600 Baud, no-parity, 8 data bits, and 1 stop bit (9600 8N1). The console port expects a terminal that is set as a DTE (Data Terminal Equipment) device.

Once the initial configurations are completed, you can remove the console connection, because it is not required to be present during routine day-to-day operations. You can perform further configurations after the wireless bridge has been assigned an IP address using Telnet, HTML, or SNMP from a remote host, browser, or management station.

Applying Power

After you install and configure the antenna, network, and console port connections, you can apply power to the wireless bridge. Power is provided by an external AC/DC power supply. The power connector is located on the side of the wireless bridge next to the console port and the On/Off power switch.

When you depress the On/Off power switch to apply power, the LED indicators for Ethernet, Status, and Radio flash in sequence to verify operation of the indicators. During operation, the Ethernet indicator is not active but becomes active in the presence of network activity, specifically, the reception and transmission of packets over the Ethernet interface. The Status indicator should always be on, providing a visual confirmation that a radio association has been established. The Radio indicator becomes active in the presence of radio activity, specifically the transmission or receipt of packets over the radio interface.

For environments deploying Cisco Aironet 350 wireless bridges, you can also provide power remotely over the Ethernet cable linking the bridge with a Cisco Catalyst switch, from a Catalyst inline power patch panel, or from a Cisco power injector. Providing power using one of these solutions eliminates the need to provide localized electrical power in difficult-to-access areas where wireless bridges may be located.

Working with Root and Non-Root Modes on a Wireless Bridge

When architecting a new wireless network, take care to define the overall wireless topology and how wired LAN segments will interface with the wireless network via the wireless bridges. As part of this exercise, one of the wireless bridges will be defined as a Root Node bridge. This Root bridge will be considered the starting point, top, or parent of the network tree. The Root bridge acts as the focal point for all of the wireless traffic generated over the wireless network, that is, all of the wireless traffic generated by each of the wireless bridges associated with the SSID of the Root bridge will pass through the Root bridge. From a network perspective, the Root Node bridge and all its Remote Node bridges will appear as a single multiport bridge.

Generally speaking, the Root bridge is usually connected to the main wired LAN or backbone of the wired network. Or, you can connect the Root bridge to the LAN segment that will generate or receive the most wireless traffic. Note that only one Root bridge can exist. All other wireless network bridges and end nodes will be considered subordinates or children of the Root (see Figure 6.7).

Figure 6.7 Wireless Network Tree Diagram

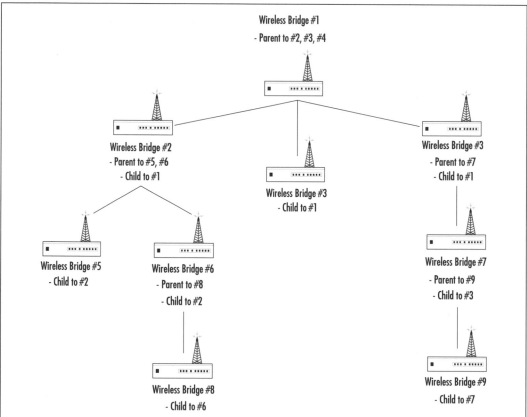

The default configuration for wireless bridges is to have Root mode set to active or "on." When implementing wireless networks with more than one wireless bridge, you can permit only one bridge to remain the root, and you must configure the other bridges to be Remote Nodes. Remote Nodes are also referred to as *repeater* bridges. Repeater bridges can establish communications with a Root bridge or other Remote/Repeater bridges. Root bridges can only establish communications with Remote bridges and not to other Root bridges. Information on how to enable and disable a bridge as a Root Node is provided in the section entitled "Using the Cisco Aironet Wireless Bridge Radio Main Menu" later in this chapter.

Overview of the Spanning Tree Protocol

The Spanning Tree Protocol (STP) was first created to assist in the deployment of bridged networks. Specifically it is used to establish precisely one path between any two nodes on the network even when alternatives are available. In complex meshed networks using bridges, the connection between the source and destination nodes may have multiple paths over which to transmit the data. These alternate paths are referred to as *loops*. Loops can be the cause of the duplication of packets whereby available network throughput can be reduced, affecting the overall network performance.

The spanning tree itself refers to all the network connections and bridges that make up the complete bridged network. The tree originates at the Root bridge and expands out to the farthest bridges. The Root bridge is determined by election or by mandate when a hard-coded assignment is in effect.

Typically, interfaces that create loops are disabled or assigned a high-cost path. When bridging network traffic, the least-cost path is always the one used while higher-cost alternatives are disregarded or available only in the event of a primary link failure. This ensures that one and only one path is ever available (see Figure 6.8). End users usually are unaware that a specific path is being used versus another.

STP was originally developed by Digital Equipment Corporation and was adapted by the IEEE 802 working groups. The Cisco Aironet wireless bridge supports the IEEE 802 STP implementation. For each network link and wireless bridge belonging to the wireless network, STP provides the following:

- **Loop detection** STP detects loops and eliminates redundant paths.

- **Automatic backup of paths** Bridges with redundant paths are assigned a backup role; that is, they are ready to be switched on in the event of a primary link failure.

- **Administrative configurations** Network Administrators can modify the configurations established by STP to address special network requirements. Special requirements can include increasing the STP path cost of expensive network segments such as those being charged per packet, or where the network link does not provide adequate facilities to support the entire throughput demands.

- **Seamless interoperability** LAN segments, servers, and end user workstations do not require special configurations to use bridged networks implementing STP.

- **Bridging of non-routable protocols** Some network protocols are nonrouting. STP provides a bridged environment supporting these protocols.

Figure 6.8 Spanning Tree

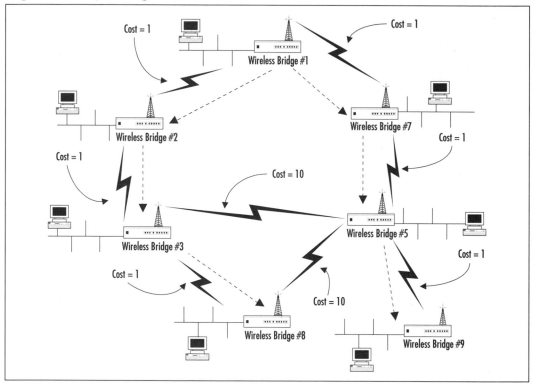

After the resolution of the Root bridge, STP establishes the hierarchy of the spanning tree via a series of bridge-to-bridge negotiations. The negotiations identify the primary interface to be used. Alternate path interfaces are either disabled or assigned path costs equating to secondary, tertiary, and so on, availability in the event of a primary link failure. Communications are passed between bridges using Bridge Protocol Data Units (BPDUs). BPDUs provide information on the bridge ID, port ID, the Root bridge ID, and the Root path cost. The bridge ID is determined based on the number of hops from the Root bridge.

When LANs are bridged by more than one bridge to other segments making up the network, the bridge with the lowest path cost and bridge ID is selected as the primary bridge and interface. The active loop interface is placed in a state referred to as *forwarding*. The remaining bridges supporting the LAN places its network interface in a *blocked* state. Blocked state ports respond only to BPDU packets. Blocked ports can change their state to forwarding in the event of a primary link failure. Bridge link failures are identified by other bridges from the lack of BPDU packet broadcasts from an active loop within the allotted time. In the event of a Root bridge failure, a new Root bridge is identified and a new spanning tree is established starting from the new Root bridge.

BPDU packets consist of the following fields:

- **Protocol Identifier** Identifies the use of STP.

- **Version** Identifies the STP version in use.

- **Message Type** Not used.

- **Flag** A one-byte field that flags the BPDU packet as a Topology Change (TC) or Topology Change Acknowledgement (TCA).

- **Root ID** Lists the Root bridge two-byte priority listing followed by its six-byte ID.

- **Root Path Cost** Identifies the path cost from the bridge originating the BPDU back to the Root bridge. Root path cost can be tailored.

- **Bridge ID** Lists the two-byte priority listing followed by the six-byte ID of the bridge originating the BPDU.

- **Port ID** Identifies the port from which the BPDU was sent. Port IDs are used to identify multiport loops and facilitates the resolution of loops.

- **Message Age** Specifies the total time since the Root bridge sent the network configuration BPDU packet from which the current BPDU packet is based.

- **Maximum Age** Specifies a two-byte time value at which time, the current BPDU should be deleted.

- **Hello Time** Identifies the time interval between Root bridge network configuration messages.

■ **Forward Delay** Identifies the time delay that must elapse before bridges can change from one state to another when a link becomes disabled. An example would be changing the status of an interface from a blocked state to a forwarding state. In this scenario, all of the appropriate bridge interfaces on all affected bridges should be changed at the same time to prevent partial network connectivity availability during a changeover.

As we have noted earlier in this chapter, after a bridge establishes a given link, it learns the MAC addresses of all the devices on each of its segment by analyzing each of the packets received. The learned MAC address is stored within a bridging table on the local bridge that identifies the network interface where the packet was received. Knowledge of this information is used to forward or filter packets that are destined to MAC addresses seen on a specific interface. Over time, the MAC address table is updated through an aging process. The aging process discards MAC addresses that have not been seen over its interfaces over a given period of time.

Designing & Planning...

Enhanced Bridging and Switching Protocols

Recent enhancements in bridging and switching protocols now offer the possibility to support concurrent loops to create a single logical multi-link path. In essence, multiple loops are aggregated into a single logical path providing the full bandwidth of all the links added together. This is beneficial for environments requiring more bandwidth than is available in a single link and for environments requiring high availability for each of its connections.

An example would be that of a bridged WAN link between two sites. Multiple links may be made available for backup and redundancy. Under normal bridging rules, only one link would remain active in a forwarding state while the remaining links would be relegated to a blocked state. The new protocol enhancements provide a capability to uniquely identify these aggregated loops and allow for the transmission of traffic over any one of the segments. The multiloop paths are managed by the protocol to ensure that one and only one active loop will transmits a given packet.

Initial Setup of the Cisco Aironet Wireless Bridge

This section discusses how to configure the Cisco Aironet wireless bridge using the command-line interface and the command menu. The initial configuration is applied upon first powerup. You need to configure the wireless bridge in order to establish a baseline of operation. You accomplish this by connecting a terminal or PC using a terminal emulation program to the Console interface.

You can perform the configuration of the wireless bridge directly via the command-line interface or by using the options menus.

Configuring the Bridge Using the Command-Line Interface

The command-line interface provides a means to enter full commands with options without navigating through the command menus. The command-line interface is the command prompt displayed below the various menu windows (see Figure 6.9). Commands are made up by combining various subcommands available from the command tree structure and appending the value to be set for that command followed by the **Enter** key. The command-line commands follow the same syntax that is provided in the various command menus. Options are also configured in the same way as listed in the various command menus. For additional information on specific command-line syntax and option configurations, refer to the appropriate command menu section in this chapter.

Additionally, you can also use the command-line interface to navigate to submenus by entering the command tree structure syntax that is directed to the desired command menu.

Configuring the Bridge Using the Command Menus

The console option menus are organized via a structure that can be expanded into further submenus and subcommands. Commands are organized in operations that configure the wireless bridge, display information about the settings, display the statistics of operation, or test the system. Navigation of the menu structure is accomplished by entering the menu option number associated with the command to be used or by typing the command at the command prompt located at the bottom of the screen. To return to the previous menu, press **Esc** (Escape) on the terminal keyboard. To return to the main menu directly from a lower sub-menu, press = (equal sign) on the terminal keyboard.

Figure 6.9 Cisco Aironet Wireless Bridge Main Command Menu

```
                             Main Menu
       Option              Value           Description
  1 - Configuration      [ menu  ]      - General configuration
  2 - Statistics         [ menu  ]      - Display statistics
  3 - Association        [ menu  ]      - Association table maintenance
  4 - Filter             [ menu  ]      - Control packet filtering
  5 - Logs               [ menu  ]      - Alarm and log control
  6 - Diagnostics        [ menu  ]      - Maintenance and testing commands
  7 - Privilege          [ write ]      - Set privilege level
  8 - Help                              - Introduction


  Enter an option number or name
  >   ◀

          Command Line Prompt
```

Each of the menus displayed consists of a standard look and feel. At a min-imum, the following are available:

- A Title Line is displayed at the top of the screen indicating which menu is being accessed.

- An Option Number is listed to the left of the screen for each command option available in that particular menu.

- A Value entry is provided for each command indicating either the setting for that option's *actual value* or that the command will drill down to another submenu **Menu**.

- A Description entry provides basic information on the use of the command.

- A command prompt at the bottom of the screen, where operational and menu navigational commands are entered.

All commands, command-line commands, or menu commands, are acted upon and saved in flash memory immediately after pressing **Enter** or by entering the menu option. Although you don't need to perform further actions or enter other commands in order to save a configuration, you can remotely store wireless bridge configurations for backup purposes and build version control. This is referred to as a *configuration dump* and is covered later in this chapter under the section titled "Backing Up Wireless Bridge Configurations."

Whenever the unit is powered up, the main menu is displayed (see Figure 6.10). The commands displayed are part of the first level of the menu structure. This menu structure is also presented when opening up a new Telnet or Web configuration session.

General Configuration Recommendations and Notes

Note that, for troubleshooting and ease of configuration, you should configure wireless bridges while in close proximity to the other wireless network devices that will share the same SSID. This will facilitate the configuration of network parameters while ensuring that strong radio signals are present. After you complete the configuration, you can then relocate the wireless bridge to its intended installation point.

Note that when a Telnet session is active, access to the main menu via the console port *will be temporarily disabled*. If a console connection is made while a Telnet session is active, a message is displayed on the console indicating that a Telnet operation is in progress and from which IP address. You can disconnect a Telnet session from the console by pressing the **Break** key. When you perform a Telnet session break, the configuration menu is returned to the console interface control. Take care to verify all active Telnet sessions before forcing a disconnection. Breaking a session can cause configuration commands to be cut off midstream or in a state of partial configurations, thereby rendering the operations of that function or perhaps the entire wireless bridge as inactive or improperly configured. This can also result in other system errors that could affect the operation of the wireless network.

Performing the Initial Configuration

This section walks you through the two most critical components to be configured during initial powerup. Using the console port of the wireless bridge, we do the following:

- Assign the Radio parameters
  - Set the root parameters

- Set the SSID

- Set the data rate

- Set the distance

■ Assign an IP address

Assigning the Radio Parameters

You must configure the Radio parameters of the wireless bridge before the wireless bridge can communicate with the other wireless network devices. Note that resetting any of the radio parameters while the wireless bridge is in operation will force a disconnect of all wireless communications and a reinitialization of the wireless bridge in question. Active sessions on that bridge will also be terminated and reinitialized.

Setting the Root Parameters

As discussed earlier, if you use two or more wireless bridges to create a wireless network, one of the bridges must be set as Root, and the other bridges must be set as Remote. Cisco Aironet 340 wireless bridges are configured as Root when shipped from the factory.

To change the setting on remote bridges, select the **Configuration** option from the main menu, then select the **Radio** option, and lastly select **Root**. A prompt will be displayed asking to verify that a change in the Root setting is to be made. When using the terminal emulator connected to the console port, pressing **Y** will toggle the setting from on to off and off to on.

Setting the SSID

The SSID is often referred to as the wireless LAN workgroup number or the wireless cell number. It is a unique, case-sensitive, and up to 32-characters-long identifier that is appended to network packets. The SSID defines the name of the wireless LAN workgroup and is used to authenticate and establish communications with other wireless bridges and wireless APs sharing the same SSID. The wireless bridge discards all transmissions received from wireless devices not sharing the same SSID.

To configure the SSID on the new wireless bridge, select the **Configuration** option from the main menu, then select the **Radio** option, and lastly select **SSID**. At the prompt, enter the SSID that is to be associated with this wireless bridge. The SSID must be the same for all wireless network devices that you intend to include within the same wireless network.

Setting the Data Rate

The Data Rate configuration defines the minimum rate at which data will be transmitted between itself and other wireless network devices such as other bridges and APs. Wireless devices within the wireless workgroup can transmit data to the wireless bridge at the minimum rate or at any other available rate. Generally speaking, when a wireless bridge communicates with a Root bridge, the rate used to communicate is the highest rate supported by both units and supported by the media/environment at that time.

To configure the data rate on the wireless bridge, select the **Configuration** option from the main menu, then select the **Radio** option, and lastly select **Rates**. At the prompt, enter the value for the rates. Be sure to select more than one rate, so as to provide fail-safe supporting communications when the media/environment changes due to weather, construction, or other potential interference. If you select only one rate and cannot maintain it, wireless communications will be terminated.

Setting the Distance

The travel distance of wireless signals between wireless bridges can be as short as a few meter (10 feet or less), as in the case of bridging between the floors of a building, or as far away as 40 kilometers (25 miles) when creating a large bridged wireless LAN between segments located in different buildings. The propagation delay of the radio signals can cause a transmitting bridge to assume that a communication never reached its intended recipient. To counter this scenario, the Root Node wireless bridge is configured with a distance parameter that adjusts system timers responsible for network and transmission control on all of the Remote Nodes under its control.

To configure the distance parameter on the wireless bridge, select the **Configuration** option from the main menu, then select the **Radio** option, and lastly select **Distance**. At the prompt, enter the longest expected radio link in terms of kilometers—not miles.

Assigning IP Information

The IP information is used to establish the network address of the wireless bridge. This address is used to remotely communicate with the wireless bridge using Telnet, HTTP, and SNMP. Although you can configure other IP information to specifically tailor the operation of the wireless bridge, this section covers only the basic configuration required to support Telnet and HTTP remote management sessions. Additional configuration options are discussed later in this chapter.

To configure the IP address and other related settings, select the **Configuration** option from the main menu, then select **Ident**. Use the **Inaddr** option to assign the IP address of the wireless bridge. Use the **Inimask** option to configure the network subnet mask. Use the **Gateway** option to configure the gateway address.

Some network configurations will require one or more of these IP address configuration fields to be defined. Please refer to your network administrator for the network configuration information specific to your wireless network environment.

After you enter the IP information, you can establish communications with the wireless bridge by using Telnet and HTTP, as shown in the following sections.

Establishing Communications Using Remote Telnet Access

The menu style and options presented during a Telnet session will be similar to the ones presented during configuration sessions established from the console. Command menu navigation is similar to console-based command menu navigation.

To access the configuration menu from the command prompt of a PC or workstation, enter the following:

```
telnet <IP address of the bridge>
```

Establishing Communications Using Remote Web Browser Access

Although the menu style presented during a Web browser session will be different from the one presented during a Telnet or console session, the options presented under each menu will be similar. Each of the menu pages contain links to command options.

To select a menu option, bring the mouse pointer to the option and click. By default, submenus are not active in terms of configuration, that is, to change any displayed parameter, you must click **Allow Config Changes** first. As mentioned earlier, configuration changes take effect immediately. As a precaution, click the **Disallow Config Changes** once configuration changes have been completed to prevent accidental reconfigurations of the wireless bridge.

Configuration commands with fixed options display the options as a list. The active choice is listed in bold. To select another option, click on the option.

Configuration commands requiring text input display text boxes. You can type information into the text box and then press **Enter**.

A HOME link is provided at the top left of each page as a convenience. Use it to return to the main menu from any submenu.

To access the configuration menu from the URL field of the Web browser software, enter the following:

```
http://<IP address of the bridge>
```

Operational Configuration of the Cisco Aironet Wireless Bridge

After you define the initial configuration , the wireless bridge will have the capability to establish elementary wireless communications with other Cisco bridges and APs. In order to support additional networking and security requirements, you may need to define advanced bridge configuration options.

Using only the network capabilities that were configured on the bridge during the initial setup, administrators can now access the bridge via one of three types of connections:

- Console
- Telnet
- Web browser

Console Access

You can establish console access by connecting a terminal or a PC running a terminal emulation program to the console port on the wireless bridge. The menus displayed are in the same format as those displayed during a Telnet session (refer to Figure 6.9).

Telnet Access

You can establish Telnet access by initiating a Telnet session with the wireless bridge by using the bridge's IP address. (for example, Telnet 10.15.22.11, where 10.15.22.11 is the address of the wireless bridge). The menus displayed are in the same format as those displayed during a console session (refer to Figure 6.9).

Web Browser Access

You can establish Web browser access by initiating a Web session with the wireless bridge by using the bridge's IP address. (for example, http://10.15.22.11, where 10.15.22.11 is the address of the wireless bridge). The top of each Web page provides links to submenu pages. The menu option displayed in each of the submenus is similar to those displayed during console and Telnet session. The formatting of information is provided within the main body of the Web page instead of posting using a new screen (see Figure 6.10).

Figure 6.10 Cisco Aironet Wireless Bridge Main Web Command Menu

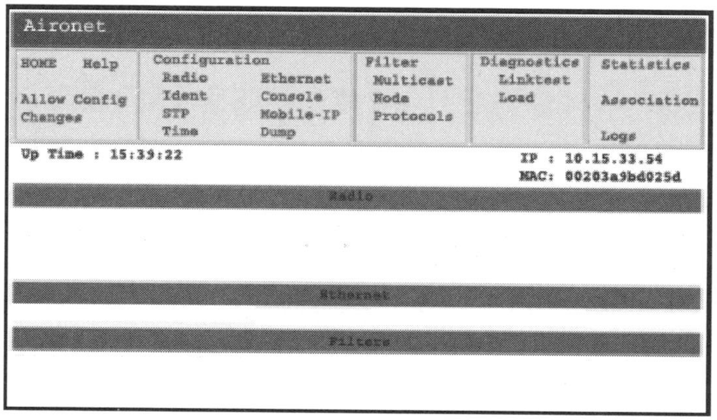

NOTE

Examples and screenshots presented for the remainder of the chapter use the command-line menu format.

You can access advanced configuration options from the wireless bridge main menu by selecting **Configuration**.

The Configuration menu provides the submenus indicated in Figure 6.11. In this section, we discuss each of the Configuration menu submenus along with each of the related parameters.

Figure 6.11 Cisco Aironet Wireless Bridge Configuration Menu

```
Configuration Menu

Option                 Value            Description

1 - Radio              [ menu ]         Radio network paramenters

2 - Ethernet           [ menu ]         Ethernet conifiguration

3 - Ident              [ menu ]         Identification information

4 - Console            [ menu ]         Control console access

5 - Stp                [ menu ]         Spanning Tree Protocol

6 - Mobile IP          [ menu ]         Mobile IP protocol configuration

7 - Time               [ menu ]         Network Time Setup

8 - Dump                                Dump configuration to console

Enter an option number or name, "=" main menu, <ESC> previous menu>
```

Using the Cisco Aironet Wireless Bridge Radio Main Menu

The Radio menu is the first menu listed within the wireless bridge Configuration menu. You can use the Radio menu to configure the options supporting the radio network (see Figure 6.12).

Figure 6.12 Cisco Aironet 340 Radio Configuration Menu

```
Configuration Radio Menu

Option                 Value            Description

1 - Ssid               [ "test" ]       Service set identification

2 - Root               [ on ]           Enable root mode

3 - Rates              [ 1_11 ]         Allowed bit rates in megabits/second

4 - Basic_rates        [ 1 ]            Basic bit rates in megabits/second

5 - Frequency          [ "auto" ]       Center frequency in MHz

6 - Distance           [ 0 ]            Maximum separation in kilometers

7 - I80211             [ menu ]         802.11 parameters

8 - Linktests          [ menu ]         Test the radio link

9 - Extended           [ menu ]         Extended parameters

Enter an option number or name, "=" main menu, <ESC> previous menu
```

> **NOTE**
>
> Several of the options were discussed within the "Performing the Initial Configuration" section earlier in this chapter. These included SSID, root, rates, and distance. They are not repeated here.

Configuring the Basic Rates Option

The Basic_rates option (Radio menu option 4) is configured on the Root Node bridge only and establishes the various supported rates within the wireless network. Normal data communications traffic will be transmitted as the highest sustainable rate available; network control packets, broadcast packets, and multicast packets are transmitted at the lowest transmission rate.

Configuring the Frequency Option

You may configure the Frequency option (Radio menu option 5) on the Root Node bridge only, and it is subject to radio regulations. By default, this option is configured for "auto" and as such supports all of the frequencies available within the local market radio jurisdiction. When initialized, the Root Node bridge will assess the frequencies available and will select an appropriate frequency. In general, you should leave this option at the default value, but you may change it to address environmental interference within a specific frequency.

Configuring the IEEE 802.11 Options

The IEEE80211 options (Radio menu option 7) menu provides configuration options over the radio protocols, power save, and other radio node management functions (see Figure 6.13). The Default settings for these options are typically appropriate for most environments.

Figure 6.13 Cisco Aironet 340 IEEE 802.11 Configuration Menu

```
Configuration Radio I80211 Menu

Option              Value        Description

1 - Beacon          [ 100 ]      Beacon period in Kusec

2 - Dtim            [ 5 ]        DTIM interval

3 - Extend          [ on ]       Allow proprietary extensions

4 - Bcst_ssid       [ on ]       Allow broadcast SSID
```

Continued

Figure 6.13 Continued

```
5 - Rts              [ 2048 ]        RTS/CTS packet size threshold
6 - Privacy          [ menu ]        Privacy configuration
7 - Encapsulation    [ menu ]        Configure packet encapsulation
Enter an option number or name, "=" main menu, <ESC> previous menu
```

Configuring the Beacon Period Option

You can use the Beacon option (IEEE 802.11 menu option 1) to configure the interval time between the broadcast of beacon packets over the network. Beacon packets are like a pulse and are used to synchronize the wireless network and the wireless nodes. While the default is generally appropriate for most environments, you can use shorter beacon interval times to increase response times of devices.

Configuring the Dtim Interval

The Dtim interval option (IEEE 802.11 menu option 1) is used to configure the Delivery Traffic Indicator Map settings. The 802.11 general MAC layer provides power saving features using Traffic Indicator Map (TIM) and Delivery Traffic Indicator Map (DTIM) "beacons". Use of TIMs and DTIMs can greatly increase the effectiveness of wireless LAN deployments using laptops. Power management can save laptop battery life and therefore extend duration of network functionality when operating without a connection to an A/C power outlet.

TIMs are sent periodically by a wireless AP or bridge. TIMs provide a listing of the identity of other wireless nodes with pending have traffic pending. Wireless NIC cards within the wireless node are set at a minimum, configured to wake upon receiving at TIM.

DTIMs are similar to TIM s but with have broad-/multicast traffic indication. DTIMs are sent at lower frequency than TIMs, such as 1 DTIM every 5 TIMs. The recommended power wake setting for NIC cards is at every DTIM. You can also use other user-defined or adaptive wake settings (see Figure 6.14).

The Cisco Aironet 340 wireless bridge provides a facility to configure the interval using the Dtim menu option.

Configuring the Network Management Extension Option

The Network Management Extension option (IEEE 802.11 menu option 3) provides for the communication of additional Cisco specific node and network management information within the management packets sent over the network.

These include enhanced bridge affiliations and communications path management. Although most non-Cisco products generally ignore this additional information, some products may attempt to interpret these extensions, causing errors. In these cases, disable this option by setting it to "off."

Figure 6.14 TIM/DTIM Interval

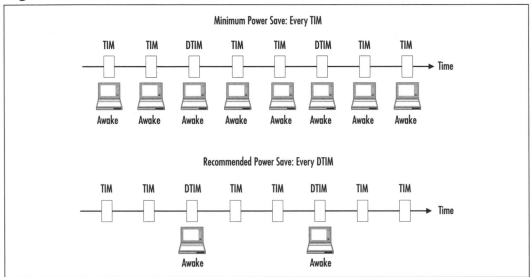

Configuring Allow Broadcast SSID Option

The broadcast SSID (IEEE 802.11 menu option 4), also referred to as no-SSID or empty SSID, is used as a default means or last resort for establishing communications over a wireless network. This option allows for the configuration of bridges to support or disallow communications using the broadcast SSID. For security reasons, you should define a SSID for the wireless network, and all clients should be required to use the appropriate SSID when communicating over the network. As such, this option should generally be disabled by setting it to "off".

Configuring the Request to Send/Clear to Send Option

You can use the RTS/CTS option (IEEE 802.11 menu option 5) to establish a formal communications channel between nodes for the transmission of packets meeting a size threshold. In essence, it is a means of preventing collisions and ensuring that the broadcast medium is used as effectively as possible. When a node is ready to send a packet meeting the predetermined size threshold, the wireless bridge sends a small Request to Send packet over the network in order to obtain a clear channel. The receiving node sends out a small Clear to Send packet over the network, thereby declaring a quiet period from all the other nodes. The transmitting node sends the packet and the network becomes available again.

This is effective in larger dispersed networks where wireless bridges may be several radio hops away from a transmitting bridge or where a bridge may not be within immediate radio range of another transmitting bridge (see Figure 6.15).

Figure 6.15 Channel Assessment

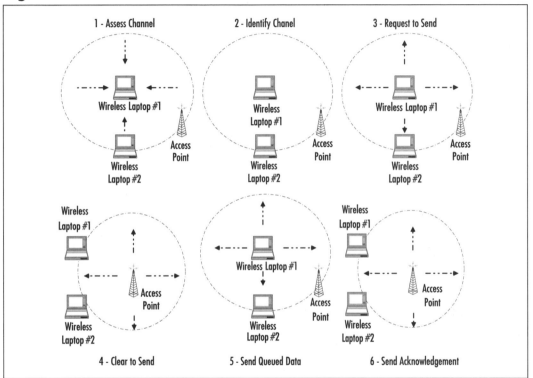

You can configure the option for packets ranging from 100–2,048 bytes. Take care to understand the types and volumes of packet data being transmitted on a regular basis in order to assess which setting is most appropriate for the given environment. Also note that the lower the packet size threshold setting, the greater the amount of RTS/CTS packets will be sent over the network. This will result in lowered network availability for the transmission of actual data packets.

Configuring the Privacy Option

You can use the Privacy option (IEEE 802.11 menu option 6) to establish an encrypted communications channel between the wireless devices that make up the network (see Figure 6.16).

Figure 6.16 Privacy Options Menu

```
Configuration Radio I80211 Privacy Menu

Option              Value           Description

1 - Encryption      [ off ]         Encrypt radio packets

2 - Auth            [ open ]        Authentication mode

3 - Client          [ open ]        Client authentication modes allowed

4 - Key                              Set the keys

5 - Transmit                         Key number for transmit

Enter an option number or name, "=" main menu, <ESC> previous menu
```

- **Encryption option (Privacy menu option 1)** By default, this option is configured to "off" and communications are not encrypted between wireless bridges. When enabled, by changing the setting to the "on" position, communications links are encrypted using the RSA RC4 symmetric encryption algorithm. A symmetric algorithm is an algorithm in which the secret key that is used to encrypt the data is also used to decrypt the data. This implies that the key installed must be the same on all wireless nodes wishing to communicate using an encrypted channel. As a result, key updates must be performed on all nodes as the same time for encrypted communications to remain available.

  Note that when set to "on," a node will participate only in communications on an encrypted channel and will discard any received packets that are not encrypted. You can configure the wireless bridge to support an environment supporting both encrypted and unencrypted communications by selecting the "mixed" setting. From a security perspective, the mixed setting is not recommended because rogue nodes can capture both encrypted and unencrypted packets and perform cryptanalysis operations to determine the secret keys in use.

- **Authentication Mode option (Privacy menu option 2)** This option specifies the type of authentication that is to be used by wireless Remote Node bridges to authenticate to the Root Node wireless bridge. Two modes are available: open and shared key. The open mode allows any Remote Nodes to authenticate to the Root Node. The shared key mode uses a challenge response token to verify that the Remote Node is to be allowed into the network. The challenge consists of the Root Node sending a data token to the Remote Node and requesting it be encrypted and returned back to the Root Node. If decryption is successful, it is deemed that the Remote Node is a valid Remote Node allowed to participate on the wireless network. It is plainly assumed that the client obtained the keys via proper channels and is not a rogue unit.

- **Client option (Privacy menu option 3)** This option is similar to Authentication Mode option in that it is used for authentication purposed and it uses the "open," "shared-key," and "both" options. It is used only by wireless bridges that have also been configured to operate as wireless APs. When operating in this mode, it specifies the authentication to be used by client nodes wishing to associate with a wireless bridge.

- **Key option (Privacy menu option 4)** The Cisco Aironet 340 wireless bridge, supports up to four programmed keys in each device. One of the keys is used at any given time to set up the encrypted session. Each of the four keys must be known to all devices sharing in the communications to ensure that data can be encrypted and decrypted by all nodes. Note that the four keys must also be entered in the same order on each of the wireless devices.

    To enter a key, select the **Key** option. A prompt will be displayed requesting the input of the key string. Key strings are made up of 10 hexadecimal characters for 40-bit keys and 26 hexadecimal characters for 128-bit keys. Key entry is repeated twice for each inputted key to guard against mistyped characters.

- **Transmit option (Privacy menu option 5)** Once the keys are entered, select the [**TRANSMIT**] option and select the desired key. You don't need to configure any "receive" option because knowledge of the key is all that is required from the receiving station to decrypt messages.

Configuring the Packet Encapsulation Option

Although in general, Cisco Aironet wireless bridges do not interoperate with other wireless networking equipment from other vendors out of the box, you can, under certain circumstances, modify the signaling and packet assembly of the Cisco Aironet Bridge to support basic transmissions. You can accomplish this by using the Packet Encapsulation option (IEEE 802.11 menu option 7).

In order for communications to successfully take place between equipment from different wireless vendors, you need to have an understanding of the vendor-specific packet encapsulation protocol being used. The encapsulation table is used to configure the specific packet build settings meeting the communications requirements. This is an advanced function and you should thoroughly investigate and test configuration options prior to deployment.

When configuring a Cisco Aironet 340–only network, you can ignore these options and leave them to their default value of 802.1H.

Configuring the LinkTests Options

The LinkTests menu options (Radio menu option 8) are discussed in the Troubleshooting section later in this chapter.

Configuring the Extended Options

The Extended options (Radio menu option 9) provide access to the various radio parameters that may be modified under certain circumstances (see Figure 6.17). Generally speaking, you should leave these options at their default settings unless environmental conditions or other network factors are causing faults within the network. The default options listed are reflective of the type of application the wireless unit is called to serve.

Figure 6.17 Radio Extended Options Menu

```
Configuration Radio Extended Menu

Option              Value            Description
1 - Bridge_mode     [ bridge_only]   Bridging mode
2 - Parentid        [ any ]           Parent node Id
3 - Parent_timeout  [ off ]          Time to look for specified parent
4 - Time_retry      [ 8 ]            Number of seconds to retry transmit
5 - Count_retry     [ 0 ]            Maximum number transmit retries
6 - Refresh         [ 100 ]          Refresh rate in 1/10 of seconds
7 - Roaming         [ directed ]     Type of roaming control packets
8 - Balance         [ off ]          Load balancing
9 - Diversity       [ off ]          Enable the diversity antennas
01 - Power          [ 20 ]           Transmit power level
```

Continued

Figure 6.17 Continued

```
02 - Fragment          [ 2048 ]          Maximum fragment size
03 - Options                             Enable radio options
Enter an option number or name, "=" main menu, <ESC> previous menu
```

- **Bridge Mode option (Radio Extended menu option 1)** This option establishes which types of communications will be supported by the wireless node. In "bridge_only" mode, wireless bridges will be the only type of unit allowed to communicate with this node. In "access_point" mode, any and all wireless devices, including wireless bridges and wireless nodes, will be allowed to communicate with this node. "Client" mode, will cause this unit to act as a standalone radio repeater and will not have any communications with other units.

- **Parentid option (Radio Extended menu option 2)** When wireless nodes are activated, they engage into a listening mode where they automatically determine a parent with which it will communicate. This is part of the hierarchy or network tree that defines the network architecture. Although this is an automatic process, circumstances may exist where a wireless bridge that has been configured as "client," should be assigned a specific parent. This option allows for the manual definition of a parent node on these bridges.

- **Parent Timeout option (Radio Extended menu option 3)** This option is used to configure the timeout period to be elapsed when communications with a parent is not available, before determining another parent. By configuring this option to the "off" setting, the wireless bridge will communicate only with its associated parent and will never attempt to define an alternate parent. Once the communications are re-established with the parent, the wireless bridge re-associates itself to its parent.

- **Time Retry option (Radio Extended menu option 4)** This option is used to define parameters affecting the retry timers of the transmitters. It is used in concurrence with the Count Retry option. If a packet cannot be transmitted to the intended recipient bridge, parent or child, within the specified time a new association may be established. In the case of the time retry counter exceeding the allowed retry time for a parent bridge, a new parent bridge will be determined. In the case of the time retry counter exceeding the allowed retry time for a child bridge, the parent/child bridge relationship will be dissolved.

You can configure the Time Retry counter from 1 second to 30 seconds.

- **Count Retry option (Radio Extended menu option 5)** This option is used to define parameters affecting the retry counters of the transmitters. It is used in concurrence with the Count Retry Option. If a packet cannot be transmitted to the intended recipient bridge, parent or child, within the specified retry count a new association may be established. In the case of the retry counter exceeding the allowed retry count for a parent bridge, a new parent bridge will be determined. In the case of the retry counter exceeding the allowed retry count for a child bridge, the parent/child bridge relationship will be dissolved.

  You can configure the Count Retry counter from 0 tries to 64 tries. A setting of 0 disables the Count Retry option. In this case, only the Time Retry option is active.

- **Refresh option (Radio Extended menu option 6)** The Refresh option is available on bridges operating as repeater bridges. You can view it as a keep-alive option that ensures long periods of inactive communications with a parent are not the result of a loss in communication. In essence, after a period of inactivity, the repeater bridge sends an empty packet to the parent that is acknowledged by the parent. The Refresh association interval is defined in tenths of a second.

- **Roaming option (Radio Extended menu option 7)** The Roaming Notification Mode is used in scenarios where an associated wireless node has the capability to roam within an environment and as such re-associate itself to a new parent node. When this re-association occurs, the parent forwards a notification to the other wireless bridges informing them of the new relationship.

  When configured in "directed" mode, the bridge will interrogate the new child and will attempt to determine the roaming node's previous parent. Once this has been determined, a packet is sent to the previous parent announcing a change in affiliations.

  Although "directed" mode generally works for most networks, circumstances may exist where it is more effective to broadcast the affiliation change to any and all wireless network devices. To activate the general broadcast, set the Roaming option to "broadcast".

- **Balance option (Radio Extended menu option 8)** The Load Balancing option is used by Root Node bridges in conjunction with the i80211 Extend options (Cisco-specific network management and control options—see Extended Options earlier in this section) to communicate load balancing configurations. The load balancing algorithm is used to balance the parent/child associations between different Remote Nodes based on traffic loads, number of existing associations and other parameters. You can configure this option to "off," "slow," or "fast". The "slow" option executes the load balancing algorithm and association assessment every 30 seconds, whereas the fast" setting executes every 4 seconds.

- **Diversity option (Radio Extended menu option 9)** The diversity option is used to inform the wireless bridge of the presence of two antennas instead of one. When the option is set to "off," the wireless bridge operates as if a single antenna is present in the right antenna connector on the back of the bridge. When set to "on," the wireless bridge is told that two antennas are present.

- **Power option (Radio Extended menu option 01)** The Power Level option is used to reduce the broadcast power of radio transmitter from full power down to 100 milliwatts or 50 milliwatts. In general, the default setting is appropriate for most operations but can be reduced if interference is caused within other devices.

- **Fragment option (Radio Extended menu option 02)** The Fragment Size option is used to determine the largest packet size allowed to be transmitted. Packets exceeding this size limit are rearranged into smaller packets meeting the size restrictions. You can configure the maximum fragment size for values ranging from 256 bytes to 2,048 bytes.

- **Options option (Radio Extended menu option 03)** The Options option is used to activate additional wireless bridge peripheral accessories, which are obtained separately. For information on these options, refer to Chapter 9.

Configuring the Ethernet Port

The Cisco Aironet wireless bridge provides an Ethernet port that can be used to connect an Ethernet LAN. The Ethernet port configurations are defined using the Ethernet menu option (Configuration menu option 2). See Figure 6.18.

Figure 6.18 Ethernet Configuration Menu

```
Configuration Ethernet Menu

Option          Value           Description

1 - Active      [ on ]          Connection active

2 - Size        [ 1518 ]        Maximum frame size

3 - Port        [ auto ]        Port selection

Enter an option number or name, "=" main menu, <ESC> previous menu
```

- **Active option (Ethernet Configuration menu option 1)** The Active option is used to enable or disable the Ethernet port on the back of the wireless bridge. The default setting is "on." When installing a wireless bridge as a repeater only or in a configuration where the Ethernet port is not intended to be used, set the setting to "off." Setting the Active option to "off" disables all bridge activity from that port, lowering the overall processor load.

- **Size option (Ethernet Configuration menu option 2)** The maximum frame size option can be used to extent the maximum frame size limit from 1,518 bytes to 4,096. Don't use this option unless operating an application requiring this change. Reconfiguring this option will require a manual reboot of the wireless bridge before settings become active.

- **Port option (Ethernet Configuration menu option 3)** This option specifies which Ethernet port is to be used. The "auto" setting uses an active scan to determine the active port. If the port is connected to an Ethernet card that is configured to perform this scan, use the manual port definition setting to activate a specific port.

Configuring the Network Identifiers

Network identifiers are used to define network address parameters, network service, and other related configurations (see Figure 6.19). The network identifiers are configured using Ident menu options (Configuration menu option 3) In addition to the configurations listed earlier in the "Performing the Initial Configuration" section, there may be requirements to define some of the advanced radio features available within the Cisco Aironet wireless bridge. These include the following:

- Domain Name Service

- Unit Naming

- DHCP

Figure 6.19 Network Identifier Menu

```
Configuration Ident Menu

Option                Value                    Description
1 - Inaddr           [ 10.053.147.031 ]      Internet address
2 - Inmask           [ 255.255.255.000 ]     Internet subnet mask
3 - Gateway          [ 10.053.147.050 ]      Internet default gateway
4 - Routing          [ menu ]                  IP routing table configuration
5 - Dns1             [ 10.053.147.254 ]      DNS server 1
6 - Dns2             [ 000.000.000.000 ]     DNS server 2
7 - Domain           [ "Wireless" ]          Domain name
8 - Name             [ "CAWB_3f_SE_P3 ]      Node name
9 - Location         [ "" ]                   System location
01 - Contact         [ "" ]                   System contact name
02 - Bootp_DHCP      [ on ]                      Use BOOTP/DHCP on startup
03 - Class           [ "" ]               DHCP class id
```

- **Inaddr, Inmask, and Gateway (Ident menu options 1,2, and 3)** These settings were discussed in the initial installation section and relate to the configuration of the IP address of the wireless bridge, the network subnet mask, and the predefined network gateway.

- **Routing option (Ident menu option 4)** The routing menu configuration defines how IP packets will be routed and forwarded.

- **DNS option (Ident menu options 5, 6, and 7)** The Domain Name Server configuration option provides an input parameter for two DNS addresses. You can obtain them from the local network administrator.

- **Name option (Ident menu option 8)** This options provide a string input parameter of up to 20 characters in length giving the wireless bridge an identity name. This name appears on all console port menus and is used to identify the wireless bridge to all of the members of the wireless network.

- **Location and Contact (Ident menu option 9 and 01)** These options provide a field to input of up to 20 characters per field of wireless bridge manager contact information. This information is read by SNMP management workstations.

- **Bootp_DHCP and Class Option (Ident menu option 02 and 03)** This option, set to the default "on" configuration allows the wireless bridge to request an IP address from a DHCP server or from a BOOTP service. The Class option defines the class of DHCP option.

Console Management Access

Access to the console and remote management features (Configuration menu option 4) can be managed through the use of tables containing user privileges and credentials information. When tables are in use, users who are authorized can access the wireless bridge configurations options and services to which they are cleared for, including Telnet, HTTP, FTP, SNMP, and TFTP, among others. Non-authorized users are denied access.

You can define and manage users through an IP address or a MAC address listing. You can create and maintain listings using the "Add," "Remove," and "Display" menu options. To prevent any form of remote access, you need to set the Remote menu option to "off." When the Remote menu option is set to "on," and no entries are made within the right management tables, privileges are deemed to be universally available, that is any user at any location can access the console.

Configuring Passwords

To configure a password for a selected privilege, select the **Configuration** option from the main menu then select **Console**. The two defined privileges are

- RPassword
- WPassword

Select the privilege for which a password is to be applied. To enter no password, type **none**. To configure a password, enter a character string of at least 5 characters but less than 10 characters. Passwords are case-sensitive. A prompt will ask for a confirmation of the password. To confirm a password, enter the chosen password a second time. After you set the password, the system will monitor for incorrect logins. Failing to enter the correct password at the prompt three consecutive times will cause the wireless bridge to drop the connection. A log entry records the failed login attempts.

> ## Security Alert!
>
> Note that passwords can be changed provided the active password is known. Passwords cannot be changed or reset if forgotten! In the event that a password is forgotten, the unit requiring a password reset will need to be returned to Cisco for maintenance.

Configuring Privileges

Note that privileges are configured directly from the main menu by selecting the **Privilege** option (main menu option 7). Users navigating from a high privilege level to a lower privilege level are not required to re-authenticate. Users navigating from a low privilege level to a higher privilege level must re-authenticate using valid credentials for that level. Three privilege levels are available:

- **Off privilege** This option provides the access level available when a user is logged off. With this configuration enabled, they are able to view the "privilege" and "help" entries of the main menu. You cannot password protect this privilege level.

- **ReadOnly privilege** This option provides read-only access to all submenu command options that display configuration, statistics, and other operational commands. Commands that can modify configurations are not available for use. You can password protect this privilege level.

- **Write privilege** This option provides read/write access to all available menus and options. You can password protect this privilege level.

SNMP Support

The Simple Network Management Protocol is used to provide a management interface on the wireless bridge to remote network management stations. SNMP configurations can be very involved in that information can be remotely obtained from and configured for well over a hundred different variables on the Cisco Aironet 340 wireless bridge.

This brief discussion provides basic configuration instructions that can be used to enable SNMP services on the wireless bridge. For NMS configurations and a listing to the available variable, please consult the Cisco documentation.

To configure SNMP, select the **Configuration** option from the main menu, then select **Console**, and lastly select **Communities**.

- **Adding an SNMP Community** To add an SNMP community on the wireless bridge, select the "add" menu option from the Communities menu. Available options include "Read Only Access," "Any NMS IP Address," and "Any NID."

- **Configuring SNMP Community Access** To configure specific access rights and privileges to an SNMP community, select the "access" menu option from the Communities menu and then select the appropriate option: "read" or "write." The "read" option supports gets and get-nexts SNMP requests from readable variables. The "write" options supports set, gets, and get-nexts on all available variables.

  The default configuration is for all SNMP communities to have "read" access only.

- **Displaying SNMP Communities** To display a SNMP community on the wireless bridge, select the "display" menu option from the Communities menu. The display will consist of the SNMP community name, access mode, NMS IP address, and NMS Node ID.

- **Removing an SNMP Community** To Remove an SNMP community on the wireless bridge, select the "remove" menu option from the Communities menu and enter the name of the community to be removed.

Configuring the Time Service

The Network Time Protocol (NTP) (Configuration menu option 7) can be used to synchronize networked equipment. The Cisco Aironet wireless bridge allows for the specification of a time server and configuration of related parameters (see Figure 6.20).

Figure 6.20 Network Time Service Menu

```
Configuration Time Menu

Option                Value                Description

1 - Time_server      [ 10.053.147.080 ]   Time protocol server

2 - Sntp_server      [ 000.000.000.000 ]  Network time server

3 - Offset           [ -300 ]             GMT offset in minutes

4 - Dst              [ on ]               Use daylight savings time

Enter an option number or name, "=" main menu, <ESC> previous menu
```

- **Time Server option (Configuration Time menu option 1)** The Time Server option defines the network address or DNS name of the time server supporting Unix time protocol. If the Time Server option is defined, leave the SNTP Server option blank.

- **SNTP Server option (Configuration Time menu option 2)** The SNTP Server option defines the network address or DNS name of the simple network time protocol server. If the SNTP Server option is defined, leave the Time Server option blank.

- **Offset option (Configuration Time menu option 3)** This option is used to calibrate the plus or minus time offset from Greenwich Mean Time (GMT) in minutes.

Setting Up Association Tables

Association tables are used to define and manage the parent/child relationship between Cisco Aironet wireless bridges and end node address information to perform traffic routing, load balancing, and other management functions. Wireless bridges acting as parents, can manage up to 2,048 subordinate entries. Entry information provides details on the child node and client name, address, device, and association type. You can manually edit table entries in order to map out a predetermined wireless network tree.

A good example of the application of association tables is in the determination of traffic routing over the wireless network. Using tables, a wireless bridge can be made aware of the Root Node bridge, Remote bridges, and dedicated repeaters. It can be aware of its parent and any child relationship other wireless nodes will have with it. Table entries may also exist for end stations connected via its own Ethernet port and those of other remote wireless bridges.

When a wireless bridge is handed a packet originating from its Ethernet interface or via the radio transmitter, it attempts to determine the destination of the packet. If the destination address is located on its own Ethernet interface, it will forward the packet directly. If the destination address is located on the Root Bridge, child bridge, or an associated dedicated repeater, the wireless bridge forward the packet directly. If the location of the destination address is not known, the wireless bridge will forward the packet to the Root Bridge for further transmission over the LAN connection it has with the main LAN, and to all associated parent bridges.

To configure the association tables, select the Association option (main menu option 3) from the main menu (see Figure 6.21).

Figure 6.21 Association Menu

```
Association Menu
Option                   Value           Description
1 - Display                              Display the table
2 - Summary                              Display the table summary
3 - Maximum              [ 1024 ]        Maximum allowable child nodes
4 - Autoassoc            [ on ]          Allow automatic table additions
5 - Add                                   Control node association
6 - Remove                                Remove association control
7 - Staletime            [ 350 ]         Backbone LAN node stale out time
8 - Niddisp              [ numeric ]     Node Ids display mode
Enter an option number or name, "=" main menu, <ESC> previous menu
```

To display existing associations, select the Display option from the Associations menu. A prompt will appear requesting the type of associations to be displayed. These include the associations shown in Table 6.2.

Table 6.2 Association Options

Type	Definition
All	Displays all of the entries contained within the table
Connected	Displays all of the entries currently connected to the wireless bridge
Hierarchy	Displays the association tree with parent and children associations

Continued

Table 6.2 Continued

Type	Definition
Static	Displays entries that were entered manually
Multicast-filters	Displays multicast entries for which filters have been defined
Node-filters	Displays node entries for which filters have been defined

- **Summary option** The Display Association Table Summary provides an abbreviated listing of direct and indirect associations for the wireless bridge.

- **Maximum option** The maximum allowed number of child nodes option provides a means to manually define the maximum number of child nodes that can be associated with the wireless bridge.

- **Autoassoc option** The auto association option enables the automatic association of parent/child relationships and maintenance of association lists on the wireless bridge. By default, the "on" setting configures the wireless bridge to allow any wireless device requesting an association to receive one. The "off" setting forces the verification of nodes against the predefined static association list.

- **Add option** The manually add association option provides a means for administrators to manually add addresses to the association list. This is useful in establishing an enhanced security policy where only predefined nodes are given the right to associate with a wireless bridge. It is also useful in defining an association tree and limiting access to services by specific nodes.

- **Staletime option** The backbone LAN node stale out time is used within the association table of devices located on Ethernet LAN interface. As a new address is added to the association table, a last seen counter is started and reset every time a packet originating from that address is received on the Ethernet LAN interface.

- **NIDdisp option** The Node Address Display option is used to define the display characteristics when displaying association table information. Options can consist of "numeric" and "name." The default "numeric" option displays the association table information in numeric format only.

The "name" option provides a means for the wireless bridge to display association table information based on the Organizational Unique Identifier.

Using Filters

Wireless network filters are used to manage and minimize wireless traffic based on predefined traffic types. They can be applied to Ethernet LAN originating traffic (*to_radio* option) or to both Ethernet LAN originating traffic and wireless network originating traffic (*both* option). As such, you can use filters to block certain types of packets and can reduce the amount unnecessary wireless transmissions.

When properly configured, filtering can extend the life of battery-operated wireless nodes by providing a means to ensure that all communications sent over the radio transmitter are genuinely required. You should configure all wireless bridges with the same filter sets to ensure a uniform management of all traffic types over the entire wireless network.

To configure the wireless bridge filters, select the **Filter** option (main menu option 4) from the main menu (see Figure 6.22).

Figure 6.22 Filter Menu

```
Filter Menu
Option                  Value          Description
1 - Multicast           [ menu ]       Multicast address filtering
2 - Node                [ menu ]        Node address filtering
3 - Protocols           [ menu ]       Protocol filters
4 - Direction           [ both ]       Packet direction affected by filters
Enter an option number or name, "=" main menu, <ESC> previous menu
```

Configuring the Multicast Option

The Multicast option provides a submenu where you can define and manage multicast filters for each multicast address:

- **Default option** The Default option establishes the filtering to be applied to multicast traffic not originating from a defined multicast address.

  - The "discard" option discards all multicast traffic not originating from a known address.

■ The "forward" option configures the wireless bridge to forward multicast traffic from unknown multicast addresses out onto the wireless network.

■ The "accesspt" option configures the wireless bridge to forward multicast traffic from unknown multicast addresses to APs and wireless bridges only.

■ The "nonsps" option configures the wireless bridge to forward multicast traffic from unknown multicast addresses to wireless devices that do not operate in power saving mode.

■ **Show option** The display filters show option displays the defined multicast filters.

■ **Add and Remove options** The Add and Remove options are used to define and remove multicast filters to multicast addresses. Adding a multicast consists of entering a multicast address and defining the type of action to be performed when a multicast packet is received. Removing a multicast filter consists of specifying which multicast address is to be removed. Once removed, the default actions specified for unknown multicast addresses will be applied to this address.

■ **Radio_Mcast option** The Radio multicast filter option provides a means of managing multicast addresses received from the wireless network.

Configuring the Node Option

The filtering node address option provides a means of filtering packets based on source node addresses. You can define default actions for addresses not contained within the table. You can populate the node address filters by using the IP address of the node in question (see Figure 6.23).

Figure 6.23 Filter Node Menu

```
Filter Node Menu

Option              Value              Description

1 - Ethdst          [ forward ]        Destination address from ethernet

2 - Raddst          [ forward ]        Destination address from radio

3 - Source          [ off ]            Source addresses

4 - Display                            Display the node address filters
```

Continued

Figure 6.23 Continued

```
5 - Ipdisplay                    Display the IP address filters
6 - Add                          Add a node address filter
7 - Remove                       Remove a node address filter
Enter an option number or name, "=" main menu, <ESC> previous menu
```

- **Ethdst option** The Ethernet destination address establishes the default actions to be performed on packets originating from the Ethernet LAN interface of the wireless bridge.

- **Raddst option** The Radio destination address establishes the default actions to be performed on packets originating from the wireless network interface of the wireless bridge.

- **Source option** The default source option is configured to the "off" setting by default, meaning that packet filtering is not active on source addresses. Valid settings for this option include "off," "forward," and "discard."

- **Add and Remove option** The Add and Remove options are used to define and remove filters to originating addresses. Adding an originating address consists of entering an address and defining the type of action to be performed when a packet is received from that address. Removing an originating address filter consists of specifying which address is to be removed. Once removed, the default actions specified for unknown addresses will be applied to this address.

- **Display option** The display node address filters is used to display the node address filter table entries. The display is similar to the association display. The display provides the source address, the filter to be applied and other related information regarding the node.

Configuring the Protocols Option

The filtering protocol option provides a means of filtering packets based on the encapsulation protocol used to wrap the packet. You can define default actions for protocols not defined within the table. Protocol filtering can minimize the transmission of protocol packets that are not used on remote wireless LAN segments. Options are similar to multicast and source address filters. Applying protocol filters can be a complex proposition and is outside of the scope of this chapter.

Event Logging

Event logging is used by the Cisco Aironet 340 wireless bridge to document actions and events which occurred during operation. The wireless bridge provides several types of logs, including the ones shown in Table 6.3.

Table 6.3 Wireless Bridge Logging

Type	Description
Information Log	Records changes in the operation of the wireless bridge
Error Log	Records self-recoverable errors such as transmission errors
Severe Error Log	Records critical errors requiring intervention from an administrator

To use the wireless bridge logs, select the **Log** option (main menu option 5) from the main menu (see Figure 6.24).

Figure 6.24 Logs Menu

```
Logs Menu
Option              Value               Description
1 - History                            Log and alarm history
2 - Clear                              Clear the history buffer
3 - Printlevel      [ all ]            Type of logs to print
4 - Loglevel        [ all ]            Type of logs to save
5 - Ledlevel        [ error/severe ]   Type of logs to light status led
6 - Statistics                         Set alarms on statistics
7 - Network         [ off ]            Log network roaming
8 - Bnodelog        [ off ]            Log backbone node changes
9 - Snmp            [ menu ]           Set-up SNMP traps
01 - Syslog         [10.053.147.131]   Unix syslogd address
02 - Syslevel       [ error/severe ]   Type of logs to send to syslog
03 - Facility       [ 16 ]             Syslog facility number to send
04 - Rcvsyslog      [ on ]             Enable reception of syslog messages
Enter an option number or name, "=" main menu, <ESC> previous menu
```

- **History option** The view log history option provides the means to review logs. Logs are maintained from the time the wireless bridge was initially activated (including power failure resets), from the last log buffer clear operation or from the oldest available record if the log file is full and is removing old entries from the 10KB logs buffer to make room for new entries.

- **Clear option** The clear logs buffer option resets the log history buffer to null.

- **Printlevel option** The type of logs to print option provides a means to define which logs are to be displayed on the console screen. You can use this to facilitate wireless bridge management in that you can specify severe errors, all errors, or print log off to be displayed.

- **Loglevel option** The type of logs to save option defines the type of logs that are to be saved into memory and available for review on the display log history menu. You can specify severe errors, all errors, and logging off for the save operation.

- **Ledlevel option** You can define the type of error to generate the indicator LED to turn amber through this option. You can specify severe errors, all errors, and logging off to trigger the LED.

- **Statistics options** The statistics parameter configuration defines how and when alarm conditions are to be triggered based on the wireless bridge statistics. You can generate logs when statistics change more quickly than specified or upon any changes within statistics, or you can disable them entirely.

- **Network option** Although the wireless bridge logs the roaming of clients to and from its domain, the log network roaming option provides a means to log to register the movement of wireless nodes between other bridges.

- **BnodeLog option** Although the wireless bridge logs all changes of clients from its own domain, the log backbone option provides a means to log changes to the backbone.

- **SNMP option** You can configure the wireless bridge to trigger SNMP traps under certain operating conditions, and you can also configure it to forward traps to a management workstation. Use the Trapdest menu option to define the IP address destination for the traps. The Trapcomm menu option defines the community to be used for the SNMP traps. The Loglevel menu option defines the type of logs which create a trap. The Authtrap menu option activates the authentication failure trap.

- **Syslog, SysLevel, Facility, and Rcvsyslog options** You can save system logs to the 10KB log buffer and simultaneously forward them to a Unix-based host running a Syslog daemon process. This can facilitate the troubleshooting of systems failures and other operational anomalies. Use these options to define the settings for the types of logs forwarded along and the address they are to be forwarded to.

  You can also configure the wireless bridge as a syslog host for the other wireless bridge making up the wireless network by using the Rcvsyslog option.

Viewing Statistics

The Cisco Aironet 340 wireless bridge provides a facility to view statistical information on several operation parameters including such as general status, throughput, error, routing, and related wireless bridge information. To use the wireless bridge logs, select the **Statistics** option from the main menu (see Figure 6.25). To refresh on-screen information, press the **Spacebar**. To clear the display and the statistics press **Shift+C**. To exit the display press **q** (lowercase Q).

Figure 6.25 Statistics Menu

```
Statistics Menu
Option                   Value          Description
1 - Throughput                          Throughput statistics
2 - Radio                               Radio error statistics
3 - Ethernet                            Ethernet error statistics
4 - Status                              Display general status
5 - Map                                 Show network map
6 - Watch                               Record history of a statistic
7 - History                             Display statistic history
8 - Nodes                               Node statistics
9 - ARP                                 ARP table
01 - Display_time     [ 10 ]            Time to re-display screens
02 - IpAdr            [ off ]           Determine client IP addresses
Enter an option number or name, "=" main menu, <ESC> previous menu
```

Throughput Option

The throughput statistics option provides a summary of wireless transmitter statistical throughput information. Display options (Statistics menu option 1) are listed in Table 6.4.

Table 6.4 Throughput Rate Display

Option	Description
Recent rate/s	Displays throughput information per second dated back up to 10 seconds
Total	Displays the throughput totals since the last reset
Average Rate	Displays the throughput total averages since the last reset
Highest Rate	Displays peak throughput since the last reset
Packets	Displays the total number of packets sent or received
Filtered	Displays the total number of filtered (discarded) packets

Radio Option

The radio error statistics menu option provides a submenu displaying an error summary of wireless transmitter and receiver. Display options (Statistics menu option 2) are listed in Table 6.5.

Table 6.5 Radio Option Display

Display	Description
Buffer Full Frame Lost	Displays the number of packets discarded due to a buffer overrun
Duplicate Frames	Displays the number of packets received more than once
CRC Errors	Displays the number of packets received with CRC errors
Retries	Displays the cumulative count of packet retransmits attempts
Max Retries / Frame	Displays the highest count of a retransmit for a packet
Queue Full Discards	Displays the number of discarded packets due transmissions to a wireless bridge not being successful

Duplicate frame errors are generally indicative of packet receive acknowledgements being lost over the network. CRC Errors, retries, and queue full discards are usually caused by interference and noise over the radio path.

Ethernet Option

The Ethernet error statistics menu provides a submenu displaying an error summary occurring over the Ethernet port. Display options (Statistics menu option 3) are listed in Table 6.6.

Table 6.6 Ethernet Display

Display	Description
Buffer Full Frames Lost	Displays the number of packets discarded due to a buffer overrun
CRC Errors	Displays the number of packets received with CRC errors
Collisions	Displays the number of collisions that have occurred
Frame Alignment Errors	Displays the number of misaligned (not a multiple of 8) packet received
Over-length Frames	Displays the number of packets received which exceeded the maximum packet size
Overruns	Displays the number of first-in-first-out (FIFO) overflow errors
Misses	Displays the number of packets lost due to lack of buffer space
Excessive Collisions	Displays the number of transmission failures do to collisions
Deferrals	Displays the number of times a packet transmission was delayed due to network collisions
Excessive Deferrals	Displays the number of times frames were discarded due to excessive deferrals
No Carrier Sense Present	Displays the number of times the Ethernet carrier was not present during a packet transmission
Carrier Sense Lost	Displays the number of times the Ethernet carrier was lost during a packet transmission
Out of Window Collision	Displays the number of times a collision indication occurred after the 64th byte of a frame was transmitted

Continued

Table 6.6 Continued

Display	Description
Underruns	Displays the number of times the transmit FIFO was empty during transmission
Bad Length	Displays the number of times a packet larger than the maximum allowed was attempted to be transmitted

Status Option

The Display Overall Ethernet Status menu option (Statistics menu option 4) displays critical operational configurations and runtime statistics for the wireless transmitter (radio), Ethernet LAN port connections, and filtering.

Map Option

The Display Network Map menu option (Statistics menu option 5) provides a means for the local wireless bridge to query the other wireless network components on their parent/child relationships and display a network tree.

Watch Option

The Watch option (Statistics menu option 6) provides a means to record selected Ethernet statistical information based on a timer. The last 20 saved events are kept.

History Option

The static history display menu option (Statistics menu option 7) displays the saved events generated from the Watch menu option configuration.

Node Option

The node information display menu option (Statistics menu option 8) provides the Ethernet details of a client, including address, signal strength, total number of transmitted and received packets, total number of bytes transmitted and received, and the total number of packets that were retransmitted due to acknowledgements not received.

ARP Option

The ARP information display menu option (Statistics menu option 9) lists the ARP table of the IP to MAC address and provides details regarding support for Ethernet Type II or IEEE 802.2 framing support.

Display Time Option

The screen display time option (Statistics menu option 01) sets the automatic refresh rate for constantly updated screens. The default refresh rate is configured at 10 seconds.

Ipadr Option

The client IP address determination option (Statistics menu option 02) configures the wireless bridge to determine the IP address of client notes that are associated.

Cisco Aironet Wireless Bridge Troubleshooting

The troubleshooting functions such as Telnet, linktests, restart, reset, and ping, among others, are available from the Diagnostics menu. To use the wireless bridge diagnostics functions, select the **Diagnostics** option from the main menu (see Figure 6.26).

Figure 6.26 Diagnostics Menu

```
Diagnostics Menu

Option            Value          Description
1 - Network       [ menu ]       Network connection commands
2 - Linktest      [ menu ]       Run a link test
3 - Restart                      Equivalent to power-up
4 - Defaults                     Return to default configuration
5 - Reset                        Default parts of the configuration
6 - Load          [ menu ]       Load new version of firmware
Enter an option number or name, "=" main menu, <ESC> previous menu
```

Network Menu Option

The Network options submenu provides network-based troubleshooting and support tools. Tools include a facility to establish a Telnet session, ping, and find a wireless bridge.

Connect Option

This option is used to start a Telnet session with another remote wireless bridge located on the wireless network. It is used to remotely access the console menu on the remote wireless bridge in order to remotely support troubleshooting and configuration operations.

You can establish the Telnet connection by using the remote wireless bridge's IP address or in some cases MAC address provided the remote wireless bridge is located on the same bridged wireless LAN. You must enable Telnet on the remote wireless bridge for the connection to be established.

As we mentioned earlier, note that when a Telnet session is active, access to the main menu via the console port *will be temporarily disabled*. This means that if an administrator attempts to initiate a console session with the wireless bridge while the Telnet session is active, a message will be displayed indicating that a Telnet session is currently active and from which IP address it is originating. You can interrupt the Telnet session from the console by pressing the **Break** key. Once the Telnet session is terminated, management control of the wireless bridge is returned to the console.

Before interrupting any active Telnet sessions, you should communicate with the user originating the session to ensure that commands are not terminated midstream or in a state of partial configuration. A possibility exists that commands that have not been completed could result in wireless bridge errors or errors in the operation of the wireless network.

To close a remote wireless bridge Telnet session for the local wireless bridge when configuration and troubleshooting is completed, enter the Telnet escape sequence. By default the escape sequence is configured for **Ctrl+Z**, but you can change it using the Escape menu.

Escape Option

The escape menu option provides a means to reconfigure the Telnet escape sequence from the default **Ctrl+Z** to another defined string up to 10 characters in length. Generally this is required only if the default escape character has an alternate meaning on the host. To enter nonprintable characters, use the following:

- To enter an escape sequence using the Ctrl key, enter the caret (^) character. Example: Enter **Ctrl+Z** as **^z.**

- To enter an escape character using a three-digit octal character number, precede the entry with a back slash. Example: **\021**.

- To enter an escape character using a two-digit hexadecimal number, precede the entry with a string. Example: **$4F**.

Find Option

In locations where several bridges are co-located or in poorly lit locations where it may be difficult to visually identify a wireless bridge, you can use the Find option to trigger the blinking of the amber LED indicators on the remote bridge. Telnet to the desired remote wireless bridge and select the **Find** option. Once you locate the bridge, disengage the find setting by pressing **Ctrl+C**.

Ping Option

You can use the ping option to verify connectivity between wireless bridges and other network devices. A standard ICMP echo request packet is sent to the remote node every 3 seconds until a reply is received or until 5 ICMP echo request packets have been sent. To stop the ping command, press **Ctrl+C**.

Linktest Menu Options

The linktest menu option is used to verify the operational quality of the wireless network. To use the wireless bridge linkstate functions, select the **Linktest** option from the **Diagnostics** menu. See Figure 6.27 for the Linkstest Menu, then read on for a description of each option.

Figure 6.27 Linktest Menu

```
Configuration Radio Linktests Menu

Option              Value          Description

1 - Strength                       Run a signal strength test

2 - Carrier                        Carrier busy statistics

3 - Multicast                      Run a multicast echo test

4 - Unicast                        Run a unicast echo test

5 - Remote                         Run a remote echo test

6 - Destination     [ any ]        Target address
```

Continued

Figure 6.27 Continued

```
7 - Size           [ 512 ]          Packet size
8 - Count          [ 100 ]          Number of packets to send
9 - Rate           [ auto ]         Data rate
01 - Errors                         Radio error statistics
02 - Autotest      [ once ]         Auto echo test
03 - Continuous    [ 0 ]            Repeat echo test once started
Enter an option number or name, "=" main menu, <ESC> previous menu
```

The first option is the Strength option. You can use the signal strength test to verify the carrier signal strength between nodes. The wireless bridge sends an echo request to its parent and to each of the wireless nodes listed in the association tables every second. An assessment of the overall signal strength is listed for each node. The signal strength option is useful for testing the initial installation and location of wireless bridges, antennas, and optional equipment.

Next is the Carrier option. The carrier busy test option is used to determine the overall level of activity present and overall availability for each available frequency. You can use it to help determine which frequency is most appropriate for the intended wireless network, and you can also use it to investigate the presence of radio signaling and jamming equipment. When a wireless bridge is performing a carrier busy test, it does not perform any of the normal wireless bridge operations, and as a result, all associations and communications will be dropped.

The Multicast, Unicast, and Remote echo test options are used to test the reception of packets on a remote wireless bridge from a local wireless bridge. During this test, packets are sent using a Cisco proprietary protocol triggering the remote node to send a reply regarding signal strength and other related parameters.

- You can use the Multicast option to verify and obtain metrics on the wireless transmissions over a local wireless network. Like regular multicast packets, the multicast test packets are sent over the network without any acknowledgement or retries other than the test report added to the test packet. The packet contains the time it was initially sent, and the time it was received again at the point of origin. A signal strength metric, expressed as a percentage of full power, provides the information on the strength of the signal at each transient point on the network.

- You can use the Unicast option to verify the path between the wireless bridge and other nodes on the wireless and Ethernet segment. The same error recovery considerations are applied to this packet as would normal user packets. The information provided in the report packet provides insight into network throughput and congestion along with the number of retry attempts.

- The Remote option provides a means of controlling a multicast link test triggered on a remote bridge, from the local bridge console. The test is the same as the standard multicast test.

The sixth through the ninth options are Destination, Size, Count, and Rate. These echo parameter menu options provide a facility to perform echo tests on wireless bridges:

- The Destination option allows the input of the intended destination for the echo test. Valid entries include the actual device infrastructure address or the value "any." The "any" value configures the wireless bridge to use the first usable entry on listed on its association table.

- The Size and Count options configure the size and number of packets to be sent. The default setting is configured to send 100 packets of 512 bytes. The packet size can be from 24 bytes to 1,500 bytes and the count can be from 1 to 999.

- The rate option specifies the packet transmit data rate. The default "auto" setting uses the maximum rate available. You can enter a specific rate to provide for specialized test case scenarios.

Next is the Errors option. The viewing errors option provides access to the radio error statistics generated during the test.

The Continuous option is the continuously running link test option, which supports the repetition of tests. The value entered configures the time in seconds between each test. A value of zero implies that tests are performed once and are not repeated.

The Autotest option controls the automatic operation of a link test when a repeater associates with its parent. The test uses the existing configured test parameters to define the test options. The acceptable values include "off," to configure that a test is never triggered, "once" to configure that a test is to be triggered only the first time a unit associates with its parent and "always" where a test is triggered every time a node associates with a parent.

When in autotest mode, the wireless bridge LED indicators will turn green in a cyclic pattern. Once the test is completed, the LEDs will be a solid pattern to indicate the results of the test. You can display the patterns shown in Table 6.7.

Table 6.7 Linktest LED Patterns

LED Pattern	Meaning
Green, green, green	Excellent
Green, green, amber	Very good
Green, green, off	Good
Green, amber, off	Satisfactory
Amber, off, off	Fair
Red, off, off	Poor

Restart Option

The restart unit menu option (Diagnostics menu option 3) reboots the Cisco Aironet 340 wireless bridge. The wireless bridge operates as it would if it had just been powered up and all currently existing associations are lost.

Default and Reset Options

The return unit to default configuration menu options (Diagnostics menu options 4 and 5) provide a means to reset the wireless bridge to full factory default using the "default" option or reset specific configuration selections, such as radio and filter, among others, back to factory default.

Loading Firmware and Configurations

The load option (Diagnostics menu option 6) displays a submenu that provides options for loading updates to firmware and configuration files from a remote host into the local main memory of the wireless bridge (see Figure 6.28). Newly downloaded files must be stored into local flash memory before becoming active. Files stored in the flash memory of the bridge are retained during power down.

You can edit configuration text files to act as command line input. These files start with the string "! CONFIGURATION". Commands that are to be executed are listed line-by-line using the standard command-line syntax and option settings.

Figure 6.28 Diagnostics Load Menu Options

```
Diagnostics Load Menu
Option              Value            Description
1 - Xmodem                           - Xmodel load from serial port
2 - Crc-xmodem                       - Xmodem-crc load from serial port
3 - FTP             [ menu ]         - Load using FTP
4 - Distribute      [ menu ]         - Distribute the firmware
5 - Bootp/DHCP      [  on  ]         - Use Bootp/DHCP on startup
6 - Class           [<value>]        - DHCP class ID


Enter an option number or name, "=" main menu, <ESC> previous menu
```

Xmodem and Crc-xmodem

The serial port download option (Diagnostics Load menu options 1 and 2) provides a means of downloading firmware and configuration files via the serial console port using Xmodem (downloads terminate with a checksum) or Crc-xmodem (downloads terminate with a cyclic redundancy checksum).

To start the download, select the appropriate download method (xmodem or crc-xmodem) on the wireless bridge. The following message will be displayed: "Ready for XMODEM download. Use several ^X's to cancel". At this time, begin the transfer using the terminal program on the device connected to the wireless bridge console port. Once the download is started, the following message will be displayed: "XMODEM received 139448 bytes in 00:02:58; 800 bytes/s transfer rate".

Once the download is complete, the firmware is validated and saved into flash memory and the wireless bridge is automatically rebooted with the new code. Upon boot up, the code integrity is verified. If the integrity check is passed, the code will be loaded and become active on the wireless bridge. If the integrity check fails, an error message is displayed indicating that the firmware needs to be reloaded.

FTP—File Transfer Protocol

FTP is used to upload and download firmware on the wireless bridge. You must configure IP addresses on all of the hosts and wireless bridges actively participating in the file transfer as a host or client. The wireless bridge supports four modes of FTP transfers, as listed in Table 6.8. See Figure 6.29 for a listing of the available menu options.

Table 6.8 FTP Transfer Options

Connection Origin	Connection Destination	Action
Local wireless bridge	Remote PC or host	Retrieve a copy of the new firmware (get)
Local wireless bridge	Remote PC or host	Send a copy of the active firmware
Local wireless bridge	Remote wireless bridge	Send or receive a copy of the active firmware
PC or host	Local wireless bridge	Send a copy of the new firmware

Figure 6.29 Diagnostics Load FTP Menu

```
Diagnostics Load Ftp Menu
Option              Value                       Description
1 - Get                                     - Load a firmware/config file
2 - Put                                     - Send a firmware file
3 - Config                                  - Send a configuration file
4 - Dest       [ 000.000.000.000 ]          - Host IP address
5 - Username   [ "" ]                       - Host username
6 - Password                                - Host password
7 - Filename   [ "" ]                       - Host filename
Enter an option number or name, "=" main menu, <ESC> previous menu>
```

- **Get (Diagnostics Load FTP menu option 1)** Used to retrieve firmware or configuration files from a remote PC or host.

- **Put (Diagnostics Load FTP menu option 2)** Used to send firmware or configuration files to a remote PC or host.

- **Config (Diagnostics Load FTP menu option 3)** Used to save local wireless bridge configuration files to a remote PC or host in a format that is compatible with FTP and BOOTP.

- **Dest, Username, Password, and Filename (Diagnostics Load FTP menu option 4, 5, 6, and 7)** Used to identify the remote PC, login to the FTP server and select the file

Distribute

The firmware distribution option (Diagnostics Load menu option 4) provides a means of distributing firmware and configuration files to one or all of the wireless bridges making up the wireless infrastructure. The distribute option provides an efficient means of updating files on remote wireless bridges. See Figure 6.30 for menu options.

Figure 6.30 Diagnostics Load Distribution Menu

```
Diagnostics Load Distribution Menu

Option              Value           Description
1 - Go                              - Start the distribution
2 - Type          [firmware]        - What to distribute
3 - Control       [ "newer"]        - How to control distributions
4 - Add                             - Change distributable configuration
5 - Remove                          - Remove change
6 - Show                            - Show changes
7 - Dump                            - Show Configuration
Enter an option number or name, "=" main menu, <ESC> previous menu>
```

- **Go (Diagnostics Load Distribution menu option 1)** Command used to start the distribution of software to other wireless bridges. The following message appears when the distribution is initiated: "Finding the other units…". At this time, the local wireless bridge sends a Cisco specific broadcast providing information on the firmware to be distributed. Remote wireless bridges opt in or opt out of the download based on the value of the distribute parameter set in the Control option. See Control option in later this list.

- **Type (Diagnostics Load Distribution menu option 2)** Defines what type of file is being distributed.

- **Control (Diagnostics Load Distribution menu option 3)** Configures the wireless bridge response used when queried about a firmware or configuration distribution. Available options include the following:

- **None** The wireless bridge will not respond to distribution queries and will not accept distributions from other wireless bridges.

- **Any** The wireless bridge defers the decision to accept or reject a distribution back to the local wireless bridge initiating the distribution.

- **Newer** The wireless bridge responds only to distributions of newer firmware. For configuration distributions, the setting is equivalent to "Any," as defined previously.

- **None of the Above** Provides a means of configuring a local authentication password on the remote wireless bridge. Wireless bridges initiating distributions must provide the local authentication password before a remote wireless bridge will accept a distribution.

- **Add, Remove, and Show (Diagnostics Load Distribution menu options 4,5, and 6)** Commands are used to add to, remove from, and display the contents of the distribution.

- **Dump (Diagnostics Load Distribution menu option 7)** Displays the configuration distribution status.

BOOTP and DHCP

The BOOTP and DHCP options (Diagnostics Load menu option 5) is used for downloading firmware from a BOOTP or DHCP server. This option is enabled by default.

Class

The Class option (Diagnostics Load menu option 6) defines the DHCP class ID to be used.

Backing Up Wireless Bridge Configurations

Whenever custom configurations are entered on the wireless bridge, you should always save a copy of the configuration on a centralized server. This is referred to as a *dump*. The dump operation involves configuring the console terminal emulator program to save or capture the screen information. Once you have configured this, select the Dump option from the main menu. Three options will be available:

- **All** The All option provides a dump of all system configurations.

- **Non-Default option** The Non-default option provides a dump of all the configuration settings that have been changed from their default settings.

- **Distributable option** The Distributable option provides a dump of all the configurations that are not considered unique to any one specific wireless bridge. Dumps can be transmitted to other wireless bridge for remote configuration. From the Distributable options menu select the type of configuration dump to be used:

  - **Standard Dump option** This provides a dump of the configurations in a standard readable text format.

  - **Encoded Dump option** The Encoded Dump Option provide a dump of the configurations using unique command identifiers instead of worded commands. This is most effective when storing configuration files for later use, in that the unique command identifiers will remain the same over the lifetime of the Cisco Aironet 340 wireless bridge product line.

Summary

This chapter provided detailed design and configuration information on Cisco Aironet wireless bridges. Wireless bridges operate at Layers 1 (Data Link) and 2 (Physical) of the OSI reference model and are used to interlink distinct LAN segments to form a single logical whole. Bridges can learn the location (local or remote) of devices using static configuration inputted by administrators, dynamic configurations generated using intelligent routing protocols, and by analyzing the flow of traffic over the various bridge interfaces. By knowing the location of devices (local or remote), the bridge can forward or filter packets on various interfaces thereby ensuring that required communications paths are available while minimizing the traffic flow to the required minimum.

You can use wireless bridges to bridge cabled LAN segments over distances ranging from a few feet to twenty or more miles. When establishing a wireless bridge network, you need to consider two factors: line of sight and Fresnel Zones. Line of sight refers to establishing a wireless path between two bridge nodes with the minimum of obstructions. A good guideline is that if you can see the target, you should be able to establish a good wireless connection.

The Cisco wireless bridge family is made up of two distinct series of components, the 340 wireless bridge and the 350 wireless bridge. The main difference between these two wireless bridge series revolves primarily around transmitter power. The 340 series wireless bridge can transmit at up to 30 milliwatts whereas the 350 series wireless bridge can transmit at up to 100 milliwatts.

Apart from this distinction and the inline power option (power obtained from the Ethernet cable connected to a Cisco Catalyst switch, power patch panel or power injector) available on the 350 series bridges, both bridges support the basic three modes of operation: point-to-point, point-to-multipoint and repeater. Point-to-point configurations refer to using two wireless bridges to interconnect two LAN segments. In Point-to-point, one cabled LAN segment is bridged to another cabled LAN segment using two wireless bridges. In this case, the wireless network is used only to send traffic between the two LANs.

In point-to-multipoint mode, three or more bridges are interlinked together to form a larger LAN. One of the wireless bridges is configured as the Root Node, whereas the others are configured as Remote Nodes. The Root Node is used to identify the start for the network or root of the network tree. The identification of the Root Node is significant to the definition of the Spanning Tree Protocol and for the establishment of parent/child relationships between each of the bridges used in the point-to-multipoint configuration. The parent/child relationship establishes a hierarchy between devices and defines rules for receiving and transmitting communications between each node.

Wireless bridges configured as repeaters simply rebroadcast transmissions from a wireless bridge for which it is acting as a parent and from the wireless bridge that is acting as it own parent.

The quick installation and configuration steps used during the initial setup of the wireless bridge involve configuring the wireless bridge from the console interface (default setting 9600 8N1) to define the base antenna, radio, and Ethernet port baseline configurations. Once complete, the initial configuration provides the wireless bridge with the basic configuration required to establish elementary communications with other wireless bridges and for using the local Ethernet port.

LEDs are provided to indicate association status, that is, if a connection is established with the wireless LAN; operational status, transmission, and receipt of packets over the wireless LAN; errors and warnings, if transmit or receive errors are encountered; and lastly, bridge failure where errors with the firmware load process occurred.

Once the wireless bridge is operational, you can access the bridge three different ways for additional configuration: through the console interface, using Telnet, and via a Web server interface. To enable Telnet, HTTP, and SNMP, you must configure a local IP address, a subnet mask, and a gateway on the bridge using the **Ident** setting under the **Configuration** option from the main menu. Although the interface access may be different, the menus displayed in each of the access modes provided a consistent layout of features and functions. In addition, you can use the command prompt to speed up command input and menu navigation. Remember that when a Telnet session is active, the console interface is temporarily disabled. You can force a Telnet disconnect from the console using the **Break** key.

The radio parameters options are used to configure the Root Node bridge and for setting the SSID, data rate, and distance. The Radio menu is found in the Configuration menu selection. More advanced options available from the Radio menu include options such as IEEE 802.11 configuration options (Beacon, DTIM), extended network protocols, privacy, and encapsulation used when integrating multiple vendor solutions within a single wireless LAN.

Advanced Ethernet options are used to define the maximum frame size and Ethernet port selection. Network identifiers are used to define DNS, DHCP, and wireless bridge naming.

Console management provides access to the wireless bridge to specific administrative and support personnel with read and write privileges. You can assign passwords to each privilege and class of administrative user by defining RPassword and WPassword. Use these passwords to secure access to the console port. Take special care to remember the password settings because the only way to recover lost password is to send the unit back to Cisco for factory reset. SNMP is supported within the wireless bridge to provide remote management and support. Using the Configuration Console Communities menu, administrators can create, remove, and list SNMP communities.

You should define Network Time Protocol to ensure the proper operation of the network and the synchronization of logged events over all the devices making up the network. It is configured using the Configuration Time menu options.

The Cisco wireless bridge uses association tables to define parent/child relationships between wireless bridges. Wireless bridges connections and relationships can be resolved as connected, hierarchy, static, multicast filters, and node filters. You can use filters to define the operation of the wireless bridge in multicast, node address, protocol, and direction filtering by using the Filter option from the main menu.

Logs and statistics are used to record and identify error and severe error events occurring within the wireless bridge. From these displays, you can review network activity information relating to throughput, radio, Ethernet, map, and ARP, among others.

The Diagnostics menu provides a facility to simplify troubleshooting activities. Network test tools available include Telnet, Ping, and Find. Linktest reports can be used to indicate signal strength; wireless carrier state; multicast, unicast, and remote echo tests; destination addresses; packet configurations, and test settings. LED pattern displays on the wireless bridge provide a local display of link test status and related error conditions when performing link tests.

The Cisco Aironet wireless bridge family can load and save firmware and configuration files. You can use the console interface to upload or download files using Xmodem and Crc-xmodem file exchange protocols. You can establish an FTP session over the cabled network Ethernet port to transfer files to and from a remote agent or a server. Lastly, the Distribute option is available for the download and installation of updated configuration and firmware files between wireless bridges over the wireless network using control management packets. You can configure a local wireless bridge to accept or reject distributions based on the Control settings defined in the Diagnostics Load Distribution Menu. For environments using centralized configuration file management and distribution, use

BOOTP and DHCP to initiate the automated remote download of configuration files.

You can initiate formal backup the wireless bridge configurations by using the Dump menu option located on the main menu. You can configure wireless bridges to provide a dump of system configurations, nondefault option, and the distributable option by using the dump command.

Solutions Fast Track

Installation of the Cisco Aironet Bridge Unit

☑ Used to interconnect LAN segments using a wireless network in between the segments.

☑ The main differences between Cisco Aironet 340 and 350 series wireless bridges is in the strength of the power transceiver (30 milliwatts for 340 and 100 milliwatts for 350) and the inline power option available to the 350 series bridges.

☑ The inline power option provides the bridge with electrical power via its Ethernet port. This option requires that a Cisco Catalyst switch, power distribution, or power injector be used at the remote end of the Ethernet segment.

☑ The Cisco Aironet wireless bridge can learn network addresses, forward packets, and file packets destined to the wireless segment or local Ethernet LAN segment.

☑ Aironet bridges can operate in point-to-point mode where the bridges provide a wireless connection between to cabled LAN segments; Point-to-multipoint mode is implemented where three or more wireless bridges are used to interconnect multiple LAN segments to form a single logical segment; repeater mode is used when a bridge is placed as an intermediary hop point for connections between remote bridges and the Root bridge.

Initial Setup of the Cisco Aironet Wireless Bridge

- ☑ The console interface supports 9600 Baud, no-parity, 8 data bits, and 1 stop bit (9600 8N1).

- ☑ The initial console setup configures the wireless bridge to support basic wireless radio communications with the wireless network, activation of the local Ethernet port, and support for remote access using Telnet and Web.

- ☑ Basic wireless communication is established by setting up and defining the antenna configuration and the SSID.

- ☑ Use a lightening arrestor when installing an antenna outdoors to prevent lightning discharges from damaging the wireless bridge.

- ☑ Three Ethernet ports are provided (10Base2, 10Base5, and 10BaseT) for maximum LAN support. You can use only one LAN port at any time.

- ☑ If you require remote management using Telnet, HTML, or SNMP, you must define an IP address, subnet mask, and gateway address for the wireless bridge.

- ☑ Wireless networks can be made up of many wireless bridges. A hierarchy is defined using parent/child relationships between wireless bridges to provide a coherent topology. Relationships can be static or dynamic depending on the network architecture requirements. A Root Node is defined to establish the start point of the network.

- ☑ SSID, data transmission rates, and distance settings are radio parameters configured for operational use.

- ☑ SSIDs are 32-character identifiers that are used to authenticate members to a wireless work group.

- ☑ Data transmission rates are used to define the minimum rate data will be transmitted between nodes on the wireless network. They range from 1 Mbps to 11 Mbps.

- ☑ The Distance setting is used to define the distance between wireless bridges. This setting is used by the wireless bridge to anticipate the amount of propagation delay that will be present when transmitting and receiving data over the wireless radio path. The range is from a few meters (few feet) to 40 kilometers (25 miles).

Operational Configuration of the Cisco Aironet Wireless Bridge

☑ You can configure the wireless bridge by using console access, Telnet access, and Web access. All of the menus displayed provide a similar menu structure. The information presented is the same with all display formats.

☑ The Radio menu provides access to the radio settings. These include SSID, Root mode, Rates, Basic Rates, Frequency, Distance, 802.11 parameters (TIM, DTIM, CTS), linktests, privacy options (link encryption and network authentication), and extended network parameters.

☑ The Ethernet Port configuration options support the enabling of the port and maximum frame size definition.

☑ The Network Identifier options are used to identify the wireless bridge over the network. Options include the IP address of the bridge, the subnet mask, the gateway, the packet routing configurations, DNS services, the wireless domain name, the local node name and location, contact information, and use of DHCP.

☑ Management console access security is provided using Rpassword and Wpassword.

☑ Association tables are used to define and manage the parent/child relationships between the wireless bridges that make up the wireless network.

☑ Filters are configured to define the wireless operation of the bridge. You can use filters to manage multicast packets, nodes, protocols, and the direction of traffic.

Event Logging

☑ Information logs, error logs, and severe error logs are used to record incidents that have occurred on the wireless bridge.

☑ Several menu options are available to assist in the display and identification of specific log records, including the types of log records to display on the screen, print, and display on the LEDs.

☑ Wireless bridge logs can be sent to a Unix-based syslogd.

Viewing Statistics

☑ Statistics are used to obtain information on the operational status of the wireless bridge. They can also be used to identify network issues and to help design and implement the wireless network radio connections.

☑ Statistics are available with information on data throughput, radio, Ethernet, general status, network mappings, specific nodes, and ARP tables.

Cisco Aironet Wireless Bridge Troubleshooting

☑ In addition to logs and statistics, the wireless bridge also provides access to network command and linktest options to troubleshoot the wireless network.

☑ Network based troubleshooting support tools include ping, Telnet, and find, used to find a specific wireless node.

☑ The Linktest options include tests to determine the signal strength between wireless bridges, carrier status, multicast echo, and unicast echo.

☑ The linktest also provides a means of initiating a test remotely from another wireless bridge.

☑ The wireless bridge can load and save firmware and configuration using Xmodem and Crc-xmodem (over a console connection), FTP (over the Ethernet port) and a bridge specific Distribution option (over the wireless network).

☑ You can also use BOOTP and DHCP to initialize automated remote download of configuration files.

☑ The Dump option provides an additional facility where you can save wireless bridge configurations and nondefault options locally.

Frequently Asked Questions

The following Frequently Asked Questions, answered by the authors of this book, are designed to both measure your understanding of the concepts presented in this chapter and to assist you with real-life implementation of these concepts. To have your questions about this chapter answered by the author, browse to **www.syngress.com/solutions** and click on the **"Ask the Author"** form.

Q: Can I use Cisco Aironet 340 and 350 wireless bridges within a single environment?

A: Yes, you can use 340 and 350 series wireless bridges to create a hybrid environment. In these scenarios, you can effectively use the 340 series wireless bridges to bridge a short distance wireless network, while you can use the 350 series wireless bridge to bridge longer distances up to 40 kilometers (25 miles).

Q: When assigning the SSID used by the wireless bridge network backbone, is it essential that all SSIDs be entered in order?

A: Yes, you should enter the SSIDs used to identify the network in the same order on each of the wireless bridges, APs, and wireless nodes. This is critical in that SSID identification is based on the SSID number and the listing.

Q: Can I print logs displayed on the console?

A: Yes, you can copy, store, and print logs displayed on a terminal emulator operating from a PC or workstation using the local print facilities supported by the PC or workstation.

Q: Once I establish the wireless network using STP, can I display a visual representation of the network to facilitate design enhancement layout?

A: Using the Map option available from the Statistics menu (option 5), you can display a visual layout of the parent/child relationship of each wireless bridges making up the network.

Q: The distribute option provides a means of distributing firmware and configuration files from one source wireless bridge out to other bridges. Is a facility available to authenticate that the wireless bridge acting as the source is really a valid host on the network?

A: The Control option available from the Diagnostics Load Distribution menu (option 2) provides a means to assign the type of distributions a local wireless bridge will accept from a distribution source wireless bridge. You can define a password so that only wireless bridges with the proper password can send distributed files to the local node.

Chapter 7

Installation and Configuration of Cisco Wireless Network Cards

Solutions in this chapter:

- Cisco Aironet Client Adapter Types
- Cisco Aironet Client Utility (ACU)
- Cisco Aironet Client Installation and Configuration
- Cisco Aironet Client Network Security Configuration
- Client Adapter Auto Installer
- Client Adapter Diagnostics

☑ Summary

☑ Solutions Fast Track

☑ Frequently Asked Questions

Introduction

The Cisco Aironet client adapter cards are versatile wireless LAN adapters that are used to establish network connections between the wireless client node and other Cisco Aironet client nodes or Cisco Aironet wireless network access points (APs). The Wireless LAN adapters are configured to operate in one of two network modes: *Infrastructure* network mode or *Ad Hoc* network mode.

When used in the Infrastructure network mode, the cards provide networking capabilities that establish and support communications between the wireless client node and one or more Cisco Aironet APs. You can configure infrastructure clients to communicate with all available wireless APs with preferred affiliations to specific wireless APs. Preferred affiliations provide network architects with the ability to better plan and engineer wireless network deployment taking into consideration issues of client node roaming and redundancy engineering.

Ad Hoc network mode provides wireless client nodes with the capability to establish peer-to-peer network connections with other wireless client nodes. When configured in Ad Hoc, infrastructure components are not required to establish the network connection. Two or more workstations configured to access the same wireless network is all that is needed. The primary use of Ad Hoc network mode configurations is for peer-to-peer file exchange between wireless clients over the wireless radio network.

The Cisco Aironet wireless LAN adapters support the use of one or more security overlays to secure communications. These consist of Service Set ID (SSID) identification, preferred AP configurations, and Wired Equivalent Protocol (WEP) session encryption. The WEP mode provides multiple modes of operation to address different network communication security requirements, including 40-bit and 128-bit cryptography and dynamic WEP key updates.

Lastly, the Cisco Aironet wireless LAN adapters can be installed in the wireless client node with or without the Aironet Client Utility (ACU). The ACU is used by administrators and end users to configure the Aironet wireless LAN adapter locally and to perform wireless network tests and general system diagnostics. The ACU can also support centralized administration and distribution wireless client node configuration files via a localized auto-installer. In this mode, administrators can predefine user configurations and issue them with the adapter and the wireless LAN adapter card driver.

This chapter provides detailed information on the installation and configuration of Cisco wireless LAN adapters, provides insight on option selections to support both Infrastructure network and Ad Hoc network modes of operations, and describes the troubleshooting features that are available on the LAN adapter itself and via the ACU.

Cisco Aironet Client Adapter Types

Cisco Aironet client adapters are available in several form factors. These include PC Card, LM Card, PC Interface (PCI), and mini PCI card (see Table 7.1). The support for multiple card form factors provides the capability to integrate a multitude of end client devices within the wireless LAN environment.

Although distinctions exist regarding the type of physical interface used by the wireless LAN adapter to connect to the client node device bus, all wireless LAN adapters, with the exception of Mini PCI adapters, possess of the same basic components. These include a wireless antenna, a network access card, status LEDs, and the various system drivers.

Table 7.1 Aironet Wireless LAN Adapter Form Factor

Client Adapter Type	Features
PC card	A PCMCIA card supporting external Personal Computer Memory Card International Association (PCMCIA) Type II or Type III interfaces. Generally used on laptops, personal digital assistants (PDAs), and other portable computing platforms.
LM card	A PCMCIA card supporting internal PCMCIA Type II or Type III interface. Generally used on handheld devices.
PCI card	A PCI card that can be inserted into a PCI card expansion slot interface. Generally used on desktop computing platforms.
Mini PCI	A mini PCI card can be inserted in an internal Type IIIa mini CI slot interface. Generally used on laptop computing platforms. Note that the Mini PCI card does not have status LEDs because it is generally installed within a device and the card is not visible from the exterior.

Comparing the Cisco Aironet 340 and 350 Series Wireless LAN Adapters

Two series of wireless LAN adapters are available for each of the form factors listed in Table 7.1, namely the 340 series and the 350 series. The 340 and 350 series of adapter and infrastructure network components, such as wireless APs, bridges and repeaters, are all interoperable. The basic difference between the two model series relates to the strength of the radio used.

The 350 series provides a more powerful radio transmitter than the 340 series. The 350 transmitter can operate at power signal strengths up to 100 milliwatts. The 340 transmitter is limited to power strengths up to 30 milliwatts. Depending on the deployment requirements, lower powered 340 series wireless adapters may suit the networking needs of most client nodes within short proximity to each other or to the wireless infrastructure components. For longer transmission distances or in areas where radio signals are impacted by environmental factors, the more powerful 350 series wireless adapters may be better suited. Choosing the right adapter for each specific environment can be facilitated by using the radio link test set provided with the ACU application. Information on how to use the test suite is provided in the section entitled "Client Adapter Diagnostics."

WARNING

You should also consider user safety precautions when employing any form of radio transmitter. Government guidelines on the use of and exposure to radio transmitters are available from the Federal Communications Commission. You can obtain reports via the Internet at www.fcc.gov.

Apart from the model line difference between the 340 and 350 series adapter, a distinction is also present within each of the model lines. The 341 and 351 model wireless LAN client adapters support 40-bit WEP encryption. The 342 and 352 model wireless LAN adapters support both 40-bit and 128-bit WEP encryption. Table 7.2 provides a matrix of the capabilities of each adapter type.

Table 7.2 Aironet Adapter Models

Aironet Adapter	Model 3x1	Model 3x2
340 series	Radio transmitter can operate up to 30 milliwatts Supports 40-bit WEP	Radio transmitter can operate up to 30 milliwatts Supports 40-bit WEP Supports 128-bit WEP

Continued

Table 7.2 Continued

Aironet Adapter	Model 3x1	Model 3x2
350 series	Radio transmitter can operate up to 100 milliwatts Supports 40-bit WEP	Radio transmitter can operate up to 100 milliwatts Supports 40-bit WEP Supports 128-1bit WEP

Note that from a configuration standpoint, you can configure all of the wireless adapters using the same ACU. Distinctions are present only within the security submenus that provide support for the added cryptographic options within the 342 and 352 adapters.

Configuring & Implementing…

Wireless LAN Adapter Specifications

The wireless LAN adapter supports 1, 2, 5.5, and 11 Mbps wireless LANs based on the IEEE 802.11b standard. When operating at 1 Mbps, the adapter users Differential Bi-Phase Shift Key (DBPSK) phase modulation, at 2 Mbps, it uses Differential Quadrature Phase Shift Keying (DQPSK), and at 5.5 and 11 Mbps it uses Complimentary Code Keying (CCK).

Transmission range for cards operating at 1 Mbps throughput is generally up to 1,500 feet for outdoor locations and up to 300 feet for indoor locations. Transmission range for cards operating at 11 Mbps throughput is generally up to 400 feet for outdoor locations and up to 100 feet for indoor locations.

Cisco Aironet Client Utility (ACU)

The Cisco ACU is the configuration application that provides the interface to configure the Cisco Aironet 340 and 350 Client adapters. Administrators can use the ACU to create profiles for users with restricted access to configuration menus. Windows XP provides a capability to configure the client adapter directly from the control panel menu. The Windows XP control panel configuration interface will not be discussed as part of this chapter.

The ACU consists of four main areas (see Figure 7.1). The command bar to the top of screen, the menu bar directly below the command bar, the main screen, and the status bar located to the bottom of the screen. The command bar provides access to configuration commands and options. The menu bar provides access to operational and troubleshooting options. The main window is where the various configuration and status screens display information. The status bar provides information on the current status of the client adapter, including if it has associated with a wireless AP, if it currently not associated, if it is inserted, if it is being flashed with new firmware, or if the status is not available.

Figure 7.1 Aironet Configuration Utility Main Screen

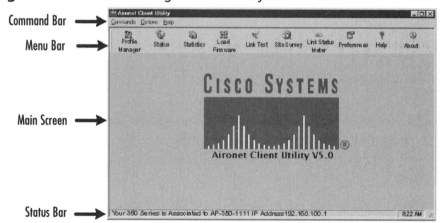

Installing and Configuring the Cisco Aironet LAN Adapter Card

The ACU is installed and configured after the Cisco Aironet LAN adapter Card and drivers have been installed. To install the card and driver, insert the Cisco Aironet 340 or 350 series wireless LAN adapter and insert the Cisco Aironet CD-ROM. Follow the on-screen instructions for the installation of the driver:

1. Upon completion of the installation of system driver files, select the **Network icon** located on the Control Panel.

2. From the **Network** screen, select the Cisco Wireless LAN adapter and click the **Properties** tab.

3. Select **Advanced | Client Name**.

4. Enter the client name that is to be associated with this machine and press **Enter**.

5. Enter the wireless network's SSID within the provided SSID text box.

6. If the wireless client will obtain a Dynamic Host Configuration Protocol (DHCP) IP address from the wireless network, click **OK** and follow the on-screen instructions to reboot.

7. If the wireless client is to use a static IP, select the **TCP/IP** tab from the **Network** screen.

8. Select **TCP/IP** then select **Cisco Wireless LAN Adapter**.

9. From the **Properties** tab, select **Specify an IP Address** and enter the wireless client's IP address.

10. Click **OK** to acknowledge the TCP/IP configuration and click **OK** to acknowledge the Network configurations.

11. Follow the on-screen instructions to reboot.

Installing the Cisco ACU

The Cisco ACU will be used to configure the Aironet LAN Adapter and to access the troubleshooting and diagnostics menus. The ACU is a typical Windows and Macintosh application. Before attempting to install the ACU, ensure that the Aironet LAN Adapter card and drivers have been installed.

Configuring & Implementing...

Linux and WinCE Configurations

Obtaining the Wireless LAN Adapter

Go to the Cisco Wireless LAN URL at http://cisco.com/public/ sw-center/sw-wireless.shtml. For Linux drivers, select the **For Linux** link; for WinCE, select the appropriate Windows CE version. Several file download options are available, including adapter drivers, ACU, and various readme files.

Installing the Linux ACU

From the For Linux wireless files page, download the drivers or ACU and save the compressed file to the local drive. Uncompress the file to a writeable directory, then type **sh /.cwinstall** and press **Enter**. The Installation screen will be displayed and will request the location of the

Continued

Web browser on the local machine. The installation script will then ask which Linux version is installed. This will be used to determine if card support is present. Follow the remaining on-screen instructions and configure the wireless LAN adapter to match the local wireless network configurations using the ACU. The ACU provides the main submenu commands from pull-down menus. The configuration screens are similar to the Windows screens provided in this chapter.

Installing the WinCE ACU

Connect the WinCE device to a PC host running ActiveSync. This will be used to exchange files between the PC and the WinCE device. Double-click the CiscoWinCExxxvxxxx.exe file to create an install directory and copy the compressed installation files. Launch the Windows CE Application Manager—CeAppMgr from ActiveSync. The installation files will be downloaded to the Windows CE device to the default location. Insert the wireless LAN adapter. The Windows CE device will configure the adapter and the Cisco ACU dialog window will be displayed. Enter the configurations for the local wireless LAN. Although the ACU provides the same configuration capabilities as those found on the Windows client, the screen displays have been minimized to support the smaller display typically found on Windows CE devices.

Perform the ACU installation by inserting the application installation CD-ROM and following the on-screen prompts. The ACU supports Windows XP, ME, 2000, NT, 98, and 95, as well as Linux and MacOS 9. Once you install the ACU and reboot the computer, the green LEDs will blink on the Aironet client adapter. This will confirm that the ACU installation was successful and communications with the Aironet Client adapter have been established.

Cisco Aironet Client Profile Manager

The ACU Profile Manager provides a facility through which you can define up to sixteen different client profiles in order to support the varying wireless network environments a client may be subject to during roaming. You can establish distinct environment configurations to support corporate wireless LAN networking, public wireless network access, home wireless network access, and ad hoc peer-to-peer networks. You can save and export configuration profiles to support remote backup in the event of system failure or to re-create installed configurations on other wireless client nodes.

Creating a New Aironet Client Profile

The create new profile function is used to define Aironet LAN Adapter configurations. To create a new client profile, follow these steps:

1. Launch the ACU, accessed from the computer's desktop or from the application menu, and select the **Profile Manager** icon located on the menu bar (refer to Figure 7.1).

2. Click **Add** and input the name of the profile that is to be configured.

3. Once completed, press **Enter**, and the profile properties screens for the new profile will be displayed. If the default values are appropriate for the new profile, click **OK**.

You can change the configurations later to match the local wireless LAN environment.

Using an Existing Aironet Client Profile

Three modes of operation are available to the wireless client for selecting the profile to be used during a session. The first is referred to as Manual Profile Selection. In this mode, you need to manually select the profile to be used during the wireless networking session from the list of available profiles provided in the drop-down profile list menu.

The second mode of operation is referred to as Auto Profile Selection. In this mode, the wireless client automatically chooses which profile to use. If the wireless LAN client becomes disassociated from the wireless network for more than 10 seconds or longer than the time defined in the Lightweight Extensible Authentication Protocol (LEAP) configuration, it will attempt to re-establish a wireless networking session using an alternate profile.

The third mode is called Allow Windows To Configure My Wireless Network Settings, which is available only to Windows XP users. This option disregards any ACU configurations and provides access to configurations defined within Windows XP. In most cases, the ACU would not be used or installed in conjunction with Windows XP for everyday wireless networking. The only benefit to installing the ACU on Windows XP platforms would be to access the advanced troubleshooting and diagnostics functions available only from the ACU.

Modifying an Existing Aironet Client Profile

You can modify profiles that you have saved within the ACU Profile Manager to address changes in configurations or to create new profiles. To access an existing profile, select the requested profile from the **Profile Manager** profile listing drop-down menu and click **Edit**. The profile properties will be displayed on the main screen. Once you have reconfigured the profile settings, you can save the profile and include it as a valid option for use with the Auto Profile Selection by clicking the **Include Profile in Auto profile Selection** checkbox. If you are using LEAP, you can only include the profile in the Auto Profile Selection if it has been saved with a LEAP username and password pair. Once the configurations are complete, click **OK** to save the configurations.

Reconfiguring Profiles with the Default Aironet Client Profile Values

At times, you may want to reset a profile to the original baseline client profile setting values. To accomplish this, select the profile from the **Profile Manager** profile listing drop-down menu and click **Use Defaults**. The system will prompt for a confirmation. Clicking **Yes** followed by **OK** will reconfigure the profile with the baseline option settings and save the profile.

Renaming Profiles Stored within the ACU

To rename an existing profile, select the profile from the **Profile Manager** profile listing drop-down menu and click **Rename**. Enter the new name information within the text box provided and click **OK** to save the profile with the new name.

Deleting Profiles Stored within the ACU

To delete profile configurations that are no longer used or required, select the profile from the **Profile Manager** profile listing drop-down menu and click **Delete**. The system will prompt for a confirmation. Clicking **Yes** followed by **OK** will delete the profile from the ACU.

Importing Profiles to the ACU

The import profile function of the ACU provides the capability to import profiles that were previously saved from the current ACU or from another ACU. This is useful for recovering profiles that have become corrupt due to a system or application fault, or to import profile configurations that are to be used on a new network or to emulate the configurations of an existing wireless node.

You can import profiles from the local hard disk, floppy, or other drive or system folder accessible from the system. To import a profile from the **Profile Manager** window, click **Import** and use the directory navigation tools to select the profile. Click the **Open** button. The ACU imports the profile and makes it available for use within the profile drop-down menu listing.

Exporting Profiles from the ACU

The export profile function of the ACU provides the capability to export profiles that have previously been configured and saved on the current ACU. This is useful for creating backup copies of configuration profiles and for distributing an existing profile to other users.

You can export profiles to the local hard disk, floppy, or other drive or system folder accessible from the system. To export a profile from the **Profile Manager** window, select a profile from the profile drop-down menu listing and click **Export**. Use the directory navigation tools to select the location where you want to save the profile. You can change the Save As name if required. Click **Save**. The ACU exports the profile to the requested location.

Restricting Profile Access to Administrative Users

The ACU installed on Windows XP, 2000, and NT operating systems supports multiple classes of users. This means that the base operating system can make a distinction between administrative users and non-administrative users (regular users). As such, you can configure the ACU to support administrative rights for administrative tasks involving profiles. In this mode, regular users are not allowed to access profile or configuration functions within the local ACU.

To modify the administrative control of the ACU parameters, log in to the system using an account with administrative rights and access the ACU. Select the **Preferences** icon on the menu bar (see Figure 7.1). Deselect the **Allow Non-Administrator Users to Use ACU to Modify Profiles** checkbox. Click **OK** to save the configuration. Regular users will not be able to use the ACU to modify profiles or configurations.

To allow regular users to access profiles and configuration screens, log in to the system using an account with administrative rights and access the ACU. Select the **Preferences** icon on the menu tab. Select the **Allow Non-Administrator Users to Use ACU to Modify Profiles** checkbox.

Click **OK** to save the configuration. Regular users will now be able to use the ACU to modify profiles or configurations.

Cisco Aironet Client Installation and Configuration

As previously mentioned, the Cisco Aironet client LAN adapter configurations are managed using profiles. When you open a profile, several configuration window tabs are available, as listed in Table 7.3 and Figure 7.2.

Table 7.3 Profile Configuration Options Description

Options	Descriptions
System Parameters	Basic wireless network settings
Radio Frequency (RF) Network	Wireless transmitter configurations
Advanced (Infrastructure)	Defines the behavior of the client within infrastructure networks
Advanced (Ad Hoc)	Defines the behavior of the client within a peer-to-peer network
Network Security	Defines the operational security settings used for authentication and encryption purposes

Figure 7.2 System Parameter Configuration Tab

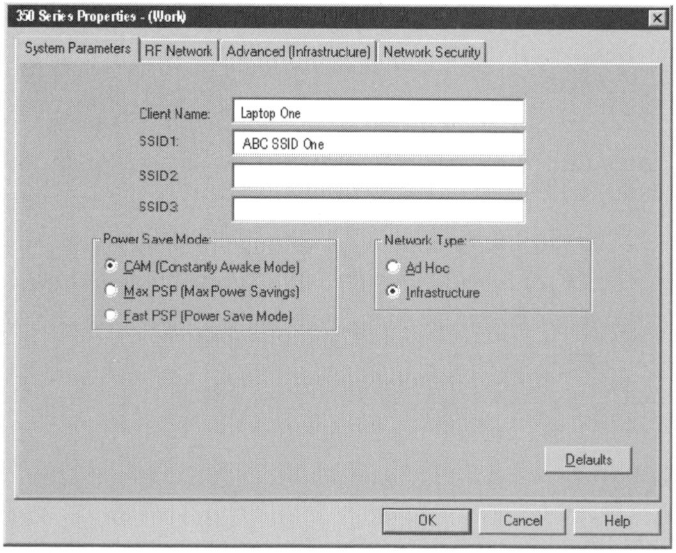

Configuring the Cisco Aironet Client System Parameter

The System Parameter configuration screen provides access to the configuration parameters that define the basic wireless operation of the Aironet client adapter over the wireless network in both Infrastructure and Ad Hoc mode. The System Parameter screen is displayed when you create a new profile or select a profile to be modified (see Figure 7.2).

The fields available for configurations include the following, which we take a closer look at in the next sections:

- Client Name
- SSID
- Power Save Mode
- Network Type

Setting the Client Name

The Client Name field is where you set the name that is to be associated with the Aironet LAN adapter. This name will be displayed within the Aironet wireless AP connections displays and on peer-to-peer networked wireless nodes. The client name is also used in cross-reference with wireless nodes Media Access Control (MAC) address. The name you enter can be up to 16 characters in length. The default value for the client name setting is empty.

Setting the SSID

The Service Set Identifiers are used to identify to which wireless networks each client node is allowed to participate. The screen provides for up to three SSID entries. The entry of multiple SSID settings provide client nodes with the capability to roam between wireless networks using a single profile. Each SSID entry can be up to 32 characters in length. Note that entries are case-sensitive. The default value for the SSID setting is empty. When left to the default value, client nodes will only be able to establish wireless network sessions with wireless APs that have been configured with no SSID.

Setting Power Save Mode

The Power Save Mode setting is used to configure the power usage of the wireless adapter and the radio transmitter. Different "keep alive" and "status check" packet modes are available for each of the power save modes. The Cisco Aironet Client node supports three power save modes:

- **Constantly Awake Mode (CAM)** The CAM mode is selected as the default power save mode. This power save mode keeps the adapter and transmitter constantly powered to keep transmission response times to a minimum. This setting is best suited for wireless client nodes such as desktop PCs that are attached to an AC power source.

- **Maximum Power Save (Max PSP)** The Max PSP setting registers the wireless client node within the AP node listing as operating in maximum power save mode. When client nodes are configured in this mode, the associated AP will buffer communications so that they are bursty and can provide a maximum efficiency in the use of the client node transmission power usage. In this mode, clients poll the AP on regular intervals between sleep mode to verify the presence of the AP and any buffered transmissions. This mode is efficient for battery powered devices with limited communication requirements. Note that when the ACU is launched on devices configured for Max PSP, the power save mode is temporarily set to Fast PSP mode in order to support configuration communications with APs. Upon terminating the ACU, the device is returned to Max PSP power save mode.

- **Fast Power Save (Fast PSP)** The Fast PSP setting configures the wireless client node to alternate between CAM and PSP mode in accordance to the network data transmission demands. When a high data throughput is required, the wireless client node reverts to CAM power save mode. When the data throughput demands are low, the wireless client node reverts to Max PSP power save mode.

Setting the Network Type

The Network Type configuration setting provides a means to define the type of wireless network that is to be configured. Two types of wireless networks are supported:

- **Infrastructure** The Infrastructure network type indicates that the wireless network the client node is using is eventually connected to a wired Ethernet network via a wireless AP or a wireless bridge. A distinct advanced configuration parameter menu is provided specifically for client nodes operating with network type set to Infrastructure. Infrastructure clients cannot configure options reserved for Ad Hoc clients.

- **Ad Hoc** The Ad Hoc Network type indicates that the wireless network the client node is using is not connected to a cabled Ethernet network. This network type is used when several wireless client nodes are creating a wireless LAN between themselves or when they connect to a wireless AP that does not have a cabled Ethernet connection. A distinct advanced configuration parameter menu is provided for client nodes specifically operating with network type set to Ad Hoc. Ad Hoc clients cannot configure options reserved for Infrastructure clients.

Cisco Aironet Client RF Network Configuration

The client RF network configuration screen provides access to the configuration parameters that define how the Aironet client node transmits data. Select it by clicking the **RF Network** tab when displaying the **System Parameters** screen (see Figure 7.3).

Figure 7.3 RF Network Parameter Configuration Tab

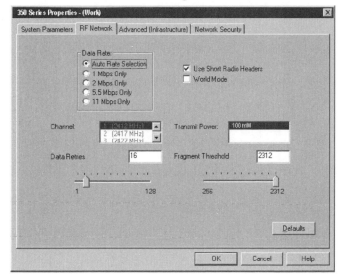

The fields available for configurations include the following:

- Data Rate
- Use Short Radio Headers
- World Mode
- Transmit Power
- Data Retries
- Fragment Threshold

These topics are covered in further detail in the following sections.

Configuring the Data Rate

The Data Rate RF Network configuration defines the data transmission rates that will be supported by the wireless client node for communications with wireless APs or other wireless client nodes. When the wireless client node has been configured for Infrastructure mode, you should configure the **Data Rate** setting to Auto Rate Selection. For wireless client nodes that are configured for Ad Hoc network mode, you should configure the **Data Rate** setting to a specific rate to minimize data rate synchronization issues. By default, the **Data Rate** setting is configured for Auto Rate Selection.

When you select Auto Rate Selection, the wireless client node will attempt to communicate using the fastest rate available (11 Mbps) and will train down to the fastest supported rate as required.

As a general observation, the 11 Mbps access rate provides the highest data transmission rate, but the shortest transmission range. The 1 Mbps data rate provides the lowest data transmission rate but the greatest range. Access rates in-between provide varying combinations of throughput and range (see Figure 7.4).

Figure 7.4 Data Throughput versus Range

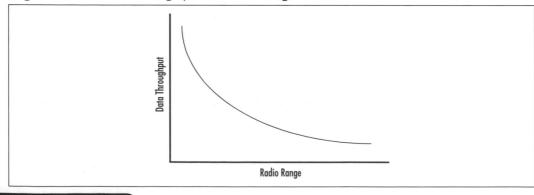

Choosing Radio Headers

The **Use Short Radio Headers** option box selection should match the **Preamble** configuration of the wireless AP. Short radio headers provide means of transmitting packets in a more efficient manner over the wireless network. Long radio headers ensure maximum interoperability with wireless devices that do not support short radio headers. By default, Short Radio Headers are enabled.

Setting World Mode

This option is available only when wireless client nodes are configured in Infrastructure mode. This setting minimizes the client configurations required to support roaming users traveling to countries approving differing radio transmission regulatory standards.

When a wireless client node and a wireless AP are both configured for World Mode, the wireless client node will support the maximum transmitter power and transmit frequencies supported by the AP. In essence, the wireless client node observes to regional radio standards as communicated by the locally configured wireless AP. By default, this option is not checked.

Selecting the Power Level

Each Cisco Aironet client adapter is configured with the maximum power output supported for the local radio transmission regulatory standard. The **Transmit Power** option provides a means of selecting the maximum power transmission option available to the region or that best fits the localized environment where the wireless client node is located. For example, operating at higher power levels increases radio range but also increases battery drain on mobile client nodes. Operating at lower power levels decreases the radio range but also decreases battery drain (see Table 7.4).

Table 7.4 Aironet 340 and 350 Transmitter Power Options

Client Adapter	Power Level Options
350 series cards	100 mW, 50 mW, 30 mW, 20 mW, 5 mW, 1 mW
340 PC cards	30 mW, 1 mW
340 PCI & LM cards	30 mW, 15 mW, 5 mW, 1 mW

Setting the Data Retries Value

The Data Retries slider and value box define the number of times a packet will be retransmitted if it is not successfully received by the wireless AP or other client node. The default setting for **Data Retries** is selected at 16, but you can configure it between 1 and 128 to match the wireless network operating environment and application protocol requirement.

Selecting Maximum Packet Size

The Fragmented Threshold is to used establish the maximum packet size that can be transmitted without being fragmented into smaller packets. Packet fragmenting provides a means to lower the retransmission requirement of large packets that are not successfully received by the intended recipient. This can save network time and power use by forcing the retransmission of only the packet fragments that have not been received. By default, the **Fragment Threshold** option is configured for 2,312, but you can configure it between 256 and 2,312 depending on the network requirements.

Configuring the Cisco Aironet Client: Advanced (Infrastructure)

The advanced infrastructure configuration screen provides any wireless client node configured with a network type setting of **Infrastructure** access to the advanced radio and wireless network parameters. Select it by clicking the **Advanced (Infrastructure)** tab when displaying the **System Parameters** screen (see Figure 7.5).

The advanced infrastructure screen provides access to infrastructure-specific configuration options. The fields available for configurations include the following:

- Antenna Mode (Receive)/Antenna Mode (Transmit)
- Specified AP
- RTS Threshold
- RTS Retry Limit

Each of these topics are covered in the following sections.

Figure 7.5 Advanced Infrastructure Parameter Configuration Tab

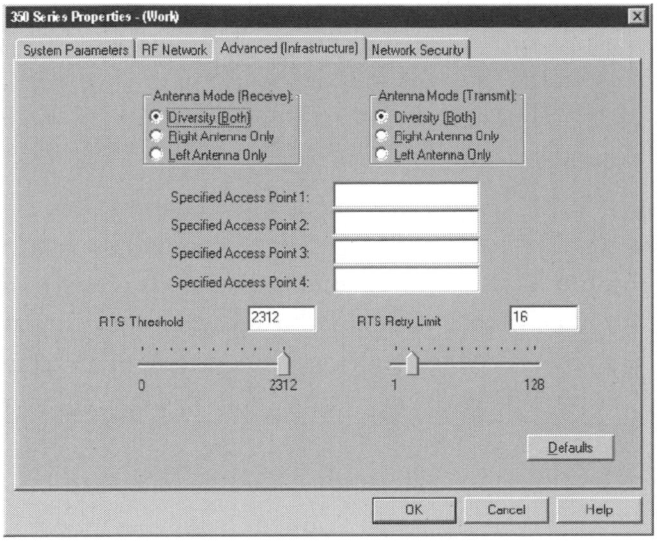

Antenna Mode (Receive)/Antenna Mode (Transmit)

The Antenna Mode selection box is used to define the antenna mode that is to be used in the current infrastructure-based wireless environment. Three options are available, including diversity, left antenna only, and right antenna only. Whereas the left and right antenna options provide similar range and transmission/reception capabilities, the diversity option provides enhanced transmission/reception for clients located in areas where wireless signals may be attenuated by the environment, as in the case of obstructions or by long radio signal travel path. The option you select should be the one that best addresses the wireless network operational conditions. Three options are provided:

- **Diversity (Both)** Configures the wireless adapter card to use both antennas and use the packets that have been received with the best available signal. This is the default option for PC card, LM card, and PCI mini card client adapters. This option is not available to PCI card client adapter cards because they only have one antenna.

- **Right Antenna Only** Configures the wireless adapter card to use only the right antenna. This is the default option for PCI card client adapters. This option is available to PC card, LM card, and PCI mini card client adapters.

- **Left Antenna Only** Configures the wireless adapter card to use only the left antenna. This option is available to PC card, LM card, PCI card, and PCI mini card client adapters.

Specified AP

The text box entries allow for the entry of four distinct preferred repeater AP MAC addresses to which the wireless client node can interface. The APs you enter should be only APs configured in repeater mode. The text boxes are empty by default. This option is useful for creating a network layout where specific wireless clients interface with specific APs to address even distribution of client nodes among the available AP. In this example, multiple APs can be co-located within a given area providing distinct wireless LANs to each user population.

RTS Threshold

RTS packets are used to establish a clear, open-channel window during which the client is the only authorized data transmitter over the wireless LAN. A clear channel is acknowledged by the AP, by sending a clear-to-send (CTS) packet over the network.

Setting this parameter can help to bring order to a network experiencing high packet collision rates. To configure this option, enter the minimum packet size required before the wireless client node sends a request-to-send (RTS) packet over the network. By default the parameter is configured for 2,312, but you can set it between 0 and 2,312 to meet local wireless network requirements. You can conduct testing by using link tests and troubleshooting tests to help define the optimum configuration for the client environment.

RTS Retry Limit

The RTS retry limit defines the number of times a wireless client node will attempt to obtain a CTS from the AP before attempting to send the packet over the network without receipt of a CTS packet. By default the parameter is configured for 16, but you can adjust it between the values of 1 and 128 to address environments where high network usage issues exist within congested areas.

Cisco Aironet Client Advanced Ad Hoc Configuration

The advanced infrastructure configuration screen provides wireless client node configured with a network type setting of Ad Hoc access to the advanced radio and wireless network parameters. Select it by clicking the **Advanced (Ad Hoc)** tab when displaying the **System Parameters** screen (see Figure 7.6).

Figure 7.6 Advanced (Ad Hoc) Parameter Configuration Tab

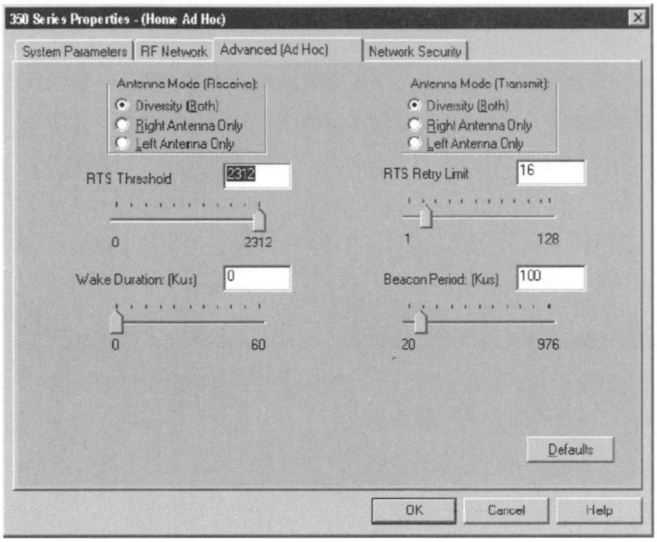

The Ad Hoc configuration tab provides many of the same configuration options as the Advanced (Infrastructure) tab.

The fields available for configurations include:

- Antenna Mode (Receive)/Antenna Mode (Transmit)
- RTS Threshold
- RTS Retry Limit
- Wake Duration (Kμs)
- Beacon Period (Kμs)

Antenna Mode (Receive)/Antenna Mode (Transmit)

The Antenna Mode selection box is used to define the antenna mode that is to be used in the current infrastructure-based wireless environment. Three options are available, including diversity, left antenna only, and right antenna only. Whereas the left and right antenna options provide similar range and transmission/reception capabilities, the diversity option provides enhanced transmission/reception for clients located in areas where wireless signals may be attenuated by the environment, as in the case of obstructions or by long radio signal travel path. The option you select should be the one that best addresses the wireless Ad Hoc network operational conditions. Three options are provided:

- **Diversity (Both)** Configures the wireless adapter card to use both antennas and use the packets that have been received with the best available signal. This is the default option for PC card, LM card, and PCI Mini card client adapters. This option is not available to PCI card client adapter cards because they have only one antenna.

- **Right Antenna Only** Configures the wireless adapter card to use only the right antenna. This is the default option for PCI card client adapters. This option is available to PC card, LM card, and PCI mini card client adapters.

- **Left Antenna Only** Configures the wireless adapter card to use only the left antenna. This option is available to PC card, LM card, PCI card, and PCI mini card client adapters.

RTS Threshold

The RTS threshold configuration operates in a similar manner to the RTS threshold setting available in Advanced Infrastructure settings. It defines the minimum packet size required before the wireless client node sends an RTS packet over the network. RTS packets are used to establish an open-channel widow during which the client is the only authorized data transmitter. A clear channel is acknowledged by the receipt of a CTS packet over the network. Setting this parameter can help to bring order to a network experiencing high packet collision rates. By default, the parameter is configured for 2,312, but you can set it between 0 and 2,312 to meet local wireless network requirements.

RTS Retry Limit

The RTS retry limit defines the number of times a wireless client node will attempt to obtain a CTS from the AP before attempting to send the packet over the networking without receipt of a CTS packet. By default, the parameter is configured for 16, but you can adjust it between the values of 1 and 128 to address network throughput issues.

Wake Duration (Kµs)

The Wake Duration settings define the period of time a wireless client node adapter will remain awake to receive an Announcement Traffic Indication

Message (ATIM) packet after a beacon. The default setting is of 5Kμs. The parameter supports settings of 0Kμs (which must be used in CAM mode) and between 5Kμs and 60Kμs (when configured in Max PSP or Fast PSP). One kilomicrosecond or 1Kμs is equivalent to 1024 microseconds or 1.024 milliseconds.

Beacon Period (Kμs)

The Beacon Period is used to define and synchronize the beacon timing periods used between Ad Hoc wireless client nodes. The default setting is configured to of 100Kμs. The parameter supports settings ranging from 20Kμs to 976Kμs.

Cisco Aironet Client Network Security Configuration

The Client Network Security configuration screen defines how the wireless client node will establish a secure connection with an AP. The settings are not used in Ad Hoc mode. Proper configuration is critical to the secure operation of the wireless network. You should use the maximum security setting whenever possible.

Note that the wireless client node and the wireless AP (in Infrastructure mode) or other wireless clients (in Ad Hoc mode) must share the same configurations settings for the security options to work and for communications to be properly established. See Figure 7.7 for the available options.

Figure 7.7 Network Security Parameter Configuration Tab

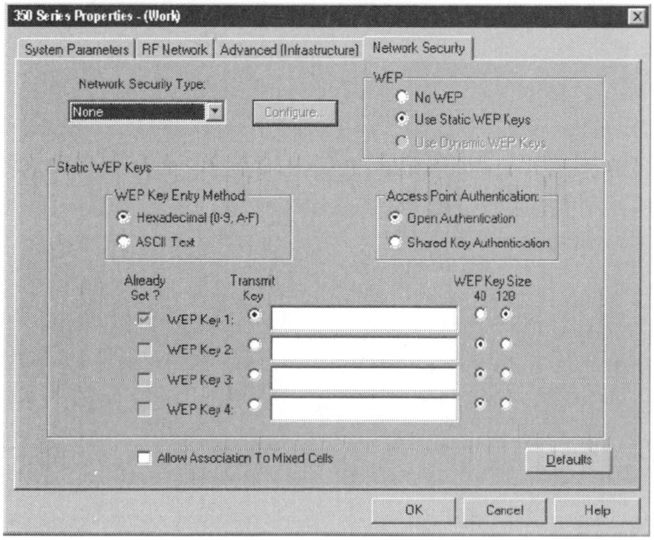

Configure the network security options by clicking the **Network Security** tab from the **System Parameters** screen. Configuration options entered on this screen *must* match the configurations entered on the AP or client. Failure to do so can result in an inoperative network or an open network. Chapter 5 provides detailed information on the security options available on the AP. We review the options in this section at a high level for chapter continuity.

Setting the Security Parameters

The static WEP keys are used to provide a basic level of security over the wireless radio link. As such, you should not consider them to be a complete security solution.

Each profile can have up to four distinct static WEP keys assigned within the Network Security options of a profile. WEP keys can be 40-bit or 128-bit. You must configure APs for full encryption for WEP keys to be effectively used. WEP keys must also be the same on all devices making up the wireless network. If a node receives a packet encrypted with a WEP key that is not available locally, the packet will be discarded.

You must enter WEP keys in the same sequence on all devices, that is, WEP key number one on the AP must also be WEP key number one on the wireless client. Once entered in the configuration screen, static WEP keys are stored in an encrypted format within the Windows Registry and are no longer readable from the WEP key configuration screen. WEP keys are downloaded to the wireless LAN adapter card upon system bootup or card insertion. This implies that if a wireless LAN card is lost or stolen, the WEP keys will not be available. You can enter WEP keys as a hexadecimal value (numbers 0–9 and letters A–F) or as ASCII text, meaning that the WEP key is made up of characters, numbers, and punctuation marks. To enter a new WEP key, re-enter the value in the appropriate WEP key field.

Authentication to the AP is performed using one of two methods: Shared Key Authentication and Open Authentication. Shared Key Authentication specifies that the client can communicate only with APs that have the same WEP key. As part of the shared authentication process, a packet is sent from the AP to the client for encryption. Once the packet has been encrypted using a WEP key, the packet is returned to the AP. If the AP can decrypt the packet, an acknowledgment is sent back to the client indicating a successful authentication. Shared key is not the recommended method of authentication due to security risks inherent in the authentication method. The default setting is Open Authentication. It allows the client node to authenticate and attempt to communicate with APs even it does not share the same WEP keys.

Allow Association to Mixed Cells

This option setting defines if the local wireless client node will be allowed to associate with wireless APs having WEP security set to "Optional." By selecting the **Allow Association to Mixed Cells**, the local wireless client node will associate with both APs that have WEP security configured to "Optional" and APs that force WEP security. By deselecting the **Allow Association to Mixed Cells**, the wireless client node will associate only with APs that have WEP security enabled using one of the predefined WEP keys. The default is for the parameter to not be enabled.

Client Adapter Auto Installer

The Aironet client LAN adapter auto installer is an executable application that can install the ACU and configure the local Aironet client LAN adapter automatically. The Auto Installer works under Windows XP, ME, 2000, NT, 98, and 95. No Auto Installer is available at this time for the MacOS platform.

The Auto Installer application is named CWUAInst.exe and can run locally on the device's hard drive or remotely on a network drive. The Auto Installer provides details regarding the installation of the ACU, firmware installation, application file location, and the name of the wireless configuration profile to be used during the client LAN adapter configuration. The client profile used during the installation and configuration must be present within the installation directory for the auto installation process to complete successfully. The installation file is an ASCII encoded file that can have an .INI or a .TXT extension.

A DOS-based configuration file encryption utility is provided for the safeguard of the INI or TXT configuration file. The utility encrypts the file by using a scrambling algorithm that can be decrypted by the Auto Installer. The utility is called EncryptIni.exe. The following provides an example for the syntax of the EncryptIni.exe:

1. Select **Start | Run**.
2. In the Open prompt, type **Command** and press **Enter**.
3. Using the DOS commands, navigate to the directory where the EncryptIni.exe and the configuration files are located.
4. Type **EncryptIni.exe** *<configuration file name>*.

Using the Auto Installer

The Auto Installer is a DOS-based installation utility. Be sure to have the Auto Installer, configuration file (encrypted or plain text), and ACU all located within the same working directory. You need to install the Aironet wireless LAN adapter driver files on the local wireless client node before initiating an Auto Install session. To execute the Auto Installer, follow these steps:

1. Select **Start | Run**.

2. In the Open prompt, type **Command** and press **Enter**.

3. Using the DOS commands, navigate to the directory where the EncryptIni.exe and the configuration files are located.

4. Type **CWUAInst** *<configuration file name>*.

Installation Configuration File Field Definition

The installation configuration file supports all of the options available within the ACU. For additional information on the available parameter options, please refer to the appropriate section in this chapter. The layout of the configuration file is provided in Table 7.5. A sample configuration file is provided in Figure 7.8.

Table 7.5 Auto Install INI File Layout

Section Name	Parameter Description
[LogFile]	Defines the location of the installation log file.
[Install Apps]	Selects if ACU is to be installed during Auto Install.
[Administrative Overrides]	Configures profile security options.
[App Parameters]	Defines LEAP operation within the ACU.
[Device Resident Wep Keys]	Defines the WEP keys to be used.
[Firmware Upgrade]	Selects the upgrade option to the firmware.
[Profile Name]	Selects the profile to be used for configuration and default use.
[<profile name>]	This section is titled with the profile name defined in the previous setting. The information provided in this section establishes the operational settings of the profile

Figure 7.8 Sample Auto Install Configuration File

```
[LogFile]
File Name = C:\Program Files\Cisco Aironet\Log\CWUA.log
[Install Apps]
ACU = yes
[Administrative Overrides]
Allow Edit Profile = yes
Allow Export Profile = no
Allow Import Profile = no
Allow Edit WEP = no
Existing Profiles = Delete
[App Parameters]
Folder Name = Cisco Aironet
Program Location = C:\Program Files\Cisco Aironet
Enable Leap = no
Allow Leap Data save = no
Create ACU icon on desk = no
Allow Non Admin to modify profiles = no
[Device Resident Wep Keys]
Save Keys to Flash = no
WepKey1 = f7390341230edfa338e88da11
WepKey1size = 128
WepKey1IsTransmit = yes
WepKey2 =
WepKey2size =
WepKey2IsTransmit =
WepKey3 =
WepKey3size =
WepKey3IsTransmit =
WepKey4 =
WepKey4size =
WepKey4IsTransmit =
[Firmware Upgrade]
Upgrade = yes
Display Flash Progress = no
Firmware Path = D:\Client\Firmware\client08.img
```

Continued

Figure 7.8 Continued

```
[Profile Names]
Office
[Office]
IsDefault = no
IsFactoryDefault = no
AutoSelect = no
NotAllowEdit = no
Not Allow Export = no
NotAllowEditWepKey = no
Client Name = walterallan
Use Logon Name = no
Use Computer Name = no
SSID1 = systempasskey
SSID2 = lockthedoor
SSID3 = cryptohaven
Power Save Mode = cam
Network Type = Infrastructure
Data Rate = auto
Data Retries = 16
Fragment Threshold = 2312
Antenna Mode Receive = Both
Antenna Mode Transmit = Both
RTS Threshold = 2312
Network Security = None_Open_Wep
WepKey2 = myfavoritedrink
WepKey2size = 40
WepKey2IsTransmit = no
WepKey3 = justforus
WepKey3size = 40
WepKey3IsTransmit = no
WepKey4 = littlesecret
WepKey4size = 0
WepKey4IsTransmit = no
```

Client Adapter Diagnostics

This section identifies the client adapter diagnostics tools available from the ACU. You can use these tools to troubleshoot the wireless connectivity between a client and an AP and between two clients and for verifying that the wireless adapter is functioning properly.

The ACU provides the following diagnostics capabilities:

- Display current status and configuration
- Display transmit and receive statistics
- Display graphic of client adapter radio link
- Perform a radio link test

Configuring ACU Diagnostics Preferences

Before performing any tests or obtaining wireless adapter configuration information, you should configure the Diagnostics preferences to ensure that displayed information is meaningful. To do this, use the **Preferences** icon in the menu bar. The preferences include settings for the screen refresh rate (1–60 seconds), signal strength display (percent of maximum power or dBm milliwatts) and link status meter options to display a graphical history of the last 50 signal transmissions (see Figure 7.9).

Figure 7.9 Diagnostics Preferences

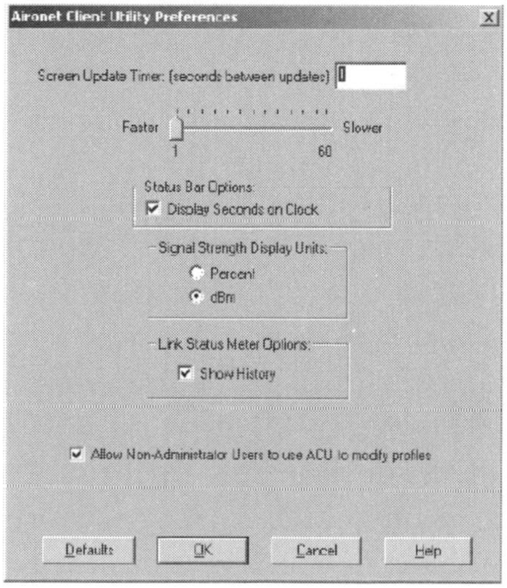

Displaying the Current Status

The wireless client node adapter status display provides a synopsis of the active configuration and the current signal strength. As such, information regarding the version number of the current firmware, default profile, authentication type, transmit power levels, data rate, and channel frequency are all listed. To view the status of the wireless LAN adapter, click **Status** on the menu bar. The status menu screen will be displayed indicating the current profile in use and the hardware settings, along with signal strength and signal quality (see Figure 7.10).

Figure 7.10 Link Status

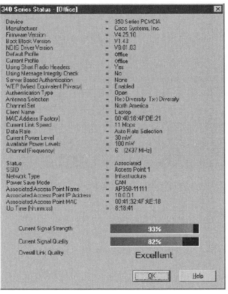

Displaying the Operational Statistics

You can view information on the number and types of packets transmitted and received by the wireless LAN adapter from the Operational Statistics screen. To display the operational statistics, select **Statistics** from the menu bar. The statistics menu screen will be displayed indicating the current profile in use and various signal and data transmission statistics. The transmit and receive statistics are obtained from querying the host. See Figure 7.11 and Table 7.6.

Generally speaking, the fewer the errors, the better the state of the overall network. The best way to identify if the wireless network is experiencing problems is by identifying a baseline of operation once the network has been operational for a few days and running routine checks to compare the latest statistics with the baseline statistics. Review errors and identify their causes by using the troubleshooting tools.

Figure 7.11 Statistics Display

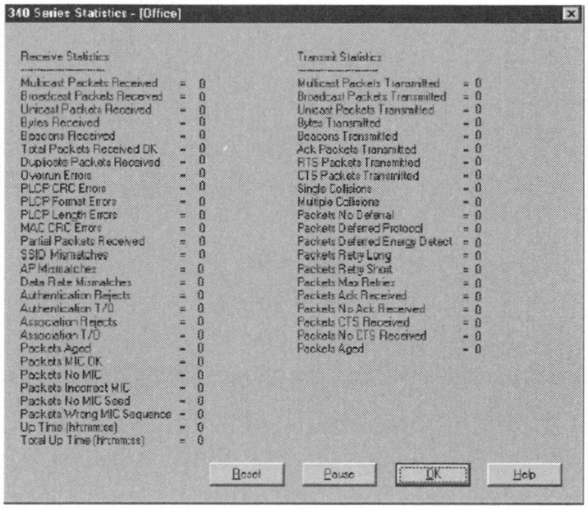

Table 7.6 Statistics Display Field Definition

Adapter Statistics	Definition
Multicast Packets Received	Total number of multicast packets successfully received.
Broadcast Packets Received	Total number of broadcast packets successfully received.
Unicast Packets Received	Total number of unicast packets successfully received.
Bytes Received	Total number of bytes successfully received.
Beacons Received	Total number of beacon packets successfully received.
Total Packets Received OK	Total number of all packets successfully received.
Duplicate Packet Received	Total number of duplicate packets successfully received.
Overrun Errors	Total number of packets received when buffers were full.
PLCP CRC Errors	Total number of times Physical Layer Convergence Protocol packets were received with invalid CRC.

Continued

Table 7.6 Continued

Adapter Statistics	Definition
PLCP Format Errors	Total number of times Physical Layer Convergence Protocol packets were received with a valid CRC but with an error within the header.
PLCP Length Errors	Total number of times Physical Layer Convergence Protocol packets were received with invalid header length.
MAC CRC Errors	Total number of Media Access Control packets with a CRC error within the packet.
Partial Packets Received	Total number of incorrect packets that were discarded to unsuccessful transmission.
SSID Mismatch	Total number of attempted to associations between the client and an AP while trying the wrong SSID.
AP Mismatches	Total of attempted associations between the client and an AP where the AP was not specified in the client.
Data Rate Mismatches	Total of attempts where the client data rate was not supported by AP.
Authentication Rejects	Total of authentication rejections by an AP.
Authentication T/O	Total of authentication response time outs for an AP.
Packets Aged	Total of packets that were discarded post successful reception due to packet fragments not arriving within 10 seconds of each other or due to the host not polling for the packet.
Packets MIC OK	Total of packets received with a valid message integrity check; MIC must be supported by the driver and configured on the AP.
Packets No MIC	Total of packets discarded due to invalid message integrity check; MIC must be supported by the driver and configured on the AP.
Packets No MIC Seed	Total of packets discarded due to missing MIC seed. MIC must be supported by the driver and configured on the AP.

Continued

Table 7.6 Continued

Adapter Statistics	Definition
Packets Wrong MIC Sequence	Total packets discarded due to wrong MIC numbering sequence; MIC must be supported by the driver and configured on the AP.
Up Time (days:hh:mm:ss)	Total uptime since last reset.
Broadcast Packets Transmitted	Total of successfully transmitted broadcast packets.
Unicast Packets Transmitted	Total of successfully transmitted unicast packets.
Bytes Transmitted	Total data bytes successfully transmitted.
Beacons Transmitted	Total beacon packets successfully transmitted. Provides data only when an Ad Hoc network is used.
Ack Packets Transmitted	Total Acknowledgement packets sent responding to unicast.
RTS Packets Transmitted	Total of RTS packets successfully transmitted.
CTS Packets Transmitted	Total of CTS packets successfully transmitted. CTS packets are sent to respond to received RTS packets.
Single Collisions	Total of packets retransmitted due to collisions.
Multiple Collisions	Total of packets retransmitted two or more times due to collision.
Packets No Deferral	Total of packets sent with no wait time.
Packets Deferred Protocol	Total of packets delayed at transmission due to 802.11 protocol.

Displaying the Link Status Meter

The ACU provides a link status meter. It displays metrics on the wireless radio link between the wireless client node and a wireless AP or other wireless client node. The Link Status Meter is useful in troubleshooting weak links. You can also use it to identify a radio network signal map outlining optimum areas where radio signal strength is at its peak. To display the link status meter, select **Link Status Meter** from the menu bar.

Signal Strength Indicator

A signal strength bar is provided vertically to the left of the display indicating the current signal strength as a percentage or dBm rating.

Signal Quality Indicator

A signal quality bar is provided horizontally to the bottom of the display indicating the current signal quality as a percentage or dBm rating

Signal Status Line

A signal status line displays the current signal status based on the signal strength and signal quality. The status can line terminate in one of four signal status regions: Poor, Fair, Good, and Excellent:

- **Poor and Fair Signal Status** Signals status identifying Poor to Fair ratings indicate that the current location does not provide radio signals than can sustain high data throughputs. High error and retransmission rates can be expected from areas supporting Poor and Fair signal status. You should move the wireless client node to an alternate location or lower the access speed.

- **Good Signal Status** Signal status identifying Good ratings indicate that the current location provides adequate radio transmission and reception to support most high-throughput communications. A low rate of errors and packet retransmissions can be expected from the current location.

- **Excellent Signal Status** Signal status identifying Excellent ratings indicate that the current location provides optimum radio transmission and signal reception to support high throughput communications with very low error rates and packet retransmissions.

Performing a Radio Frequency Link Test

You can use radio frequency link test to send network pings to obtain metrics on the performance of the radio network from the current wireless client node location. When you perform this test from various locations, you can establish a radio access map for troubleshooting and network architecture purposes. You can quickly identify troubled areas and relocate wireless repeaters or APs to address the issues.

To initiate a link test, select **Link Test** from the menu bar. Enter the IP address of the device to be pinged within the **IP Address of AP**. The address can be that of a wireless AP if operating in Infrastructure mode or that of a wireless client node if operating in Ad Hoc mode.

You can specify the number of ping packets (from 1 to 1000) to be sent in the **Number of Packets** field. The default value is 4. Alternately, you can use the **Continuous Link Test** mode if a long duration test is to be performed. In this mode, the **Number of Packets** entry is ignored.

Specify the packet size (from 64 to 2,048) to be sent in the **Packet Size** field. The default value is 100. Note that the TCP/IP stack will fragment packets that are more than 512 bytes. In this case, the display indicating the number of packets sent versus the number of packets received can be dissimilar.

To start the test, click **Start**.

To stop the test, click **Stop**.

The test display provides statistical information, as provided in Table 7.7.

Table 7.7 Statistics Field Information

Statistic	Definition
Packets Received OK	Total packets successfully received during the test.
Packets Transmitted OK	Total packets successfully transmitted during the test.
Status	Displays the current operational status of the wireless client adapter. Can be displayed as Associated, Not Associated, Ad Hoc, Configured, and Error.
Current Link Speed	Displays the data transmission rate (1 Mbps, 2 Mbps. 5.5 Mbps, or 11 Mbps).
Associated AP Name	Displays the name of the AP associated to by the client when configured in Infrastructure mode.
Associated AP MAC	Displays the MAC address of the AP associated to by the client when configured in Infrastructure mode.
Current Signal Strength	Displays the signal strength of received packets. The display can be defined in terms of percentage (1%–100%) or dBm (–95dBm–45dBm).
Current Signal Quality	Displays the signal quality of received packets. (0%–100%).
Current Noise Level	Displays the total background radio nose level within the 2.4 GHz band (–100 dBm to –45dBm).

Continued

Table 7.7 Continued

Statistic	Definition
Overall Link Quality	Provides a rating of the radio link quality. See "Displaying the Link Status Meter" section earlier in this chapter for indicator value meanings. Rating values are Not Associated, Poor, Fair, Good, and Excellent.
Signal to Noise Ratio	Provides an analysis of the overall signal strength versus the background noise. The rating indicates how well the wireless client node adapter will be able to send and receive information over the wireless link. Rating value is 0dB to 90dB.

Client Adapter Indicator LEDs

The Aironet client adapter card provides two LEDs to display card and link status information:

- **Link Integrity/Power LED** The link integrity and power LED provides visual confirmation that the adapter is receiving power (green) and that it is associated with the wireless network (green and blinks slowly).

- **Link Activity LED** The link activity LED provides a visual display of the level of transmit and receive activity from the client node radio transmitter. During normal operation, the amber LED blinks quickly and erratically in synch with network traffic. When a device error occurs, the amber LED blinks in a pattern according to the type of error encountered.

LED Display Patterns

Both LEDs blinking quickly indicates that the adapter is powered, the self-test did not report any errors, and the client node is attempting to communicate with the wireless network (see Table 7.8).

Table 7.8 LED Patterns

LED Pattern	Description
Green slow blink/amber quick blink	When the green power LED blinks slowly and the amber activity LED blinks quickly, the client adapter is powered and associated with a wireless AP.
Green slow blink or on/amber blink	When the green power LED blinks slowly or is continuously on and the amber activity LED is blinking, the client adapter is associated with an AP and is transmitting or receiving data.
Green off/amber quick blink	When the green power LED is off and the amber activity LED is blinking quickly, the client adapter is operating in power save mode.
Green on/amber quick blink	When the green power LED is solidly lit and the amber activity LED is blinking quickly, the client adapter is operating in Ad Hoc mode
Green off/amber off	When the green power LED is off and the amber activity LED is off, the client adapter is operating not powered or an error condition has occurred.
Green off/amber blink every 2 seconds	When the green power LED is off and the amber activity LED blinks once every 2 seconds, the client adapter has experienced a RAM failure. Cisco technical support is required to address this error condition.
Green off/amber 2 fast blink every 2 seconds	When the green power LED is off and the amber activity LED blinks 2 times quickly every 2 seconds the client adapter has experienced a Flash boot block checksum failure. Cisco technical support is required to address this error condition.
Green off/amber 3 fast blink every 2 seconds	When the green power LED is off and the amber activity LED blinks 3 times every 2 seconds, the client adapter has experienced a firmware checksum failure. To resolve the error condition, reload the adapter firmware.

Continued

Table 7.8 Continued

LED Pattern	Description
Green off/amber 4 fast blink every 2 seconds	When the green power LED is off and the amber activity LED blinks 4 times every 2 seconds, the client adapter has experienced an error while reading the MAC address on the adapter chip. To resolve the error condition, reload the adapter firmware.
Green off/amber 5 fast blink every 2 seconds	When the green power LED is off and the amber activity LED blinks 4 times every 2 seconds the client adapter has experienced a physical layer access error. Cisco technical support is required to address this error condition.
Green off/amber 6 fast blink every 2 seconds	When the green power LED is off and the amber activity LED blinks 6 times every 2 seconds the client adapter indicates that the firmware that was attempted to be loaded is incompatible with the adapter. To resolve the error condition, reload the appropriate adapter firmware.

Summary

This chapter provided a practical exposition on the implementation of wireless clients using Cisco Aironet 340 and 350 series client adapters.

Four form factors of wireless client adapter cards make up the Cisco Aironet adapter family specifically the PC card, the LM card, the PCI card, and lastly the Mini PCI card. The PC card form factor is a PCMCIA card that can be used in external type II and III PCMCIA interfaces typically found on laptops, PDAs, and other portable platforms. The LM card is also a PCMCIA card, but this one is intended for devices that have internal type II or III PCMCIA interfaces. The PCI card is intended for desktop computing platforms with PCI card support. Lastly, the Mini PCI card is used on devices possessing internal type IIIa mini PCI slots.

There are two series of Cisco Aironet wireless adapters: the 340 and the 350 series. The 350 series cards (Aironet 351 and 352) possess more powerful transmitters capable of transmitting a signal with a signal power up to 100 milliwatts, whereas the 340 series cards (Aironet 341 and 342) supported transmitters with up to 30 milliwatts. The $3x1$ (Aironet 341 and 351) support WEP encryption modes of operation consisting of 40-bit keys, whereas the $3x2$ cards (Aironet 342 and 352) support 40-bit and 128-bit WEP.

The Aironet Client Utility (ACU) is a GUI that provides a configuration and maintenance interface used to support all of the Aironet client adapters. The ACU provided four informational sections consisting of the command bar, the menu bar, the main screen, and the status bar.

The ACU can preconfigure and manage user profiles or identities used to access one or more wireless LAN deployments. You can import and export use profiles for backup and recovery purposes by using the Profile Manager Import/Export function. Widows XP, 2000, and NT operating systems have the added capability to restrict access to the profiles to administrative users only by using the Preferences options and deselecting **Allow Non-Administrator Users to User ACU to Modify Profiles**.

Client name, SSIDs, type of power save modes, and network type are defined using the System Parameter screen. Three types of power save modes were available for the client, namely Constantly Awake Mode (CAM), Maximum Power Save (Max PSP), and Fast Power Save (Fast PSP).

The RF Network Parameters are used configure the minimum data throughput rates (1 Mbps to 11 Mbps), radio channels, transmit power, data retries, and packet fragment threshold. The RF Network Parameters are also used to select the use of Short Radio Headers and world mode activation for international infrastructure network roaming.

The Advanced (Infrastructure) menu display is used to define the parameter configurations specific to wireless LAN clients operating with APs. The configurable parameters for Infrastructure mode clients includes the selection of receive and transmit antenna mode (the left, right, or both antennas) preferred APs, Ready To Send (RTS) threshold, and retry limits.

The Advanced (Ad Hoc) menu display is used to define parameter configuration specific to wireless LAN clients operating in a peer-to-peer network of wireless clients. Receive and transmit antenna modes and Ready To Send (RTS) threshold and retry limits are defined in a similar way to Advanced (Infrastructure)–based clients. Ad Hoc clients, however, are also provided with access to configure the Wake Duration and Beacon Period in thousands of microseconds. These settings are used by the client adapter to help to structure the communications and operations of the peer-to-peer wireless network.

The Network Security screen is where you define wireless network security configurations. The parameters configured on this screen select the WEP mode (static or dynamic), the type of AP authentication scheme, and the WEP key entry in hexadecimal or ASCII text.

The Aironet Auto Client Installer is used by administrators to install and configure client wireless LAN adapter software and firmware without the need to configure each option individually from menus. To initiate the Auto Installer, use the *CWUAInst <configuration file name>* command. LAN adapter configuration parameters are defined in a standard text file. Client adapter diagnostics utilities are used to verify and troubleshoot the operations of the network. Configuration preferences are available to define screen update times, status bar, and the percent and dBm display modes for the signal strength indicator. The current status of the client adapter can be displayed by selecting the **Status** option on the menu bar. Adapter statistics can be displayed using the **Statistics** option. The **Link Status Meter** is used to display a graph of the overall state of the wireless link. Frequency Link Tests are used to obtain metrics on the performance of the radio network.

Link integrity/power and link activity LEDs are used to display the operational status of the wireless LAN adapters. Color and blink patterns are used to identify specific network, communication, and firmware errors.

Solutions Fast Track

Cisco Aironet Client Adapter Types

☑ The Cisco Aironet client adapter can be used in Infrastructure (with an AP) or in Ad Hoc mode (without AP).

☑ The Ad Hoc mode allows for the configuration of wireless networks using peer-to-peer networking.

☑ There are four types of Aironet client adapter cards: PC card, LM card, PCI card, and Mini PCI card.

☑ The Cisco Aironet 341 and 342 adapters can send signals at up to 40 milliwatts; the 351 and 352 adapters can send signals at up to 100 milliwatts.

☑ The Cisco Aironet 341 and 351 adapters support 40-bit WEP encrypted sessions while the 342 and 352 adapters support both 40-bit WEP and 128-bit WEP.

Cisco ACU

☑ The Aironet Client Utility (ACU) is used to configure the Aironet client adapters.

☑ There are four main sections to the ACU display—the command bar, the menu bar, the main screen, and the status bar.

☑ The Profile Manager can be used to manage multiple profiles (a.k.a wireless configurations) that are used by the wireless client adapter to establish a networking session with wireless networks.

☑ Profiles can be individually imported and exported in order to safeguard and recover from system errors or to duplicate client settings.

☑ Access to profiles can be restricted to users possessing system Administrator privileges on Windows XP, 2000, and NT operating systems.

☑ The ACU provides access to configuration settings using the five option screens: System Parameter, RF Network, Advanced (Infrastructure), Advanced (Ad Hoc), and Network Security.

Cisco Aironet Client Installation and Configuration

☑ The System Parameter configuration tab provides access to the Client Name, SSIDs, Power Save, and Network Type options.

☑ The RF Network Parameter Configuration tab provides input for network Data Rate, selection of Short Radio Headers, World Mode radio signal selection, Transmit Power, Data Retries, and Fragment Threshold.

☑ The Advanced (Infrastructure) tab provides input for the configuration of network parameters used in wireless networks with Access points.

☑ The receive and transmit Antenna Modes, the configuration of selected APs, the RTS Threshold, and Retry Limits are configured using the Advanced (Infrastructure) tab.

☑ The Advanced (Ad Hoc) tab provides input for the configuration of network parameters used in wireless networks without APs.

☑ Ad Hoc networks are entirely built up using client nodes only.

☑ The receive and transmit Antenna Modes, the configuration of selected APs, the RTS Threshold, and Retry Limits, along with the Wake Duration and Beacon Period, are configured using the Advanced (Ad Hoc) tab.

Cisco Aironet Client Network Security Configuration

☑ The Network Security Parameter configuration tab is where the WEP cryptographic key information is entered.

☑ This includes the selection of no WEP, Static WEP and Dynamic WEP, the WEP key themselves in hexadecimal and ASCII text along with the type of AP configuration: Open Authentication or Shared Key Authentication.

☑ This screen is used to configure the client to associate with only authenticated APs or both Authenticated and Open Authentication APs.

Client Adapter Auto Installer

☑ The Client Adapter Auto Install is used to preconfigure the installation of client software on user desktops. Administrators can predefine user profile settings to support a given environment.

Client Adapter Diagnostics

☑ The ACU Diagnostics Preferences screen configures the screen refresh rate, the status clock display, the signal strength display units in percent or dBm, and the link status meter options.

☑ The Link Status Display provides information on the current operation of the client adapter including device configurations and signal strength and quality indicators.

☑ The Statistics Display screen provides detailed metrics on the throughput performance of the client adapter in terms of packets and bytes transmitted and received.

☑ Provides information on the signal strength and signal quality.

☑ Provides a rating system of Poor, Fair, Good, and Excellent of the overall RF signal.

☑ Provides a means to configure and initiate a frequency link test.

☑ Link test configurations can include a specific number of packets to be used or continuous until stopped.

☑ Packet size and AP IP Address information can also be specified.

☑ Two LEDs are provided: Link Integrity/Power LED and Link Activity LED.

☑ Display patterns indicate the overall status of the client adapter.

Frequently Asked Questions

The following Frequently Asked Questions, answered by the authors of this book, are designed to both measure your understanding of the concepts presented in this chapter and to assist you with real-life implementation of these concepts. To have your questions about this chapter answered by the author, browse to **www.syngress.com/solutions** and click on the **"Ask the Author"** form.

Q: What is Message Integrity Check (MIC) and how is it used?

A: MIC is a protocol that prevents bit-flip attacks on encrypted packets transmitted between wireless clients and APs supporting MIC. MIC adds integrity check bits the packet, rendering it tamper-proof. Encrypted packets that are modified during transit by an attacker are identified as being tampered, and a retransmit packet request is sent to the originating station.

Q: Where are the multiple profiles stored within Profile Manager?

A: Profiles are stored within the Aironet client adapter registry entry. Registry entries are organized by the type of radio transmitter selected—that is, 340 series or 350 series adapters.

Q: Are there any restrictions regarding the use of the Auto Profile Feature?

A: You need to consider several points using Auto Profile, the first is that two or more profiles must exist on the local client. Second, if a profile is configured to use LEAP authentication, it must have a user name and password associated with it before being added to the Auto Profile list. Lastly, when using LEAP in conjunction with login scripts for a profile configured in Auto Profile, ensure that network connectivity is fully established before the scripts are initiated. If the scripts are initiated prior to full network connectivity, the scripts will not activate.

Q: How can I find out if my network is operating properly?

A: All network deployments are different. Each has its own characteristics that can be identified only by obtaining and reviewing operational baseline statistics on a regular basis. Some wireless links cover short distances. When wireless nodes are within close proximity to each other, a strong signal is expected, and a low number of errors should be indicated. For wireless links covering longer distances, a weaker signal is expected along with a higher number of reported errors. Weather, construction, and other environment variables can play a large part in the overall health of a wireless network. Only through diligent status checking can you identify problems and treat them early.

Chapter 8

Cisco Wireless Security

Solutions in this chapter:

- **Understanding Security Fundamentals and Principles of Protection**

- **MAC Filtering**

- **Reviewing the Role of Policy**

- **Implementing WEP**

- **Addressing Common Risks and Threats**

- **Sniffing, Interception, and Eavesdropping**

- **Spoofing and Unauthorized Access**

- **Network Hijacking and Modification**

- **Denial of Service and Flooding Attacks**

☑ Summary

☑ Solutions Fast Track

☑ Frequently Asked Questions

Introduction

There is not much indication of anything slowing down the creation and deployment of new technology to the world any time in the near future. With the constant pressure to deploy the latest generation of technology today, little time is allowed for a full and proper security review of the technology and components that make it up.

This rush to deploy, along with the insufficient security review, not only allows age-old security vulnerabilities to be reintroduced to products, but creates new and unknown security challenges as well. Wireless networking is not exempt from this, and like many other technologies, security flaws have been identified and new methods of exploiting these flaws are published regularly.

Utilizing security fundamentals developed over the last few decades, you can review and protect your wireless networks from known and unknown threats. In this chapter, we recall security fundamentals and principles that are the foundation of any good security strategy, addressing a range of issues from authentication and authorization, to controls and audit.

No primer on security would be complete without an examination of the common security standards, which are addressed in this chapter alongside the emerging privacy standards and their implications for the wireless exchange of information.

We also look at how you can maximize the features of existing security standards like Wired Equivalent Protocol (WEP). We also examine the effectiveness of Media Access Control (MAC) and protocol filtering as a way of minimizing opportunity. Lastly, we look at the security advantages of using virtual private networks (VPNs) on a wireless network, as well as discuss the importance of convincing users of the role they can play as key users of the network.

You'll also learn about the existing and anticipated threats to wireless networks, and the principles of protection that are fundamental to a wireless security strategy. And although many of the attacks are similar in nature to attacks on wired networks, you need to understand the particular tools and techniques that attackers use to take advantage of the unique way wireless networks are designed, deployed, and maintained. We explore the attacks that have exposed the vulnerabilities of wireless networks, and in particular the weaknesses inherent in the security standards. Through a detailed examination of these standards, we identify how these weaknesses have lead to the development of new tools and tricks that hackers use to exploit your wireless networks. We look at the emergence and threat of "war driving" technique and how it is usually the first step in an attack on wireless networks.

Understanding Security Fundamentals and Principles of Protection

Security protection starts with the preservation of the *confidentiality*, *integrity*, and *availability* (CIA) of data and computing resources. These three tenets of information security, often referred to as "The Big Three," are sometimes represented by the CIA triad, shown in Figure 8.1.

Figure 8.1 The CIA Triad

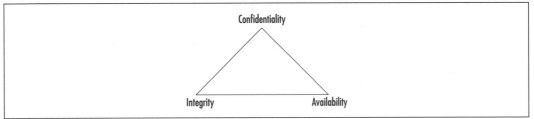

As we describe each of these tenets, you will see that in order to provide for a reliable and secure wireless environment, you will need to ensure that each tenet is properly protected. To ensure the preservation of The Big Three and protect the privacy of those whose data is stored and flows through these data and computing resources, The Big Three security tenets are implemented through tried-and-true security practices. These other practices enforce The Big Three by ensuring proper authentication for authorized access while allowing for nonrepudiation in identification and resource usage methods, and by permitting complete accountability for all activity through audit trails and logs. Some security practitioners refer to Authentication, Authorization, and Audit (accountability) as "AAA." Each of these practices provides the security implementer with tools which they can use to properly identify and mitigate any possible risks to The Big Three.

Ensuring Confidentiality

Confidentiality attempts to prevent the intentional or unintentional unauthorized disclosure of communications between a sender and recipient. In the physical world, ensuring confidentiality can be accomplished by simply securing the physical area. However, as evidenced by bank robberies and military invasions, threats exist to the security of the physical realm that can compromise security and confidentiality.

The moment electronic means of communication were introduced, many new possible avenues of disclosing the information within these communications were created. The confidentiality of early analog communication systems, such as the telegraph and telephone, were easily compromised by simply having someone connect to the wires used by a sender and receiver.

When digital communications became available, like with many technologies, it was only a matter of time until knowledgeable people were able to build devices and methods that could interpret the digital signals and convert them to whatever form needed to disclose what was communicated. And as technology grew and became less expensive, the equipment needed to monitor and disclose digital communications became available to anyone wishing to put the effort into monitoring communication.

With the advent of wireless communications, the need for physically connecting to a communication channel to listen in or capture confidential communications was removed. Although you can achieve some security by using extremely tight beam directional antennas, someone still just has to sit somewhere in between the antennas to be able to monitor and possibly connect to the communications channel without having to actually tie into any physical device.

Having knowledge that communications channels are possibly compromised allows us to properly implement our policies and procedures to mitigate the wireless risk. The solution used to ensure The Big Three and other security tenets is *encryption*.

The current implementation of encryption in today's wireless networks use the RC4 stream cipher to encrypt the transmitted network packets, and the WEP to protect authentication into wireless networks by network devices connecting to them (that is, the network adapter authentication, not the user utilizing the network resources). Both of which, due mainly to improper implementations, have introduced sufficient problems that have made it possible to determine keys used and then either falsely authenticate to the network or decrypt the traffic traveling across through the wireless network.

With these apparent problems, those in charge of wireless network security should utilize other proven and properly implemented encryption solutions, such as Secure Shell (SSH), Secure Sockets Layer (SSL), or IPSec.

Ensuring Integrity

Integrity ensures the accuracy and completeness of information throughout its process methods. The first communication methods available to computers did not have much in place to ensure the integrity of the data transferred from one to another. As such, occasionally something as simple as static on a telephone line could cause the transfer of data to be corrupted.

To solve this problem, the idea of a checksum was introduced. A *checksum* is nothing more than taking the message you are sending and running it through a function that returns a simple value which is then appended to the message being sent. When the receiver gets the complete message, they would then run the message through the same function and compare the value they generate with the value that was included at the end of the message.

The functions that are generally used to generate basic checksums are usually based upon simple addition or modulus functions. These functions can sometimes have their own issues, such as the function not being detailed enough to allow for distinctly separate data that could possibly have identical checksums. It is even possible to have two errors within the data itself cause the checksum to provide a valid check because the two errors effectively cancel each other out. These problems are usually addressed through a more complex algorithm used to create the digital checksum.

Cyclic redundancy checks (CRCs) were developed as one of the more advanced methods of ensuring data integrity. CRC algorithms basically treat a message as an enormous binary number, whereupon another large fixed binary number then divides this binary number. The remainder from this division is the checksum. Using the remainder of a long division as the checksum, as opposed to the original data summation, adds a significant chaos to the checksum created, increasing the likelihood that the checksum will not be repeatable with any other separate data stream.

These more advanced checksum methods, however, have their own set of problems. As Ross Williams wrote in his 1993 paper, A Painless Guide to CRC Error Detection Algorithms (www.ross.net/crc/crcpaper.html), the goal of error detection is to protect against corruption introduced by noise in a data transfer. This is good if we are concerned only with protecting against possible transmission errors. However, the algorithm provides no means of ensuring the integrity of an intentionally corrupted data stream. If someone has knowledge of a particular data stream, altering the contents of the data and completing the transaction with a valid checksum is possible. The receiver would not have knowledge of the changes in the data because their checksum would match and it would appear as if the data was transferred with no errors.

This form of intentional integrity violation is called a "Data Injection." In such cases, the best way to protect data is to (once again) use a more advanced form of integrity protection utilizing cryptography. Today, this higher level of protection is generally provided through a stronger cryptographic algorithm such as the MD5 or RC4 ciphers.

Wireless networks today use the RC4 stream cipher to protect the data transmitted as well as provide for data integrity. It has been proven that the 802.11 implementation of the RC4 cipher with its key scheduling algorithm introduces enough information to provide a hacker with enough to be able to predict your network's secret encryption key. Once the hacker has your key, they are not only able to gain access to your wireless network, but also view it as if there was no encryption at all.

Ensuring Availability

Availability, as defined in an information security context, ensures that access data or computing resources needed by appropriate personnel is both reliable and available in a timely manner. The origins of the Internet itself come from the need to ensure the availability of network resources. In 1957, the United States Department of Defense (DoD) created the Advanced Research Projects Agency (ARPA) following the Soviet launch of Sputnik. Fearing loss of command and control over U.S. nuclear missiles and bombers due to communication channel disruption caused by nuclear or conventional attacks, the U.S. Air Force commissioned a study on how to create a network that could function with the loss of access or routing points. Out of this, packet switched networking was created, and the first four nodes of ARPANET were deployed in 1968 running at the then incredibly high speed of 50 kilobits per second.

The initial design of packet switched networks did not take into consideration the possibility of an actual attack on the network from one of its own nodes. As the ARPANET grew into what we now know as the Internet, many modifications have been made to the protocols and applications that make up the network, ensuring the availability of all resources provided.

Wireless networks are experiencing many similar design issues, and due to the proliferation of new wireless high-tech devices, many are finding themselves in conflict with other wireless resources. Like their wired equivalents, there was little expectation that conflicts would occur within the wireless spectrum available for use. Because of this, very few wireless equipment providers planned their implementations with features to ensure the availability of the wireless resource in case a conflict occurred.

Ensuring Privacy

Privacy is the assurance that the information a customer provides to some party will remain private and protected. This information generally contains customer personal nonpublic information that is protected by both regulation and civil liability law. Your wireless policy and procedures should contain definitions on how to ensure the privacy of customer information that might be accessed or transmitted by your wireless networks. The principles and methods here provide ways of ensuring the protection of the data that travels across your networks and computers.

Ensuring Authentication

Authentication provides for a sender and receiver of information to validate each other as the appropriate entity they are wishing to work with. If entities wishing to communicate cannot properly authenticate each other, then there can be no trust of the activities or information provided by either party. It is only through a trusted and secure method of authentication that we are able to provide for a trusted and secure communication or activity.

The simplest form of authentication is the transmission of a shared password between the entities wishing to authenticate with each other. This could be as simple as a secret handshake or a key. As with all simple forms of protection, once knowledge of the secret key or handshake was disclosed to nontrusted parties, there could be no trust in who was using the secrets anymore.

Many methods can be used to acquire a simple secret key, from something as simple as tricking someone into disclosing it, to high-tech monitoring of communications between parties to intercept the key as it is passed from one party to the other. However the code is acquired, once it is in a nontrusted party's hands, they are able to utilize it to falsely authenticate and identify themselves as a valid party, forging false communications, or utilizing the user's access to gain permissions to the available resources.

The original digital authentication systems simply shared a secret key across the network with the entity they wished to authenticate with. Applications such as Telnet, File Transfer Protocol (FTP), and POP-mail are examples of programs that simply transmit the password, in clear-text, to the party they are authenticating with. The problem with this method of authentication is that anyone who is able to monitor the network could possibly capture the secret key and then use it to authenticate themselves as you in order to access these same services. They could then access your information directly, or corrupt any information you send to other parties. They may even be able to attempt to gain higher privileged access with your stolen authentication information.

Configuring & Implementing…

Clear-Text Authentication

Clear-text (non-encrypted) authentication is still widely used by many people today who receive their e-mail through the Post Office Protocol (POP), which by default sends the password unprotected in clear-text from the mail client to the server. You can protect your e-mail account password in several ways, including connection encryption as well as not transmitting the password in clear-text through the network by hashing with MD5 or some similar algorithm.

Encrypting the connection between the mail client and server is the only way of truly protecting your mail authentication password. This will prevent anyone from capturing your password or any of the mail you might transfer to your client. SSL is generally the method used to encrypt the connection stream from the mail client to the server and is supported by most mail clients today.

If you just protect the password through MD5 or a similar cryptocipher, anyone who happens to intercept your "protected" password could identify it through a brute force attack. A brute force attack is where someone generates every possible combination of characters running each version through the same algorithm used to encrypt the original password until a match is made and your password is found.

Authentication POP (APOP) is a method used to provide password-only encryption for mail authentication. It employs a challenge/response method defined in RFC1725 that uses a shared timestamp provided by the server being authenticated to. The timestamp is hashed with the username and the shared secret key through the MD5 algorithm.

There are still a few problems with this, the first of which is that all values are known in advance except the shared secret key. Because of this, there is nothing to provide protection against a brute-force attack

Continued

on the shared key. Another problem is that this security method attempts to protect your password. Nothing is done to prevent anyone who might be listening to your network from then viewing your e-mail as it is downloaded to your mail client.

You can find an example of a brute-force password dictionary generator that can produce a brute-force dictionary from specific character sets at www.dmzs.com/tools/files.

To solve the problem of authentication through sharing common secret keys across an untrusted network, the concept of Zero Knowledge Passwords was created. The idea of Zero Knowledge Passwords is that the parties who wish to authenticate each other want to prove to one another that they know the shared secret, and yet not share the secret with each other in case the other party truly doesn't have knowledge of the password, while at the same time preventing anyone who may intercept the communications between the parties from gaining knowledge as to the secret that is being used.

Public-key cryptography has been shown to be the strongest method of doing Zero Knowledge Passwords. It was originally developed by Whitfield Diffie and Martin Hellman and presented to the world at the 1976 National Computer Conference. Their concept was published a few months later in their paper, New Directions in Cryptography. Another crypto-researcher named Ralph Merkle, working independently from Diffie and Hellman, also invented a similar method for providing public-key cryptography, but his research was not published until 1978.

Public-key cryptography introduced the concept of having keys work in pairs, an encryption key and a decryption key, and having them created in such a way that generating one key from the other is infeasible. The encryption key is then made public to anyone wishing to encrypt a message to the holder of the secret decryption key. Because identifying or creating the decryption key from the encryption key is infeasible, anyone who happens to have the encrypted message and the encryption key will be unable to decrypt the message or determine the decryption key needed to decrypt the message.

Public-key encryption generally stores the keys or uses a certificate hierarchy. The certificates are rarely changed and often used just for encrypting data, not authentication. Zero Knowledge Password protocols, on the other hand, tend to use Ephemeral keys. *Ephemeral keys* are temporary keys that are randomly created for a single authentication, and then discarded once the authentication is completed.

Note that the public-key encryption is still susceptible to a chosen-ciphertext attack. This attack is where someone already knows what the decrypted message is and has knowledge of the key used to generate the encrypted message. Knowing the decrypted form of the message lets the attacker possibly deduce what the secret decryption key could be. This attack is unlikely to occur with authentication systems because the attacker will not have knowledge of the decrypted message: your password. If they had that, they would already have the ability to authenticate as you and not need to determine your secret decryption key.

Currently 802.11 network authentication is centered on the authentication of the wireless device, not on authenticating the user or station utilizing the wireless network. Public-key encryption is not used in the wireless encryption process. Although a few wireless vendors have dynamic keys that are changed with every connection, most wireless 802.11 vendors utilize shared-key authentication with static keys.

Shared key authentication is utilized by WEP functions with the following steps:

1. When a station requests service, it sends an authentication frame to the access point (AP) it wishes to communicate with.

2. The receiving AP replies to the authentication frame with its own, which contains 128 octets of challenge text.

3. The station requesting access encrypts the challenge text with the shared encryption key and returns to the AP.

4. The access decrypts the encrypted challenge using the shared key and compares it with the original challenge text. If they match, an authentication acknowledgement is sent to the station requesting access, otherwise a negative authentication notice is sent.

As you can see, this authentication method does not authenticate the user or any resource the user might need to access. It is only a verification that the wireless device has knowledge of the shared secret key that the wireless AP has. Once a user has passed the AP authentication challenge, that user will then have full access to whatever devices and networks the AP is connected to. You should still use secure authentication methods to access any of these devices and prevent unauthorized access and use by people who might be able to attach to your wireless network.

To solve this lack of external authentication, the IEEE 802.11 committee is working on 802.1x, a standard that will provide a framework for 802-based networks authenticating from centralized servers. Back in November 2000, Cisco introduced Light Extensible Authentication Protocol (LEAP) authentication to their wireless products, which adds several enhancements to the 802.11 authentication system, including the following:

- Mutual authentication utilizing Remote Access Dial-In User Service (RADIUS).

- Securing the secret key with one-way hashes that make password reply attacks impossible.

- Policies to force the user to re-authenticate more often, getting a new session key with each new session. This will help to prevent attacks where traffic is injected into the data stream.

- Changes to the initialization vector used in WEP encryption that make the current exploits of WEP ineffective.

Not all vendors support these solutions, so your best bet is to protect your network and servers with your own strong authentication and authorization rules.

Extensible Authentication Protocol (EAP)

The Extensible Authentication Protocol (EAP) was designed to provide authentication methods within the Point-to-Point-Protocol (PPP). EAP allows for the integration of third-party authentication packages that use PPP. EAP can be configured so that it can support a number of methods for authentication schemes, such as token cards, public key, certificates, PINs, and on and on.

When you install PPP/EAP, EAP will not select a specific authentication method at the Link Control Protocol (LCP) Phase, but will wait until the Authentication Phase to begin. What this does is allow the authenticator the ability to request more information, and with this information it will decide on the method of authentication to use. This delay will also allow for the implementation of a server on the backend that can control the various authentication methods while the PPP authenticator passes through the authentication exchange.

In this way, network devices like APs or switches do not need to understand each request type, because they will simply act as a conduit, or passthrough agent, for a server on a host. The network device will only need to see if the packet has the success or failure code in order to terminate the authentication phase.

EAP is able to define one or more requests for peer-to-peer authentication. This can happen because the request packet includes a type field, such as Generic Token, one-time password (OTP), or an MD5 challenge. The MD5 challenge is very similar to the Challenge Handshake Authentication Protocol (CHAP).

EAP is able to provide you with a flexible, link-layer security framework (see Figure 8.2), by having the following features:

- EAP mechanisms are IETF standards–based and allow for the growth of new authentication types when your security needs change:
    - Transport Layer Security (TLS)
    - Internet Key Exchange (IKE)
    - GSS_API (Kerberos)
    - Other authentication schemes (LEAP)
- There is no dependency on IP, because this is an encapsulation protocol.
- There is no windowing as this is a simple ACK/NAK protocol.
- No support for fragmentation.
- Can run over any link layer (PPP, 802.3, 802.5, 802.11, and so on).
- Does not consider a physically secure link as an authentication method to provide security.
- Assumes that there is no reordering of packets.
- Retransmission of packets is the responsibility of authenticator.

Figure 8.2 The EAP Architecture

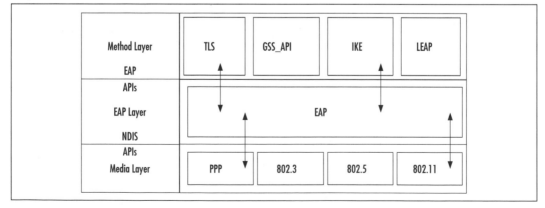

802.1x and EAP

One type of wireless security is focused on providing centralized authentication and dynamic key distribution area. By using the IEEE 802.1x standard, the EAP, and the Cisco Lightweight Extensible Authentication Protocol (LEAP) as an end-to-end solution, you can provide enhanced functionality to your wireless network. Two main elements are involved in using this standard:

- EAP/LEAP allows all wireless client adapters the capability to communicate with different authentication servers such as RADIUS and Terminal Access Controller Access Control System (TACACS+) servers that are located on the network.

- You implement the IEEE 802.1x standard for network access control that is port based for MAC filtering.

When these features are deployed together, wireless clients that are associated with APs will not be able to gain access to the network unless the user performs a network logon. The user will need to enter a username and password for network logon, after which the client and a RADIUS server will perform authentication, hopefully leading to the client being authenticated by the supplied username and password and access to the network and resources.

How this occurs is that the RADIUS server and client device will then receive a client-specific WEP key that is used by the client for that specific logon session. As an added level of security, the user's password and session key will never be transmitted in the open, over the wireless connection.

Here is how Authentication works and the WEP key is passed:

1. The wireless client will associate with an AP located on the wireless network.

2. The AP will then prevent all other attempts made by that client to gain access to network until the client logs on to the network.

3. The client will supply a username and password for network logon.

4. Using 802.1x standard and EAP/LEAP, the wireless client and a RADIUS server perform authentication through the AP. The client will then use a one-way hash of the user-supplied password as a response to the challenge, and this will be sent to the RADIUS server. The RADIUS server will then reference its user table and compare that to the response from the client. If there is a match, the RADIUS server

authenticates the client, and the process will be repeated, but in reverse. This will enable the client to authenticate the RADIUS server.

(If you are using LEAP, the RADIUS server will send an authentication challenge to the client.)

After authentication completes successfully, the following steps take place:

1. The RADIUS server and the client determine a WEP key that is unique for the client and that session.

2. The RADIUS server transmits this WEP key (also known as a session key), across the wired LAN to the AP.

3. The AP will encrypt the broadcast key and the session key so that it can then send the new encrypted key to the client. The client will then use the session key to decrypt it.

4. The client and AP then activates the WEP. The APs and clients will then use the session and broadcast WEP keys for all communications that occur during the session.

5. For enhanced security, the session key and broadcast key are regularly changed at regular periods that are configured in the RADIUS server.

A more simplified version is included in Figure 8.3.

Figure 8.3 Cisco Security Solution Using Session-Based Encryption Keys

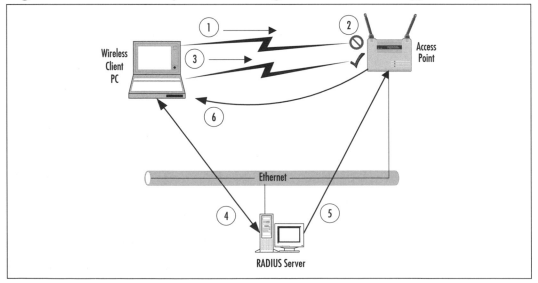

An Introduction to the 802.1x Standard

In order to better understand 802.1x, you must also understand the enhancements of current IEEE 802.11b security products and features. The current IEEE 802.11b standard is severely limited because it is available only for the current open and shared key authentication scheme, which is non-extensible.

Some of these requirements for the future security include the following:

- The creation of new 802.11 authentication methods.

- These authentication methods must be independent of the underlying 802.11 hardware.

- Authentication methods should be dynamic because hard coding it makes it difficult to fix security holes when they are found.

- It must have the ability to support Public Key Infrastructure (PKI) and certificate schemes.

Project Authorization Request (PAR) for 802.1x

Currently, no standard mechanism allows access to and from a network segment based only on the authenticated state of a port user. The problem is that network connectivity allows for the anonymous access to company data and the Internet. When 802-based networks are deployed in more accessible areas, you will need a method to authenticate and authorize basic network access. These types of projects provide for common interoperable solutions that use standards-based authentication and authorization infrastructures like those that are commonly supporting schemes such as dial-up access already.

The Objectives of the 802.1x Standard

The IEEE 802.1x Working Group was created for the purpose of providing a security framework for port-based access control that resides in the upper layers. The most common method for port-based access control is to enable new authentication and key management methods without changing current network devices.

The benefits that are the end result of this group are as follows:

- There is a significant decrease in hardware cost and complexity.

- There are more options, which allows you to pick and choose your security solution.

- You can install the latest and greatest security technology, and it should still work with your existing infrastructure.

- You are able to respond to security issues as quickly as they arise.

802.1x in a Nutshell

When a client device connects to a port on an 802.1x switch and AP, the switch port can determine the authenticity of the devices. Due to this and, according to the protocol specified by 802.1x, the services offered by the switch can be made available on that port. Only EAPOL (see the following list) frames can be sent and received on that port until the authentication is complete. When the device is properly authentication, the port switches traffic as though it were a regular port.

Here is some terminology for the 802.1x standard that you should familiarize yourself with:

- **Port** A port is a single point of connection to the network.

- **Port Access Entity (PAE)** The PAE controls the algorithms and protocols that are associated with the authentication mechanisms for a port.

- **Authenticator PAE** The authenticator PAE enforces authentication before it will allow access resources located off of that port.

- **Supplicant PAE** The supplicant PAE tries to accesses the services that are allowed by the authenticator.

- **Authentication Server** The Authentication Server is used to verify the supplicant PAE. It decides whether the supplicant is authorized to access the authenticator or not.

- **Extensible Authentication Protocol Over LAN (EAPOL)** The 802.1x defines a standard for encapsulating EAP messages so that they can be handled directly by a LAN MAC service. 802.1x tries to make authentication more encompassing, rather than enforcing specific mechanisms on the devices. Because of this, 802.1x uses Extensible Authentication Protocol to receive authentication information.

- **Extensible Authentication Protocol Over Wireless (EAPOW)** When EAPOL messages are encapsulated over 802.11 wireless frames, they are known as EAPOW.

Making it Come Together—User Identification and Strong Authentication

With the addition of the 802.1x standard, clients are identified by usernames, not the MAC address of the devices. This was designed to not only enhance security, but to streamline the process for authentication, authorization, and accountability for your network. 802.1x was designed so that it could support extended forms of authentication, using password methods (such as one-time passwords, or GSS_API mechanisms like Kerberos) and nonpassword methods (such as biometrics, Internet Key Exchange [IKE], and smart cards).

Key Derivation Can Be Dynamic

You can also use per-user session keys, because the 802.1x standard allows for the creation of them. Because you don't need to keep WEP keys at the client device or AP, you can dispense per-user, and/or per session–based WEP keys. These WEP keys will be dynamically created at the client for every session, thus making it more secure. The Global key, like a broadcast WEP key, can be encrypted using a unicast session key and then sent from the AP to the client in a much more secure manner.

Mutual Authentication

When using 802.1x and EAP, you should use some form of mutual authentication. This will make the client and the authentication servers mutually authenticating end-points and will assist in the mitigation of attacks from man in the middle types of devices. To enable mutual authentication, you could use any of the following EAP methods:

- **TLS** This requires that the server supply a certificate and establish that it has possession of the private key.

- **IKE** This requires that the server show possession of preshared key or private key (this can be considered certificate authentication).

- **GSS_API (Kerberos)** This requires that the server can demonstrate knowledge of the session key.

NOTE

Cisco Systems has also created a lightweight mutual authentication scheme, called LEAP (discussed later), so that your network is able to support operating systems that do not normally support EAP. LEAP also offers the capability to have alternate certificate schemes such as EAP-TLS.

Per-Packet Authentication

EAP can support per-packet authentication and integrity protection, but this authentication and integrity protection is not extended to all types of EAP messages. For example, NAK (negative acknowledgment) and notification messages are not able to use per-packet authentication and integrity. Per-packet authentication and integrity protection works for the following (packet is encrypted unless otherwise noted):

- TLS and IKE derive session key
- TLS ciphersuite negotiations (not encrypted)
- IKE ciphersuite negotiations
- Kerberos tickets
- Success and failure messages that use derived session key (through WEP)

Designing & Planning...

Preventing Dictionary Attacks Using EAP

EAP was designed to support extended authentication. When you implement EAP, you can avoid dictionary attacks by using nonpassword-based schemes such as biometrics, certificates, OTP, smart cards, and token cards.

You should be sure that if you are using password-based schemes that they use some form of mutual authentication so that they are more protected against dictionary attacks.

Possible Implementation of EAP on the WLAN

There are two main authentication methods for EAP on your wireless LAN: One is EAP-MD5, and the other is to use Public Key Infrastructure (PKI) with EAP-TLS. EAP-MD5 has a couple of issues because it does not support the capability for mutual authentication between the access server and the wireless client. The PKI schemes also has drawbacks, because it is very computation-intensive on the client systems, you need a high degree of planning and design to make sure that your network is capable of supporting PKI, and it is not cheap.

Cisco Light Extensible Authentication Protocol (LEAP)

LEAP is an enhancement to the EAP protocol, and as you remember, the EAP protocol was created in an effort to provide a scalable method for a PPP-based server to authenticate its clients and, hopefully allow for mutual authentication. An extensible packet exchange should allow for the passing of authentication information between the client devices and the PPP servers. The thing is that PPP servers usually rely on a centralized authentication server system that can validate the clients for them. This is where a RADIUS or a TACACS+ server usually comes into play.

This reason that the servers can work is that the servers have a protocol that will enable them to pass EAP packets between the authentication server and the PPP server. Essentially this makes the PPP server a passthrough or a relay agent, so that the authentication process happens between the client and the RADIUS server. The RADIUS server will then tell the PPP server the results of the authentication process (pass/fail) that will allow the client to access the network and its resources.

To make sure that all types of network access servers could be implemented to validate clients to network resources, the EAP protocol was created. Because we are talking about wireless connections though, the link between the AP and the client is not PPP but WLAN.

When the 802.11 specifications were standardized, it allowed for the encryption of data traffic between APs and clients through the use of a WEP encryption key. When it was first implemented, the AP would have a single key, and this key had to be configured on each client. All traffic would be encrypted using this single key. Well, this type of security has a lot of issues. In current implementations that use EAP authentication, the client and RADIUS server have a shared secret; generally this is some permutation of a username and password combination. The server will then pass certain information to the AP so that the client and AP can derive encryption keys that are unique for this client-AP pair. This is called Cisco LEAP authentication.

The previous section discussed the implementation methods of EAP (EAP-MD5, and PKI with EAP-TLS), and some of the issues that you can expect to see when you plan to implement them. LEAP may be a better option because it can offer mutual authentication, it needs only minimal support from the client's CPU, it can support embedded systems, and it can support clients whose operating system does not have the support for native EAP or allow for the use of the PKI authentication.

LEAP authentication works through three phases: the *start phase*, the *authenticate phase*, and the *finish phase*. The following sections show the process that the client and AP go through so that the client can also talk to the RADIUS server.

Start Phase for LEAP Authentication

In the start phase, information (in packet form) is transferred between the client and APs:

1. The EAPOW-Start (this is also called EAPOL-Start in 802.1x for wired networks) starts the authentication process. This packed is sent from the client to the AP.

2. The EAP-Request/Identity is sent from the AP to the client with a request for the clients Identity.

3. The EAP-Response/Identity is sent from the client to the AP with the required information.

Authentication Phase for LEAP Authentication

This sequence will change based on the mutual authentication method you choose for the client and the authentication server. If you were to use TLS for the transfer of certificates in a PKI deployment, EAP-TLS messages will be used, but because we are talking about LEAP, it would go more like this:

1. The client sends an EAP-Response/Identity message to the RADIUS server through the AP as a RADIUS-Access-Request with EAP extensions.

2. The RADIUS server then returns access-request with a RADIUS-challenge, to which the client must respond.

Cisco LEAP authentication is a mutual authentication method, and the AP is only a passthrough. The AP in the authenticate phase forwards the contents of the packets from EAP to RADIUS and from Radius to EAP.

The (Big) Finish Phase of LEAP Authentication

The steps for the finish phase are as follows:

1. If the client is considered invalid, the RADIUS server will send a RADIUS deny packet with an EAP fail packet embedded within it. If the client is considered to be valid, the server will send a RADIUS request packet with an EAP success attribute.

2. The RADIUS-Access-Accept packet contains the MS-MPPE-Send-Key attribute to the AP, where it obtains the session key that will be used by client.

The RADIUS server and client both create a session key from the user's password, when using LEAP. The encryption for the IEEE 802.11 standard can be based on a 40/64-bit or 104/128-bit key. Note that the key derivation process will create a key that is longer than is required. This is so that when the AP receives the key from the RADIUS server (using MS-MPPE-Send-Key attribute), it will send an EAPOL-KEY message to the client. This key will tell the client the key length and what key index that it should use.

The key value isn't sent because the client has already created it on its own WEP key. The data packet is then encrypted using the full-length key. The AP will also send an EAPOL-KEY message that gives information about the length, key index, and value of the multicast key. This message is encrypted using the full-length session unicast key from the AP.

Configuration and Deployment of LEAP

In this section, we talk about the installation and requirements for a LEAP solution that consists of a client, an AP and a RADIUS server for key distribution in your network.

Client Support for LEAP

You can configure your client to use LEAP mode in one of two modes:

- **Network Logon Mode** In Network Logon Mode, an integrated network logon provides for a single-sign on for both the wireless network as well as Microsoft Networking. This will provide users with a transparent security experience. This is probably the most common method of authenticating into the wireless network (or the wired network).

■ **Device Mode** In Device Mode, the wireless LAN stores the username/password identification, so that you can get non-interactive authentication into the wireless LAN. You will often see this on wireless appliances where the devices that can authenticate themselves through these preconfigured credentials are enough security.

Access Point Support for LEAP

Access points can provide 802.1x for 802.11 Authenticator support. In order to make this work, you need to take the following two steps in setting up 802.1x authenticator support:

■ You need to configure the AP to use 40/64- or 104/128-bit WEP mode.

■ You must give the LEAP RADIUS server address and configure the shared secret key that the AP and RADIUS server use, so that they can communicate securely.

Configuring your RADIUS server for LEAP

To configure the RADIUS server for authentication and key distribution users, you will need to do the following:

■ You need to create the user databases.

■ You need to configure the APs as Network Access Servers (NASs). This will enable users that are configured with Cisco-Aironet RADIUS extensions on the NAS to use RADIUS. RADIUS requests from the AP with EAP extensions are passed as described earlier.

Ensuring Authorization

Authorization is the rights and permissions granted to a user or application that enables access to a network or computing resource. Once a user has been properly identified and authenticated, authorization levels determine the extent of system rights that the user has access to.

Many of the early operating systems and applications deployed had very small authorization groups. Generally, only user groups and operator groups were available for defining a user's access level. Once more formal methods for approaching various authorization levels were defined, applications and servers started offering more discrete authorization levels. You can observe this by simply looking at any standard back-office application deployed today.

Many of them provide varying levels of access for users and administrators. For example, they could have several levels of user accounts allowing some users access to just view the information, while giving others the ability to update or query that information and have administrative accounts based on the authorization levels needed (such as being able to look up only specific types of customers, or run particular reports while other accounts have the ability to edit and create new accounts).

As shown in the previous authentication example, Cisco and others have implemented RADIUS authentication for their wireless devices. Now, utilizing stronger authentication methods, you can implement your authorization policies into your wireless deployments.

However, many wireless devices do not currently support external authorization validation. Plus, most deployments just ensure authorized access to the device. They do not control access to or from specific network segments. To fully restrict authorized users to the network devices they are authorized to utilize, you will still need to deploy an adaptive firewall between the AP and your network.

This is what was done earlier this year by two researchers at NASA (for more information, see www.nas.nasa.gov/Groups/Networks/Projects/Wireless). To protect their infrastructure, but still provide access through wireless, they deployed a firewall segmenting their wireless and department network. They most likely hardened their wireless interfaces to the extent of the equipments' possibilities by utilizing the strongest encryption available to them, disabling SID broadcast, and allowing only authorized MAC addresses on the wireless network.

They then utilized the Dynamic Host Configuration Protocol (DHCP) on the firewall, and disabled it on their AP. This allowed them to expressly define which MAC addresses could receive an IP address, and what the lease lifetime of the IP address would be.

The researchers then went on to turn off all routing and forwarding between the wireless interface and the internal network. If anyone happened to be able to connect to the wireless network, they would still have no access to the rest of the computing resources of the department. Anyone wishing to gain further access would have to go to an SSL protected Web site on the firewall server and authenticate as a valid user. The Web server would authenticate the user against a local

RADIUS server, but they could have easily used any other form of user authentication (NT, SecurID, and so on).

Once the user was properly authenticated, the firewall would change the firewall rules for the IP address that user was supposed to be assigned to, allowing full access to only the network resources they are authorized to access.

Finally, once the lease expired or was released for any reason from the DHCP assigned IP address, the firewall rules would be removed and that user and their IP would have to re-authenticate through the Web interface to allow access to the network resources again.

MAC Filtering

In order to fully discuss the advantages and disadvantages of MAC filtering, let's have a short review on what a MAC address is. The term *MAC* stands for Media Access Control, and forms the lower layer in the Data-Link layer of the OSI model. The purpose of the MAC sublayer is to present a uniform interface between the physical networking media (copper/fiber/radio frequency) and the Logical Link Control portion of the Data-Link layer. These two layers are found onboard a NIC, whether integrated into a device or used as an add-on (PCI card or PCMCIA card).

What Is a MAC Address?

In order to facilitate delivery of network traffic, the MAC layer is assigned a unique address, which is programmed into the NIC at the time of manufacture. The operating system will associate an IP address with this MAC address, which allows the device to participate in an IP network. Because no other NIC in the world should have the same MAC address, it is easy to see why it could be a secure way to equate a specific user with the MAC address on his or her machine.

Now, let's look at an actual MAC address. For example, my laptop has a MAC address of 00-00-86-4C-75-48. The first three octets are called the organizationally unique identifier (OUI). The Institute of Electrical and Electronic Engineers controls these OUIs and assigns them to companies as needed. If you look up the 00-00-86 OUI on the IEEE's Web site (http://standards.ieee.org/regauth/oui/index.shtml), it will state that the manufacturer of this NIC is the 3Com Corporation.

Corporations can own several OUIs, and often acquire additional OUIs when they purchase other companies. For example, when Cisco purchased Aironet

Wireless Communications in 1999, they added the 00-40-96 OUI to the many others they have.

Some other OUIs you could see on your WLAN might be the following:

- **00-02-2D** Agere Communications (previously known as ORiNOCO)
- **00-10-E7** Breezecom
- **00-E0-03** Nokia Wireless
- **00-04-5A** Linksys

The remaining three octets in a MAC address are usually burned into the NIC during manufacture, thus assuring that duplicate addresses will not exist on a network. We say "usually" because this rule has a few exceptions. For example, in some redundancy situations, one NIC on a machine is able to assume the MAC address of the other NIC if the primary NIC fails. Some early 802.11 PCMCIA cards also had the capability to change their MAC address. Although not necessarily easy to do, changing the MAC address gives a user the ability to spoof the MAC address of another PCMCIA card. This could be used to circumvent MAC filtering or be employed in a denial of service (DoS) attack against a specific user.

Where in the Authentication/Association Process Does MAC Filtering Occur?

When a wireless device wants to connect to a WLAN, it goes though a two-part process called authentication and authorization. After both have been completed, the device is allowed access to the WLAN.

As mentioned earlier, when a wireless device is attempting to connect to a WLAN, it sends an authentication request to the AP (see Figure 8.4). This request will contain the SSID of the target network, or a null value if connecting to an open system. The AP will grant or deny authentication based on this string. Following a successful authentication, the requesting device will attempt to associate with the AP. It is at this point in time that MAC filtering plays its role. Depending on the AP vendor and administrative setup of the AP, MAC filtering either allows only the specified MAC addresses—blocking the rest, or it allows all MAC addresses—blocking specifically noted MACs. If the MAC address is allowed, the requesting device is allowed to associate with the AP.

Figure 8.4 MAC Filtering

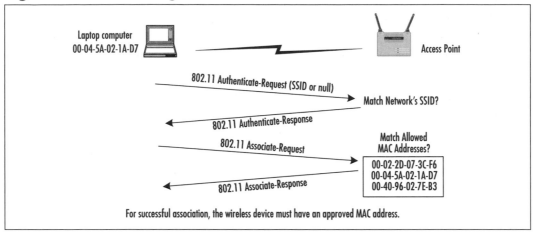

For successful association, the wireless device must have an approved MAC address.

Determining MAC Filtering Is Enabled

The easiest way to determine if a device has failed the association process due to MAC filtering is through the use of a protocol analyzer, like Sniffer Pro or AiroPeek. The difficulty here is that other factors besides MAC filtering could prevent association from occurring. RADIUS or 802.1x authentication, or an incorrect WEP key could also prevent this. These of course are costly mechanisms commonly seen in large corporate environments. Due to the costs involved with setting up the higher forms of non–AP-based authentication, most small businesses or home installations will use MAC filtering to limit access (if they use anything at all).

MAC Spoofing

If you discover that your MAC address is not allowed to associate with the AP, don't give up. There are other ways into the network besides the front door.

First off, just because you can't associate with the AP doesn't mean you can't sit there and passively watch the traffic. With 802.11b protocol analysis software, your laptop can see all the other stations' communication with any AP within range. Because the MAC addresses of the other stations are transmitted in clear text, it should be easy to start compiling a list of the MAC addresses allowed on the network.

Some early runs of 802.11 PCMCIA cards had the capability to modify their MAC addresses. Depending on the card and the level of firmware, the method to change your MAC address may vary. There are sites on the Internet that can give you more specific information on altering these parameters.

Once you have modified the MAC address, you should be able to associate it with the AP. Keep in mind however, that if the device bearing the MAC address you have stolen is still operating on the network, you will not be able to use your device. To allow the operation of two duplicate MAC addresses will break ARP tables and will attract a level of attention to your activities that is undesirable. The advanced hacker we are discussing would realize this. In attempts to subvert the security mechanisms, traffic would be monitored to sufficiently pattern the intended victim whose MAC address and identification are to be forged in order to avoid detection.

Ensuring Non-Repudiation

Repudiation is defined by West's Encyclopedia of American Law as "the rejection or refusal of a duty, relation, right or privilege." A repudiation of a transaction or contract means that one of the parties refuses to honor their obligation to the other as specified by the contract. Non-repudiation could then be defined as the ability to deny, with irrefutable evidence, a false rejection or refusal of an obligation.

In their paper "Non-Repudiation in the Digital Environment," Adrian McCullagh and William Caelli put forth an excellent review of the traditional model of non-repudiation and the current trends for crypto-technical non-repudiation. The paper was published online by First Monday—you can find it at www.firstmonday.dk/issues/issue5_8/mccullagh/index.html.

The basis for a repudiation of a traditional contract is sometimes associated with the belief that the signature binding a contract is a forgery, or that the signature is not a forgery but was obtained via unconscionable conduct by a party to the transaction, by fraud instigated by a third party, or undue influence exerted by a third party. In typical cases of fraud or repudiated contracts, the general rule of evidence is that if a person denies a particular signature, the burden of proving that the signature is valid falls upon the receiving party.

Common law trust mechanisms establish that in order to overcome false claims of non-repudiation, a trusted third party needs to act as a witness to the signature being affixed. Having a witness to the signature of a document, who is independent of the transactions taking place, reduces the likelihood that a signor is able to successfully allege that the signature is a forgery. However, there is always the possibility that the signatory will be able to deny the signature on the basis of the situations listed in the preceding paragraph.

A perfect example of a non-repudiation of submissions can be viewed by examining the process around sending and receiving registered mail. When you send a registered letter, you are given a receipt containing an identification number for the piece of mail sent. If the recipient claims that the mail was not sent, the receipt is proof that provides the non-repudiation of the submission. If a receipt is available with the recipient's signature, this provides the proof for the non-repudiation of the delivery service. The postal service provides the non-repudiation of transport service by acting as a Trusted Third Party (TTP).

Non-repudiation, in technical terms, has come to mean the following:

- In authentication, a service that provides proof of the integrity and origin of data both in an unforgeable relationship, which can be verified by any third party at any time; or

- In authentication, an authentication that with high assurance can be asserted to be genuine, and that cannot subsequently be refuted.

The Australian Federal Government's Electronic Commerce Expert group further adopted this technical meaning in their 1998 report to the Australian Federal Attorney General as:

> Non-repudiation is a property achieved through cryptographic methods which prevents an individual or entity from denying having performed a particular action related to data (such as mechanisms for non-rejection or authority (origin); for proof of obligation, intent, or commitment; or for proof of ownership.

In the digital realm, a movement is in place to shift the responsibility of proving that a digital signature is invalid to the owner of the signature, not the receiver of the signature, as is typically used in traditional common law methods.

In only a few examples does the burden of proof fall upon the alleged signer. One such example is usually found in taxation cases where the taxpayer has made specific claims and as such is in a better position to disprove the revenue collecting body's case. Another example would be in an instance of negligence. In a negligence action, if a plaintiff is able to prove that a defendant failed to meet their commitment, the burden of proof is in effect shifted to the defendant to establish that they have met their obligations.

The problem found in the new digital repudiation definitions that have been created is that they take into consideration only the validity of the signature itself. They do not allow for the possibility that the signor was tricked or forced into signing, or that their private key may be compromised, allowing the forgery of digital signatures.

With all the recent cases of Internet worms and viruses, it is not hard to imagine that one might be specifically built to steal private keys. A virus could be something as simple as a Visual Basic macro attached to a Word document, or an e-mail message that would search the targets hard drive looking for commonly named and located private key rings that could then be e-mailed or uploaded to some rogue location.

With this and other possible attacks to the private keys, it becomes difficult, under the common law position, for someone attempting to prove the identity of an alleged signatory. This common law position was established and founded in a paper-based environment where witnessing became the trusted mechanism utilized to prevent the non-repudiation of a signature. For a digital signature to be proven valid, however, it will need to be established through a fully trusted mechanism.

Thus, for a digitally signed contract to be trusted and not susceptible to repudiation, the entire document handling and signature process must take place within a secured and trusted computing environment. As we will see in some of the documentation to follow, the security policies and definitions created over the years have established a set of requirements necessary to create a secure and trusted computer system.

If we follow the definitions established in the Information Technology Security Evaluation Certification (ITSEC) to create a trusted computing environment of at least E3 to enforce functions and design of the signing process and thus prevent unauthorized access to the private key, the common law position for digitally signed documents can be maintained. E3 also ensures that the signing function is the only function able to be performed by the signing mechanism by having the source code evaluated to ensure that this is the only process available through the code. If these security features are implemented, it can be adequately assessed that under this mechanism the private key has not been stolen and as such that any digital signature created under this model has the trust established to ensure the TTP witness and validation of any signature created, preventing any possible repudiation from the signor.

One such example of a secure infrastructure designed and deployed to attempt to provide a digitally secure TTP are the PKI systems available for users of unsecure public networks such as the Internet. PKI consists of a secure computing system that acts as a certificate authority (CA) to issue and verify digital certificates. Digital certificates contain the public key and other identification information needed to verify the validity of the certificate. As long as the trust in the CA is maintained (and with it, the trust in the security of the private key), the digital certificates issued by the CA and the documents signed by them remain trusted. As long as the trust is ensured, then the CA acts as a TTP and provides for the non-repudiation of signatures created by entities with digital certificates issued through the CA.

Accounting and Audit Trails

Auditing provides methods for tracking and logging activities on networks and systems, and it links these activities to specific user accounts or sources of activity. In case of simple mistakes or software failures, audit trails can be extremely useful in restoring data integrity. They are also a requirement for trusted systems to ensure that the activity of authorized individuals on the trusted system can be traced to their specific actions, and that those actions comply with defined policy. They also allow for a method of collecting evidence to support any investigation into improper or illegal activities.

Most modern database applications support some level of transaction log detailing the activities that occurred within the database. This log could then be used to either rebuild the database if it had any errors or create a duplicate database at another location. To provide this detailed level of transactional logging, database logging tends to consume a great deal of drive space for its enormous log file. This intense logging is not needed for most applications, so you will generally have only basic informative messages utilized in system resource logging.

The logging features provided on most networks and systems involve the logging of known or partially known resource event activities. Although these logs are sometimes used for analyzing system problems, they are also useful for those whose duty it is to process the log files and check for both valid and invalid system activities.

To assist in catching mistakes and reducing the likelihood of fraudulent activities, the activities of a process should be split among several people. This segmentation of duties allows the next person in line to possibly correct problems simply because they are being viewed with fresh eyes.

From a security point of view, segmentation of duties requires the collusion of at least two people to perform any unauthorized activities. The following guidelines assist in assuring that the duties are split so as to offer no way other than collusion to perform invalid activities:

■ **No access to sensitive combinations of capabilities** A classic example of this is control of inventory data and physical inventory. By separating the physical inventory control from the inventory data control, you remove the unnecessary temptation for an employee to steal from inventory and then alter the data so that the theft is left hidden.

- **Prohibit conversion and concealment** Another violation that can be prevented by segregation is ensuring that supervision is provided for people who have access to assets. An example of an activity that could be prevented if properly segmented follows a lone operator of a night shift. This operator, without supervision, could copy (or "convert") customer lists and then sell them off to interested parties. Instances have been reported of operators actually using the employer's computer to run a service bureau at night.

- **The same person cannot both originate and approve transactions** When someone is able to enter and authorize their own expenses, it introduces the possibility that they might fraudulently enter invalid expenses for their own gain.

These principles, whether manual or electronic, form the basis for why audit logs are retained. They also identify why people other than those performing the activities reported in the log should be the ones who analyze the data in the log file.

In keeping with the idea of segmentation, as you deploy your audit trails, be sure to have your logs sent to a secure, trusted, location that is separate and non-accessible from the devices you are monitoring. This will help ensure that if any inappropriate activity occurs, the person can't falsify the log to state that the actions did not take place.

Most wireless APs do not offer any method of logging activity, but if your equipment provides the feature, you should enable it and then monitor it for inappropriate activity using tools such as logcheck. Wireless AP logging should, if it's available, log any new wireless device with its MAC address upon valid WEP authentication. It should also log any attempts to access or modify the AP itself.

Using Encryption

Encryption has always played a key role in information security, and has been the center of controversy in the design of the WEP wireless standard. But despite the drawbacks, encryption will continue to play a major role in wireless security, especially with the adoption of new and better encryption algorithms and key management systems.

As we have seen in reviewing the basic concepts of security, many of the principles used to ensure the confidentiality, integrity, and availability of servers and services are through the use of some form of trusted and tested encryption. We also have seen that even with encryption, if we get tied up too much in the acceptance of the hard mathematics as evidence of validity, it is possible to be tricked into accepting invalid authorization or authentication attempts by someone who has been able to corrupt the encryption system itself by either acquiring the private key through cryptanalysis or stealing the private key from the end user directly.

Cryptography offers the obvious advantage that the material it protects cannot be used without the keys needed to unlock it. As long as those keys are protected, the material remains protected. There are a few potential disadvantages to encryption as well. For instance, if the key is lost, the data becomes unavailable, and if the key is stolen, the data becomes accessible to the thief.

The process of encryption also introduces possible performance degradation. When a message is to be sent encrypted, time must be spent to first encrypt the information, then store and transmit the encrypted data, and then later decode it. In theory, this can slow a system by as much as a factor of three.

Until recently, distribution and use of strong encryption was limited and controlled by most governments. The United States government had encryption listed as munitions, right next to cruise missiles! As such, it was very difficult to legally acquire and use strong encryption through the entire Internet. With the new changes in trade laws, however, it is now possible to use stronger encryption for internal use as well as with communications with customers and other third parties.

Encrypting Voice Data

Voice communications have traditionally been a very simple medium to intercept and monitor. When digital cell and wireless phones arrived, there was a momentary window in which monitoring voice communications across these digital connections was difficult. Today, the only equipment needed to monitor cell phones or digital wireless telephones can be acquired at a local Radio Shack for generally less than $100.

Most voice communication systems are not designed to ensure the privacy of the conversations on them, so a new industry was created to facilitate those needs. Originally designed for government and military usage, telephone encryption devices give people the option of encrypting their daily calls. A few of these devices are starting to make their way into the commercial market. Although a few are being slowed down by organizations such as the National Security Agency (NSA) and the Federal Bureau of Investigation (FBI), who argue that it will prevent their "legal" monitoring of criminal activities, consumer market needs should eventually push these devices into the mainstream.

The Internet, being a communications network, offers people the ability to communicate with anyone, anywhere. Because of this, it didn't take long for the appearance of applications enabling voice communications across the Internet. Many of the early versions, like all budding technologies, did not offer any protection methods for their users. As a result, people utilizing Internet voice communications programs could have their communications monitored by someone with access to the data stream between parties. Fortunately, encryption is making its way into some of these programs, and if you're careful, you should be able to find one that uses modern tested and secure encryption algorithms such as Twofish, a popular and publicly-available encryption algorithm created by Bruce Schneier.

Encrypting Data Systems

Data networks have traditionally been susceptible to threats from a trusted insider. However, as soon as someone connects their network to another entity, it introduces possible security compromises from outside sources. Remember, all forms of data communications, from simple modem lines to frame-relay and fiber-optic connections, can be monitored.

Reviewing the Role of Policy

Good policy is your first line of defense. A properly designed policy examines every threat (or tries to) and ensures that confidentiality, integrity, and availability are maintained (or at least cites the known and accepted risks). As we shall see, policy definition begins with a clear identification and labeling of resources being utilized that will build into specific standards that define acceptable use in what's considered an authorized and secure manner. Once a basic standard is defined, you start building specific guidelines and procedures for individual applications and services.

Many wireless manufacturers have responded to security threats hampering their initial product versions by releasing upgrades to their software and drivers. Your security policy should always require that all technology, either existing or newly deployed, have the latest security patches and upgrades installed in a timely manner. However, because the development and release of patches takes time, policy and its proper implementation tend to be the first layer of defense when confronting known and unknown threats.

A well-written policy should be more than just a list of recommended procedures. It should be an essential and fundamental element of your organization's security practices. A good policy can provide protection from liability due to an employee's actions, or can form a basis for the control of trade secrets. A policy or standard should also continue to grow and expand as new threats and technologies become available. They should be constructed with the input of an entire organization and audited both internally and externally to ensure that the assets they are protecting have the controls in place as specified in the standards, policies, and guidelines.

Designing & Planning...

The Management Commitment

Management must be aware of their needed commitment to the security of corporate assets, which includes protection of information. Measures must be taken to protect it from unauthorized modification, destruction, or disclosure (whether accidental or intentional), and ensure its authenticity, integrity, availability and confidentiality.

Fundamental to the success of any security program is senior management's commitment to the information security process and their understanding of how important security controls and protections are to the enterprise's continuity.

The senior management statement usually contains the following elements:

- An acknowledgment of the importance of computing resources to the business model

- A statement of support for information security throughout the enterprise

- A commitment to authorize and manage the definition of the lower level standards, procedures, and guidelines

Part of any policy definition includes what is required to ensure that the policy is adhered to. The prime object of policy controls is to reduce the effect of security threats and vulnerabilities to the resources being protected. The policy definition process generally entails the identification of what impact a threat would have on an organization, and what the likelihood of that threat occurring would be. Risk analysis (RA) is the process of analyzing a threat and producing a representative value of that threat.

Figure 8.5 displays a matrix created using a small x–y graph representing the threat and the corresponding likelihood of that threat. The goal of RA is to reduce the level of impact and the likelihood that it will occur. A properly implemented control should move the plotted point from the upper right to the lower left of the graph.

Figure 8.5 Threat versus Likelihood Matrix

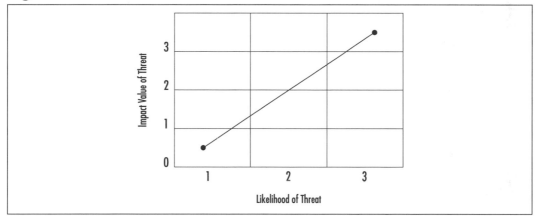

An improperly designed and implemented control will show little to no movement in the plotted point before and after the control's implementation.

Identifying Resources

To assess and protect resources, they must first be identified, classified, and labeled so that in the process of performing your risk analysis you are able to document all possible risks to each identified item and provide possible solutions to mitigate those risks.

Security classification provides the following benefits:

■ Demonstrates an organization's commitment to security procedures

- Helps identify which information is the most sensitive or vital to an organization

- Supports the tenets of confidentiality, integrity, and availability as it pertains to data

- Helps identify which protections apply to which information

- May be required for regulatory, compliance, or legal reasons

In the public sector, the common categories utilized in the classification of resources are the following:

- **Public** These are no-risk items that can be disclosed to anyone, as long as they do not violate any individual's right to privacy, and knowledge of this information does not expose an organization to financial loss or embarrassment, or jeopardize security assets. Examples of public information include marketing brochures, published annual reports, business cards, and press releases.

- **Internal Use** These are low-risk items that due to their technical or business sensitivity are limited to an organization's employees and those contractors covered by a nondisclosure agreement. Should there be unauthorized disclosure, compromise, or destruction of the documents, there would only be minimal impact on the organization, its customers, or employees. Examples of Internal Use information include employee handbooks, telephone directories, organizational charts, and policies.

- **Confidential** These are moderate-risk items whose unauthorized disclosure, compromise, or destruction would directly or indirectly impact an organization, its customers, or employees, possibly causing financial damage to an organization's reputation, a loss of business, and potential legal action. They are intended solely for use within an organization and are limited to those individuals who have a "need-to-know" security clearance. Examples of confidential items include system requirements or configurations, proprietary software, personnel records, customer records, business plans, budget information, and security plans and standards.

- **Restricted** These are high-risk critical items whose unauthorized disclosure, compromise, or destruction would result in severe damage to a company, providing significant advantages to a competitor, or causing penalties to the organization, its customers, or employees. It is intended solely for restricted use within the organization and is limited to those with an explicit, predetermined, and stringent "business-need-to-know." Examples of restricted data include strategic plans, encryption keys, authentication information (passwords, PINs, and so on), and IP addresses for security-related servers.

All information, whether in paper, spoken, or electronic form should be classified, labeled, and distributed in accordance to your information classification and handling procedures. This will assist in the determination of what items have the largest threat, and as such, should determine how you set about providing controls for those threats.

Your wireless network contains a few internal items that should be identified and classified, however the overall classification of any network device comes down the level of information that flows through its channels. While using e-mail systems or accessing external sites through your wireless network, you will likely find that your entire network contains restricted information. However, if you are able to encrypt the password, the classification of your network data will then be rated based upon the non-authentication information traveling across your wireless network.

Understanding Classification Criteria

To assist in your risk analysis, you can use a few additional criteria to determine the classification of information resources:

- **Value** Value is the most commonly used criteria for classifying data in the private sector. If something is valuable to an individual or organization, that will prompt the data to be properly identified and classified.

- **Age** Information is occasionally reclassified to a lower level as time passes. In many government organizations, some classified documents are automatically declassified after a predetermined time period has passed.

- **Useful Life** If information has become obsolete due to new information or resources, it is usually reclassified.

- **Personal Association** If information is associated with specific individuals or is covered under privacy law, it may need to be reclassified at some point.

Implementing Policy

Information classification procedures offer several steps in establishing a classification system, which provides the first step in the creation of your security standards and policies. The following are the primary procedural steps used in establishing a classification system:

1. Identify the administrator or custodian.

2. Specify the criteria of how the information will be classified and labeled.

3. Classify the data by its owner, who is subject to review by a supervisor.

4. Specify and document any exceptions to the classification policy.

5. Specify the controls that will be applied to each classification level.

6. Specify the termination procedures for declassifying the information or for transferring custody of the information to another entity.

7. Create an enterprise awareness program about the classification controls.

Once your information and resources are properly identified and classified, you will be able to define the controls necessary to ensure the privacy and security of information regarding your employees and customers. Many industries are required, either by regulation or civil law, to ensure that proper policy is in place to protect the security and privacy of nonpublic personal information. This relationship of policy, guidelines, and legal standards is shown in Figure 8.6.

Figure 8.6 The Hierarchy of Rules

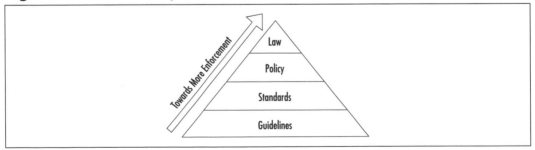

Guidelines refer to the methodologies of securing systems. Guidelines are more flexible than standards or policies and take the varying nature of information systems into consideration as they are developed and deployed, usually offering specific processes for the secure use of information resources. Many organizations have general security guidelines regarding a variety of platforms available within them: NT, SCO-Unix, Debian Linux, Red Hat Linux, Oracle, and so on.

Standards specify the use of specific technologies in a uniform way. Although they are often not as flexible as guidelines, they do offer wider views to the technology specified. Usually, standards are in place for general computer use, encryption use, information classification, and others.

Policies are generally statements created for strategic or legal reasons, from which the standards and guidelines are defined. Some policies are based on legal requirements placed on industries such as health insurance, or they can be based upon common law requirements for organizations retaining personal nonpublic information of their customers.

Policies, standards, and guidelines must be explicit and focused, and they must effectively communicate the following subjects:

- Responsibility and authority
- Access control
- The extent to which formal verification is required
- Discretionary/mandatory control (generally relevant only in government or formal policy situations)
- Marking/labeling
- Control of media
- Import and export of data
- Security and classification levels
- Treatment of system output

The intent of policy is to delineate what an organization expects in the information security realm. Reasonable policy should also reflect any relevant laws and regulations that impact the use of information within an organization.

The System Administration, Networking, and Security Institute (SANS) offers excellent resources for implementing security standards, policies, and guidelines. You can find more information on policy implementation at the SANS Web site at www.sans.org/newlook/resources/policies/policies.htm. There you'll find example policies regarding encryption use, acceptable use, analog/ISDN lines, anti-virus software, application service providers, audits, and many others.

In this section's sidebar, "Sample Wireless Communication Policy," you will find the example wireless policy that defines the standards used for wireless communications.

Designing & Planning…

Sample Wireless Communication Policy

1.0 Purpose

This policy prohibits access to *<Company Name>* networks via unsecured wireless communication mechanisms. Only wireless systems that meet the criteria of this policy or have been granted an exclusive waiver by InfoSec are approved for connectivity to *<Company Name>*'s networks.

2.0 Scope

This policy covers all wireless data communication devices (for example, personal computers, cellular phones, PDAs, and so on) connected to any of *<Company Name>*'s internal networks. This includes any form of wireless communication device capable of transmitting packet data. Wireless devices and/or networks without any connectivity to *<Company Name>*'s networks do not fall under the purview of this policy.

3.0 Policy

To comply with this policy, wireless implementations must: maintain point-to-point hardware encryption of at least 56 bits; maintain a hardware address that can be registered and tracked (for instance, a MAC address); support strong user authentication which checks against an external database such as TACACS+, RADIUS, or something similar.

Exception: a limited-duration waiver to this policy for Aironet products has been approved if specific implementation instructions are followed for corporate and home installations.

4.0 Enforcement

Any employee found to have violated this policy may be subject to disciplinary action, up to and including termination of employment.

5.0 Definitions

Terms	Definitions
User Authentication	A method by which the user of a wireless system can be verified as a legitimate user independent of the computer or operating system being used.

6.0 Revision History

Addressing the Issues with Policy

Wireless users have unique needs that policy must address. The administrator must take diligent care in creating effective policy to protect the users, their data, and corporate assets. But just what is an effective policy for wireless users? Let's look at some common sense examples of good wireless policy.

First, wireless LANs are an "edge" technology. As such, policy should reflect a standard consistent with end users attempting to gain access to network resources from "the edge." In the case of wired LANs, typically you would set some standard physical access restrictions. This type of restriction would protect the LAN from certain types of attacks. You might also create group policy on the PC for authentication and access restrictions to corporate domains, and so long as there is no inside threat, the LAN is secured. (This scenario is unlikely in that disgruntled employees are representative of a solid portion of network hacking/misuse.) If you can't physically access the media, you cannot break in. If you do not furnish a valid username and password despite physical access, in most cases you cannot break in. Certainly some other methods of attack exist so long as you have physical access, but for all intents and purposes in this discussion, the typical, aspiring hacker is locked out. This assists in implementing the more stringent rule set as required by edge and remote access.

In a wireless environment, the rules change. How do you stop access to RF? RF travels through, around, and is reflected off objects, walls, and other physical barriers. RF doesn't have the feature-rich security support that the typical wired network has. Even though you can use the features of the wired Ethernet/IP security model after you are connected to the LAN, what about the signal from the AP to the client and vice-versa? Because of this access methodology, wireless poses some interesting policy challenges.

You can overcome one of these challenges—ease of capture of RF traffic—by preventing the broadcast of the Secure Set Identifier (SSID) to the world from the AP. Much like the Network Basic Input/Output System (NETBIOS) in the Windows world that broadcasts shares, the AP typically broadcasts the SSID to allow clients to associate. This is an advertisement for access to what you would like to be a restricted WLAN. Therefore, a good policy in the WLAN space is to prevent the AP from broadcasting this information. Instead, set up the AP to respond only to clients that already have the required details surrounding the Basic Service Set (BSS). This means that when the client attempts to associate, the AP challenges the client for the SSID and WEP encryption key information before allowing access. Of course, there are still ways to capture the traffic, but with this minor policy rule, the level of difficulty has been exponentially increased from the default implementation.

This security policy works well in the WLAN space until a technically savvy, but security ignorant, user installs a rogue AP because they wish to have their own personal AP connected to the WLAN. This poses a strong threat to the overall network security posture and must be prohibited.

What's in a name? It's imperative that you set in place a standard naming convention and WEP policy to prevent the standard defaults from being utilized. You wouldn't want your password published to the world in a set of instructions on how to access your PC, but that is exactly the case when speaking of WLAN defaults. They are published, documented, and presented as the default settings of the wireless space built from that specific hardware, and this is a *good* thing. Without this information, you would not be able to implement the hardware. However, to prevent unauthorized access, it's critical that you do not leave the default settings in place. A further consideration would be not using easily guessed names such as the company name. This should be part of your security policy for new hardware/software integration and goes toward assisting in the mitigation of capturing RF traffic.

With respect to roaming needs, these policies should not change from room to room or AP to AP. A consistent rule set (more stringent than normally internally trusted users) should be put in place across all APs where users are likely to roam while connected wirelessly. When choosing your AP, you can also add to ease of use for your wireless users by getting hardware that supports true roaming as opposed to having to lose connectivity momentarily while re-associating with another AP. The temporary loss of connectivity could lead to account lock out and the need to re-authenticate in upper layers.

Finally, strong authentication and encryption methods makes attacking the access mechanisms even more difficult, which is why the organization must include the appropriate use of authentication and encryption in its policy. Use of RADIUS or VPN solutions for authentication and tunneling sits nicely in the gap for the added protection. These authentication tools even serve as a standalone security feature for open networks where disabling the SSID is not an option.

All in all, policy should reflect these general guidelines if you intend to secure the WLAN access to corporate assets. We explore each in detail throughout this chapter to give you the information you need to secure your WLAN. Don't make the mistake of using just one of these options. Instead, look at your security policy as a tightly bound rope consisting of multiple threads. Each thread is another layer of security. In this case, your security policy will remain strong despite the failure of one or two threads. At no time do you want one solution to be the only boundary between maintaining your valuables and losing them.

Implementing WEP

Despite its critics, WEP still offers a reasonable level of security, providing that all its features are used properly. This means greater care in key management, avoiding default options, and making sure adequate encryption is enabled at every opportunity.

Proposed improvements in the standard should overcome many of the limitations of the original security options, and should make WEP more appealing as a security solution. Additionally, as WLAN technology gains popularity, and users clamor for functionality, both the standards committees as well as the hardware vendors will offer improvements. This means that you should make sure to keep abreast of vendor-related software fixes and changes that improve the overall security posture of your WLAN.

Most APs advertise that they support WEP in at least 40-bit encryption, but often the 128-bit option is also supported. For corporate networks, 128-bit encryption–capable devices should be considered as a minimum. With data security enabled in a closed network, the settings on the client for the SSID and the encryption keys have to match the AP when attempting to associate with the network, or it will fail. In the next few paragraphs, we discuss WEP as it relates to the functionality of the standard, including a standard definition of WEP, the privacy created, and the authentication.

Defining WEP

802.11, as a standard, covers the communication between WLAN components. RF poses challenges to privacy in that it travels through and around physical objects. As part of the goals of the communication, a mechanism needed to be implemented to protect the privacy of the individual transmissions that in some way mirrored the privacy found on the wired LAN. Wireless Equivalency Privacy is the mechanism created in the standard as a solution that addresses this goal. Because WEP utilizes a cryptographic security countermeasure for the fulfillment of its stated goal of privacy, it has the added benefit of becoming an authentication mechanism. This benefit is realized through a shared key authentication that allows the encryption and decryption of the wireless transmissions. Many keys can be defined on an AP or a client, and they can be rotated to add complexity for a higher security standard for your WLAN policy. This is a must!

WEP was never intended to be the absolute authority in security. Instead, the driving force was privacy. In cases that require high degrees of security, you should utilize other mechanisms, such as authentication, access control, password protection, and virtual private networks.

Creating Privacy with WEP

Let's look at how WEP creates a degree of privacy on the WLAN. WEP comes in several implementations: no encryption, and 40-bit and 128-bit encryption. Obviously, no encryption means no privacy. Transmissions are sent in the clear, and they can be viewed by any wireless sniffing application that has access to the RF propagated in the WLAN. In the case of the 40- and 128-bit varieties (just as with password length), the greater the number of characters (bits), the stronger the encryption. The initial configuration of the AP will include the setup of the shared key. This shared key can be in the form of either alphanumeric, or hexadecimal strings, and is matched on the client.

WEP uses the RC4 encryption algorithm, a stream cipher developed by noted cryptographer Ron Rivest (the "r" in RSA). Both the sender and receiver use the stream cipher to create identical pseudorandom strings from a known shared key. The process entails the sender to logically XOR the plaintext transmission with the stream cipher to produce the ciphertext. The receiver takes the shared key and identical stream and reverses the process to gain the plaintext transmission.

A 24-bit initialization vector (IV) is used to create the identical cipher streams. The IV is produced by the sender, and is included in the transmission of each frame. A new IV is used for each frame to prevent the reuse of the key weakening the encryption. This means that for each string generated, a different value for the RC4 key will be used. Although a secure policy, consideration of the components of WEP bear out one of the flaws in WEP. Because the 24-bit space is so small with respect to the potential set of IVs, in a short period of time, all keys are eventually reused. Unfortunately, this weakness is the same for both the 40- and 128-bit encryption levels.

To protect against some rudimentary attacks that insert known text into the stream to attempt to reveal the key stream, WEP incorporates a checksum in each frame. Any frame not found to be valid through the checksum is discarded. All in all this sounds secure, but WEP has well-documented flaws, which we cover in later sections. Let's review the process in a little more detail to gain a better understanding of the behind-the-scenes activities that are largely the first line of defense in WLAN security.

The WEP Authentication Process

Shared key authentication is a four-step process that begins when the AP receives the validated request for association. After the AP receives the request, a series of management frames are transmitted between the stations to produce the authentication. This includes the use of the cryptographic mechanisms employed by WEP as a validation.

Strictly with respect to WEP, in the authorization phase, the four steps break down in the following manner:

1. The requestor (the client) sends a request for association.

2. The authenticator (the AP) receives the request, and responds by producing a random challenge text and transmitting it back to the requestor.

3. The requestor receives the transmission, ciphers the challenge with the shared key stream, and returns it.

4. The authenticator decrypts the challenge text and compares the values against the original. If they match, the requestor is authenticated. On the other hand, if the requestor doesn't have the shared key, the cipher stream cannot be reproduced, therefore the plaintext cannot be discovered, and theoretically, the transmission is secured.

WEP Benefits and Advantages

WEP provides some security and privacy in transmissions to prevent curious or casual browsers from viewing the contents of the transmissions held between the AP and the clients. In order to gain access, the degree of sophistication of the intruder has to improve, and specific intent to gain access is required. Let's view some of the other benefits of implementing WEP:

- All messages are encrypted using a checksum to provide some degree of tamper resistance.

- Privacy is maintained via the encryption. If you do not have the key, you can't decrypt the message.

- WEP is extremely easy to implement. Set the encryption key on the AP, repeat the process on each client, and voilà! You're done!

- WEP provides a very basic level of security for WLAN applications.

- WEP keys are user definable and unlimited. You do not have to use pre-defined keys, and you can and should change them often.

WEP Disadvantages

As with any standard or protocol, WEP has some inherent disadvantages. The focus of security is to allow a balance of access and control while juggling the advantages and disadvantages of each implemented countermeasure for security gaps. The following are some of the disadvantages of WEP:

- The RC4 encryption algorithm is a known stream cipher. This means it takes a finite key and attempts to make an infinite pseudorandom key stream in order to generate the encryption.

- Once you alter the key—which you should do often—you have to tell everyone so they can adjust their settings. The more people you tell, the more public the information becomes.

- Used on its own, WEP does not provide adequate WLAN security.

- WEP has to be implemented on every client as well as every AP to be effective.

The Security Implications of Using WEP

From a security perspective, you have mitigated the curious hacker who lacks the means or desire to really hack your network. If you have enabled WEP as instructed in the previous pages, someone has to be actively attempting to break into your network in order to be successful. If that is the case, using the strongest form of WEP available is important. Because WEP relies on a known stream cipher, it is vulnerable to certain attacks. By no means is it the final authority and should not be the only security countermeasure in place to protect your network—and ultimately your job!

Implementing WEP on the Cisco Aironet AP 340

As you can see in the following, the Cisco AP340 supports 128-bit encryption. It is configured with either a HTTP connection pictured here, or a serial connection. The serial interface is cryptic and in no way intuitive. If you plan on administering many Cisco wireless devices, use the Web interface. In Figure 8.7, you see the Web interface for an AP340. By using the drop-down menu, you can select

Full Encryption and then **128 bit** for the key size. Finally, select the **WEP Key** radio button for the transmission key and type the string.

Figure 8.7 WEP Configuration on the Aironet

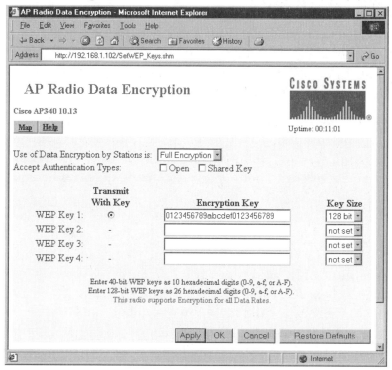

Exploiting WEP

There have been a number of well-publicized exploitations and defeats of the security mechanisms at the heart of WEP, from weaknesses in the encryption algorithm to weaknesses in key management. Although steps have been taken to overcome these weaknesses, attackers are not suffering from a lack of networks to exploit.

The first warnings regarding WEP's vulnerability to compromise came in the fall of 2000 when Jesse Walker published a document called "Unsafe at any Size: An Analysis of the WEP Encryption." In this document, Walker underscored the main weakness of WEP—the fact that it reinitializes the encrypted data stream every time an Ethernet collision occurs. Even though the 802.11 protocol attempts to avoid them with CDMA/CA, collisions are a reality that will occur. If someone is listening in on the wireless conversation, they capture the IV information transmitted with each frame and in a matter of hours have all the data needed to recover the WEP key.

Although many experts have made similar discoveries regarding this and other ways to recover WEP keys, these were usually academic and only showed that the potential for vulnerability existed. This all changed with the introduction of AirSnort and WEPCrack. Both of these programs saw an initial release in the summer of 2001, and moved the recovery of WEP keys from being a theoretical to something anyone could do—if they had a wireless card based on the Prism2 chipset.

Security of 64-Bit versus 128-Bit Keys

It might seem obvious to a nontechnical person that something protected with a 128-bit encryption scheme would be more secure than something protected with a 64-bit encryption scheme. This, however, is not the case with WEP. Because the same vulnerability exists with both encryption levels, they can be equally broken within similar time limits.

With 64-bit WEP, the network administrator specifies a 40-bit key—typically ten hexadecimal digits (0–9, a–f, or A–F). A 24-bit IV is appended to this 40-bit key, and the RC4 key scheme is built from these 64-bits of data. This same process is followed in the 128-bit scheme. The Administrator specifies a 104-bit key—this time 26 hexadecimal digits (0–9, a–f, or A-F). The 24-bit IV is added to the beginning of the key, and the RC4 key schedule is built.

As you can see, because the vulnerability comes from capturing predictably weak IVs, the size of the original key would not make a significant difference in the security of the encryption. This is due to the relatively small number of total IVs possible under the current WEP specification. Currently, there are a total of 2^{24} possible IV keys. You can see that if the WEP key was not changed within a strictly-defined period of time, all possible IV combinations could be heard off of a 802.11b connection, captured, and made available for cracking within a short period of time. This is a flaw in the design of WEP, and bears no correlation to whether the wireless client is using 64-bit WEP or 128-bit WEP.

Acquiring a WEP Key

As mentioned previously, programs exist that allow an authenticated and/or unassociated device within the listening area of the AP to capture and recover the WEP key. Depending on the speed of the machine listening to the wireless conversations, the number of wireless hosts transmitting on the WLAN, and the number of IV retransmissions due to 802.11 frame collisions, the WEP key could be cracked as quickly as a couple of hours. Obviously, if an attacker attempts to listen to a WEP-protected network when there was very little network traffic, it would take much longer to be able to get the data necessary to crack WEP.

Armed with a valid WEP key, an intruder can now successfully negotiate association with an AP, and gain entry onto the target network. Unless other mechanisms like MAC filtering are in place, this intruder is now able to roam across the network and potentially break into servers or other machines on the network. If MAC filtering is occurring, another procedure must be attempted to get around this. This was covered earlier in the "MAC Filtering" section.

WARNING

Because WEP key retrieval is now possible by casual attackers, keeping the same static WEP key in a production role for an extended period of time does not make sense. If your WEP key is static, it could be published into the underground by a hacker and still be used in a production WLAN six months to a year later.

One of the easiest ways to mitigate the risk of WEP key compromise is to regularly change the WEP key your APs and clients use. Although this may be an easy task for small WLANs, the task becomes extremely daunting when you have dozens of APs and hundreds of clients to manually rekey.

Both Cisco and Funk Software have released Access Control servers that implement rapid WEP rekeying on both APs as well as the end-user client. Utilizing this form of software, even if a WEP key was to be discovered, you could rest assured that within a specified period of time, that particular key would no longer be valid.

Addressing Common Risks and Threats

The advent of wireless networks has not created new legions of attackers. Many attackers will utilize the same attacks for the same objectives they used in wired networks. If you do not protect your wireless infrastructure with proven tools and techniques, and do not have established standards and policies that identify proper deployment and security methodology, you will find that the integrity of your wireless networks may be threatened.

Finding a Target

Utilizing new tools created for wireless networks and thousands of existing identification and attack techniques and utilities, attackers of wireless networks have many avenues to your network. The first step to attacking a wireless network involves finding a network to attack. The first popular software to identify wireless networks was NetStumbler (www.netstumbler.org). NetStumbler is a Windows application that listens for information, such as the SSID, being broadcast from APs that have not disabled the broadcast feature. When it finds a network, it notifies the person running the scan and adds it to the list of found networks.

As people began to drive around their towns and cities looking for wireless networks, NetStumbler added features such as pulling coordinates from Global Positioning System (GPS) satellites and plotting that information on mapping software. This method of finding networks is very reminiscent of a way hackers would find computers when they had only modems to communicate. They would run programs designed to search through all possible phone numbers and call each one looking for a modem to answer the call. This type of scan was typically referred to as *war dialing*; driving around looking for wireless networks has come to be known as *war driving*.

NetStumbler.org created place that people can upload the output of their war drives for inclusion in a database that can graph the location of wireless networks that have been found (www.netstumbler.org/nation.php). See Figure 8.8 for output of discovered and uploaded wireless networks as of January 2002.

Similar tools soon became available for Linux and other UNIX-based operating systems, which contained many additional utilities hackers use to attack hosts and networks once access is found. A quick search on www.freshmeat.net or www.packetstormsecurity.com for "802.11" will reveal several network identification tools as well as tools to configure and monitor wireless network connections.

Finding Weaknesses in a Target

If a network is found without encryption enabled, which reports are showing to be more than half of the networks found so far, the attacker has complete access to any resource the wireless network is connected to. They can scan and attack any machines local to the network, or launch attacks on remote hosts without any fear of reprisal, as the world thinks the attack is coming from the owner of the wireless network.

If the network is found with WEP enabled, the attacker will need to identify several items to reduce the time it will take to get onto the wireless network.

First, utilizing the output of NetStumbler or one of the other network discovery tools, the attacker will identify the SSID, network, MAC address, and any other packets that might be transmitted in cleartext. Generally, NetStumbler results include vendor information, which an attacker can use to determine which default keys to attempt on the wireless network.

Figure 8.8 Networks Discovered with NetStumbler (as of January 2002)

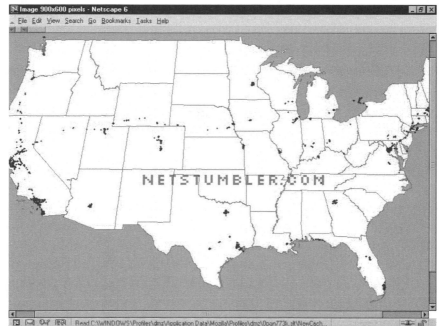

If the vendor information has been changed or is unavailable, the attacker can still use the SSID and network name and address to identify the vendor or owner of the equipment (many people use the same network name as the password, or use the company initials or street address as their password). If the SSID and network name and address has been changed from the default setting, a final network-based attempt could be to use the MAC address to identify the manufacturer.

If none of these options work, there is still the possibility of a physical review. Many public areas are participating in the wireless revolution. An observant attacker will be able to use physical and wireless identification techniques—such as finding antennas, APs, and other wireless devices that are easily identified by the manufacturer's casing and logo.

Exploiting Those Weaknesses

A well-configured wireless AP will not stop a determined attacker. Even if the network name and SSID are changed and the secret key is manually reconfigured on all workstations on a somewhat regular basis, the attacker will still take other avenues to compromise the network.

If easy access is available near to the wireless network, such as a parking lot or garage next to the building being attacked, the only thing an attacker needs is patience and AirSnort or WEPCrack. When these applications have captured enough "weak" packets (IV collisions, for example) they are able to determine the secret key currently in use on the network. Quick tests have shown that an average home network can be cracked in an overnight session. This means that to ensure your network protection, you would need to change your WEP key at least two times per day, or keep your eyes open for any vehicles that look suspicious (with an antenna sticking out the window, for instance) parked outside your home or business for hours or days at a time.

If none of these network tools help in determining which default configurations to try, the next step is to scan the traffic for any cleartext information that might be available. Some manufacturers, such as Lucent, have been known to broadcast the SSID in cleartext even when WEP and closed network options are enabled. Using tools such as Ethereal (www.ethereal.com) and TCPDump (www.tcpdump.org) allow the attacker to sniff traffic and analyze it for any cleartext hints they may find.

As a last option, the attacker will go directly after your equipment or install their own. The number of laptops or accessories stolen from travelers is rising each year. At one time these thefts were perpetrated by criminals simply looking to sell the equipment, but as criminals become more savvy, they are also after the information contained within the machines. Once you have access to the equipment, you are able to determine what valid MAC addresses can access the network, what the network SSID is, and what secret keys are to be used.

An attacker does not need to become a burglar in order to acquire this information. A skilled attacker will utilize new and specially designed malware and network tricks to determine the information needed to access your wireless network. A well-scripted Visual Basic script that could arrive in e-mail (targeted spam) or through an infected Web site can extract the information from the user's machine and upload it to the attacker.

With the size of computers so small today (note the products at www.mynix .com/espace/index.html and www.citydesk.pt/produto_ezgo.htm), it wouldn't take much for the attacker to simply create a small AP of their own that could be attached to your building or office and look just like another telephone box. Such a device, if placed properly, will attract much less attention than someone camping in a car or van in your parking lot.

Sniffing, Interception, and Eavesdropping

Originally conceived as a legitimate network and traffic analysis tool, sniffing remains one of the most effective techniques in attacking a wireless network, whether it's to map the network as part of a target reconnaissance, to grab passwords, or to capture unencrypted data.

Defining Sniffing

Sniffing is the electronic form of eavesdropping on the communications that computers have across networks. In the original networks deployed, the equipment tying machines together allowed every machine on the network to see the traffic of others. These repeaters and hubs, while very successful for getting machines connected, allowed an attacker easy access to all traffic on the network by only needing to connect to one point to see the entire network's traffic.

Wireless networks function very similar to the original repeaters and hubs. Every communication across the wireless network is viewable to anyone who happens to be listening to the network. In fact, the person listening does not even need to be associated with the network to sniff!

Sample Sniffing Tools

The hacker has many tools available to attack and monitor your wireless network. A few of these tools are Ethereal and AiroPeek (www.wildpackets.com/products/airopeek) in Windows, and TCPDump or ngrep (http://ngrep.sourceforg.net) within a UNIX or Linux environment. These tools work well for sniffing both wired and wireless networks.

All of these software packages function by putting your network card in what is called *promiscuous mode*. When in this mode, every packet that goes past the interface is captured and displayed within the application window. If the attacker is able to acquire your WEP password, they can then utilize features within AiroPeek and Ethereal to decrypt either live or post-capture data.

Sniffing Case Scenario

By running NetStumbler, the hacker will be able to find possible targets. As shown in Figure 8.9, we have found several networks that we could attack.

Figure 8.9 Discovering Wireless LANS with NetStumbler

MAC	SSID	C.	Vendor	No.	S.	Latitude	Lon
00022D0...	04464e	1	Agere (Lucent) ...	-95	9	N37.67...	W12
00022D0...	045841	1	Agere (Lucent) ...	-95	8	N37.69...	W12
00022D2...	Apple Netw...	1	Agere (Lucent) ...	-96	6	N37.68...	W12
00045A...	COMPAQ	6	Linksys	-93	7	N37.69...	W12
004005D...	default	6	D-Link	-96	11	N37.69...	W12
0040964...		1	Cisco (Aironet)	-98	23	N37.70...	W12
000124F...	home	6		-97	17	N37.69...	W12
0040964...	labaccessp...	6	Cisco (Aironet)	-97	25		
00045A...	linksys	6	Linksys	-96	6	N37.69...	W12
00045A...	linksys	4	Linksys	-95	3	N37.69...	W12
00045A...	linksys	6	Linksys	-96	6	N37.69...	W12
00055D...	linksys	6	D-Link	-94	7	N37.69...	W12
0002A56...	protest	10		-95	15	N37.68...	W12
0040964...		6	Cisco (Aironet)	-97	25	N37.68...	W12
0030AB...	Tiger	6	Delta Networks	-97	12	N37.69...	W12
0040963...	TJALL	6	Cisco (Aironet)	-96	19	N37.69...	W12
0040964...	TJPOS	1	Cisco (Aironet)	-146	54	N37.69...	W12
00045A0...	tsaumi	6	Linksys	-95	10	N37.69...	W12
00022D3...	WaveLAN	10	Agere (Lucent) ...	-97	11	N37.68...	W12
0030AB...	Wireless	6	Delta Networks	-97	7		
0090D10...	WLAN	11	Addtron	-97	17	N37.68...	W12

Once the hacker has found possible networks to attack, one of the first tasks is to identify who the target is. Many organizations are "nice" enough to include their name or address in the network name. For those that do not display that information, we can gather a lot from their traffic that allows us to determine who they could be.

Utilizing any of the mentioned network sniffing tools, the unencrypted network is easily monitored. Figure 8.10 shows our network sniff of the traffic on the wireless network. From this, we are able to determine who their Domain Name System (DNS) server is, and what default search domain and default Web home page they are accessing. With this information, we can easily identify who the target is and determine if they are worth attacking.

If the network is encrypted, the first place to start is locating the physical location of the target. NetStumbler has the capability to display the signal strength of the networks you have discovered (see Figure 8.11). Utilizing this information, the attacker needs to just drive around and look for where the signal strength increases and decreases to determine the home of the wireless network.

Figure 8.10 Sniffing with Ethereal

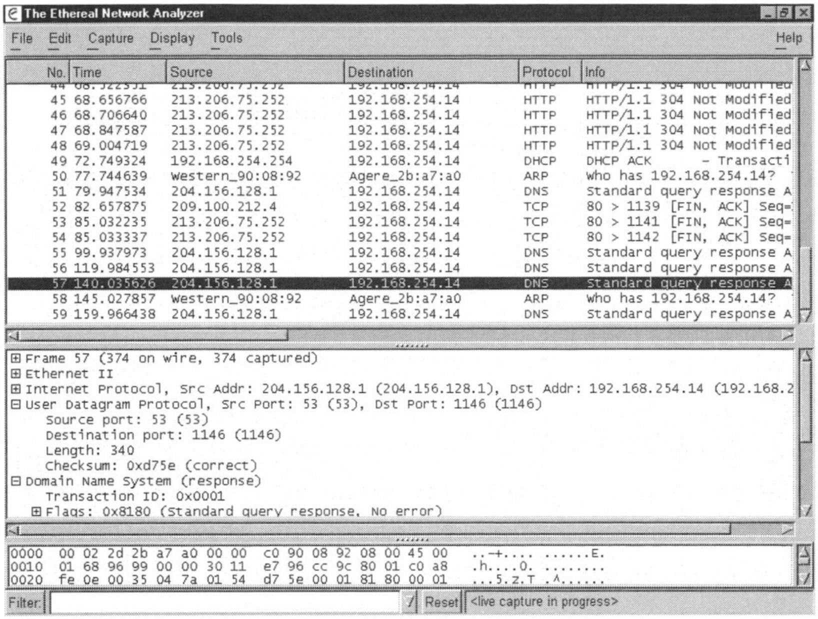

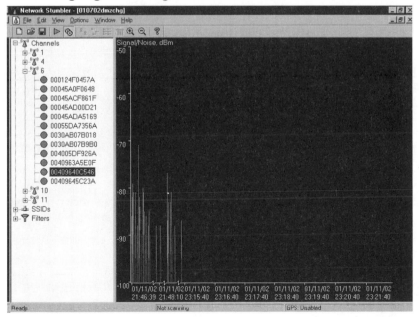

Figure 8.11 Using Signal Strength to Find Wireless Networks

To enhance the ability to triangulate the position of the wireless network, the attacker can utilize directional antennas to focus the wireless interface in a specific direction. An excellent source for wireless information, including information on the design of directional antennas is the Bay Area Wireless Users Group (www.bawug.org).

Protecting Against Sniffing and Eavesdropping

One protection available to wired networks was the upgrade from repeaters and hubs to a switched environment. These switches would send only the traffic intended over each individual port, making it difficult (although not impossible) to sniff the entire network's traffic. This is not an option for wireless due to the nature of wireless itself.

The only way to protect your wireless users from attackers who might be sniffing is to utilize encrypted sessions wherever possible: Use SSL for e-mail connections, SSH instead of Telnet, and Secure Copy (SCP) instead of FTP.

To protect your network from being discovered with NetStumbler, be sure to turn off any network identification broadcasts, and if possible, close down your network to any unauthorized users. This will prevent tools such as NetStumbler from finding your network to begin with. However, the knowledgeable attacker will know that just because you are not broadcasting your information does not mean that your network can't be found.

All the attacker needs to do is utilize one of the network sniffers to monitor for network activity. Although not as efficient as NetStumbler, it is still a functional way to discover and monitor networks. Even encrypted networks will show traffic to the sniffer, even if you are not broadcasting who you are. Once they have identified your traffic, the attacker will then be able to utilize the same identification techniques to begin an attack on your network.

Spoofing and Unauthorized Access

The combination of weaknesses in WEP, and the nature of wireless transmission, has highlighted the art of *spoofing* as a real threat to wireless network security. Some well publicized weaknesses in user authentication using WEP have made authentication spoofing just one of an equally well tested number of exploits by attackers.

Defining Spoofing

One definition of spoofing is where an attacker is able to trick your network equipment into thinking that the connection they are coming from is one of the valid and allowed machines from its network. Attackers can accomplish this several ways, the easiest of which is to simply redefine the MAC address of your wireless or network card to be a valid MAC address. This can be accomplished in Windows through a simple Registry edit. Several wireless providers also have an option to define the MAC address for each wireless connection from within the client manager application that is provided with the interface.

There are several reasons that an attacker would spoof your network. If you have closed out your network to only valid interfaces through MAC or IP address filtering, if an attacker is able to determine a valid MAC or IP address, he could then reprogram his interface with that information, allowing him to connect to your network impersonating a valid machine.

IEEE 802.11 networks introduce a new form of spoofing: authentication spoofing. As described in their paper "Intercepting Mobile Communications: The Insecurities of 802.11," the authors identified a way to utilize weaknesses within WEP and the authentication process to spoof authentication into a closed network. The process of authentication, as defined by IEEE 802.11, is a very simple process. In a shared-key configuration, the AP sends out a 128-byte random string in a cleartext message to the workstation wishing to authenticate. The workstation then encrypts the message with the shared key and returns the encrypted message to the AP. If the message matches what the AP is expecting, the workstation is authenticated onto the network and access is allowed.

As described in the paper, if an attacker has knowledge of both the original plaintext and ciphertext messages, it is possible to create a forged encrypted message. By sniffing the wireless network, an attacker is able to accumulate many authentication requests, each of which includes the original plaintext message and the returned ciphertext-encrypted reply. From this, the attacker can easily identify the keystream used to encrypt the response message. She could then use it to forge an authentication message that the AP will accept as a proper authentication.

Sample Spoofing Tools

The wireless hacker does not need many complex tools to succeed in spoofing a MAC address. In many cases, these changes are either features of the wireless manufacturers or easily changed through a Windows Registry modification. Once a valid MAC is identified, the attacker need only reconfigure his device to trick the AP into thinking they are a valid user.

The ability to forge authentication onto a wireless network is a complex process. There are no known "off the shelf" packages available that will provide these services. An attacker will need to either create their own tool or take the time to decrypt the secret key by using AirSnort or WEPCrack.

If the attacker is using Windows 2000, and his network card supports recon-figuring the MAC address, there is another way to reconfigure this information. If your card supports this feature, you can change it from the Control Panel by clicking the **System** icon. Once the System Properties dialog box appears, select the **Hardware** tab and choose **Device Manager**. Within the Device Manager, under the **Network Adaptors**, you should find your interface. If you open the properties to this interface, you should have an **Advanced** tab. Many network adaptors allow you to reconfigure the MAC address of the card from this area.

Now that the hacker is utilizing a valid MAC address, he is able to access any resource available from your wireless network. If you have WEP enabled, the hacker will have to either identify your secret key, or as you will see shortly, cap-ture the key through malware or stealing the user's notebook.

Protecting Against Spoofing and Unauthorized Attacks

Little can be done to prevent these attacks. The best protection involves several additional pieces to the wireless network. Using an external authentication source, such as RADIUS or SecurID, will prevent an unauthorized user from accessing the wireless network and resources it connects with.

If the attacker has reconfigured her machine to use a valid MAC address, little can be done, except the additional external authentication. The only additional protection that you can provide is if you utilize secure connections for all host services accessed by the network. If you use SSH and SSL, you can require valid client certificates to access those resources. Even if a hacker were able to access the network, this would keep her from accessing your critical systems.

However, note that even with this, and without utilizing either a dynamic firewall or RADIUS WEP authentication, an attacker could be able to get onto your network. Even if you protect your critical systems, the attacker will still have access to all workstations on the network, as well as all networks that are con-nected to the wireless network. She could then compromise those resources and acquire the valid information needed to access your systems.

Network Hijacking and Modification

Numerous techniques are available for an attacker to "hijack" a wireless network or session. And unlike some attacks, network and security administrators may be unable to tell the difference between the hijacker and a legitimate passenger.

Defining Hijacking

Many tools are available to the network hijacker. These tools are based upon basic implementation issues within almost every network device available today. As TCP/IP packets go through switches, routers, and APs, each device looks at the destination IP address and compares it with the IP addresses it knows to be local. If the address is not in the table, the device hands the packet off to its default gateway.

This table is used to coordinate the IP address with what MAC addresses are local to the device. In many situations, this list is a dynamic list that is built up from traffic that is passing through the device and through Address Resolution Protocol (ARP) notifications from new devices joining the network. There is no authentication or verification that the request received by the device is valid. So a malicious user is able to send messages to routing devices and APs stating that their MAC address is associated with a known IP address. From then on, all traffic that goes through that router destined for the hijacked IP address will be handed off to the hacker's machine.

If the attacker spoofs as the default gateway or a specific host on the network, all machines trying to get to the network or the spoofed machine will connect to the attacker's machine instead of where they had intended. If the attacker is clever, he will only use this to identify passwords and other necessary information and route the rest of the traffic to the intended recipient. This way the end user has no idea that this "man-in-the-middle" has intercepted her communications and compromised her passwords and information.

Another clever attack that is possible is through the use of rogue APs. If the attacker is able to put together an AP with enough strength, the end users may not be able to tell which AP is the real one to use. In fact, most will not even know that another is available. Using this, the attacker is able to receive authentication requests and information from the end workstation regarding the secret key and where they are attempting to connect.

These rogue APs can also be used to attempt to break into more tightly configured wireless APs. Utilizing tools such as AirSnort and WEPCrack requires a large amount of data to be able to decrypt the secret key. A hacker sitting in a car in front of your house or office is easily identified, and will generally not have enough time to finish acquiring enough information to break the key. However, if they install a tiny, easily hidden machine, this machine could sit there long enough to break the key and possibly act as an external AP into the wireless network it has hacked.

Sample Hijacking Tools

Attackers who wish to spoof more than their MAC addresses have several tools available. Most of the tools available are for use under a UNIX environment and can be found through a simple search for "ARP Spoof" at http://packetstormse-curity.com. With these tools, the hacker can easily trick all machines on your wireless network into thinking that the hacker's machine is another machine. Through simple sniffing on the network, an attacker can determine which machines are in high use by the workstations on the network. If they then spoof themselves as one of these machines, they could possibly intercept much of the legitimate traffic on the network.

AirSnort and WEPCrack are freely available. And while it would take additional resources to build a rogue AP, these tools will run from any Linux machine.

Hijacking Case Scenario

Now that we have identified the network to be attacked, and spoofed our MAC address to become a valid member of the network, we can gain further information that is not available through simple sniffing. If the network being attacked is using SSH to access their hosts, just stealing a password might be easier than attempting to break into the host using any exploit that might be available.

By just ARP spoofing their connection with the AP to be that of the host they are wishing to steal the passwords from, all wireless users who are attempting to SSH into the host will then connect to the rogue machine. When they attempt to sign on with their password, the attacker is then able to, first, receive their password, and second, pass on the connection to the real end destination. If the attacker does not do the second step, it will increase the likelihood that their attack will be noticed because users will begin to complain that they are unable to connect to the host.

Protection against Network Hijacking and Modification

You can use several different tools to protect your network from IP spoofing with invalid ARP requests. These tools, such as ArpWatch, will notify an administrator when ARP requests are seen, allowing the administrator to take appropriate action to determine if indeed someone is attempting to hack into the network.

Another option is to statically define the MAC/IP address definitions. This will prevent the attacker from being able to redefine this information. However, due to the management overhead in statically defining all network adaptors' MAC address on every router and AP, this solution is rarely implemented. In fact, many APs do not offer any options to define the ARP table, and it would depend upon the switch or firewall you are using to separate your wireless network from your wired network.

There is no way to identify or prevent any attackers from using passive attacks, such as from AirSnort or WEPCrack, to determine the secret key used in an encrypted wireless network. The best protection available is to change the secret key on a regular basis and add additional authentication mechanisms such as RADIUS or dynamic firewalls to restrict access to your wired network once a user has connected to the wireless network. However, if you have not properly secured every wireless workstation, an attacker need only go after one of the other wireless clients to be able to access the resources available to it.

Denial of Service and Flooding Attacks

The nature of wireless transmission, and especially the use of spread spectrum technology, makes a wireless network especially vulnerable to *denial of service* (DoS) attacks. The equipment needed to launch such an attack is freely available and very affordable. In fact, many homes and offices contain equipment necessary to deny service to their wireless network.

Defining DoS and Flooding

A denial of service occurs when an attacker has engaged most of the resources a host or network has available, rendering it unavailable to legitimate users. One of the original DoS attacks is known as a *ping flood*. A ping flood utilizes misconfigured equipment along with bad "features" within TCP/IP to cause a large number of hosts or devices to send an ICMP echo (ping) to a specified target. When the attack occurs it tends to use much of the resources of both the network connection and the host being attacked. This will then make it very difficult for any end users to access the host for normal business purposes.

In a wireless network, several items can cause a similar disruption of service. Probably the easiest is through a confliction within the wireless spectrum by different devices attempting to use the same frequency. Many new wireless telephones use the same frequency as 802.11 networks. Through either intentional or unintentional uses of this, a simple telephone call could prevent all wireless users from accessing the network.

Another possible attack would be through a massive amount of invalid (or valid) authentication requests. If the AP is tied up with thousands of spoofed authentication attempts, any users attempting to authenticate themselves would have major difficulties in acquiring a valid session.

As you saw earlier, the attacker has many tools available to hijack network connections. If a hacker is able to spoof the machines of a wireless network into thinking that the attackers machine is their default gateway, not only will the attacker be able to intercept all traffic destined to the wired network, but they would also be able to prevent any of the wireless network machines from accessing the wired network. To do this the hacker need only spoof the AP and not forward connections on to the end destination, preventing all wireless users from doing valid wireless activities.

Sample DoS Tools

Not much is needed to create a wireless DoS. In fact, many users create these situations with the equipment found within their homes or offices. In a small apartment building, you could find several APs as well as many wireless telephones. These users could easily create many DoS attacks on their own networks as well as on those of their neighbors.

A hacker wishing to DoS a network with a flood of authentication strings will also need to be a well skilled programmer. Not many tools are available to create this type of attack, but as we have seen in the attempts to crack WEP, much of the programming required does not take much effort or time. In fact, a skilled hacker should be able to create such a tool within a few hours. When done, this simple application, when used with standard wireless equipment, could possibly render your wireless network unusable for the duration of the attack.

Creating a hijacked AP DoS will require additional tools that can be found on many security sites. See the earlier section "Sample Hijacking Tools" for a possible starting point to acquiring some of the ARP spoofing tools needed. These tools are not very complex and are available for almost every computing platform available.

DoS and Flooding Case Scenario

Many apartments and older office buildings do not come prewired for the high-tech networks that many people are using today. To add to the problem, if many individuals are setting up their own wireless networks, without coordinating the installs, many problems can occur that will be difficult to detect.

Only so many frequencies are available to 802.11 networks. In fact, once the frequency is chosen, it does not change until someone manually reconfigures it.

With these problems, it is not hard to imagine the following situation from occurring.

A person goes out and purchases a wireless AP and several network cards for his home network. When he gets home to his apartment and configures his network he is extremely happy with how well wireless actually works. Then all of a sudden none of the machines on the wireless network are able to communicate. After waiting on hold for 45 minutes to get though to tech support for the device, the network magically starts working again so he hangs up.

Later that week the same problem occurs, only this time he decides to wait on hold. While waiting he goes onto his porch and begins discussing his frustration with his neighbor. During the conversation his neighbor's kids come out and say that their wireless network is not working.

So they begin to do a few tests (still waiting on hold, of course). First the man's neighbor turns off his AP (which is generally off unless the kids are online, to "protect" their network). Once this is done the wireless network starts working again. Then they turn on the neighbor's AP again and the network stops working again.

At this point, tech support finally answers and he describes what has happened. The tech-support representative has seen this situation several times and informs the user that he will need to change the frequency used in the device to another channel. He explains that what has happened is that the neighbor's network is utilizing the same channel, causing the two networks to conflict. Once he changes the frequency, everything starts working properly.

Protecting Against DoS and Flooding Attacks

There is little that you can do to protect against DoS attacks. In a wireless environment the attacker does not need to even be in the same building or neighborhood. With a good enough antenna, the attacker is able to send these attacks from a great distance away. There is no indication that there is any reason for the disruption.

This is one of the valid times to use NetStumbler in a nonhacking context. By using NetStumbler, you can identify any other networks that might be conflicting with your network configuration. However, NetStumbler will not identify other DoS attacks or other equipment that is causing conflicts (such as wireless telephones).

Summary

Only through a solid understanding of security fundamentals, principles, and procedures will you be able to fully identify today's security risks. From this understanding, which is built upon "The Big Three" tenets of security (confidentiality, integrity, and availability, or CIA) come the basis for all other security practices. The essential practices usually associated with security build upon the concepts of "The Big Three," which provide tools for actually implementing security into systems. The ability to properly authenticate a user or process, before allowing that user or process access to specific resources, protect the CIA directly. If you are able to clearly identify the authenticated user through electronic non-repudiation techniques usually found in encryption tools such as public-key encryption, you can ensure that the entities attempting to gain access are who they say they are. Finally, if you log the activities performed, a third party can monitor the logs and ensure that all activity happening on a system complies with the policy and standards defined, and that all inappropriate activity is identified, allowing for possible prosecution or investigation into the invalid activity.

Following these practices, through the use of tested and proven identification and evaluation standards, you can fully understand the security risks associated with any object. Once you know the risks, you can provide solutions to diminish these risks as much as possible.

The standard solution is to create a formal security policy along with detailed guidelines and procedures. These guidelines describe the actual implementation steps necessary for any platform to comply with the established security procedure.

By using these standard methods to protect your wireless network, you should be able to develop a clear and concise wireless security plan that incorporates the needs of your organization's highest levels. This plan will allow for the deployment of a wireless network that's as secure as possible and will provide clear exception listings for areas where the risks to your infrastructure cannot be fully controlled.

Through a careful examination of the design of WEP, we identified significant weaknesses in the algorithm. These weaknesses, along with implementation flaws, have lead to the creation of many new tools that can be used to attack wireless networks. These tools allow for the attacker to identify a wireless network through *war driving* and then crack the secret key by passively listening to the encrypted transmissions. Once they have access to the secret key, only those that have deployed additional security measures will have some additional protection for the rest of their infrastructure.

Even if you have a incident response plan and procedure defined in your security standards, if an attack is not known to be happening, there is little you can do to mitigate or rectify the intrusion. The entire discovery and WEP-cracking process is passive and undetectable. Only at the point of attacking other wireless hosts or spoofing their attacking machine as a valid host does the attack becomes noticeable. However, many installations do not implement system logging, nor do they have standards and practices requiring monitoring of those logs for inappropriate activity.

None of these actions will provide protection against one of the oldest attacks known—theft. There is little you can do to protect your resources if critical information, such as network passwords and access definitions, can be acquired by only gaining access to notebooks or backups. High-tech criminals are creating custom malware that can access this information through spam or disguised Web sites.

Although wireless networks are making computing easier and more accessible, understanding the design and implementation weaknesses in 802.11 will help you in preventing attacks. And at times when attacks are unavoidable, by knowing how and where the attackers will come, you may be able to identify when they are attempting to gain access and respond as defined in your standards and incident response practices.

Solutions Fast Track

Understanding Security Fundamentals and Principles of Protection

- ☑ "The Big Three" tenets of security are: *confidentiality*, *integrity*, and *availability*.

- ☑ Requirements needed to implement the principles of protection include proper authentication of authorized users through a system that provides for a clear identification of the users via tested non-repudiation techniques.

- ☑ Internal or external auditors can use logging or system accounting to ensure that the system is functioning and being utilized in accordance to defined standards and policies.

☑ Logging can also be the first place to look for evidence should an attack does occur. Ensure that logging is going to a trusted third-party site that cannot be accessed by personnel and resources being logged.

☑ These tools are essential to protecting the privacy of customer, partner, or trade secret information.

☑ Encryption has provided many tools for the implementation of these security fundamentals.

☑ Encryption is not the definitive solution to security problems. For example, a known secret key could be stolen, or one of the parties utilizing encryption could be tricked or forced into performing the activity, which would be seen as a valid cryptographic operation because the system has no knowledge of any collusion involved in the generation of the request.

MAC Filtering

☑ Media Access Control (MAC) filtering is effective against casual attackers.

☑ MAC filtering can be circumvented by changing the MAC address on the client device.

☑ It is difficult to determine if the lack of association is due to MAC filtering or other reasons like an incorrect Wired Equivalent Protocol (WEP) key.

Reviewing the Role of Policy

☑ Once basic fundamentals and principles are understood, through the creation of policies and standards an organization or entity is able to clearly define how to design, implement, and monitor their infrastructure securely.

☑ Policies must have direct support and sign-in by the executive management of any organization.

☑ A properly mitigated risk should reduce the impact of the threat as well as the likelihood that that threat will occur.

☑ A clear and well-defined classification and labeling system is key to the identification of resources being protected.

☑ Information classification techniques also provide a method by which the items being classified can then have the proper policy or standards placed around them depending on the level or importance, as well as the risk associated with each identified item.

☑ Some organizations are required by their own regulations to have clear and well defined standards and policies.

Implementing WEP

☑ To protect against some rudimentary attacks that insert known text into the stream to attempt to reveal the key stream, WEP incorporates a check sum in each frame. Any frame not found to be valid through the check sum is discarded.

☑ Used on its own, WEP does not provide adequate wireless local area network (WLAN) security.

☑ WEP has to be implemented on every client as well as every Access Point (AP) to be effective.

☑ WEP keys are user definable and unlimited. You do not have to use predefined keys, and you can and should change them often.

☑ Implement the strongest version of WEP available and keep abreast of the latest upgrades to the standards.

Addressing Common Risks and Threats

☑ By examining the common threats to both wired and wireless networks, you can see how a solid understanding in the basics of security principles allows you to fully assess the risks associated with using wireless and other technologies.

☑ Threats can come from simple design issues, where multiple devices utilize the same setup, or intentional denial of service attacks which can result in the corruption or loss of data.

☑ Not all threats are caused by malicious users. They can also be caused by a conflict of similar resources, such as with 802.11b networks and cordless telephones.

☑ With wireless networks going beyond the border of your office or home, chances are greater that your actions might be monitored by a third party.

☑ Unless your organization has clear and well-defined policies and guidelines, you might find yourself in legal or business situations where your data is either compromised, lost, or disrupted. Without a clear plan of action that identifies what is important in certain scenarios, you will not be able to address situations as they occur.

Sniffing, Interception, and Eavesdropping

☑ Electronic eavesdropping, or *sniffing*, is passive and undetectable to intrusion detection devices.

☑ Tools to sniff networks are available for Windows (such as Ethereal and AiroPeek) and UNIX (such as tcpdump and ngrep).

☑ Sniffing traffic allows attackers to identify additional resources that can be compromised.

☑ Even encrypted networks have been shown to disclose vital information in cleartext, such as the network name, that can be received by attackers sniffing the WLAN.

☑ Any authentication information that is broadcast can often be simply replayed to services requiring authentication (NT Domain, WEP authentication, and so on) to access resources.

☑ The use of virtual private networks, Secure Sockets Layer (SSL), and Secure Shell (SSH) helps protect against wireless interception.

Spoofing and Unauthorized Access

☑ Due to the design of Transmission Control Protocol/Internet Protocol (TCP/IP), there is little that you can do to prevent MAC/IP address spoofing.

☑ Only through static definition of MAC address tables can you prevent this type of attack. However, due to significant overhead in management, this is rarely implemented.

☑ Wireless network authentication can be easily spoofed by simply replaying another node's authentication back to the AP when attempting to connect to the network.

☑ Many wireless equipment providers allow for end-users to redefine the MAC address within their cards through the configuration utilities that come with the equipment.

☑ External two-factor authentication such as Remote Access Dial-In User Service (RADIUS) or SecurID should be implemented to additionally restrict access requiring strong authentication to access the wireless resources.

Network Hijacking and Modification

☑ Due to the design of TCP/IP, some spoof attacks allow for attackers to hijack or take over network connections established for other resources on the wireless network.

☑ If an attacker hijacks the AP, all traffic from the wireless network gets routed through the attacker, so they are then able to identify passwords and other information other users are attempting to use on valid network hosts.

☑ Many users are easily susceptible to these man-in-the-middle attacks, often entering their authentication information even after receiving many notifications that SSL or other keys are not what they should be.

☑ Rogue APs can assist the attacker by allowing remote access from wired or wireless networks.

☑ These attacks are often overlooked as just faults in the user's machine, allowing attackers to continue hijacking connections with little fear of being noticed.

Denial of Service and Flooding Attacks

☑ Many wireless networks within a small space can easily cause network disruptions and even denial of service (DoS) for valid network users.

☑ If an attacker hijacks the AP and does not pass traffic on to the proper destination, all users of the network will be unable to use the network.

☑ Flooding the wireless network with transmissions can also prevent other devices from utilizing the resources, making the wireless network inaccessible to valid network users.

☑ Wireless attackers can utilize strong and directional antennas to attack the wireless network from a great distance.

☑ An attacker who has access to the wired network can flood the wireless AP with more traffic than it can handle, preventing wireless users from accessing the wired network.

☑ Many new wireless products utilize the same wireless frequencies as 802.11 networks. A simple cordless telephone could create a DoS situation for the network more easily than any of these other techniques.

Frequently Asked Questions

The following Frequently Asked Questions, answered by the authors of this book, are designed to both measure your understanding of the concepts presented in this chapter and to assist you with real-life implementation of these concepts. To have your questions about this chapter answered by the author, browse to **www.syngress.com/solutions** and click on the **"Ask the Author"** form.

Q: Do I really need to understand the fundamentals of security in order to protect my network?

A: While you are able to utilize the configuration options available to you from your equipment provider, without a solid background in how security is accomplished you will never be able to protect your assets from the unknown threats that will come against your network through either misconfiguration, backdoors provided by the vendor, or new exploits that have not been patched by your vendor.

Q: Am I required by law to have a security policy?

A: If your organization is a video store, deals with children's records, or is associated with the health care or financial industries (and you are located in the United States), you are most likely required by federal regulation to have a defined security policy, and in some cases you are required to have complete third-party audits of your configuration and policies. If you are not required by legislation, you might still find yourself liable under civil law to provide proper protection for customer or partner information contained within your system.

Q: Is 128-bit WEP more secure than 64-bit WEP?

A: Not really. This is because the WEP vulnerability has more to do with the 24-bit initialization vector than the actual size of the WEP key.

Q: If I am a home user, can I assume that if I use MAC filtering and WEP, that my network is secure?

A: You can make the assumption that your home network is more secure than if it did not utilize these safeguards. However, as shown in this chapter, these methods can be circumvented to allow for intrusion.

Q: Where can I find more information on WEP vulnerabilities?

A: Besides being one of the sources who brought WEP vulnerabilities to light, www.isaac.cs.berkeley.edu has links to other Web sites that cover WEP insecurities.

Q: Can my customers really sue me or my company for being hacked and having their information leaked or misused?

A: In any situation, if you have an established trust with a customer to maintain their information securely and someone breaks into the building or into their corporate servers, a a customer can possibly pursue litigation against you if you did not have any policies or procedures in place to address the risk associated with this and other threats to the customer's information.

Q: If someone can be forced into performing an activity, why should I bother setting up complex security applications?

A: Without those applications in place, you would find that it does not take direct force to attack you or your information. There has always been the possibility that threats could force individuals in key positions to reveal damaging information and secrets, but there is a greater chance that someone will trick a user into disclosing their password or some other security key. Proper training and education are the best defenses in these situations.

Q: I added a firewall to my design. Why should I also need both a policy and external auditing?

A: Again, a firewall may protect you initially, but what do you do as technology changes, or your staff is replaced? Policies and standards ensure that current and future implementations are built in accordance to the definitions laid out by the organization. Adding logging, as well as internal and third-party auditing of the implemented resources helps ensure that the implementations are built in accordance to policy, and that all activity occurring within the environment is in compliance with your standards, guidelines, and policies.

Q: If I have enabled WEP, am I now protected?

A: No. Certain tools can break all WEP keys by simply monitoring the network traffic for generally less than 24 hours.

Q: Is there any solution available besides RADIUS to perform external user and key management?

A: No, plans are available from manufacturers to identify other ways of performing the user/key management, but to date nothing is available.

Chapter 9

Cisco Aironet Accessories

Solutions in this chapter:

- Antenna Accessories

- Bridge and Access Point Accessories

- Cabling, Connectors, and Bulkhead Extenders

- Radio Country Options

☑ Summary

☑ Solutions Fast Track

☑ Frequently Asked Questions

Introduction

You have now designed your wireless installation, found the perfect spot for your bridge, evaluated antenna solutions, and are ready to do begin the installation. But wait, what are you going to use to attach the antenna to the roof? How are you going to connect the antenna to the bridge? Do you have the right connectors? Is there an appropriate power source nearby? Are you going to just set the bridge on the ground or mount it on a wall? What are you going to do about lightning protection?

All of these questions and more are addressed in this chapter. Specifically, we also examine the mounting options for Yagi and dipole style antenna. We also look at the functioning of the Cisco lightning arrestor with grounding ring and how to properly incorporate this piece of safety equipment into your wireless solution.

At this point, we shift the focus from the antenna accessories and look at some of the available options for the access points (APs) and bridges themselves. Though the APs and bridges have been covered in detail in previous chapters, this chapter looks specifically at the appropriate locations to mount these devices. We also look at the options available for mounting both out of the box as well as add-on mounting kits. In addition to the mounting options, we also examine the spare power supplies that are available, including the inline power injector that is now available for the 350 series bridges and APs. We then continue this section of the chapter with a discussion of the use of the console port on the back of the AP or bridge. Finally, we wrap up this section with a look at the various types of National Electrical Manufacturers Association (NEMA) enclosures and how they are used.

From the discussion on the accessories, we move on to look at the cabling that you can use for connecting the APs or bridges to the antenna. We look at the different types of cabling that is available and the merits of each. In addition to the cabling, we also spend some time looking at the connectors that go on this cabling. In this examination, we pay added attention to the Reverse Polarity Threaded-Neill-Concelman (RP-TNC) connector, which is the most common connector type used by Cisco on its wireless equipment. We conclude this section of the chapter by looking at the use of bulkhead extenders.

The final section of this chapter looks at the Radio Country options that are available for Cisco wireless solutions. With the global economy becoming more vital to the success of any company, Cisco needs to sell its products in numerous different countries around the world. Because each country has specific regulations as to the strength of signal that a wireless solution can use, as well as the range in which it can operate, Cisco developed the Radio Country options to differentiate the equipment and country in which it can be used. In addition to the local restrictions, export restrictions are also placed on devices that have greater than 128-bit encryption. Because many of the wireless components sold by Cisco fall into this category, Cisco must be careful to obtain export rights before shipping equipment to a particular country.

Antenna Accessories

As was mentioned in the previous chapters, one of the items that can greatly increase the range and usability of a wireless system is an appropriate antenna. Now that you have chosen an antenna for your given application, we need to look at the accessories that are available for it. Specifically, we examine two types of accessories in this section: lightning suppression and mounting kits. The specific mounting kits that we look at are the Yagi articulating mount and the magnetic mount.

Yagi Articulating Mount

As the name implies, this mounting kit is for the Yagi antenna. As was covered earlier, the Yagi antenna is a directional antenna and as such needs to be properly aligned in order to function optimally. The Yagi articulating mount (shown in Figure 9.1) allows for mounting of a Yagi antenna on either a flat surface or a mast. This mount then allows for both horizontal and vertical adjustment of the antenna to assist in the alignment process. Proper use of this mount will also allow the Yagi antenna to retain its wind rating of 110 miles per hour.

Figure 9.1 Yagi Articulating Mount

Magnetic Mount

The magnetic mount adapter (see Figure 9.2) is a replacement mount for the dipole antenna mount, which Cisco stopped selling in October of 2001. The magnetic mount not only has a connection for the dipole antenna, it also has a coaxial RG-58 pigtail that is approximately a foot long to allow for an easy connection to in-house wiring. (See the "RG-58 and RG-8 Cabling" section later in this chapter for more details on RG-58 cabling.) The mount that the antenna attaches to is the jack end of an RP-TNC connector; the end of the pigtail is a plug end of an RP-TNC connector. (See the "Connectors" section later in this chapter for more details on RP-TNC connectors.) The base of the mount is cylindrical and approximately 5.25 inches in diameter and approximately 2 inches high without an antenna attached. The base houses a magnet that will firmly attach the mount with antenna to a flat metallic surface. The magnet is strong enough to hold the antenna on a wall or even upside-down. The base has a thin rubber coating to protect the surface on which the mount is installed.

Figure 9.2 Magnetic Mount

Lightning Arrestor with Grounding Ring

When you are planning any wireless systems, you should always consider lightning protection. The protection plan you choose should not only cover the exterior equipment but also the interior equipment. When you are developing this plan, as with any business decision, cost is one of the driving factors. The costs involved include not only the equipment or protection itself but also the cost of downtime that could result from not putting in the protection.

When installing exterior antennas, some simple steps, such as installing them in areas that are less likely to be directly hit by lightning or the addition of lighting rods, can go a long way to protect the antenna. Though prior planning will reduce the possibility of a strike, additional protection such as the Cisco lightning arrestor with grounding ring (see Figure 9.3) will assist in the protection of interior equipment should a strike occur.

The lightning arrestor is an inline device that connects to the coaxial cable running between the antenna and the Cisco wireless device. It has a 50-ohm transmission line and is equipped with a gas discharge tube that will create a connection to ground in the presence of an electrical surge. Should such a surge occur, this transition takes place in approximately 100 nanoseconds. The lightning arrestor will provide protection for transient spikes of up to 5,000 amperes, insuring that the surge to the equipment connected to the line is limited to a maximum of 50 volts.

NOTE

The intention of the lightning arrestor is to protect equipment from nearby lightning strikes. It does not provide protection from direct lightning strikes.

Installation of the lightning arrestor is relatively straightforward. As with most inline devices, disconnect or power off any powered components connected to the coaxial cable before beginning the installation. As far as where to install the lightning arrestor, you should install it indoors, as close to the bulkhead as is convenient. You can also install the arrestor in a protected area outside, such as a cable enclosure, if no indoor locations are appropriate. In addition to the connections going to the antenna and the Cisco wireless device, you need to connect the lightning arrestor to an earth ground (usually an 8-foot copper or steel rod, placed 6 or 7 feet into the ground). You should make this connection with the ground lug attached to the lightning arrestor and with at least a #6 copper wire. Once these connections are complete, ensure the connections are sound, power on or connect the equipment, and it is ready for use.

Figure 9.3 Lightning Arrestor with Grounding Ring

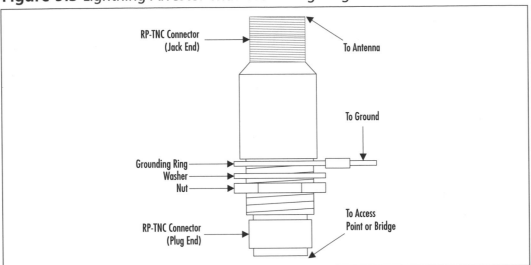

Bridge and Access Point Accessories

We look at three major types of bridge and AP accessories in this section: mounting kits, power supplies, and the serial configuration cable. Whether you are installing the AP on a plywood backboard, on drywall, or on a pole, the mounting kits allow for the installation of the AP or bridge in numerous different ways. When installing the AP or bridge be sure to choose a location that is free from large metal structures (such as filing cabinets or shelving), microwave ovens, and 2 GHz cordless phones, because these items could interfere with the performance of the AP or bridge. The spare power supplies described here are an inexpensive spare that are easy to replace—keeping one on-hand can help you minimize the downtime of your wireless system. The final accessory, the AP or bridge serial cable, allows for the configuration of the AP even when the network to it is unavailable.

Bridge Mounting Kit

You can mount an AP or bridge several different ways. The easiest method is to simply put a couple of screws into either a plywood backboard or drywall and attaching the AP or bridge to them. Depending on the type of AP or bridge you have, you will need either two or four screws and wall anchors to properly use this approach.

If you have an AP with a plastic case, you need only two #6 metal screws and two #6–#8 wall anchors. The first step is to download the mounting template, which you can retrieve from Cisco's Web site at: www.cisco.com/univercd/cc/td/doc/product/wireless/airo_350/350wgb/wgbrdgmi.htm.

Print the template and use it to determine placement of the holes for drilling. After you print it, ensure that the template holes are indeed 4.75 inches apart. Once you verify this, you can place the template in the location you wish to mount the AP and mark the holes for drilling. If for whatever reason you cannot retrieve the template, you can approximate the location you wish to mount the AP or bridge and install the wall anchors and screws 4.75 inches apart, in a horizontal or vertical configuration depending on your particular installation. Once you mark the drilling location, use a 3/16-inch bit to drill a 1-inch deep hole for each wall anchor. Then install the wall anchors and screws, making sure to leave a small gap between the wall anchor and screw head. You can then position the mounting holes on the back of the AP or bridge over the screws and slide it into place.

The design of the metal case APs and bridges use low smoke producing characteristics and have enhanced fire resistance. Though you still need to install these APs and bridges indoors, the plenum-rated case gives you the ability to place the AP or bridge in suspended ceilings and in other environmental air space. The metal case also extends the operating temperature range of the AP or bridge from the normal 32 to 122 degrees Fahrenheit (0 to 50 degrees Celsius) to −4 to 131 degrees Fahrenheit (−20 to 55 degrees Celsius). Mounting the metal case AP or bridges requires four #6 metal screws, and four #6–#8 wall anchors. As was true with the plastic case AP or bridge, the first thing that you need for mounting of the metal case AP or bridge is a template for drilling. You can retrieve the template for the metal case installation at Cisco's Web site at www.cisco.com/univercd/cc/td/doc/product/wireless/airo_350/accsspts/apmi/apbrmnt.htm.

Once you retrieve and print it, you must verify that the centerlines on the template are indeed 5.5 and 3.5 inches apart. If you cannot download the template, or if it is not printing to scale, you can place the AP in the location you wish to install use it to mark the locations to drill. Or you can draw a rectangle 5.5 inches long by 3.5 inches wide at the mounting location and drill at the corners of the rectangle. Once you drill the holes, insert all of the wall anchors and the three screws that correspond to the mounting holes in the AP or bridge leaving a small gap between the head of the screw and the anchor. Finally, slide the AP or bridge over the screws then install the fourth screw in the hole provided.

If you have a more complex mounting issue than a flat surface, another alternative is to obtain a Cisco 340 Series Bridge Mounting Kit (see Figure 9.4). This kit contains a metal back plate that is approximately 7.25 inches by 4.75 inches and has predrilled screw holes that will allow for the attachment of the 340 to the plate. You can then fasten this plate to a flat surface, or you can use some of the other fasteners that come with the kit. Specifically, you can attach a set of beam clamps to the metal back plate allowing you to attach the bridge to an I-beam or similar surface. Alternately, you can use the antenna clamp kit to attach the back plate to a pole or mast that is up to 1.5 inches in diameter.

Figure 9.4 340 Series Mounting Kit

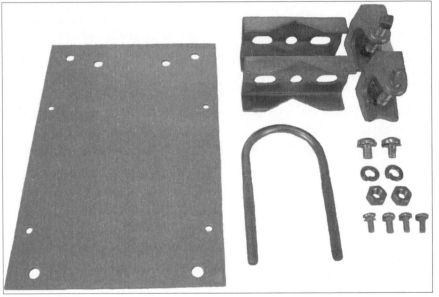

Bridge Slide Mount Kit

The bridge slide mount kit (see Figure 9.5) is another method that you can use to attach the bridge to a flat surface. This kit consists of a metal mounting plate that has predrilled holes and notches cut in it, and a plastic mounting plate that has tabs specifically designed to fit in the metal plate. In addition, the kit comes with four 8-32-inch by 5/16-inch mounting screws. You can use these screws to attach the plastic plate to the back of the bridge. Following this, you fasten the metal plate to any flat surface in the area in which you wish to mount the AP or bridge. With the bridge attached to the plastic plate, you can slide the tabs of the plastic plate into the slots in the metal plate, and then lock it into place. Once complete, you have securely mounted the bridge to the metal plate. In fact, the first couple of times you install or remove the bridge, you may find it difficult to lock or unlock the tabs in place.

Figure 9.5 Slide Mounting Kit

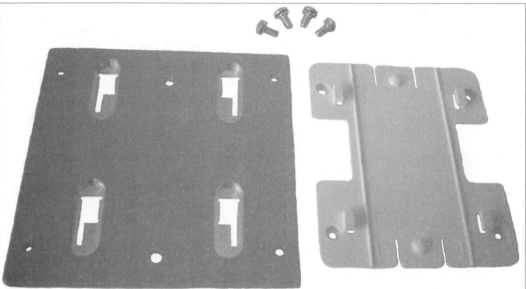

Configuring & Implementing…

Equipment Placement

When installing the Cisco AP, bridge, or any device for that matter, placement of the device can greatly affect long term stability and consistent service. In larger installations, with raised floor space specifically set aside for networking and other technology equipment, this is not much of an issue. However, in smaller installations where you put the networking equipment in a back closet that was chosen only because it had a power source, some forethought can be invaluable.

In these smaller installations, one of the most important items in choosing an installation location, is to try to keep the equipment out of heavily traveled areas as well as away from doorways. In both of these cases, there is a higher probability that the equipment will be bumped or knocked off its mounting platform. The potential issue in a high traffic area is relatively easy to see, the more people that are walking by

Continued

a location, the greater the probability that someone will accidentally come in contact with the device. The reason to be careful when installing by a doorway is twofold. First, as the door is opened and closed, the wall to which the door is attached will vibrate slightly. If the equipment is mounted to this wall, over time this vibration could affect its performance. The second reason to be careful when installing around a doorway, is similar to the issue with the high traffic area. As people come through a door, they can not necessarily see what is on the other side, and if they are in a hurry and trying to avoid an obstacle, they could run into the device or the mounting platform. Or, if they are struggling to open the door while carrying something, an accident could happen.

Another issue with placement comes into play when networking items are installed on a shelf. In many smaller offices, space is usually at a premium. As a result, if there is room above, below, or around the network equipment it will eventually be used by the office staff for storage. Such activity could not only have an immediate impact on the system by disrupting power or a cable, it could have a delayed impact due to the vents of the equipment being covered causing the device to overheat. To alleviate this potential issue, either put the networking equipment in a small enclosure, or if that is not an option, try to find a shelf that is out of the way and closely matches the dimensions of the equipment being installed.

Finally, in many smaller offices, especially those in strip malls or small, freestanding buildings, power fluctuations can be a problem. These can range from blackouts to power sags and power spikes. For electrical equipment such as lights and fans, this fluctuation does not affect them in the long term. However, these fluctuations can affect delicate networking equipment that is expecting clean uninterrupted power. Therefore, if you are in a situation such as this, a small uninterruptible power supply (UPS) may be of benefit to you. Simply plug the UPS into the building power and plug your networking equipment into the UPS. The goal of this setup is not only to keep the network equipment functioning in the event of a short outage, but also to condition the power being supplied to the networking equipment. Though the UPS may not fully condition the power, it will flatten out the peaks and valleys. In addition, many UPS units now come with management software and Simple Network Management Protocol (SNMP) capabilities. This then gives you a simple tool to determine the overall power stability in a new location or one that is having problems and can help you in making a decision as to whether or not the expense is necessary. For example, when a new location is installed, put in the UPS unit and

Continued

> software and monitor it for three to six months. If the power is solid, and you see few or no sags or spikes, take the UPS out and move it to another location where this fluctuation is occurring. Contact your local power company to resolve any problems and keep the UPS in place until they are resolved.

As you can see, the value to using this solution comes in the ease of upgrades, component replacement, or normal maintenance. Because you are able to remove the bridge from the mount without any tools, you can easily take it down to work on it. In addition, because the plastic plate attaches directly to the bridge, in the event of a bridge replacement, you can easily attach this plate at your desk or workbench then snap the entire component back into place when the replacement is complete.

Access Point / Bridge Spare Power Supplies

One of the easiest and most inexpensive spare components to keep in your inventory is a spare power supply for your AP or bridge. Having such a spare can mean the difference between a minor short term outage and having a long-term outage that has a major impact on your business. You have several options for spare power supplies. You can obtain power supplies that fit either 110 or 220 current depending on your need.

WARNING

Though newer power injectors have protection against supplying power to a standard Ethernet port, older power injectors did not. Therefore, do not plug a power injector into a standard Ethernet port because it could damage the power injector as well as the network equipment.

The 350 series bridge and AP have another option: an inline power injector (see Figure 9.6). The power injector is connected to both the to the AP or bridge via a standard Category 5 UTP cable. In addition, another Category 5 UTP cable is connected to the other side of the injector and runs to your hub or switch. The Ethernet connection between the AP or bridge and your hub or switch is made via this path. In addition to carrying the Ethernet signal to and from the AP or bridge, the UTP cable connecting the AP or bridge to the injector also carries the power needed to run the AP or bridge. The power injector supplies this power by utilizing the unused pairs in the Cat5 cable. Specifically, the negative current is sent on the cables on pins 4 and 5, and the positive is sent on the cables on pins 7 and 8. By using the power injector, you are able to put the AP or bridge in an area that is not near a power source.

Figure 9.6 In-Line Power Injector

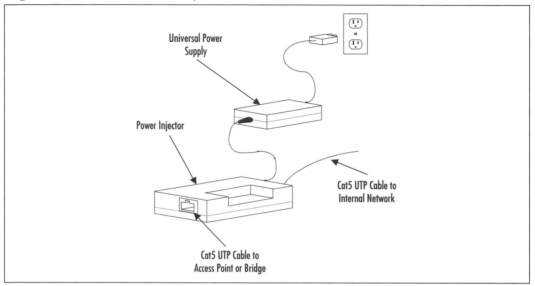

In addition to the power injector, the 350 series products can also obtain their power from inline power capable Catalyst 3524-PWR-XL switch or by using an inline power patch panel. As was the case with the power injector, these solutions also send the power via the Cat5 UTP cable.

Access Point / Bridge Serial Cable

You can establish remote configuration of your AP or bridge by using, Telnet, Hypertext Transfer Protocol (HTTP), File Transfer Protocol (FTP), Trivial File Transfer Protocol (TFTP), or SNMP, depending on the device being accessed. You can use the serial cable (see Figure 9.7) that comes with the AP or bridge, or sold separately, for local access to the device. This cable is a straightthrough cable that has a male DB-9 connector on one end and a female DB-9 connector on the other.

Connect the male end of the cable to the AP or bridge and the female end to the COM1 or COM2 port on your PC. Then using a dumb terminal emulator

(DTE), such as HyperTerminal, set the port settings for the appropriate COM port to: 9600 bits per second, 8 data bits, no parity, 1 stop bit, and set flow control to Xon/Xoff. Once you set these and make a connection, you will be able to access and manage the AP or bridge. For reference, Table 9.1 shows the standard pinout and function of a PC serial port. Note that the pinouts and signal direction referenced in the table is from the PC's or DTE's perspective.

Table 9.1 DB-9 Pinouts and Signal Description from PC's (DTE) Perspective

Pin Number	Use	Description	Signal Direction
1	DCD	Carrier detect	AP/bridge to PC
2	RXD	Receive data	AP/bridge to PC
3	TXD	Transmit data	PC to AP/bridge
4	DTR	Data terminal ready	PC to AP/bridge
5	GND	Ground	NA
6	DSR	Data set ready	AP/bridge to PC
7	RTS	Request to send	PC to AP/bridge
8	CTS	Clear to send	AP/bridge to PC
9	RI	Ring indicator	AP/bridge to PC

Figure 9.7 Serial Configuration Cable

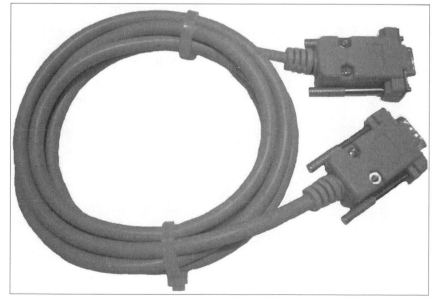

NEMA Enclosures

In areas where your bridge or AP is exposed to wide ranges of temperatures or is likely to be exposed to weather such as rain, snow, and so on, you may need to house the devices within a *NEMA enclosure*. In general, NEMA enclosures are typically watertight boxes used to mount equipment outside to protect it from the elements. NEMA enclosures are available that are heated and/or cooled.

Specifically, a NEMA enclosure is any enclosure that confirms to the National Electrical Manufacturers Association guidelines. Though NEMA defines specifications for numerous types of electrical equipment, specification 250–1997 describes the applications and feature available specifically for enclosures (with a power rating under 1,000 volts). You can get an overview of these guidelines free of charge from the NEMA Web site at www.nema.org. In addition to the overview, you can purchase the entire specification, as well as manufacturing specifications at this site. This document divides enclosures into different types according to the type of protection they are designed to provide. Table 9.2 gives a summary of these types.

Table 9.2 NEMA Enclosure Classifications

Enclosure Type	Location	Indoor/ Outdoor	General Use/ Comments
1	Non-hazardous	Indoor	Provides a degree of protection against contact with enclosed equipment.
2	Non-hazardous	Indoor	Provides some protection from small amounts of falling water and dirt.
3	Non-hazardous	Outdoor	Provides protection against wind-blown dust, rain, sleet, and external ice formation.
3R	Non-hazardous	Outdoor	Provides protection against falling rain, sleet, and external ice formation.
3S	Non-hazardous	Outdoor	Provides protection against wind-blown dust, rain, sleet, and operation of the external components of the enclosure when ice-laden.

Continued

Table 9.2 Continued

Enclosure Type	Location	Indoor/ Outdoor	General Use/ Comments
4	Non-hazardous	Either	Provides protection against wind-blown dust, and rain, and splashing or hose directed water.
4X	Non-hazardous	Either	Provides protection against wind-blown dust, rain, and splashing or hose-directed water; corro-sion-resistant.
5	Non-hazardous	Indoor	Provides protection from settling dust, falling dirt, and dripping (noncorrosive) liquids.
6	Non-hazardous	Either	Provides protection against the entry of water during temporary submersion in water at a limited depth.
6P	Non-hazardous	Either	Provides protection against the entry of water during prolonged submersion in water at a limited depth.
7	Hazardous	Indoor	For use in locations classified as a Class I (Groups A, B, C, D) as defined in the National Electrical Code. Will contain internal explo-sion without causing an external hazard.
8	Hazardous	Either	For use in locations classified as a Class I (Groups A, B, C, D) as defined in the National Electrical Code. Will prevent combustion through the use of oil-immersed equipment.
9	Hazardous	Indoor	For use in locations classified as a Class II (Groups E, F, G) as defined in the National Electrical Code. Will prevent the ignition of combustible dust.

Continued

www.syngress.com

Table 9.2 Continued

Enclosure Type	Location	Indoor/ Outdoor	General Use/ Comments
10	Hazardous	Either	Meet applicable requirements of the Mine Safety and Health Administration. Will contain internal explosion without causing an external hazard.
11	Non-hazardous	Indoor	Provides protection, by oil immersion, from the corrosive effects of liquids and gases
12	Non-hazardous	Indoor	Provides some protection from settling dust, falling dirt, and dripping (noncorrosive) liquids.
12K	Non-hazardous	Indoor	Provides protection from settling dust, falling dirt, and dripping (noncorrosive) liquids. 12K enclosures contain knockouts. This protection does not apply to the knockout area.)
13	Non-hazardous	Indoor	Provides protection from dust, and spraying water, oil, and noncorrosive coolant.

Because Cisco does not offer NEMA enclosures, if required for an installation, you will need to obtain a NEMA enclosure from another source. In general, you can obtain these enclosures through your cabling or electrical supply vendor. By going through them first, they may be aware of enclosures that meet your specifications and that are specifically designed for the cabling or equipment you are using. If you are unable to obtain the type of enclosure you are looking for through these sources, you can check national electrical or telecommunications supply companies, such as Anixter (www.anixter.com). In addition, if you know the specifics on the enclosure that you wish to purchase, try searching the Internet search to find a retailer that has exactly what you are looking for.

Cabling, Connectors, and Bulkhead Extenders

When you are installing a wireless system, especially one with an external antenna, a number of things within and outside your control can affect the systems performance. Once you take the items outside your control (for example, weather, line of site, and so on) into account, the design of a wireless system shifts to items within your control. We have already looked at antenna choices; therefore, the next item to examine is how the signal gets to and from the antenna. This communications occurs over cabling and through connectors and bulkheads. Each of which we examine in the course of this section.

Cabling

It may seem strange that wiring can have an impact on a wireless system, but choosing the wrong cabling could mean the difference between the success or failure of your wireless system. Specifically, the cabling being referred to is the cabling between the AP and the antenna. This cabling carries both the signals from the AP or bridge to the antenna and from the antenna to the AP or bridge.

The cabling that is used in most installations for this purpose is coaxial, or coax, cable (see Figure 9.8). Coaxial cable comes in many different varieties and sizes, but all of these different types share a common construction. In the center of a coaxial cable is a single conductor. This conductor may be solid, stranded, or in some rare instance, a tube, and is usually made of copper. Surrounding this conductor is a dielectric material that acts as an insulator. One common dielectric that is used for this purpose is solid or foam-based polyethylene. On top of this dielectric, a shielding layer is added. This layer can be a wire braid, a foil wrap, a metal tube, or a combination of these items. Though a metal tube provides the best overall performance, the overall flexibility of the cable suffers. In many instances, a foil wrap is used in conjunction with a wire braid to allow for cable flexibility as well as good protection. Finally, an outer jacket is added to the cable. A common material for this jacket is Polyvinyl Chloride (PVC). This jacket protects the outer most conductor in the cable.

Figure 9.8 Standard Coaxial Cable

Figure reprinted with the permission of Belden, Inc. (www.belden.com)

The signal on a coaxial cable travels on the center conductor of the coaxial cable. The outer conductor, whether that be a wire braid, foil, or both, acts a shield from outside interference as well as a ground for the cable. The dielectric compound that separates the two parts acts as an insulator and ensures that the center conductor stays in or very close to the center of the cable. This combination of the outer conductive shielding and insulating material allows the cable to carry signals with minimal interference and distortion.

The impedance of coaxial cable can range from 35 to 185 ohms, however, the most common values are 50, 75, and 93 ohms. For use with the Cisco wireless devices, you should use 50-ohm cable. This is because the Cisco wireless devices are manufactured with 50 ohm components, and for most efficient energy transfer, all parts of a system; transmitter, cabling, and receiver should have the same impedance values.

RG-58 and RG-8 Cabling

Though the origin of the acronym RG can not be determined for certain, the general belief is that it was derived from U.S. military terminology and stands for "Radio Grade." This is because, the basis of the RG grading values is U.S. military specifications, specifically MIL-C-17. From these general specification, cable manufacturing companies produce multiple different variations of these cables that have different performance characteristics. Many characteristics can change from cable to cable, including attenuation, shielding type and quality, dielectric type and quality, flexibility of the cable, bend radius, center conductor material, shielding material, and outer cover material. All of these characteristics have an impact on the overall cable performance.

The two most common cable types used for Cisco wireless systems are RG-58 and RG-8. Both RG-58 and RG-8 are have 50-ohm impedance values, matching the impedance that is found on the AP or bridge. Though very similar, the major difference between RG-58 and RG-8 is the center conductor size. The RG-8 center conductor is almost twice as large as the RG-58 center conductor is. Because of this size difference, RG-8 cabling has better transmission qualities for the frequency range that the APs and bridges use. Therefore, for longer runs or runs that need to have a higher quality cable, RG-8 is preferred. However, in some situations, the performances of standard RG-58 or RG-8 cabling will still not meet the installation requirements. In these cases, you should look at the possibility of using specially designed low-loss or ultra low-loss coaxial cabling,

9913 Cabling

9913 cabling is a low-loss coaxial cable specifically designed and manufactured by Belden cable. Due to its success, many other cable manufacturing companies manufacture their cable to the Belden 9913 specifications. This cable will perform substantially better than a normal RG-58 or RG-8 cable, but the RG-58 or RG-8 cable will cost less. However, you can easily justify the additional cost if you require high performance or have a long run to the antenna. The cable itself is a 50–ohm RG-8 coaxial cable and comes in two separate varieties, the 9913 and the newly released 9913F. Though both of these cables are low-loss, and use the same outer conductor design, there are some differences in how they are constructed.

The 9913 cable by Belden (See Figure 9.9) has a single copper conductor that is 9.5 AWG (American Wire Gauge). The dielectric that is used is a semisolid polyethylene in a helical construction. Due to this construction technique, the cable has numerous air pockets. In an outdoor environment, in the event of a faulty termination or cable slice, there is a possibility for water to collect in these pockets rendering the cable useless. Therefore, when using this cable outside, you should be careful to keep the cable watertight. Finally, the outer coating of the 9913 is PVC.

Figure 9.9 Belden 9913 Low-Loss Coaxial Cable
Figure reprinted with the permission of Belden, Inc. (www.belden.com)

By contrast, the 9913F (see Figure 9.10), also manufactured by Belden has a stranded center conductor made up of 19 tightly wound cables to give an overall conductor size of 10 AWG. The dielectric used in the 9913F is a nitrogen gas-injected foam polyethylene. This process creates a solid dielectric layer with minimal difference from the 9913 cable in attenuation loss at higher frequencies. The solid dielectric also helps the cable stand up better in wet conditions. The final difference between the 9913 and the 9913F is that the outer sheath on the 9913F is made out of Belflex, which was created by Belden for added ruggedness and flexibility.

Figure 9.10 Belden Low-Loss 9913 F Coaxial Cable
Figure reprinted with the permission of Belden, Inc. (www.belden.com)

Designing & Planning…

Transmission and Transmission Media Terminology

In the course of this chapter, as well as in the book, we have used some terms in describing the characteristics of transmission media that were not necessarily explained. Therefore, we wanted to take this opportunity to further explain what some of these terms mean. For this discussion, we focus primarily on the terms that affect cabling and connectors.

The first of these terms that you hear quite often is *decibels*, or *dB*. The dB scale is used to measure the power of a signal and is logarithmic in nature. In general, every 3 dB increase in signal strength doubles the power of a signal. For example, increasing the signal strength from 10 dB to 13 dB doubles the power of the signal. This can then be applied to the transmit power ratings associate with the Cisco wireless devices. For example, a 100 milliwatt transmit power setting translates to a 20 dBm (m standing for milliwatt) signal. A 50-milliwatt transmit power setting translates to a 17-dBm signal. Moreover, the progression continues with the 20, 5, 2, and 1 milliwatt corresponding to 13, 7, 3 and 0 dBm respectively. You may also hear dB referred to as dBi. The "i" in this case refers to comparing the signal to a theoretical isotope that radiates energy equally in all directions. For example, an antenna that is rated at 6 dBi will enhance the signal strength by fourfold.

The impedance of a cable has been described as the AC equivalent to resistance. The specific impedance of any cable is determined at the time of manufacturing. You can obtain the impedance value of a cable or connector by examining the voltage and current characteristics of the cable or conductor over the operating frequency range of the cable. This information is then put into a formula that determines the overall impedance of the cable. As was mentioned in the cabling section, impedance should match across all components used in a system.

Another term that is used quite often is *attenuation*. This is nothing more than the reduction of the amplitude of the electrical signal. Attenuation is affected not only by material type, but also by length of cable as well as the frequency at which the signal is transmitted. All things being equal, a lower frequency signal will have a lower attenuation of the length of a cable but will also be able to transmit less data. Obviously, in your installations the lower the attenuation the better.

Finally, we discuss the term *Voltage Standing Wave Ratio* (VSWR). Due to irregularities in cabling and connectors, the signal on a cable will

Continued

be reflected back onto itself. These reflections cause dips and peaks in the amplitude of the signal. VSWR is simply a measure of the ratio of peak to dip voltage. If there were no reflections in the cable the VSWR would be 1:1, however, not many devices are perfect, so when looking at devices, one with a lower VSWR ratio has better transmission qualities.

Connectors

Along with the cabling, one of the items that can have the largest impact on the quality of the signal that the bridge or AP receives is the connector that is used. Connectors are used to interface the cabling with the AP or bridge as well as the antenna or bulkhead. As was previously discussed, the primary type of cabling used to connect the AP or bridge to the antenna is coaxial. Therefore, for the purpose of this book, we discuss only coaxial connectors. Because coaxial cable is used for numerous applications, you can find a wide variety of connectors, coming in different shapes, sizes, and containing different characteristics. As was the case with the cabling, you need to choose a connector that matches the impedance of the system being installed and that is capable of handling the power and frequency range of this system. When selecting a connector, you also need to ensure that you use one that is appropriate for the environment in which it will be installed. For example, you should not use a connector rated for indoor use in an exterior installation. Some of the more popular types of coaxial conductors are *BNC, F, N*, and *TNC*.

RP-TNC Connectors

As the introduction stated, there are many different varieties of coaxial connectors, however, the Cisco APs, bridges, and accessories use primarily the RP-TNC connector (see Figure 9.11). You may have noticed that the RP-TNC connector was not in the list of popular types. This is because FCC regulations (part 15.203) state that all wireless devices with removable antenna are required to have "nonstandard" connectors. The meaning of *nonstandard* has been debated, however for our case, it means that Cisco APs, bridges, and antennas come with RP-TNC connectors.

At first glance, the design of the RP-TNC connector looks exactly like a TNC connector. This is because it was based on the TNC design. The TNC connector was first made in the 1950s as an improvement upon the Bayonet-Neill-Concelman (BNC) connector. The TNC connector is usually a little over .5

inches in diameter and has a threaded connection. The threads allow for a consistent fit that will not be easily compromised by movement or vibration. The TNC as well as the RP-TNC connector can handle frequencies up 11 GHz, well within the range used by Cisco wireless devices.

The difference between a normal TNC connector and a RP-TNC connector comes in where the female and male contacts are located. Specifically, in a TNC connector, the male contact is in the plug connector and the female connector is in the jack. In the RP-TNC, the contacts are reversed. In this manner, it is assured that equipment not suited for wireless use can not be accidentally connected to an AP or bridge.

Figure 9.11 RP-TNC Connectors (Jack on the Left, Plug on the Right)

Bulkhead Extenders

Bulkhead extenders are cables that have a normal connector, such as an RP-TNC, on one end and a bulkhead connector on the other. Because we have already discussed normal connectors, we focus on the bulkhead connector at this point. A bulkhead is nothing more than a mounting style of connector. Primarily bulkheads are inserted through a premade panel or precut hole and secured by a nut screwed onto the end of the connector. By installing a bulkhead, you are able to attach a cable or antenna pigtail to a secure point that will not move around and ensure a watertight fit around the connector. You can use bulkhead extenders to easily move a bulkhead connector to another location, such as onto another panel or from the inside to the outside of an NEMA enclosure. This methodology allows for a watertight seal around the cable that can easily be relocated if necessary. This seal is crucial in environments where sensitive electronic equipment is installed in locations that are outside the normal operating specifications of the equipment. The main bulkhead extender that Cisco sells for use with its APs and bridges is a 60-inch extender (see Figure 9.12). This bulkhead extender is made from RG-58 cable with RP-TNC connectors. The jack side of the RP-TNC connector has the bulkhead connector on it.

Figure 9.12 60-Inch Bulkhead Extender

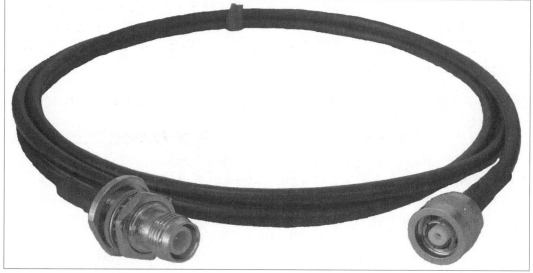

Radio Country Options

Due to differing regulations in each country, different RF frequencies are allowed to be used by wireless devices. In addition, because many of the items shipped have encryption greater than 64-bit, special export regulations need to be followed, or in some cases, certain products can't be exported to particular countries at all. To accommodate these needs, Cisco originally created an individual country option or "Air Country" code for each country. For example the country option for France was, AIR-05-FRANCE, the code for Italy was AIR-18-ITALY, and the code for the US was AIR-01-US. In total, approximately 70 country codes were defined.

   To simplify stocking as well as customer support, Cisco decided to alter this system. Specifically, the change was to group the countries into areas that all had similar requirements. After analyzing the different products that each country allows, it was determined that the countries fell into three different groups, the Americas, Europe, and Japan (see Table 9.3). Though not all of the countries fit exactly in the groupings for their geographic area, most did. Cisco then changed their part numbers to reflect these groupings as well as to indicate which products had greater than 64-bit encryption by adding information to the end of the existing part number. For example, part number AIR–BR350–E–K9 still refers to a 350 Bridge (part #AIR–BR350), however the "–E" means that it used the "European" frequencies and power and the "–K9" means that the encryption is greater than 64 bits.

Table 9.3 Radio Country Groupings and Number of Channels

Group	Abbreviation	# of RF Channels
Americas	A	11
Europe	E	13
Japan	J	14

Finally, to ensure that products were not being shipped to countries where they are prohibited, Cisco created a product/country matrix showing which products are approved for shipment to which country as well as the group that each country belongs to. Table 9.4 contains information from some selected locations. Products that are approved for order and shipment to a country are marked in the table as "Permitted." Products that are not approved for order and shipment to a country are marked in the table as "—." If you would like a more detailed list of products as well as countries, please see the Cisco Web site at www.cisco.com/warp/public/779/smbiz/wireless/approvals.html.

Table 9.4 Selected Products and Country Codes

Country	Group	Product 340 Bridge	350 Bridge	340 AP	350 AP
Argentina	A	Permitted	Permitted	Permitted	Permitted
Australia	A	Permitted	Permitted	Permitted	Permitted
Austria	E	Permitted	Permitted	Permitted	Permitted
Brazil	A	Permitted	Permitted	Permitted	Permitted
Canada	A	Permitted	Permitted	Permitted	Permitted
China	A	Permitted	—	Permitted	—
France	E	Permitted	Permitted	Permitted	Permitted
Germany	E	Permitted	Permitted	Permitted	Permitted
Greece	E	Permitted	Permitted	Permitted	Permitted
Hong Kong	A	Permitted	Permitted	Permitted	Permitted

Continued

Table 9.4 Continued

Country	Group	Product 340 Bridge	350 Bridge	340 AP	350 AP
India	A	Permitted*	Permitted*	Permitted*	Permitted*
Italy	E	Permitted	Permitted	Permitted	Permitted
Japan	J	Permitted	Permitted	Permitted	Permitted
Mexico	A	Permitted	—	Permitted	Permitted
Norway	E	Permitted	Permitted	Permitted	Permitted
Peru	A	Permitted	—	Permitted	Permitted
Russian Fed.	E	Permitted	Permitted	Permitted	Permitted
South Africa	E	Permitted	Permitted	Permitted	Permitted
Spain	E	Permitted	Permitted	Permitted	Permitted
Sweden	E	Permitted	Permitted	Permitted	Permitted
Taiwan	E	Permitted	Permitted	Permitted	Permitted
Turkey	E	Permitted*	Permitted*	Permitted*	Permitted*
UK	E	Permitted	Permitted	Permitted	Permitted
US	A	Permitted	Permitted	Permitted	Permitted
Venezuela	A	Permitted	Permitted	Permitted	Permitted

* Approved for some resellers or individual user license required

Summary

By now, you should be well on your way to answering the questions posed at the beginning of the chapter and completing your installation. The information covered in this chapter gave specific details on antenna accessories, AP, and bridge accessories, cabling and connectors, as well as Radio Country options.

The antenna accessories covered in this chapter include mounting kits for Yagi and dipole antennas, as well as a discussion on the appropriate use of the lightning arrestor with grounding ring. The Yagi articulating mount allows for the installation and position of a Yagi antenna because it can move on both the horizontal and vertical plane. Because the Yagi antenna is a directional antenna, this movement is critical to getting the antenna properly aligned. The magnetic mount that you can purchase from Cisco is specifically designed for dipole antennas. This magnetic base mount allows it to be easily installed, repositioned, or removed from a metallic surface. Lightning protection is an important concerns for any wireless installation. The lightning arrestor with grounding ring will provide protection from nearby lightning strikes but not a direct strike. Due to this care, should be taken when installing your antenna to ensure it is located in a place that has a low likelihood of being directly struck by lightning.

Numerous accessories are available for the Cisco 340 and 350 series bridges and APs. Though you can mount these APs on a simple flat surface with nothing more than a couple of screws, mounting kits are available that will allow for them to be mounted on I-beams or on poles or masts. In addition, the Slide Mounting kit will allow for the AP or bridge to be taken down for service or repair without any tools. Once the service is complete, you can then remount it, once again without the need for any tools. The serial cable that comes with the AP or bridge is nothing more than a straightthrough cable with a male and female DB-9 connector, which you can connect to the COM port of any PC to allow for local access to the AP or bridge. NEMA enclosures come in many different variations that you can install to fit just about any installation need. They can be heated or cooled, if needed, and depending on type, provide different levels of protection for the equipment. Though Cisco does not sell NEMA enclosures, you can get them from your local cable or electrical supply dealer, from a national electrical or cable supply company, or through an Internet search.

Cabling and connectors are an integral part of the overall wireless solution. Specifically, the cabling and connectors connect the antenna to the AP or bridge. The cabling is a coaxial cable that has a 50-ohm impedance. In most cases, the specific type of cabling is either RG-8 or RG-58. In cases where you need longer cabling runs or higher performance, you should use low-loss or ultra low-loss coaxial cabling such as Belden's 9913 and 9913F. You must use connectors to attach the cabling to the antenna, AP, or bridge. In most cases with Cisco's wireless solution, the connector of choice is the RP-TNC. The RP-TNC connector is a normal TNC connector that has been modified to fit FCC regulations. Specifically the RP-TNC is still a threaded connector, but instead of the male contact being in the plug end of the connector, it is in the jack end. Finally, we examined bulkheads. A bulkhead is nothing more than a connector that has the capability to be mounted to a surface. Usually, the bulkhead already has a cable attached to it. This configuration allows you to securely connect a cable to a jack that will not move or drift over time while providing a watertight seal around the connector.

In the final section of this chapter, we looked at the Radio County options. Due to differing international laws and restrictions on the use and implementation of wireless devices, Cisco developed the Radio Country options to differentiate the type of product that is permitted in each country. Because of the streamlining of this process, Cisco took over 70 different country specific options and put each country into one of three categories: the Americas, Europe, and Japan. This streamlined approach allowed Cisco to better track which feature set goes in which country. Along with the restrictions applied in each country, Cisco also must deal with export restrictions due to the 128-bit encryption on some of their components. To deal with this issue, they created a table that shows which device type is allowed by type and by country. A sampling of this table as well as a link to the table itself is provided in the Radio Country section of this chapter.

Solutions Fast Track

Antenna Accessories

- ☑ When installing your Yagi antenna, you can position the antenna correctly by using the Yagi articulating mount, which adjusts on both the vertical as well as horizontal planes.

- ☑ The magnetic antenna mount sold by Cisco is specifically used for dipole antenna and is the replacement for the older style dipole mounts.

- ☑ Consider lightning protection when planning any wireless system. The lightning arrestor with grounding ring can provide protection for the interior equipment in the event of a nearby lightning strike.

Bridge and Access Point Accessories

☑ You can mount the Cisco 340 or 350 series AP or bridge to a flat surface with nothing more than a few screws and a template from the Cisco Web site. However, if you have a unique mounting requirement or want greater flexibility, a number of mounting kits are available from Cisco.

☑ Spare power supplies are available form Cisco that you can use as field replacements for existing power supplies. This includes the inline power injector that allows power to be supplied to the 350 bridge or AP via a Category 5 UTP cable.

☑ The serial cable used to configure the 340 and 350 series APs and bridges is a straightthrough cable with a male and female DB-9 connector of the respective ends.

☑ NEMA enclosures can provide appropriate levels of protection for wireless equipment that needs to be installed in locations that are not suitable for electronic equipment. This can be due to excessive dust, dirt, water, other foreign material, temperature range, or a combination of these factors.

Cabling, Connectors, and Bulkhead Extenders

☑ There are a number of cabling options for connecting the AP or bridge to the antenna. For longer runs or in situations where high performance is required, you should use special low-loss cabling.

☑ The main connector used by Cisco in their wireless solution is the RP-TNC connector. This allows for a secure connection between components that will not be affected by normal movement or vibration.

☑ A bulkhead connector is a connector that can be attached to a flat surface or panel. This allows for a stable connection point for cabling that will not require addition fasteners to keep it from moving or drifting, while providing a watertight seal around the connector.

Radio Country Options

- ☑ Due to differing regulations in different countries, the frequency ranges used for transmission of the Cisco APs and bridges vary based on the destination country.

- ☑ The three main groupings of AP types are the Americas, Europe, and Japan. The Americas version of the AP has 11 RF channels, the Europe version has 13 RF channels, and the Japan version has 14 RF channels.

- ☑ Cisco must follow special export regulations when exporting equipment that has greater than 64-bit encryption. As a result, not all of the Cisco 340 and 350 series product lines can be sold in every country.

Frequently Asked Questions

The following Frequently Asked Questions, answered by the authors of this book, are designed to both measure your understanding of the concepts presented in this chapter and to assist you with real-life implementation of these concepts. To have your questions about this chapter answered by the author, browse to **www.syngress.com/solutions** and click on the **"Ask the Author"** form.

Q: Where do I go to find more information about the performance characteristics of my specific cable and connectors?

A: The best place to start looking for this information is with the cable or connector manufacturer. They should have detailed specification sheets available for each of their product lines. You can also talk to a cabling Value Added Reseller (VAR). Many VARs have specification sheets from a number of manufacturers that they can provide you.

Q: Where can I find more information on lightning protection?

A: We recommend reading two articles. These are both from a journal called *QST*, which is published by the American Radio Relay League (AARL), the national association for amateur radio. They cover a fair amount of information by themselves but also give further references if you wish to get more information on a particular subject. These articles (available online along with other lightning protection material at www.arrl.org/tis/info/lightning.html) are Mike Tracy's "Lab Notes—Lightning Protection—Part 1", *QST*, October

1994, pp. 81–82, and "Lab Notes—Lightning Protection—Part 2", *QST*, December 1994, pp. 45–46.

Q: Can I connect my terminal server to my Cisco terminal server?

A: Yes. Because the standard terminal server has RJ-45 connectors and the console connection on the 340 or 350 is a DB-9, you will need to use a RJ-45 to male DB-9 shell. The pinouts to use for the shell are shown in Table 9.5.

Table 9.5 RJ-45 to DB-9 Pinouts

RJ-45 Pin	Term Server Use	DB-9 Pin	Comment
1	CTS	8	
2	DSR/DCD	1	
3	RXD	2	
4	RXD-	5	To DB-9 Ground
5	TXD-	5	To DB-9 Ground
6	TXD	3	
7	DTR	4	
8	RTS	7	

Q: Can I reterminate my cabling and bulkheads with non–RP connectors?

A: No, you cannot legally reterminate this cabling with non–RP connectors and use it in a wireless installation.

Q: Can I use the inline power injector with my Cisco 340 series bridge?

A: No, the power injector is compatible only with the 350 series bridges and APs.

Index

SYNGRESS SOLUTIONS...

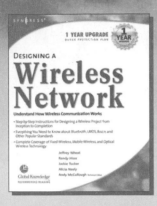

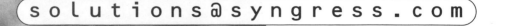